Through the Labyrinth

LEADERSHIP FOR THE
COMMON GOOD

HARVARD BUSINESS SCHOOL PRESS
CENTER FOR PUBLIC LEADERSHIP
JOHN F. KENNEDY SCHOOL OF GOVERNMENT
HARVARD UNIVERSITY

The Leadership for the Common Good series represents
a partnership between Harvard Business School Press and
the Center for Public Leadership at Harvard University's
John F. Kennedy School of Government. Books in the series
aim to provoke conversations about the role of leaders in
business, government, and society, to enrich leadership theory
and enhance leadership practice, and to set the agenda for
defining effective leadership in the future.

OTHER BOOKS IN THE SERIES

Changing Minds
by Howard Gardner

Predictable Surprises
by Max H. Bazerman and
Michael D. Watkins

Bad Leadership
by Barbara Kellerman

Many Unhappy Returns
by Charles O. Rossotti

Leading Through Conflict
by Mark Gerzon

Five Minds for the Future
by Howard Gardner

Through the Labyrinth

THE TRUTH ABOUT HOW
WOMEN BECOME LEADERS

Alice H. Eagly

Linda L. Carli

Harvard Business School Press
Boston, Massachusetts

From Alice H. Eagly

To Bob, who encourages me and provides the love that makes everyday life joyful.

To Ingrid and Ursula, who inspire me to understand the challenges that young women face.

To the memory of my parents, Josara and Harold, and of my brother, Tom, who made up the family that taught me to work hard and think independently.

And to the graduate students and collaborators whose insights and discoveries appear frequently on the pages of this book.

From Linda L. Carli

To my parents, Dollie and Victor, who instilled in me confidence, curiosity, and a love of learning

To Michael, who supports me in everything I do, and whose skill as a writer and generous spirit inspire me.

To Rance, who has always encouraged me with his optimism and good humor.

And to Alexander, who brings me joy and always knows how to make me laugh.

Library of Congress Cataloging-in-Publication Data

Eagly, Alice Hendrickson.

    Through the labyrinth : the truth about how women become leaders / Alice H. Eagly, Linda L. Carli.

      p. cm.

    Includes bibliographical references.

    ISBN-13: 978-1-4221-1691-3 (hardcover : alk. paper)

    ISBN-10: 1-4221-1691-3

    1. Women executives. 2. Women—Promotions. 3. Leadership in women. I. Carli, Linda. II. Title.

HD6054.3.E34 2007

658.4'092082—dc22

                                2007009123

The paper used in this publication meets the requirements of the American National Standard for Permanence of Paper for Publications and Documents in Libraries and Archives Z39.48-1992.

CONTENTS

The intellectual journey that resulted in *Through the Labyrinth* began years before we envisioned writing a book, when both of us initiated research on how gender affects leadership and social influence. It was the 1980s, when such topics were entirely new territory in our field of social psychology. Leadership had been largely neglected by the feminist scholars who began research on gender in the 1970s. Many of these researchers viewed leadership as something men do and therefore not a prime topic for the new research on women. For us, however, the lack of women in positions of power and authority demanded an explanation. Leadership, we were certain, is an essential topic for scholars of gender. Today many scholars and researchers share our view, as shown by the profusion of research on how gender affects leadership. Without this body of research, we could not have written this book.

Answering the question of why women have been excluded from leadership is a complex undertaking that cuts across many disciplines. Tackling the question—and the related question of why women have gained increasing access to leadership—demanded that we broaden our perspective well beyond our own discipline of psychology. In the process, we have studied the contributions of economists, sociologists, anthropologists, political scientists, and experts on management and organizations. We have benefited from insights that have emerged across the social sciences. And the diversity of methods that social scientists have brought to bear on gender and leadership lends strength to the conclusions of this book.

We invoke a labyrinth metaphor throughout the book to symbolize the situations that women face as leaders and potential leaders. The labyrinth image has a long and varied history in ancient Greece, India, and Nepal; native North and South America; medieval Europe; and elsewhere. As a contemporary symbol, the labyrinth conveys the idea of a complex journey that entails challenges and offers a goal worth striving for. Passage through a labyrinth is not simple or direct, but requires persistence, awareness of one's progress, and a careful analysis of the puzzles that lie ahead. It is this meaning that we intend to convey. For women who aspire to attain leadership, routes to this goal exist but can present both unexpected and expected twists and turns. Because all labyrinths have a viable route to their center, it is understood that goals are attainable. But passing through a labyrinth is more demanding than traveling a straight path. Thus, the labyrinth provides an encouraging metaphor for aspiring women and recognition of the challenges that these women face.

Some readers may be surprised that the subtitle of this book boldly asserts that we present the truth about how women become leaders. Our postmodernist readers may consider it naïve or presumptuous for social scientists to claim that a book offers the truth. Certainly the truths of this book are contingent on the available scientific evidence. By invoking a full range of the best social science, we offer a far more adequate and complete analysis than any that have appeared earlier.

Through the Labyrinth should help readers understand not merely leadership by women and men, but much about the feasibility of attaining gender equality in our time. If women are to achieve equality, women and men will have to share leadership equally. However, even highly industrialized societies are very far from reaching this goal. It is therefore crucial that people understand why equality has not been reached, despite substantial improvement in the status of women.

The project of writing this book took shape over several years. The first efforts (by Alice Eagly) were directed toward a monograph that might be read by professors and graduate students. After that initial start, the two of us began to work together. This collaboration started with our editing of a 2001 thematic issue of *Journal of Social Issues* on "gender, hierarchy, and leadership." We then received an invitation to write an overview chapter on gender and leadership for an edited book, *The Nature of Leadership*, which appeared in 2004. This opportunity pushed us to develop an analysis that went far beyond our previous research. We followed up with yet another overview, which appeared in *Leadership Quarterly* in 2005. It was only after completing these projects that we finally launched the writing of this book.

We have worked hard to make this book accessible and interesting to readers who are not social scientists or students of social science. We have described the abundant research without the technical jargon that often plagues such presentations. We describe studies' findings with enough detail to give readers an accurate understanding of the evidence that we cite. Citations for the research appear in the book's endnotes, so that interested readers can follow up by reading studies in their entirety. The electronic revolution in library access means that the majority of these materials are available online. We also include a substantial amount of qualitative material—much of it consisting of statements by women leaders. We offer these passages not as evidence for our conclusions, but as illustrations of the principles that we present.

Progress toward this book was facilitated by three academic leaves that Alice Eagly received. The first, for the fall of 1994, was awarded by Purdue University and facilitated the initial steps toward a book on gender and leadership. In 1998–1999, Eagly received a fellowship from the James McKeen Cattell Foundation that enabled a year's stay at the Radcliffe Institute for Advanced Study and work on several journal articles and chapters that enter into this book. Finally, the writing of the book was aided by a sabbatical leave granted by Northwestern University for 2005–2006. The hospitality of Agneta Fischer and other colleagues at the University of Amsterdam during this year provided an excellent environment for developing the book.

Many people have given us advice on this book, and we thank them for their contributions. First of all, we owe a debt to the many collaborators in our own research that is cited. These individuals include Blair Johnson, Steven Karau, Mona Makhijani, Bruce Klonsky, Wendy Wood, Mary Johannesen-Schmidt, Marloes van Engen, and Claartje Vinkenburg. Those who read and commented on the entire book include Renee Engeln-Maddox, Barbara Gutek, Anne Koenig, and Shelly Chaiken. Those who read specific chapters and provided helpful advice include Claartje Vinkenburg, Marloes van Engen, Wendy Wood, Ronit Kark, John Antonakis, Amanda Diekman, Catherine Weinberger, Susan Thistle, Kingsley Browne, Elizabeth Knowles, and Jennifer Rappaport. Anonymous reviewers of the manuscript also provided valuable feedback. Other people offered important insights at key points, including Bruce Klonsky, Anne McGuire, and Agneta Fischer. Student assistants LaTanya James, Jennifer Steele, deJohn Allen, Susan Ritacca, and Dominique Gagnon aided in checking sources and references and organizing research materials. The generous help of all of these individuals has greatly improved the book.

We thank the excellent staff of Harvard Business School Press. Senior Editor Jacque Murphy has provided advice and encouragement, and Assistant Editor Brian Surette provided organizational assistance. Senior Production

Editor Marcy Barnes-Henrie helped us clarify and sharpen numerous points in the book.

We owe the greatest debt of gratitude to our families. Our husbands, Robert Eagly and Michael Dorsey, read all the chapters more than once and provided excellent advice on content and writing style. They encouraged us to keep going and never lose sight of our goals for the book. Our children Ingrid Eagly, Ursula Eagly, and Alexander Carli-Dorsey were exceedingly understanding when we constantly repeated, "I am working on the book." Ingrid and Ursula each read chapters and offered helpful feedback. Alex, a high school student, spent hours engaged in the tedious but important work of helping to check chapter notes. Ursula, a choreographer of contemporary dance, and Ingrid, an attorney and mother of two young children, also serve as examples of how talented young women successfully cope with the challenges of the labyrinth. We admire their intelligent striving and that of thousands of other women we have come to know among our students, friends, and relatives.

CHAPTER ONE

Is There Still a Glass Ceiling?

MORE THAN A FEW women have risen to positions as corporate chief executives, university presidents, state governors, and presidents of nations. Although women's progress in attaining power and authority is unmistakable, even now the presence of women in elite leadership positions is unusual enough that it evokes a sense of wonder. Leaders such as Secretary of State Condoleezza Rice remain exceptions, and their rise to powerful government positions would have been unthinkable even twenty years ago. Given these realities, two questions loom: why have women now gained more access to powerful leadership positions? Why do men continue to have far more access than women do? We answer these questions in this book.

Women's rarity in powerful roles has most often been ascribed to the glass ceiling, but this explanation no longer fits. The glass ceiling metaphor conveys a rigid, impenetrable barrier, but barriers to women's advancement are now more permeable. Although men have long monopolized leadership, especially in the more powerful roles, this is changing. In the United States and many other nations, women have gained new access to a wide range of leadership roles.

Prejudice and discrimination that slow or sometimes completely block women's advancement have surely not disappeared, but the idea of a glass ceiling, with its portrayal of inflexible limits, has lingered too long. The facts demand a new image. In this book, we offer a new metaphor, the *labyrinth*, that captures the varied challenges confronting women as they travel, often on indirect paths, sometimes through alien territory, on their way to leadership.

Stages in Women's Access to Leadership

We begin this analysis of women's leadership by considering three types of barriers that have obstructed women's advancement: the concrete wall, the glass ceiling, and the labyrinth. The first, the concrete wall, is long gone in the United States. The second type of barrier, the glass ceiling, has eroded considerably in recent years, to be replaced by the more navigable but still challenging routes to leadership symbolized by the labyrinth.

The Concrete Wall

Clearly, the most effective way to prevent people from advancing is to block their path with overt, absolute barriers. For most of human history, barriers to women's leadership consisted of explicit rules and clear-cut norms. Even in the beginning of the 20th century, women lacked legal and political equality and were not even allowed to vote, let alone hold political office.

Although American women gained the right to vote in 1920, they still confronted many absolute barriers to leadership as recently as the middle of the twentieth century. Consider the example of Supreme Court Justice Ruth Bader Ginsburg, who graduated first in her class from Columbia University's Law School in 1959. Men who demonstrated such exceptional ability typically obtained a prestigious Supreme Court clerkship or a job with a major New York law firm, but Ginsburg did not.[1] There was, of course, no law that prohibited the hiring of women by Supreme Court justices or law firms. It just wasn't done, and everyone understood that.

In some cases, women could not even gain the same credentials as men because educational opportunities were closed to them. Until the 1960s, women were denied access to many of the most selective universities in the United States. Although state universities were coeducational, only a few Ivy League universities admitted women, and generally only to women's colleges that were affiliated with those universities. The Harvard Business School became coeducational in 1963, Yale and Princeton universities in 1969, and the U.S. military academies in 1976.[2] Degrees from such schools provide credentials for access to many leadership positions.

The views that exemplify the concrete wall appear in some of President Richard Nixon's unguarded comments, captured on White House audiotapes and later made public through the Freedom of Information Act. When explaining why he would not consider appointing a woman as justice of the

Supreme Court, Nixon said, "I don't think a woman should be in any government job whatsoever . . . The reason why I do is mainly because they are erratic. And emotional. Men are erratic and emotional, too, but the point is a woman is more likely to be."[3] With such opinions widely shared in the culture, women had virtually no chance of attaining influential leadership roles. Women were warmly welcomed for their able service as secretaries and clerks, and they had to settle for such positions.

Even in the early 1970s, many organizations refused to interview women for entry-level positions in management, law, accounting, academia, and other professional fields. Women also were excluded from most male-dominated trades and blue-collar occupations such as plumber, construction worker, and firefighter. It did not matter that some potential female candidates had excelled in educational and training programs that gave them the same—or better—credentials than their male counterparts. Recruiters visiting university campuses were known to post notices stating, "No women need apply."[4] It was exclusion that lacked any subtlety.

For careers in business, even an MBA and other excellent credentials could serve merely to disqualify a woman from employment. Consider the response that one woman received in the early 1970s when she moved to a new city and applied for positions: "Someone at one of the places where I really wanted to work said, 'I'm sorry, but there are five things wrong with you: You're a woman, you have an MBA, you were an officer at another bank, you were highly paid, and you're intelligent.' I said, 'But I thought that was all the good stuff I had.'"[5] Such outstanding credentials presumably disqualified this woman from the clerical and bank teller positions that were open to women.

The concrete wall rested on a division of labor dictating that men should be breadwinners and women should be homemakers. Women were denied entry to prestigious careers because of the assumption that their proper work was in the home. Here is how an executive responding to a survey published by the *Harvard Business Review* in 1965 put the matter: "The majority of American men and women still believe in home and family, so it is necessary that only one person in the family pursue a career. Because of women's biological role, it is more practical for the man to hold that one position."[6]

In the era of the concrete wall, the division of labor between women and men struck most people as part of the natural order. Although some individual women fought against this wall, most people simply accepted the absolute barriers that it implied.

The Glass Ceiling

The method of exclusion began to change in the 1970s. Barriers shifted so that they no longer totally excluded women from all positions of authority—only those at the higher levels. This was the period of the "glass ceiling." Two journalists—Carol Hymowitz and Timothy Schellhardt—introduced this label in the *Wall Street Journal*: "Even those women who rose steadily through the ranks," they wrote in a 1986 article, "eventually crashed into an invisible barrier. The executive suite seemed within their grasp, but they just couldn't break through the glass ceiling."[7] The accompanying drawing of a woman pushing against such a ceiling represented this metaphor (see figure 1-1).

The term quickly caught on, capturing the less obvious manner in which women were excluded from high-level leadership roles. Nevertheless, the glass ceiling still implied an absolute barrier—a solid roadblock that prevents access to high-level positions. At the same time, the image of a "glass" obstruction suggested that women were being misled about their opportunities because the impediment was not easy for them to see from a distance.

The U.S. Congress acknowledged the public's interest in the glass ceiling by establishing a commission to investigate it. In its 1995 reports, the Glass Ceiling Commission declared that this type of discrimination followed from beliefs about women that restricted their access to higher-level employment opportunities.[8] Central to these beliefs was the conviction that it would be risky to invest in women because they might well quit their jobs to raise a family. Such assumptions about a division of labor continued to disqualify women. As one executive said, "As long as I can get a satisfactory

FIGURE 1-1

Drawing accompanying *Wall Street Journal* article by Hymowitz and Schellhardt (1986) that introduced the term *glass ceiling*

© Douglas Smith, 1986.

man who will work full-time for life (and I assume as much for all men), I'll take him every day of the week over a much better woman."[9]

Women who had young children or who disclosed that they planned to have children were penalized especially severely. Some interviewers designed elaborate stratagems to discover women's present and anticipated family status, despite legislation that enjoined them from making such inquiries. A 1989 *Wall Street Journal* article disclosed "job interviewers' dirty little secret" about surreptitiously obtaining information about women's family status.[10]

One method involved having a clerk inquire (between official interviews) about the kind of health insurance coverage the applicant might prefer (individual, husband-and-wife, or family). Another approach involved using an informal lunch setting to entice the candidate to discuss the interviewer's own family situation. Conversation could casually turn to difficulties of car pool or daycare arrangements. A trusting candidate might then disclose that she already had one or more children or hoped to have a child and so was concerned about childcare arrangements. Direct inquiries about candidates' family situation were also common—but so were women's guarded responses to questions that they regarded as inappropriate and illegal. Savvy women removed their wedding rings when going to interviews.[11]

Even though women increasingly attained lower-level positions, they remained excluded from most positions at higher levels. Although the most popular justification for not promoting women may have been that they might leave the workplace to have children, there were other excuses. For example, some employers claimed that clients and customers would not want to work with women. A male CEO of an executive search company made this sentiment clear in talking to an interviewer from the Glass Ceiling Commission: "Listen, I'm meeting my bottom line and I want to find people that the client wants. My reputation is based on my track record of getting them candidates they are comfortable with. I can't bring in too many minorities and women."[12] It is obvious that such rationales served to block women's ascent to elite leadership positions, even as more gained entry to lower-level positions.

The Labyrinth

In 2004, the *Wall Street Journal* published a special section titled "Through the Glass Ceiling." In this report, journalist Carol Hymowitz, the lead author of the 1986 article that had introduced the glass ceiling metaphor, described women who were rising fast or had already made it to the top of their business organizations. On the front page of the section were the smiling faces of fifty highly successful executive women, with not one struggling, frustrated woman among them. The report described a burgeoning cadre of women "making their mark on the corporate front lines." The newspaper responsible for the glass ceiling metaphor sent a clear message that this barrier was a thing of the past.[13] The glass ceiling had broken.

The *Wall Street Journal* got it right once again. The situation had morphed from the complete exclusion of women, symbolized by the concrete wall, to the exclusion of women from more advanced positions, symbolized by the glass ceiling. With continuing change, the obstacles that women face have become more surmountable, at least by some women some of the time. Paths to the top exist, and some women find them. The successful routes can be difficult to discover, however, and therefore we label these circuitous paths a *labyrinth*.[14]

The labyrinth contains numerous barriers, some subtle and others quite obvious, such as the expectation that mothers will provide the lion's share of childcare. Yet there are almost no exclusionary laws and few clear-cut, widely endorsed norms of exclusion. Glass ceiling beliefs that deny women high positions solely on the basis of their sex now strike most decision makers as unfair. And denying women opportunities because of their capacity to reproduce or because some people "have a problem" with powerful women raises the red flag of sexism. The glass ceiling metaphor now falls short in multiple respects.

Many women are aware that barriers are no longer absolute. For instance, approximately half of the female leaders in the Boston area polled in 1998 thought that women have the same advancement opportunities as men. A majority of female executives from ten large, global companies polled in 2002 agreed that "women have made a great deal of progress in obtaining senior positions." Upon becoming CEO of Hewlett-Packard in 1999, Carly Fiorina famously said, "I hope that we are at the point that everyone has figured out that there is not a glass ceiling."[15] Although victims of discrimination often minimize actual discrimination (see chapter 10), many women now doubt the presence of the types of barriers symbolized by the glass ceiling.

As new industries have sprung up, they have not been bound by traditional norms that disqualify women and minorities from higher positions. David Parker, CEO of an executive search firm, put it this way: "In newer industries, like technology, it's strictly qualifications that get you where you

SEVEN REASONS THE GLASS CEILING METAPHOR IS MISLEADING

1. It erroneously implies that women have equal access to entry-level positions.

2. It erroneously assumes the presence of an absolute barrier at a specific high level in organizations.

3. It erroneously suggests that all barriers to women are difficult to detect and therefore unforeseen.

4. It erroneously assumes that there exists a single, homogeneous barrier and thereby ignores the complexity and variety of obstacles that women leaders can face.

5. It fails to recognize the diverse strategies that women devise to become leaders.

6. It precludes the possibility that women can overcome barriers and become leaders.

7. It fails to suggest that thoughtful problem solving can facilitate women's paths to leadership.

want to go. That's why you're more likely to see women and minorities in senior positions than in old-line, entrenched industries such as insurance, banks, steel, or manufacturing."[16] It may be no accident that many of the most powerful female CEOs in the United States have served or are serving in high-tech corporations: Meg Whitman of eBay, Anne Mulcahy of Xerox, Patricia Russo of Alcatel-Lucent, and Carly Fiorina, formerly of Hewlett-Packard.

We show in this book that women are still excluded more frequently than men, but the processes underlying this result are varied and not necessarily as obvious as they were in the past. Although many people still believe that women differ from men in personality and temperament in ways that affect leadership, these assumptions have become fuzzier. And beliefs that the sexes should occupy separate spheres have weakened as women and men have become more similar in their participation in the labor force and their household responsibilities (see chapters 2 and 4). Still, not everything is equal; a weakened division of labor remains. Women who have children still face difficult decisions that pit the demands of parenthood against the demands of their careers.

Most Americans want people to be hired and promoted in the workplace based on their abilities and accomplishments. They believe that people should not be disqualified from positions at any level merely because of their gender, race, or religion.[17] With progress toward equal opportunity, the barriers that women now encounter no longer take the form of an exclusionary wall or a rigid ceiling at a particular level. Instead, women can attain high positions, but finding the pathways demands considerable skill and some luck.

Some women have great skill, and a few also have tremendous good luck. They negotiate these labyrinthine paths to positions of power, authority, and prestige, regardless of the discriminatory impediments that they may encounter along the way. Some women find roundabout or discontinuous or nontraditional routes to authority. Who would have predicted, for example, that Hillary Clinton's role as First Lady would provide a means of becoming a senator and a presidential candidate? And many women are not deterred or embittered by the special challenges that they have faced. Consider Christine Todd Whitman, who served as governor of New Jersey and head of the Environmental Protection Agency. She said: "I believe, deep down, 'Yeah, a lot of the tough stuff may be because I'm a woman, but I'm not going to spend my whole time thinking and complaining about it, because then I won't get anything done. All I will do is concentrate on the fact that the road's a little harder because I'm a woman.' After all, there are lots of people for whom it's much harder than it is for me."[18]

Why Are Women Not Equally Represented as Leaders?

The labyrinth metaphor symbolizes the complexity of the causes of women's current situation as leaders. The chapters of this book elaborate this metaphor by analyzing all the possible causes of women's limited but increasing access to power and authority. Understanding causes can enable women to negotiate the labyrinth, as we spell out in chapter 10. But to begin this analysis, we must first state what we mean by leadership.

Our working definition of *leader* is simple and straightforward: a person who exercises authority over other people. This definition encompasses leaders who emerge informally in organizations and groups as well as those who hold managerial or governmental roles. *Leadership* entails being in charge of other people in multiple ways. It consists of influencing, motivating, organizing, and coordinating the work of others. In groups, organizations, and nations, leadership involves bringing people together to enable them to work toward shared goals. In motivating people to work together, leaders encourage them to set aside narrow self-interest. In short, leaders influence and inspire the activities of others to foster the progress of a group, organization, or nation toward its goals.[19]

Organizations depend on effective managerial leadership. Managers have control over the organization of work as well as the hiring and firing of lower-level employees. Some scholars of leadership distinguish between leadership and management by viewing managers as organizing and controlling the flow of work in an organization without necessarily undertaking the leadership activities of setting new directions, inspiring innovations, and enabling successful adaptation to challenges. Even though this distinction between leadership and management can be useful, the two types of activities are intertwined in organizations. And whether managers bring about successful innovation and adaptation to challenges becomes clear only after the fact. Therefore, we use the terms *leader* and *manager* interchangeably in discussing organizational leadership. We also extend our analysis to encompass leadership in small groups and in larger units such as cities and nations.[20]

The increasing presence of women leaders has raised many questions. Debates fester about whether prejudice and discrimination still limit women's opportunities to lead. Opinions vary on whether women opt out of leadership because it conflicts with their family obligations. Disagreements continue on whether organizations set up barriers that unfairly block women's access to leadership roles or instead merely suffer from a lack of qualified women—that is, a "pipeline problem." To resolve such issues, our book accounts for the multiple forces that have produced, maintained, and subsequently weakened men's dominance of leadership positions.

Evidence for Understanding Gender and Leadership

Our analysis is founded on scientific research from psychology, economics, sociology, anthropology, political science, communication studies, and management science. We ground our conclusions in research, but we invoke a broad range of other sources—including anecdotes, journalists' reports, biographies, memoirs, and individuals' personal recollections—to illustrate the principles that emerge from research. We use concrete examples to clarify the ways that research findings are reflected in people's lives.

We derive our conclusions from a variety of research approaches. Some studies involve surveys of representative samples of respondents, and other studies examine behavior within organizations. We cite research that mines archives such as government data on employment and wages. Other research is based on laboratory experiments that create different conditions of some variable of interest and assign people at random to the resulting conditions. Because all these methods have strengths as well as weaknesses, we take the sensible approach of considering all methods while keeping in mind each method's limitations. We ask readers to do the same.

One strength of scientific research is that tests of hypotheses can be repeated to establish whether findings generalize across various settings and types of participants. Because replications of research can result in an abundance of studies, a technique known as *meta-analysis* has become popular. Meta-analysis involves statistically combining a number of studies to produce a general answer to a question.[21] Given the ability of this method to clarify similarities and differences in the findings of related studies, we place considerable weight on the outcomes of high-quality meta-analyses.

Despite this profusion of scientific research, political implications are never far from the surface in discourse on gender and sex differences. Politics enters because of the profound implications that questions about gender have for social life and public policy. And in writing about leadership, we move to the very core of these implications. Not surprisingly, people from across the political spectrum have quite different views on the desirability of men and women sharing leadership.

Scientific methods reduce the influence of investigators' own political biases by requiring that their research be open to scrutiny and accompanied by detailed descriptions of findings and methods. Yet even with the checks provided by the scientific tradition, bias can be present. Fortunately, because the topic of women's leadership attracts scholars with divergent political orientations, the resulting debates help prevent blatantly biased conclusions.[22]

So now our story begins. Each chapter answers a distinct question. Chapter 2 answers the question of how far women have actually come as leaders. Chapter 3 addresses the fundamental question of whether women are underrepresented as leaders because nature has endowed men, but not women, with the qualities needed for effective leadership. Chapter 4 answers another fundamental question—whether women limit their paid work and feel less committed to their careers because of their domestic responsibilities. Chapter 5 evaluates whether clear evidence exists for discrimination against women as leaders. Chapter 6 answers the question of whether stereotypes and prejudices limit women's opportunities as leaders.

Chapter 7 determines whether people resist women's leadership more than men's, and chapter 8 assesses whether men and women differ in leadership style. Chapter 9 considers whether organizations have traditions and practices that create inherent obstacles to women's leadership. Chapter 10 answers the question of how some women successfully negotiate the labyrinth to reach positions of power and authority. And, finally, chapter 11 addresses the bottom-line question of what the consequences are of having women hold leadership positions at all levels.

All these analyses are informed by research and examples from the United States, in part because we know a lot about our own nation. Also, U.S. scholars and scientists have produced the greatest amount of relevant research. Nonetheless, we strive to place this research in a global context by including research and examples from other nations.

Leadership matters. Therefore, the mission of this book is extremely important. The best leadership is found by choosing leaders from the largest pool of talent, and that includes women. Opening doors for women fosters equal opportunity and can help a society to allocate its human resources optimally. With excellence in leadership in short supply, no group, organization, or nation should tolerate the losses that follow from unfairly restricting women's access to leadership roles. This book evaluates whether such restrictions are present and, if they are present, what can be done to eliminate them.

CHAPTER TWO

Where Are the Women Leaders?

THE POWER ELITE in organizations and politics does not "look like America," to borrow a phrase from former president Bill Clinton.[1] Nevertheless, the power elite looks a lot more like America than it did in the past. In this chapter, we identify where women have most advanced as leaders and where they still lag behind.

Despite expanding opportunities, it is rare to find women in very high positions, and they receive an extraordinary amount of media attention. Leaders such as eBay CEO Meg Whitman and Speaker of the House Nancy Pelosi are constantly in the news because of their gender. The continuing reports of "the first woman" to hold a prominent position show that some women are finding their way through the labyrinth but that equality remains a somewhat distant goal. As one corporate lawyer remarked, "At the leadership summit, we sat in a room full of phenomenal women. We were surrounded by trailblazers . . . who have broken through the glass ceiling. We were in a room full of firsts . . . It's depressing because we're in the third millennium and we are still counting firsts for 50 percent of the earth's population."[2]

The absence of equality is obvious. Yet women have gained access to most lower- and middle-level leadership positions and some access to many top leadership positions. In fact, when all types of organizations are taken into account (including, for example, charitable foundations, social service agencies, health organizations, and corporations), women now occupy 23 percent of chief executive positions in the United States.[3]

That women are "only" 23 percent of chief executives is not an appropriate reaction, given that before the 1980s, few women were allowed to begin careers that could lead to these roles. In fact, this figure reflects enormous social change in the past decades. Before landmark federal legislation was passed in the 1960s, most of the paths toward chief executive positions were closed to women. In the era of the concrete wall, sex-based discrimination was not only tolerated but also written into the legal code. Opportunities for women improved greatly after Title VII of the Civil Rights Act of 1964 made employment discrimination unlawful on the basis of sex as well as race, color, national origin, and religion.[4] Compliance with this law took hold only gradually. Some organizations voluntarily opened jobs to women, and others had to be challenged by legal action.

To shed light on the substantial changes that have occurred, this chapter considers the ways in which women's employment, education, and representation in leadership roles have changed. A wealth of facts and figures exists for the United States, and we provide comparisons with statistics from other nations. We also look at leadership in small work groups, in juries, and in students' high school activities.

Changes in Women's Employment and Education

It is remarkable how much the labor force participation of women and men has converged in the United States since the beginning of the twentieth century. As figure 2-1 shows, the proportion of women who are in the labor force increased greatly in the twentieth century, and the proportion of men in the labor force fell. Although the increase in women's employment slowed in the 1990s, women now constitute 46 percent of all full-time and part-time workers, somewhat short of their 51 percent share of the population. Similar employment trends have been observed in many other nations, although everywhere women's participation rate has remained somewhat lower than men's.[5]

In addition, there is a difference in the number of hours that employed women and men are on the job: some 25 percent of employed women in the United States are part-time workers, compared with only 11 percent of employed men. These statistics on part-time work have shown little change in recent decades.[6]

In education, women now have a substantial advantage. Young women attain not only much more education than their mothers and grandmothers but also more education than young men. Women's share of bachelor's degrees increased in the twentieth century until the immediate post–World

FIGURE 2-1

Civilian labor force participation of men and women in the United States, 1900–2005

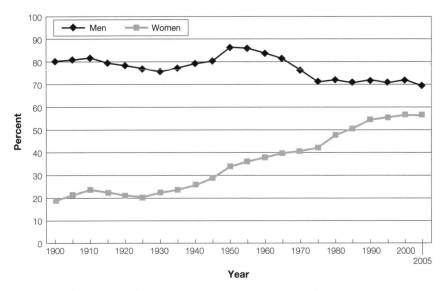

Source: Adapted from U.S. Census Bureau, 1975. Statistical Abstract of the United States: 1973, series D11–25; 2007, Statistical Abstract of the United States: 2007, table 575.

War II period, when large numbers of war veterans entered the universities. After 1950, women's share of bachelor's degrees rose rapidly and passed the 50 percent mark in 1981–1982 (see figure 2-2).[7]

This pattern of increasing female education holds for advanced degrees as well. Along with 57 percent of bachelor's degrees, women now earn 59 percent of master's degrees and 48 percent of PhDs (53 percent of PhDs if the percentage is calculated without international students). Women also receive 49 percent of law degrees and 42 percent of MBAs, degrees that often provide entry to political and organizational leadership.[8] These changes, especially in advanced degrees, reflect extraordinary shifts in social patterns. Considering people of all ages combined, the percentage of men with bachelor's degrees still slightly exceeds that of women in the United States, but the trend continues to shift in favor of women.[9]

Women's growing educational advantage is not limited to the United States, where for every 100 men enrolled in all types of post-secondary

FIGURE 2-2

Percentage of bachelor's degrees awarded to women in the United States, 1900–2004

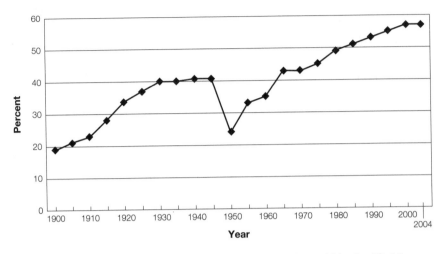

Source: Adapted from U.S. National Center for Education Statistics, 2005. Digest of Educational Statistics, table 246.

education, there are 139 women. Elsewhere the situation is similar: for every 100 men in post-secondary education, there are 155 women in Sweden, 151 in Argentina, 137 in the United Kingdom, 136 in Canada, 128 in France, and 122 in Spain.[10] With only 89 women for every 100 men in post-secondary education, Japan is a rare exception among highly industrialized nations. Despite the overall growth of women's education, it remains true that women still earn fewer degrees than men in many technical and scientific fields. In general, however, women are no longer held back by limited education. Instead, they now have the edge. Women's increasing education predicts their future workplace advancement.

Women and Men as Organizational Leaders

Now let's take a look at the leadership positions that men and women hold. Are women leaders now common—or at least more numerous than in earlier periods? Are women found in some types of leader roles but rarely in others?

The Statistics

Women's employment in the United States has shown the greatest increase in managerial and administrative occupations.[11] Figure 2-3 shows this increase for the years 1983 through 2006, with a leveling off at around 42 percent women in this category. This situation stands in stark contrast to the 18 percent of managers who were women in 1972.[12] The United States is not an exception. Women have also made considerable inroads into management in many other nations. According to United Nations data, in the United States, 42 percent of "legislators, senior officials, and managers" are women, compared with 35 percent in Germany, 33 percent in the United Kingdom, 31 percent in Sweden, 32 percent in Spain, 25 percent in Argentina, and 10 percent in Japan.[13]

Overall in the United States, 13 percent of all employed women have management positions, compared with 16 percent of employed men, and white and Asian women are better represented in management than African American and Hispanic women. At first glance, it might seem that women must be displacing men as managers, but this is not the case. Managerial

FIGURE 2-3

Percentage of women employees in management, business, and financial operations occupations in the United States, 1983–2006

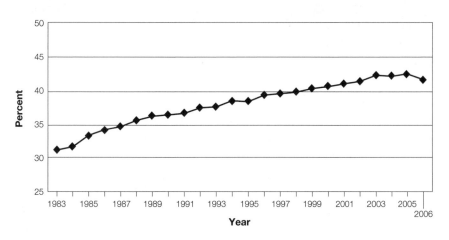

Source: Adapted from U.S. Bureau of Labor Statistics, 2007a. Historical CPS Employment for 1983–99 on the 2002 Census Industry and Occupational Classifications, Series LNU02032202 and LNU02032527.

occupations have expanded greatly, especially at lower and middle levels, making room for more workers. In addition to management positions, many women hold jobs at lower levels of organizational leadership as "first-line supervisors," mainly of office and administrative staff and retail sales workers.[14]

A substantial number of women hold middle management positions in large corporations, but relatively few are executives. Counts of women in corporate executive leadership are provided by Catalyst, an organization founded to promote the advancement of women in business and the professions. Catalyst researchers focus on the *Fortune 500*. In these corporations, women occupy 16 percent of the executive positions (2 percent are women of color). Only ten years earlier, when Catalyst conducted its first count, women of all races and ethnicities constituted only 9 percent of corporate officers.[15] So the trend is upward.

The most complete census of top business executives, conducted by management researchers Constance Helfat, Dawn Harris, and Paul Wolfson, evaluated the entire *Fortune* 1000 as of the year 2000. This survey found that only 8 percent of the executives were women. Although approximately one-fourth of the corporations had more than one woman executive, another one-fourth had only one, and half had no women executives at all. In the firms that had one or more female executives, these women were younger than the male executives and had been in their positions and with their companies for shorter periods of time. It thus appears that some corporations recently began recruiting women and promoting them into the executive ranks.[16]

Corporate officers hold either line or staff positions. Executives in *line* positions have responsibility for profits and losses or are in direct contact with clients—for example, in sales, manufacturing, and operations. In contrast, executives in *staff* positions provide support to the line operations. Because those in line positions make the critical strategic decisions that directly affect a company's financial outcomes, they are more often promoted to top corporate positions than are staff executives. The most recent Catalyst survey found that women in the *Fortune* 500 hold only 11 percent of line officer positions, but 21 percent of staff officer positions, especially concentrated in functional areas such as public relations, human resources, legal services, and accounting. As one woman executive wrote, "Women have been shunted off into support areas for the last 30 years, rather than being in the business of doing business, so the pool of women trained to assume leadership positions in any large company is very small. In MBA programs and undergraduate business schools, there should be overt messaging to encourage women students to insist on line jobs when they enter the workforce."[17] And even when male and female managers are in comparable positions in organizations, the positions held by women tend to be structured so that the women wield less authority over others than the men.[18]

At the very top of *Fortune* 500 companies are the most highly paid officers—executives who have titles such as chairman, president, chief operating officer, and chief executive officer. Of this group, only 6 percent are women. Most notably, only 2 percent of *Fortune* 500 CEOs are women. Yet even this small percentage represents an increase: in the 1970s, only two women held such positions: Katharine Graham of the *Washington Post* and Marian Sandler of Golden West Financial.[19]

Boards of directors monitor and oversee the policies and activities of corporations. In the *Fortune* 500, women hold 15 percent of the seats on boards of directors (including 3 percent by women of color), an improvement over the 10 percent that Catalyst reported in 1995. Although almost 90 percent of these companies have at least one female board member, she is often the sole representative of her sex on an otherwise all-male board. In these boards, women are somewhat underrepresented as committee chairs, especially on auditing and compensation committees. In general, female board members do not sit at the center of power.[20]

In industrialized countries other than the United States, women likewise have few positions at the highest corporate levels.[21] In the top five hundred Canadian companies, 14 percent of corporate officers, 3 percent of CEOs, and 11 percent of board members are women. In the fifty largest publicly traded corporations in each nation of the European Union, women make up, on average, 11 percent of the top executives and 4 percent of the CEOs and the presidents of boards of directors.[22] *Fortune* magazine's list of the Global 500 reveals seven female CEOs, or 1 percent; of these seven, four lead U.S. companies.[23]

In the United States, women's chances of becoming business executives are much higher outside the *Fortune* 500, where wages and capital investments are lower.[24] In this economic sector, women often own the businesses that they lead. In the United States, women hold at least half ownership in 10.4 million companies. Although the majority of firms owned by women are small, with only about 3 percent earning $1 million or more annually, they make a substantial contribution to the economy. These firms constitute approximately 40 percent of all privately held firms in the nation, employ 12.8 million workers, and generate $1.9 trillion in sales. Women-owned firms grew at twice the rate of all privately held firms in the past two decades.[25]

Education is one field in which women have gained substantially in leadership. Currently, 64 percent of educational administrators are women, including 23 percent of college and university presidents. Women now lead many prestigious universities such as Massachusetts Institute of Technology, Princeton University, Harvard University, University of Michigan, and University of Pennsylvania. And a few women are among the most highly paid university presidents in the United States.[26]

Women constitute 27 percent of the federal government's Senior Executive Service, which consists of the highest positions that are not politically appointed. Women have made some progress in law firms, where 17 percent of the partners are women. Also, 23 percent of the federal district court judges and 24 percent of the federal circuit court (court of appeals) judges are women. However, women are less well represented as military leaders, accounting for 15 percent of all officers and only 5 percent of the officers at the level of brigadier general and rear admiral or higher.[27]

Women have gained top leadership roles in many foundations. Among 802 U.S. foundations and giving programs, women are 55 percent of the chief executives, including, for example, the presidents of the Ford Foundation and the Rockefeller Foundation.[28] In the film industry, four of the six major studios have women in the top creative decision-making roles, although male executives predominate in the companies that own the studios.[29] And despite the sharp increase in women musicians in symphony orchestras after blind auditions became the norm, women remain rare as music directors—that is, principal conductors—of symphony orchestras: among the top twenty-six orchestras in the United States, only one is led by a woman.[30]

In summary, the numbers of female managers have skyrocketed even though women remain rare in some executive roles. Women now constitute a majority of managers in many areas, with the greatest concentrations in medical and health services (68 percent), human resources (66 percent), social and community services (66 percent), and education (64 percent).[31]

What Do the Statistics Mean?

Our statistics make it clear that women have gained considerable authority in the workplace even though they still have far to go in corporate leadership. Few women have ever been listed among "the best and most powerful" corporate leaders. In 2005, only two women appeared in *BusinessWeek*'s list of the best managers: Anne Mulcahy, CEO of Xerox; and Meg Whitman, CEO of eBay.[32] *Fortune*'s 2004 list of the twenty-five most powerful people in business included only three women: Carly Fiorina, then CEO of Hewlett-Packard; Meg Whitman; and Abby Johnson, who was presented with her father, the chairman of Fidelity, and described as his heir apparent.[33]

Clearly, the number of women in the corporate power elite is small, and many of their positions are peripheral to the centers of power. Sometimes companies award executive titles to women just to give the appearance of diversity. One broadcasting executive disclosed, "We gave vice president titles to women who were in corporate communications, publicity, and even the librarian, and we congratulated ourselves on having women at the senior executive levels. But the truth is we'd never let any women into sales, engineering, or programming."[34] This phenomenon may account for at least some of the discrepancy between the 16 percent of corporate officers who are women and the smaller percentages of women in line and top executive positions.

One reason that women leaders are more numerous outside the *Fortune* 500 is that slow advancement in large corporations has inspired them to start their own businesses. In fact, the most common reason that women give for striking out on their own is that they desire to advance in their careers. For example, one female entrepreneur who had left a corporate position complained about "having what you say ignored or dismissed until it's later said by a man, in which case it was determined to be a brilliant idea."[35] Labyrinthine corporate barriers have motivated women to seek opportunities in less obstructed domains.

Some commentators attribute the shortage of women in elite corporate management to the lack of women in the executive pipeline.[36] However, such claims ignore the dramatic increase in the percentage of MBAs awarded to women after 1975.[37] The executive pipeline can no longer be described as devoid of women. Because many women with MBAs are now at or approaching the life stage of maximum eligibility for top executive leadership, the representation of women as corporate executives should continue to increase.

Predictions, however, should be made with caution. Upbeat forecasts about women breaking into the corporate elite have been common. Numerous times in the past twenty-five years, *BusinessWeek*, the *Wall Street*

Journal, and *Fortune* have published lists of top corporate women and predicted that many would ascend to become CEOs. Few of these women in fact became CEOs, and that outcome is consistent with systematic research on the pipeline to CEO. Based on counts of the numbers of female corporate executives in the ranks below CEO, the most accurate forecast is that the representation of women CEOs will rise slowly in the coming decade.[38]

Countering journalists' usual optimism about women's ascent, a "female dropout" theme emerged a few years ago. In *Fortune*'s 2003 presentation of the fifty most powerful women in business, the accompanying article discussed whether women really want power: "Many fast-track women are surprisingly ambivalent about what's next. Dozens of powerful women we interviewed tell us that they don't want to be Carly Fiorina . . . many don't want to run a huge company."[39] The *New York Times Magazine* featured a similar article in 2003, accompanied by provocative headlines on the cover: "Q: Why don't more women get to the top? A: They choose not to—Abandoning the climb and heading home." *Fast Company* and *Time* joined the chorus with articles questioning women's commitment to top positions.[40]

Quickly contradicting this dropout theme, other journalists maintained that women are continuing to rise. The *Wall Street Journal*'s 2004 feature on the demise of the glass ceiling asserted that women are "now changing the leadership landscape in corporations." This report argued that, right below the very top executives, there are many women who are likely to rise. The *Wall Street Journal*'s 2006 feature article on "the 50 women to watch" also weighed in: "Women are running operations and devising strategy in virtually every industry, from heavy manufacturing, chemicals and computer technology to consumer products, fashion and media."[41] *Fortune* labeled 2005 an outstanding year for women in business and declared, "America's leading businesswomen are calling the shots more than ever before." *Fortune* then followed with a 2006 feature on the fifty most powerful women in business, presenting five full-page photographic displays of these women in a single issue, all labeled as "cover pages"—to draw attention to the increasing prominence of women among top corporate executives.[42]

Despite this mix of optimism and pessimism about women as corporate leaders, the growing educational advantage of women over men predicts an increase in their leadership at all levels and in all types of organizations. In subsequent chapters, we document other reasons women should continue to advance, especially the increasing gender equality in family responsibilities and changes in the psychology of women.

Women and Men as Political Leaders

How do women fare as political leaders? In the U.S. government, the representation of women is no greater than that of executives in the corporate sector. In the U.S. Congress, women hold 16 percent of the seats in both the House of Representatives and the Senate.[43] In 2007, Nancy Pelosi became the first to hold the top leadership position in the House of Representatives.

These figures for the Congress place the United States slightly lower than the international average of 17 percent of women in national parliaments, and far below many other industrialized nations—for example, 47 percent in Sweden, 31 percent in Spain, and 25 percent in Switzerland.[44] The countries with markedly higher percentages of women usually have quota systems ensuring a certain percentage of women candidates, either mandated by their governments or instituted voluntarily by political parties. Sometimes governments reserve a certain proportion of seats in the parliament for women.[45] Lacking any of these provisions, the U.S. electoral system does not facilitate the election of women.

The very top of the U.S. federal executive hierarchy was briefly touched by the presence of Geraldine Ferraro, the vice presidential candidate in Walter Mondale's unsuccessful 1984 campaign. Upon receiving this nomination Ferraro said, "American history is about doors being opened," but she remains the only woman vice presidential or presidential candidate nominated by a major party in the United States.[46] However, women have served or are serving as presidents or prime ministers in many other countries: twenty-five women achieved these offices in the 1990s, and seven presidents and five prime ministers are in office at this writing.[47]

In the United States, women are no longer unusual in presidential cabinets. The first woman in the cabinet, Frances Perkins, was secretary of labor in the Franklin Roosevelt administration. The second, Oveta Culp Hobby, was secretary of health, education, and welfare in the Eisenhower administration. After Hobby's term ended in 1955, there was a twenty-year gap in women's cabinet service until President Gerald Ford appointed Carla Anderson Hills as secretary of housing and urban development. Presidents Carter, Reagan, and George H. W. Bush each appointed four women to such posts. President Clinton appointed fourteen. At this writing, President George W. Bush has appointed eight women. Especially nontraditional are the appointments of women to the powerful role of secretary of state, with Madeleine Albright serving from 1997 to 2001, and Condoleezza Rice beginning in 2005.[48]

Women do somewhat better at the state level. To some extent, state offices, especially governorships, serve as a pipeline to federal offices. Currently, 18 percent of governors are women, with the first female governor, Ella Grasso, elected in Connecticut in 1974. In addition, women hold 24 percent of the statewide elective executive offices and 24 percent of the seats in state legislatures, with some states having substantial minorities of female legislators—for example, Vermont, with 37 percent. In the one hundred largest U.S. cities, 12 percent of the mayors are women.[49]

Some reports about women's progress in politics have been downbeat. In an article in the *New York Times Magazine*, journalist Gail Collins described the slow gains in office-holding by women from the 1970s onward. Collins explained the larger representation of women in state legislatures by the relatively low pay and unattractiveness of the positions. She maintained, "One reason that women are having trouble winning the top political offices is that those are the jobs men want to keep. The offices most accessible to women are those too cheap to be interesting to male [politicians]."[50]

Countering this pessimism was the upward bump in women's congressional representation in 1992, inspired at least in part by the all-male Senate Judiciary Committee's harsh treatment of Anita Hill during the hearings for the nomination of Clarence Thomas to the Supreme Court.[51] Since that year, women's congressional representation has continued to increase slowly.

Women and Men as Leaders in Other Settings

Now we turn to the microcosm of small work groups without formally appointed leaders. Research on such groups can reveal how social interactions enable people to attain leadership. Who emerges as a group leader depends on group members' behaviors and their beliefs about what type of person would make a good leader. Most of these studies are conducted by researchers in social psychology or organizational behavior, almost always with university students serving as research participants. Some of these studies are laboratory experiments involving group discussions or problem solving, and others examine longer-term groups that meet for an entire semester.

Researchers typically identify the leader by asking group members who their leader was or by selecting the person in each group who behaved most like a leader—by influencing, motivating, or coordinating the group. According to a meta-analysis of fifty-eight studies that assessed leaders' emergence, men become the overall leaders of their groups more often than women do. Women emerge more often than men as the social facilitators—that is, as persons who help other members get along with one another. Although these facilitators are generally well liked, they are not usually the most influential person in their group.[52]

As with organizational and political leadership, men's advantage has been shrinking over the years in these small-group studies. And the male advantage also weakens when groups meet over a number of weeks or work on tasks that require complex social coordination or traditionally feminine expertise, such as a sewing activity. These conditions favor women.[53]

The spontaneous emergence of leaders has also been tallied in one important natural setting: juries assembled to hear court cases. Juries choose their leader, the foreperson, at the beginning of the deliberation, after the evidence has been heard. In the small number of studies that have tallied male and female forepersons, men were chosen more often than women. For example, in two federal district courts in the Southwest during 1971–1974, women emerged as forepersons only one-fifth as often as would be expected by their number. However, in a 1997 study of mock juries composed of university students or of jury-eligible citizens, women and men were equally likely to emerge as forepersons.[54] Whether this more recent study reflects an actual trend in the selection of female forepersons would require systematic analyses of court records.

Finally, we consider high school student leaders in sports, student government, student publications, school-sponsored clubs, and the performing arts. These leaders may be elected or appointed, or they may emerge informally. As figure 2-4 shows, in surveys of high school seniors in selected years, approximately equal percentages of white boys and girls are leaders. Boys are more likely than girls to be leaders in sports, and girls in other activities. Notable is a decline since 1982 in the percentage of black student leaders, especially black girls, although the causes of this trend are unclear. Among other groups, however, high school leadership appears to be approximately equally shared between the sexes.[55]

In summary, small-group studies conducted in universities show that men emerge as leaders more than women, but this predominance of male leaders has decreased over the years. Men have also been the majority of jury forepersons, but information is too limited to show whether this leadership gap has changed over the years. In high schools, student leadership

FIGURE 2-4

Percentage of high school seniors who have served in school leadership roles in the United States, displayed by race and sex, 1972–2004

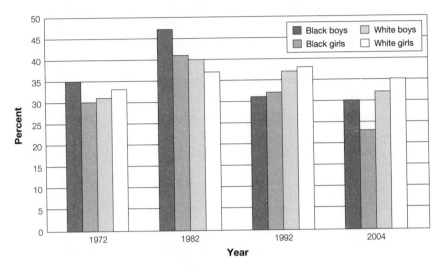

Source: Adapted from C. Weinberger, "Are There Racial Gaps in High School Leadership Opportunities?" Working Paper, University of California, Santa Barbara, 2006. Used with permission.

roles appear to have been approximately equally shared between the sexes, at least since the early 1970s.

Conclusions

Women have made very substantial progress but still have quite far to go to achieve equal representation as leaders. Few women hold the very top positions in corporations or governments, either in the United States or in other nations. Nevertheless, in the United States, women now occupy more than 40 percent of all managerial positions and hold nearly one-fourth of chief executive positions when all organizations are considered. These statistics demonstrate considerable social change and show that women's careers have become far more successful than they were in the past. Men still have more authority and higher wages, but women have been catching up.[56]

Because some women have moved into the most elite leadership roles, absolute barriers are a thing of the past. A small number of women have successfully negotiated the labyrinth that impedes most women's progress on the path toward these positions. Among them are women who have become CEOs of large corporations, presidents of universities and foundations, senators, members of presidential cabinets, and governors of states.

In the chapters that follow, we reveal the forces responsible for this increasing presence of women as well as for the continuing predominance of men, especially at the higher levels. In chapter 3, we consider (and reject) the idea that the predominance of men might be due to a fundamental psychological cause: an evolved, hard-wired biological drive to dominate that is intrinsic only to men.

CHAPTER THREE

Are Men Natural Leaders?

ARE MEN NATURAL LEADERS, shaped by evolution to attain power and status? If that were so, the scarcity of women leaders would reflect fundamental sex differences in personality and motivation, and consequently women would never attain equal access to leadership roles. Our labyrinth metaphor would be superfluous.

In this chapter we reject the idea that men, but not women, have a naturally dominant and competitive psychology that facilitates leadership. We present, and then critique, the argument that men are natural leaders. We also summarize the known sex differences and similarities in dominant traits such as aggressiveness, assertiveness, and competitiveness. Finally, we identify the personality traits that are in fact correlated with leadership, and we evaluate whether they are more prevalent in one sex than the other. This research shows that the psychological portrait of good leaders is neither masculine nor feminine but includes traits from both of these domains in approximately equal measure.

The Evolutionary Psychology Theory of Male Dominance

Many evolutionary psychologists claim that leadership is inherent in the male psyche.[1] They maintain that men are naturally more dominant and competitive than women and therefore more likely to gain authority roles. Consider the following succinct statement of this logic by Kingsley Browne, a leading proponent of this view: "Human sex differences are products of the same selective forces that cause behavioral sex differences in other species . . . Across human history, male status has led to greater reproductive success, leading to a predisposition among males to engage in the kinds of status competition that today so often have workplace implications."[2]

The basic claim is that leadership, and dominance more generally, stems from traits that are built into the male of the human species through adaptation to the primeval environments in which humans evolved. If true, such evolved dispositions would forever limit women's potential as leaders. On this point, Browne is clear: "If high-status roles are found exclusively in the extra-domestic sphere—a sphere in which men's temperament gives them an advantage—then women will be forever consigned to lower status."[3] By this reasoning, nature has doomed women to cede power and status to men except in the kitchen and the nursery.

The essential argument of evolutionary psychologists is that men and women have different personalities because they evolved different behavioral strategies for reproduction in eons past. This theorizing concerns *sexual selection*: the strategies by which men and women choose partners for mating. The central starting point for evolutionary psychologists is the observation that males and females differ in their personal investment of time and energy in their offspring. Specifically, in humans and other mammalian species, females' gestation and nursing of infants demand a considerable investment, which limits the number of offspring that they can conceive and care for. In contrast, males' provision of sperm takes relatively little time and effort, giving a man the potential to conceive many more offspring than a woman without necessarily providing subsequent investment in them. By this argument, females' high investment caused them to became choosy about potential mates. This choosiness, in turn, forced males to compete with one another for sexual access to females, especially to fertile females. The men who prevailed in this competition were then more likely to have their genes carried on to the next generation.[4]

According to evolutionary psychology, men are psychologically prepared for leadership because ancestral men competed with one another for access to fertile women. In these reproductive contests, aggressive, risk-taking, competitive men presumably were more successful and would have passed along their genes to more offspring. By this reasoning, current-day male psychology contains the vestige of ancestral men's competition with one another for access to women.

According to this theory, women's mating strategy shaped the female psyche. Ancestral women were better able to reproduce and survive if they developed a preference for mates who could provide resources to support them and their children. By this argument, women's preference would in turn have led men to evolve tendencies to acquire resources, presumably through prevailing in competitions for status, authority, and wealth.

Some evolutionary psychologists further reason that women's greater investment in their offspring had additional effects on their psychology. Because children relied more on care by their mothers than their fathers, the survival of offspring depended primarily on the survival of their mothers. Therefore, women presumably evolved a strong concern with their own personal safety as well as tendencies to be fearful and anxious and to avoid danger and risk.[5]

In brief, for many evolutionary psychologists, contemporary men's efforts to dominate one another and to control women are innate "fossils" of the selection pressures that shaped the human species in its distant evolutionary past.[6] By this reasoning, nature has endowed men more than women with aggressive, competitive, controlling, and status-striving qualities that facilitate leadership. Francis Fukuyama, a public policy expert, used these ideas to argue that women's rise toward equality is sharply limited by men's biologically given competitiveness and drive for power: "Despite the rise of women, men will continue to play a major, if not dominant, part in the governance of postindustrial countries, not to mention less-developed ones. The realms of war and international politics in particular will remain controlled by men . . . ?"[7] This reasoning rests on a cluster of assumptions about relations between the sexes in primeval times, assumptions that cannot be tested directly. We now turn to evaluating their plausibility.[8]

What's Wrong with the Evolutionary Psychology Analysis of Leadership?

One vulnerability of this theory stems from its limited sources of data. To hope to understand the origins of human traits, scientists must observe behavior in a wide variety of cultures, and particularly in small-scale, non-industrial societies. Although such societies are not the same as the groups in which humans evolved, they are much more similar to them than industrialized societies are. However, most research by evolutionary psychologists consists of studies of university students in the United States and sometimes of students in other nations. These limited sources of data have allowed these investigators to ignore evidence that the foraging and pastoral societies studied by anthropologists are less likely than modern industrialized societies to show the very sex differences that they predict.[9]

Universal dominance by men over women is one such prediction.[10] If aggressiveness and competitiveness are innate male dispositions, men would be dominant over women—everywhere and forever—although the extremity of male dominance would vary with cultural conditions. However, anthropological evidence suggests that in approximately one-third of small-scale societies with simple socioeconomic systems, men and women are about equal in authority and power even though they have somewhat different responsibilities. This finding disputes the claim that authority and dominance are inherent in men's nature.[11]

One example of an egalitarian society is the Vanatinai, a small-scale foraging and horticultural society located on a small, remote island southeast of New Guinea. This society lacks ideologies of male superiority. Because kinship is matrilineal—that is, determined by the female line—women have considerable access to material resources. Couples and their children alternate their residences between the hamlets of the wife's and the husband's families. Although there are no chiefs with formal authority, both sexes have access to a "big man" or "big woman" leadership role that confers informal power and authority. Ethnographic records show that "men have no formal authority or powers of coercion over women except for the physical violence that both sexes abhor and that is rare in the extreme."[12] The Vanatinai, like other societies, have a male–female division of labor in terms of typical activities. However, this society's division of labor does not produce an overall power advantage of men over women.

Another claim of evolutionary psychologists is that evolution endowed women with a motive to seek mates with resources and endowed men with a motive to impress women by acquiring these resources in competitions with other men.[13] This reasoning neglects women's own substantial productive contributions to subsistence activities in most nonindustrial societies and likely also in early human societies. As a result, reproductive success and survival of *both sexes* would have depended on having a mate who provided resources. Which sex was more dependent on the other sex for basic subsistence reflected whether a society's food derived mainly from gathering plants or from hunting and fishing. Cross-culturally, women were generally the gathering specialists and men the hunting and fishing specialists, especially for larger prey. In some ecological circumstances, foraging societies were dependent primarily on gathering, producing conditions in which men depended to a considerable extent on women for their basic subsistence.[14]

As more complex economies developed, people acquired new productive roles (for example, in farming and mining), including many roles requiring work outside the household. These new roles increasingly required training, intensive energy expenditure, and travel away from the home. Because men did not have the responsibilities of gestation and nursing infants, it was easier for them to fill many of these new roles. Men's greater size, upper-body strength, and speed also gave them advantages in fulfilling the particular roles associated with many preindustrial production tasks, including intensive agriculture, smelting of ores, lumbering, and warfare. As men assumed these roles, they gained control over resources and amassed social power.

As gender hierarchies formed in these new economies, men gained power over women. There is little need to explain this outcome as arising from an inborn motive of men to dominate. This result is more plausibly explained by men's freedom from childbearing and their physical prowess, which suited them to many of the productive activities that were required for survival as societies advanced toward more complex economies. Men's physical attributes positioned them to occupy the roles that provided access to wealth and power as these more complex economies developed. Women, in turn, became increasingly confined to a domestic role involving childcare and the production of goods for the immediate family through activities such as cooking, sewing, weaving, and grinding grain. Thus, patriarchy is not an inherent feature of human societies but emerged along with a variety of economic and social developments, including intensive agriculture and warfare.

As societies advanced economically, women as a group became identified as the nurturing and domestic sex because they more often cared for children and produced domestic goods for their own families. However important these activities were to families, they did not yield nearly as much power and wealth as the activities in which men increasingly specialized. Because men produced more goods that could be traded or exchanged in the marketplace, they acquired power and influence well beyond the family. And because people's expectations about social groups emerge from their observations of what behaviors are typical of a group (see chapter 6), social expectations about men and women diverged accordingly.

In general, the sex differences emphasized by evolutionary psychologists have appeared more often in societies with relatively complex economies. In an evolutionary time frame, such societies are much more recent than the societies in which humans emerged in their modern form, both ana-tomically and psychologically. In these more recent agricultural and in-dustrial societies, men typically serve as the primary resource providers for their families, and women obtain many resources from men. In the tradi-tional foraging societies that predominated prior to these more complex economies, subsistence patterns were more varied, and patriarchy was not necessarily present. Yet, any hard-wired psychological traits such as male competitiveness and desire for power would have been present in these simpler societies. The lack of consistent evidence for patriarchy in simpler societies thus raises questions about the plausibility of the evolutionary psychology claims about men's contemporary predominance as leaders.

How do evolutionary psychologists come to their conclusions about the origins of sex differences? They first assume that behavioral patterns that we observe in men and women must have been adaptive for our human ancestors and therefore became ingrained as hard-wired evolved disposi-tions. They then reason backward in time, applying what is sometimes called "reverse engineering" to figure out the adaptive problems our ances-tors might have faced that could have produced inborn psychological adap-tations favoring these patterns of behavior.[15] This popular but specula-tive type of reasoning underlies the argument that men are natural leaders because evolution endowed men, but not women, with dominance and competitiveness.

Biosocial Origins of Psychological Sex Differences

Presenting an alternative evolutionary theory, called the *biosocial origin the-ory*, Wendy Wood and Alice Eagly argue that psychological sex differences derive mainly from the types of roles filled by men and women within soci-eties.[16] Each sex develops behavioral tendencies that are appropriate for its typical roles. These roles are not fixed but change over time, reflecting the ability of each sex to perform important tasks in its particular culture. His-torically, the ability to perform various roles depended fundamentally on inherited physical attributes, especially women's childbearing and nursing of infants and men's greater size, speed, and upper-body strength.

These physical differences between the sexes have varying effects on roles, because their impact depends on a society's social structure, econ-omy, ecology, and technology. Both men and women are role specialists and learn to do what is needed to perform their roles. When one sex can perform particular roles more efficiently than the other, the more efficient sex will come to fill the majority of those roles. As societies change (for example, as they develop advanced technology), the distribution of women and men into roles often changes. Changes in the psychology of women and men follow from changes in their roles.

Contemporary highly industrialized societies present remarkably altered conditions. Birthrates have decreased substantially, thereby freeing women to work outside their homes. Medical technology facilitates control over reproduction. Occupations have changed dramatically. Few high-status occupations now favor men's greater size and strength, thus removing one of women's earlier impediments to gaining power and status. There are no height or bench-press requirements for being a lawyer, business executive, or university professor. With the lessening of the biosocial barriers that women once faced because of their reproductive activity and their lesser size and strength, women have entered a wide variety of paid occupations. In postindustrial economies, where the service sector dominates, women have entered many high-status roles in large numbers.[17]

As we explain in chapter 6, the roles occupied by men and women have powerful effects on their behavior and personalities. No one should be surprised by the continuing existence of some psychological sex differences as long as men and women continue to divide important life tasks (for example, childcare) by sex.[18]

The ability to tell a story about the possible adaptiveness of certain psychological sex differences in primeval times hardly constitutes convincing evidence of their evolutionary origins. Evolutionary theorists are mostly mute about the intervening causal processes that could produce current-day sex differences in traits relevant to leadership. For example, if women are innately less competitive than men, there should be evidence that this difference is mediated by sex-specific hormonal processes, specific sex-differentiated genes, differential expression of genes, or other mechanisms. For the most part, such issues remain to be addressed in scientific research.[19]

Psychological Sex Differences That Enhance Leadership According to Evolutionary Psychology

Now we turn to the aggressive and dominant tendencies that evolutionary psychologists most often claim can explain the prevalence of men in leadership roles. First, we ask whether men and women differ in these traits, regardless of whether any differences reflect mainly nature or mainly nurture. Then we consider whether these traits facilitate leadership.

Aggressiveness

When aggressiveness is understood as the tendency to engage in behavior that is intended to harm others, meta-analytic reviews of numerous studies have found men to be more aggressive than women overall. Men's verbal aggression, such as insulting someone, is only slightly higher than women's. Where men show quite a bit more aggression than women is in physical aggressiveness that inflicts pain or injury, such as hitting someone. Men, particularly younger men, exceed women most strongly in physical aggression toward their own sex. In natural settings, men's violence toward other men takes many forms, including assaults and homicide.[20] In the United States, men currently account for 82 percent of arrests for violent crime and 89 percent of arrests for murder and non-negligent manslaughter.[21]

Aggression need not involve direct physical or verbal assault. Instead, people can damage others' status or relationships through roundabout social maneuvers, such as gossiping and spreading damaging rumors.[22] Although girls sometimes appear to be more aggressive than boys in these indirect ways, findings have been mixed.[23]

Among adults in the workplace, aggression is often indirect but takes a wide range of forms. Hostile and damaging actions can include, for example, evaluating others' performance unfairly, failing to transmit information needed by others, and stealing company funds or property. In general, workplace aggression is more common in men than in women.[24]

In summary, the hundreds of studies that have been conducted on aggression yield a few clear-cut conclusions: specifically, men exceed women in physical aggression expressed toward same-sex peers but are only slightly more verbally aggressive than women. Men also engage in more workplace aggression than women.

Dominance, Assertiveness, and Competitiveness

Potentially important for leadership are more positive forms of dominance, including assertiveness and competitiveness, which do not necessarily involve harm to others. On personality tests of dominance or assertiveness, there is a small to moderate tendency for men to score higher than women.[25] Assertiveness tends to have different contours in men compared with women. Men generally assert themselves in a forceful or controlling manner, and women more often in a manner that acknowledges the rights of others as well as their own rights. Women also often express their dominance and assertiveness through group-oriented behaviors that facilitate the work of others, such as sharing the limelight with them at a meeting or helping them develop their talents. Assertive behavior that promotes oneself over others is more typical of men.[26]

Men seem to prefer to assert themselves in hierarchical relationships more than women do. For example, male managers report somewhat more interest than female managers in managing in a traditional command-and-control style. This greater attraction of men than women to social hierarchies also emerges in men's greater *social dominance*, a personality trait defined by the desire for one's own group to dominate other groups and be superior to them.[27]

Competitiveness, which evolutionary psychologists believe is inherent in male psychology, has been researched primarily in experiments on bargaining and negotiation. These laboratory games reveal only slightly greater male competitiveness—and greater female cooperativeness.[28] Ideally, competitiveness would be investigated in natural settings and not solely in laboratory games. Economist Uri Gneezy produced such a study by observing Israeli children running races in a physical education classes. He concluded that boys are more competitive than girls because boys increased their speed when running against another child, but girls did not. However, this interpretation failed to acknowledge boys' generally greater psychological investment in athletics.[29] Valid conclusions about competitiveness await study of a variety of tasks that include some that appeal more to females, some more to males, and some equally to males and females.

Change Over Time in Women's Tendencies to Be Dominant

Claims about men's greater dominance, expressed in aggressive, assertive, and competitive behavior, are arguable, not only because these differences are not large but also because women have been gaining on men. It is possible that women are somewhat catching up even in physical aggressiveness, consistent with crime statistics. In the face of an overall decline in violent crime in recent years in the United States, females showed a slight increase. From 1995 to 2004, the rates of arrest for violent crime for men decreased 20 percent, and those for women rose 3 percent.[30] Lending cultural endorsement to female aggressiveness, the entertainment industry has featured many physically aggressive female characters in the form of, for example, warrior princesses (*Xena*), James Bond-type spies (Mrs. Smith in *Mr. and Mrs. Smith*), and killers of abusive husbands (the Dixie Chicks' hit song "Goodbye Earl").[31]

Examination of women's reports of their own assertiveness yields clear evidence of change over time. Women now describe themselves as having more of these traditionally masculine qualities than women did in the past: more ambitious, self-reliant, and assertive. At the same time, women do not describe themselves as any less feminine than in the past—for example, not less affectionate or understanding. On the same measures, men show little change over time.[32]

Trends in women's assertiveness and dominance suggest that shifts in their access to various life roles underlie the observed changes. In a meta-analysis of twentieth-century studies of personality tests of dominance and assertiveness, psychologist Jean Twenge established that women increased in assertiveness and dominance from 1931 to 1945, declined from 1946 to 1967, and increased again from 1968 to 1993, while men remained relatively unchanged. These shifts coincided with women's changing roles: before and during World War II, barriers fell that had restricted women's access to higher-status roles; in the postwar era, barriers rose as traditional family structure prevailed. Finally, in the late twentieth century, women's access to high-status roles increased substantially. The recent surge in women's assertiveness that followed their increasing opportunities is great enough that the sex difference has become quite small in many studies.[33] Consistent with our biosocial theory of the origins of sex differences, the most important story told by these research findings is that women have been gaining in assertiveness and dominance in recent decades.

What Does Dominance Have to Do with Leadership?

The impact of these trends on leadership depends on whether dominance is actually the key to leadership. Physical aggressiveness, which is greater in males than females, is relevant to the leadership of teenage and young adult male groups that center on criminal gang activity or on sports such as football and basketball. Also, the ability to aggress physically is understandably relevant to many forms of military participation. However, physical aggression is unacceptable as a means of leading in virtually every other context. Also, workplace aggression is condemned and, in its more extreme forms, makes individuals unemployable.

More important for leadership might be verbal aggression, which appears to be slightly greater in males. If this sex difference extends to organizations, male bosses would show somewhat more verbal aggression than female bosses. But such a tendency would hardly produce a male advantage. Verbally intimidating behavior has limited value in enhancing bosses' effectiveness.[34] Even though there are some bullying bosses, this type of dominance generally elicits negative reactions and lowers evaluations of competence and leadership. As stated by Peter Crist, chairman of an executive search firm, "There are two traits now that in the corporate world are the kiss of death: intellectual arrogance and bullying."[35]

In summary, evolutionary psychologists claim that men's "natural" tendencies to be aggressive, dominant, and competitive are the key to understanding why men predominate as leaders. Although neither physical nor verbal aggressiveness appear to enhance leadership in most contexts, positive forms of dominance (such as assertiveness) do foster leadership, as we show in the next section. Yet, many experts emphasize that effective leadership requires a good measure of people skills. Some managerial writers even extol the nurturing skills associated with mothering.[36] So what does research tell us about which traits actually enhance leadership?

Personality Traits Actually Associated with Leadership

Personality *is* important to leadership. One hint that this is so is that an inclination to lead tends to emerge by adolescence. Specifically, a study of boys showed that those who had occupied leadership roles by the tenth grade were more likely to become managers as adults and to receive a wage premium for their leadership skills.[37] This consistency of attraction to leadership across the life span is congenial to explanation in terms of personality traits.

Research also suggests that about one-third of the variation in who occupies leadership roles can be explained by genetic factors, with environmental factors accounting for the other two-thirds. So leaders are to some extent "born" as well as "made."[38] But evidence for some degree of genetic predisposition to leadership (as yet not identified with specific genes) does not imply that genetic differences between the sexes underlie men's predominance as leaders. If men, and not women, were genetically programmed to lead, boys should predominate even in high school leadership roles. However, as chapter 2 indicates, leadership is shared approximately equally by girls and boys in high schools.[39]

Psychologists know a lot about the personality traits that affect leadership.[40] These investigations tell a much different story from what can be pieced together from evolutionary psychologists' claims about aggressiveness and competitiveness. This research shows that general intelligence is one quality that enhances individuals' chances of becoming leaders, just as it enhances occupational attainment and job performance in general.[41] But intelligence is not enough—good leaders generally evince a particular constellation of personality traits along with intelligence.

Which personality traits enhance leaders' emergence and effectiveness? An efficient answer comes from organizing personality traits into five classes—the famous scheme known in psychology as the *Big Five*. These five types of traits are assessed by carefully designed and validated personality tests in which people describe their typical behaviors and preferences. Using this scheme, organizational psychologists Timothy Judge, Joyce Bono, Remus Ilies, and Megan Gerhardt examined how personality traits relate to two outcomes: emerging as a leader and performing effectively as a leader.[42] Their findings appear in figure 3-1. A positive relationship means that a personality trait improves chances for leadership, and a negative relationship lessens chances. The first thing to notice is that none of these relationships between the Big Five traits and leadership emergence and effectiveness is statistically very strong, showing that personality is only one among many influences on leadership.

The Big Five Personality Traits

1. NEUROTICISM: exhibiting poor emotional adjustment and negative emotions

2. EXTRAVERSION: exhibiting sociability, assertiveness, activity, and positive emotions

3. OPENNESS TO EXPERIENCE: exhibiting creativity, nonconformity, autonomy, and unconventional qualities

4. AGREEABLENESS: exhibiting caring, trusting, compliant, and gentle qualities

5. CONSCIENTIOUSNESS: exhibiting achievement orientation and dependability

Among the Big Five traits, conscientiousness and extraversion are the strongest predictors that a person will emerge as a leader, but openness to experience and extraversion are the strongest predictors that a person will become effective in a leadership role. So overall, extraversion most

FIGURE 3-1

Personality traits associated with the emergence and effectiveness of leaders

The vertical axes display (standardized) regression coefficients that are averaged across the available studies. A positive value indicates that a trait is associated with more emergence or effectiveness; a negative value indicates that a trait is associated with less emergence or effectiveness.

Prediction of leader emergence

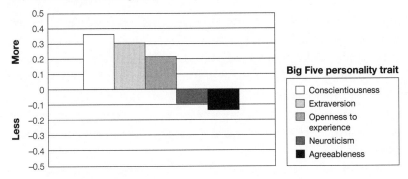

Prediction of leader effectiveness

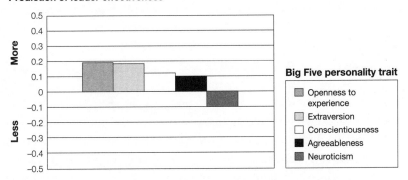

Source: Adapted from T. A. Judge et al., "Personality and Leadership: A Qualitative and Quantitative Review," *Journal of Applied Psychology* 87 (2002): 765–780. Data from table 6. Used with permission.

consistently predicts leadership. Openness to experience and conscientiousness are also important, and agreeableness and neuroticism are the least important.[43] The consistent importance of extraversion is confirmed by research on related psychological traits such as need for power, political skill, emotional intelligence, and empathy. Researchers have also established positive relationships between these traits and effective leadership.[44]

What's so special about extraversion? Extraverted people combine gregariousness with assertiveness. Extraverts like to spend time with other people and to work with them toward shared goals. They initiate action to solve the problems faced by groups and organizations. Such individuals generally have a good aptitude for leadership. They build teams, motivate others, and exert influence.[45]

Consistent with research on extraversion, study of the lives of many successful leaders often reveals their excellent people skills. For example, Franklin Roosevelt excelled in these qualities even as a student when he served as president of Harvard's student-run newspaper, the *Crimson*. A classmate and subsequent *Crimson* president noted that Roosevelt "liked people . . . and made them instinctively like him," adding that "in his geniality was a kind of frictionless command."[46] Sandra Day O'Connor, a highly influential former justice of the Supreme Court, is renowned for her excellent political skills and abilities as a negotiator: "Diligent, alert, energetic, and adept at politicking, she was a master of the telephone call and the handwritten note."[47]

This is not to say that leaders *must* be extraverted: it is not unusual to find some introverts among successful leaders. For example, Microsoft chairman Bill Gates, by reputation, is introverted. Nevertheless, extraversion eases the route to leadership because it fosters a desire to work with other people.[48]

Some degree of risk taking can be important to leadership and may be linked to the Big Five trait of openness to experience.[49] Leaders must be willing to move in new directions or, in business parlance, to "think outside the box." Especially in fast-changing environments, leaders can gain by creatively seeking new directions and moving ahead under conditions of uncertainty, although overly risky actions can, of course, be counterproductive. Leaders also should be dependable and persistent—qualities linked to the Big Five trait of conscientiousness.

The recent business scandals in the United States and elsewhere have put a spotlight on leaders' ethical qualities. Unethical leaders risk dishonor, removal from their leadership roles, revolts by followers, and, under some circumstances, imprisonment. Empirical evidence shows that positive moral qualities generally facilitate good leadership: effective leaders are regarded as trustworthy and display integrity and mature moral reasoning.[50]

In summary, along with general intelligence, relationship-building capabilities produce the most consistent associations with the emergence and effectiveness of leaders. However, intelligence and extraversion are not sufficient. Excellent leaders are creative and put forward new ideas—qualities that reflect the Big Five trait of openness to experience. Leaders also need to display the follow-through that is required to bring projects to completion—a quality that reflects the Big Five trait of conscientiousness. Honesty matters, too, because unethical behavior can derail leaders.

All in all, a certain profile of personal qualities favors leadership, even though many successful leaders do not excel on the full range of these qualities. And of course, the situation in which leadership is exerted shapes the types of leaders who are optimal, as we explain in later chapters.

Comparisons of Women and Men on Traits Actually Associated with Leadership

What does this research on traits say about whether men and women have what it takes to become successful leaders? The answer depends on whether men and women differ in the traits that promote or detract from leadership. There is no need to speculate on this point, because a great deal of research has assessed women and men on measures of intelligence and personality.[51]

Intelligence and the Big Five Personality Traits

Men and women differ little in the traits and abilities that are most relevant to leadership. Specifically, general intelligence, which is associated with leadership, is equal in women and men. On personality traits, we show data collected by psychologists Paul Costa, Antonio Terracciano, and Robert McCrae, which display a typical pattern of findings. Their study compared the scores of one thousand male and female U.S. adults on a personality test designed to assess the Big Five as well as more specific traits (called "facets") that are components of these broad classes of traits (see figure 3-2).[52]

The most important of these findings is that extraversion, which most consistently predicts the emergence and effectiveness of leaders, exists at approximately the same level in men and women, although differences are present in some of its components. As shown in figure 3-2, these components consist of warmth, positive emotions, gregariousness, activity, assertiveness, and excitement seeking. Men exceed women on assertiveness and excitement seeking, and women exceed men on warmth, positive emotions, gregariousness, and activity.[53] So neither men nor women have

FIGURE 3-2

Sex differences for 1,000 U.S. adults on extraversion, openness to experience, and conscientiousness

The vertical axes display (standardized) differences in the d effect size metric. Positive effect sizes indicate higher scores among women than men, and negative effect sizes indicate higher scores among men.

Sex differences in extraversion

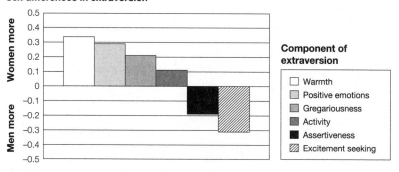

Sex differences in openness to experience

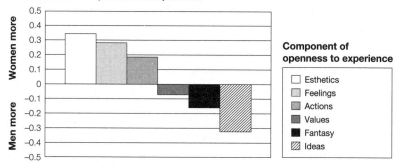

Sex differences in conscientiousness

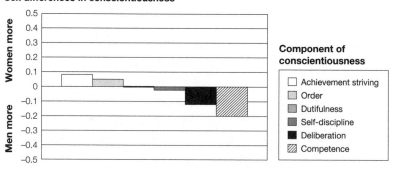

Source: Adapted from P. T. Costa Jr., A. Terracciano, and R. R. McCrae, "Gender Differences in Personality Traits Across Cultures: Robust and Surprising Findings," *Journal of Personality and Social Psychology* 81 (2001): 322–331. Data from table 2. Used with permission.

an overall advantage in the qualities that make up extraversion. Male leaders could gain from more emphasis on the more feminine aspects of extraversion such as warmth, and women could benefit from more emphasis on the more masculine aspects such as assertiveness.

The other traits that most favor leadership—openness to experience and conscientiousness—display similarly mixed patterns of sex differences across their components, with conscientiousness showing the most similarity in women and men (see figure 3-2). Among the Big Five traits, agreeableness and neuroticism show the largest sex differences, with women appearing to be both more agreeable and more neurotic than men across all of these dimensions' components.[54] Because agreeableness and neuroticism relate only weakly to leadership (see figure 3-1), we do not display their sex differences. Neither women's greater agreeableness nor men's lesser neuroticism apparently yields much benefit for leadership.

In summary, comparisons of men and women on extraversion, openness to experience, and conscientiousness—the Big Five traits that most promote leadership—indicate a rough gender balance. Women are somewhat advantaged on some aspects of these traits, and men on others.

Other Personal Qualities

Emotional intelligence and empathy, which may enhance managers' job performance, appear to be somewhat greater in women than men.[55] A need for power, which is also associated with managerial success, has proven to be equally strong in men and women. However, this research also shows that men and women tend to think about power differently; men construe it as more competitive and hierarchical, and women as more cooperative and interdependent.[56]

Research has established greater risk taking in men than women in various types of studies.[57] However, this sex difference is in general quite small, and it has become smaller over time. Moreover, it is not clear what the desirable level of risk taking is for leaders. Patricia Vaz, executive director of British company BT Retail, shared her insights on this matter:

I met a scuba diver once on holiday in the West Indies . . . He said to me that he preferred to train a woman rather than a man in scuba diving. He said, because a man will go to death's door, he will see it in front of him and swim up to it—the macho thing is: "I can do this." Whereas a woman will always say, "Can we avoid the danger, what if, can we find a way of overcoming this,

can we be safe?" Checking for understanding enables you to expose the weak-
nesses and the risks in what you are trying to do. If you can expose them, then
you can devise a strategy that mitigates those risks.[58]

Taking reasonable risks that consider potential gains and losses can be more effective than risk for its own sake.

Ethical Qualities

Men and women differ in some ethical qualities. Women, more than men, disapprove of a wide range of morally nontraditional behaviors and policies, including extramarital relationships, divorce, suicide, and the legalization of marijuana. This ethical theme is consistent with women's greater religiosity. Women also express more compassion for less-fortunate individuals and focus on implications for close relationships in resolving moral dilemmas.[59]

Directly relevant to the workplace is evidence that women, more than men, disapprove of unethical business practices such as the use of insider information, although this sex difference is smaller among managers than nonmanagers. Women are also less accepting than men of unscrupulous negotiation tactics, such as misrepresenting facts, feigning friendship to gain information, and making promises with no intention of honoring them. Similarly, a survey of values in forty-three nations found that in most nations women were less tolerant than men of dishonest or illegal behaviors such as taking bribes.[60] Also, assessments of integrity frequently included in personnel selection tests show greater self-reported integrity in women.[61]

Behaviorally, women are less likely than men to engage in most types of criminal activity. And because morality often demands resistance to temptation, it is revealing that girls and women manifest more resistance to temptation than boys and men in experiments that forbid people to play with, touch, look at, or eat one or more tempting objects.[62]

All in all, women differ from men in several aspects of ethics and morality. These findings are consistent with the prevalence of women among the whistle-blowers who have exposed major ethical violations in the United States in recent years. For example, one of these women, Sherron Watkins of Enron, became famous for her memos to CEO Kenneth Lay describing the company's misrepresentation of its finances.[63] Although few women become whistle-blowers, more may face ethical misgivings of the sort voiced by one female executive in a large retail company:

I was totally naïve. I thought everything you read should be true. I thought everything you do should be done properly. I thought everything that occurred should be reported as it happened. I had no idea that the news had to come out a certain way so that it fit into the big picture. But it's strategically necessary to report a gain before fourth-quarter earnings ... Here I was, working for this big retail chain, and it too was dirty. I had a hard time admitting to myself that I was now in the dirty world of business.[64]

Especially with heightened concern about ethics in business and politics, these moral differences could give women an advantage as leaders. Even though there is little research relating specific ethical qualities to leadership, it is convincing enough that some management researchers have suggested that including more women among executives should decrease fraud by top management.[65]

Also, the public perception that women are less likely to suffer ethical lapses can facilitate the choice of female executives, as apparently was the case when Patricia Woertz became CEO of Archer Daniels Midland. After exposure of this corporation's corrupt culture resulted in the imprisonment of some top executives and payment of hundreds of millions of dollars in fines and settlements, Woertz, an outsider and a woman, was chosen as CEO. In the words of one industrial analyst, "The company had a bit of a Mafioso image, and this [appointment of Woertz] put a friendly face on it. I think that it was a brilliant move by the board."[66] Similarly, after financial giant Smith Barney was exposed for fraudulent financial research and also had to pay very large fines, Sallie Krawcheck became its chief executive. "Dubbed 'Mrs. Clean' thanks to her frank demeanor and focus on ethics," Krawcheck proved successful in this role and further ascended to higher executive roles at Citicorp, the Smith Barney parent company.[67]

Conclusions

Assertions that men and women have different personalities have been a traditional ground for denying leadership roles to women. Challenging this outdated logic, psychological research has illuminated sex differences and similarities in personality traits and the associations of these traits with the emergence and effectiveness of leaders. Research demonstrates small sex differences in some of the traits that are relevant to good leadership—for example, assertiveness, gregariousness, risk taking, and moral integrity. These findings imply female advantage at least as often as male advantage and refute the conclusion that, as Browne wrote, "The dearth of women in high places can be understood only against the backdrop of fundamental sex differences in temperament."[68]

Arguments by evolutionary psychologists that aggressiveness and dominance are of overriding importance for leadership are particularly out of sync with contemporary organizations. As we elaborate in later chapters, what is considered good leadership has changed over the years. For example, a survey from Right Management Consultants, a large outplacement firm, shows that the skill that companies most often seek in managers is the "ability to motivate and engage others."[69] As author, editor, and commentator David Gergen wrote, "Command-and-control leadership has given way to a new approach, often called an influence model of leadership . . . The new leader persuades, empowers, collaborates, and partners."[70]

Consistent with such views, scientific research has demonstrated that some personality traits and general intelligence relate to leadership, although of course leadership is affected by many other factors. Successful leaders most often have an androgynous balance of traits that includes gregariousness, positive initiative and assertion, social skills, intelligence, conscientiousness, integrity, trustworthiness, and the ability to persuade, inspire, and motivate others. In short, effective leadership surely is not enhanced only by feminine qualities or only by masculine qualities. In fact, people who have extremely masculine or extremely feminine personalities are likely to be at a disadvantage for leadership in most contemporary settings.[71]

Thus, the fact that there are few women in some leadership roles cannot be explained by claims about inborn psychological traits. Yet, newspaper articles presenting evolutionary psychology narratives about hard-wired psychological sex differences increase the plausibility of these claims.[72] These ideas can erode confidence that women have what it takes to be good leaders and contribute to the dead ends and misleading turns in the labyrinth that women traverse on the route to leadership.

In chapter 4, we continue to explore the structure of the labyrinth. We address the fundamental issue of whether women's chances to lead are compromised by their domestic responsibilities. Do women avoid leadership or receive fewer promotions than men because they are more burdened by childcare and household responsibilities?

CHAPTER FOUR

Do Family Responsibilities Hold Women Back?

HOW DO WOMEN'S family responsibilities affect their ability to become leaders? Does caring for children and households hold women back? If men's nature can't explain why they occupy most of the leadership positions, perhaps the division of labor in the home can. In this chapter, we show that women's domestic responsibilities *do* contribute to their lesser access to power and authority in society. However, men increasingly share housework and childrearing, and there are signs that these changes toward greater equality are likely to continue. Nevertheless, women are currently responsible for the bulk of domestic work. This situation lessens women's prospects for advancement through the labyrinth. For women to achieve full access to leadership in society, men will have to step up and share more equally in family responsibilities.

Domestic Responsibilities of Women and Men

Women's domestic work far exceeds that of men. Women spend more time doing housework and caring for children than men do. Typically, women are also responsible for making appointments for family members, caring for old or sick family members, and arranging children's activities. They provide the glue that holds families together by maintaining connections with extended family, preparing celebrations for family events, sending cards, visiting with neighbors, and so on.[1]

Housework

The best evidence concerning the time people devote to housework and other activities comes from time diary studies, in which people record what they are doing during each hour of a twenty-four-hour day. Evidence from time diaries completed by representative samples of Americans shows that women's share of housework has declined, and men's has increased. As figure 4-1 indicates, married women devoted a whopping 34 hours per week to housekeeping in 1965, but their housework dropped to 19 hours by 2005. Over the same period, married men increased their housework from 5 to 11 hours per week. Housework is now shared more equally than ever before, but for every hour that men work, women put in about 1.7 hours. Although there probably are many factors contributing to the decline in housework, women's increased employment cannot be one of them because the decline was greater for women without jobs than employed women.[2]

Despite this converging trend in men's and women's housework, married women still perform more of the basic "core" tasks of cooking, cleaning,

FIGURE 4-1

Average weekly housework of married women and men ages 25–64 in the United States, 1965–2005

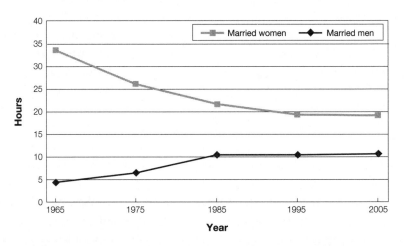

Source: Adapted from S. M. Bianchi, M. A. Milkie, L. C. Sayer, and J. P. Robinson, "Is Anyone Doing the Housework? Trends in the Gender Division of Household Labor," *Social Forces* 79 (2000): table 1. Used with permission. U.S. Bureau of Labor Statistics, 2006b, News: American Time-Use Survey—2005 Results Announced by BLS, table 3.

and laundry, and married men do more yard work, home maintenance, and bill paying.[3] Women's tasks are more frequent, routine, and difficult to skip, and this lack of flexibility contributes to women's burden.

Paradoxically, having a male partner in the home does not reduce women's housework, nor does a woman's bigger paycheck increase men's housework. In fact, married women do more housework than single women. And the proportion of family income that women bring home typically has little effect on how much work their partners do around the house. However, women who earn more of the family income or work longer hours for pay manage to reduce their own housework, probably by purchasing more goods and services.[4]

Childcare

Most men living with young children provide basic care, such as feeding, diapering, and bathing.[5] Men can often be seen by themselves pushing baby carriages or walking in public places with young children. And many men's restrooms have diaper changing tables. These changes are reflected in men's attitudes about caring for their children, as suggested by one father of two children: "I am a dad. I am their dad. I chose consciously to be a father. I mean they [his two children] are the best things that ever happened to me, and as far as bathing them and changing them and cooking for them and doing all that, I don't consider that a chore; it is just a pleasure to be around them, and I spend time with them doing those sorts of things."[6]

Time diary studies confirm men's increasing involvement in childrearing. Fathers of the Baby Boom generation increased their role in childcare compared with men of previous generations. Generation X fathers perform substantially more childcare than Baby Boomer fathers, and Generation Y fathers perform the most of all. Despite these substantial changes, married women still do 2.1 hours of childcare for every hour contributed by married men. Even women world leaders at the top of their professions in government and business perform more childcare than their male counterparts.[7]

Many female executives therefore face challenges in balancing work and family that few male executives face. The key to this difference is that most male executives have wives who are not employed, but most female executives have employed husbands. Only a minority of high-powered female executives—such as Carly Fiorina, ex-CEO of Hewlett-Packard; Anne Mulcahy, president of Xerox; and Karen Garrison, ex-president of Pitney-Bowes

Management Services—have had stay-at-home husbands. Because female executives less often have the support of a stay-at-home spouse, far more of them forgo having children or delay childbearing.[8]

Changes in attitudes about fathers' childcare responsibilities have outpaced changes in behavior. In a recent survey of American couples, a majority of women and men endorsed the egalitarian notion that mothers and fathers should equally share responsibility for everyday childcare. Such attitudes are especially prevalent among educated men and women. Among Americans generally, there has been increasing approval for both husband and wife contributing to the family income and even mothers of preschoolers having jobs. Americans also increasingly indicate that employed mothers can have just as warm a relationship with their children as mothers without jobs.[9]

Despite this greater endorsement of equality as a general principle, couples base their division of labor mainly on their ideas about what would be fair for them personally. The more that wives and husbands believe that they should share domestic duties in their own families, the more equally they share domestic work and wage labor. Yet more husbands than wives are satisfied with the wife doing more of the work, and husbands have more influence than wives on who actually does what.[10] One woman employed as a shift supervisor voiced a common complaint:

> My husband's a great help watching our baby. But as far as doing housework or even taking the baby when I'm at home, no. He figures he works five days a week . . . But he doesn't stop to think that I work seven days a week . . . On his weekends off, I have to provide a sitter for the baby so he can go fishing. When I have a day off, I have the baby all day long without a break. He'll help out if I'm not here, but the minute I am, all the work at home is mine.[11]

Although it is common knowledge that mothers provide more childcare than fathers, few people realize that mothers provide more childcare than in earlier generations. In fact, in the United States both fathers and mothers spend more time in childcare than in the past, as shown by four national time diary studies that tracked parents' childcare from 1965 through 2000 (see figure 4-2).[12] This increase in the time demands of childcare somewhat offsets the gains that mothers experience from fathers' greater participation.

Historically, mothers were busy with tasks such as baking, cooking, washing and ironing clothes, sewing, tending gardens, and, in the more distant past, spinning and weaving. They were available to their children but

FIGURE 4-2

Average weekly childcare hours for married mothers and fathers in the United States, 1965–2000

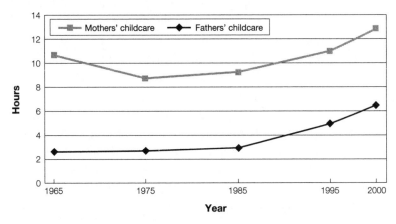

Source: Adapted from Suzanne M. Bianchi, John P. Robinson, and Melissa A. Milkie, *Changing Rhythms of American Family Life*, table 4.1, 64. © 2006 Russell Sage Foundation, 112 East 64th Street, New York, NY, 10021. Used with permission.

too busy to devote themselves to interacting with them. Even during the 1960s, when female employment was relatively low, women did not spend more time interacting with their children than women do now. Mothers often were doing housework while the children occupied themselves with play.[13] As one seventy-year-old grandmother noted,

> My daughter spends more time with her son than I did with my kids, and I spent more time with my kids than my mother did. My mother really didn't have the time. She had to work on the farm so she didn't help with homework, spend time playing with us, or take us places . . . Even when they have jobs, a lot of women today are pressured. They have to spend lots of time with their children, to make them happier, smarter . . . to give them every advantage.[14]

Cultural changes have made it seem increasingly important for mothers to spend quality time with children.[15] The trend toward more mother care began after World War I, when most affluent families lost access to servants and came to rely on mothers for raising their children.[16] The belief in the unique importance of mother care emerged particularly in the 1920s and 1930s and gained credibility throughout the twentieth century, inspired in part by childrearing manuals such as Dr. Benjamin Spock's *Baby and Child Care.* More recent books, such as Berry Brazelton's *What Every Baby Knows*, have continued to emphasize children's need for individualized maternal care.[17]

Many American women, especially better educated and wealthier women, consider motherhood to be highly rewarding, time-consuming, and intensive. And most mothers report spending too little time with their children, even though they spend more time than mothers of previous generations.[18] In fact, employed mothers in 2000 spent as much time interacting with their children as mothers without jobs did in 1975. One mother reflected on her childrearing approach with her four-year-old daughter: "[We do] a lot of negotiating, kind of, trying to set some limits, but we don't say no to her. We try and do more of just working with her [rather] than the old, 'I'm the parent and what I say goes' . . . I mean these are the things that make your life very time consuming and draining, and emotionally you're exhausted. And the older they get, the better negotiator they become. And she's become a terrific negotiator."[19]

According to research, mothers commonly believe that to facilitate healthy child development, motherhood should be selfless and "emotionally absorbing." Because intensive mothering is challenging, mothers are often critical of their parenting skills. Only about one-third of the mothers surveyed by the Pew Research Center felt "very satisfied" with their performance as mothers, and dissatisfaction was especially great among college-educated women.[20] This self-criticism is one symptom of the pressure on women to raise perfect children. As stated by *New York Times* columnist and writer Ellyn Spragins, "Moms are graded by which toddlers share toys in the sandbox and who's on the honor roll. Once upon a time, adults waited until children were grown before judging how they turned out. Now they must trace a perfect trajectory of success at every age to reflect well on their parents and their employment choices."[21]

Ironically, although educated women are especially critical of their parenting, they spend more time with their children than their less well-educated counterparts.[22] One consequence of this pattern is that parenting pressures are most intense among mothers having the most career potential, adding to the challenges that these women face in negotiating the labyrinth.

Given the importance placed on good parenting, mothers who are employed differ relatively little from those who are not employed in the time they spend interacting with their children. In a 2000 time diary study, mothers without jobs spent five more hours per week interacting with their children than employed mothers.[23]

Implications of the Division of Domestic Labor

Domestic responsibilities create time pressures that challenge women seeking advancement in their paid jobs. Employed mothers are particularly time stressed and put in considerable time fulfilling their employment and domestic duties. In a national study, among dual-career married parents with at least some college education, women had a longer total work week. Combining all hours of work, including paid employment and unpaid domestic work, fathers put in 67 hours of work per week, and mothers put in 71 hours.[24]

The demands of intensive parenting contribute to the tensions that employed mothers often experience between their jobs and their families. Women compensate for their time away from home by giving up leisure activities and solitary pursuits to be with their children. The more hours mothers work at their jobs, the less time they spend in solitary leisure and in social activities and the more time they spend in leisure and household activities while also interacting with their children. Having children under age six reduces women's leisure time by an hour a day, and so does marriage. Yet men's leisure is not affected by children or marriage.[25] Compared with men, women have a leisure deficit. In the United States, married men have several hours more leisure per week than married women, amounting to 212 hours more leisure per year, the equivalent of almost five 40-hour work weeks.[26]

Because of the demands of employment and family, women feel more rushed and time-crunched than men do. The more hours that women spend at their jobs, the more dissatisfied they feel with the amount of time they have for themselves and for their other duties, especially if they have children. In contrast, the hours that men spend at their jobs have little effect on their feelings of time pressure.[27]

The most intense time conflicts between jobs and family surface among women in managerial and professional positions because of the long hours such jobs can require (see chapter 9). Job demands often creep into personal lives, with weekend work expected. And phone calls, e-mail, and other contacts commonly intrude on home life.[28] One female lawyer described her difficulty in finding time for family life while working at a prestigious law firm: "When I came back to work after . . . maternity leave and realized that I could not maintain my pre-child work hours (weekends, nights) the partners became extremely upset. When I tried to discuss a part-time arrangement, the head partner suggested that I didn't truly want to be a 'real criminal lawyer.' I quit . . . Oh, by the way, all the 'real criminal lawyer' partners had full-time, stay-at-home wives."[29]

In general, marriage and parenthood place different demands on women than on men. Because women do more domestic work, mothers and wives are less likely to be employed. Having children leads mothers to reduce their hours of paid work but leads fathers to increase their hours. The more children women have, the less time they devote to their jobs.[30]

These inequalities reflect conventional ideas about the roles of mothers and fathers. Traditionally, being a good father meant being a good provider, and being a good mother meant providing children nurturance and care. Even though only a minority of Americans now endorse this division of labor, its influence continues to linger. When home responsibilities are not shared equally between husbands and wives, it is the wives who suffer workplace disadvantage and have more difficulty in advancing to positions that yield greater income and prestige.[31]

Of course, single parents fulfill both the provider and the caretaker roles. As a result, the employment patterns of single mothers and single fathers are more similar than those of married couples, where the discrepancy in men and women is greatest. Yet, even among single parents, the mothers work fewer hours than the fathers. Single fathers are able to undertake more paid work than single mothers because most of them live with their parents or other adults who can share domestic responsibilities, but most single mothers do not have this advantage.[32]

Continuity in the Employment of Women and Men

For many women, family demands conflict with job obligations, resulting in women's less continuous employment, which in turn lessens their opportunities for workplace advancement. We now compare these employment patterns in men and women.

Taking Breaks from Employment

Some women, even those with excellent career prospects, make time for family responsibilities by relinquishing their jobs entirely. For example, in one study, 37 percent of the women with strong educational credentials— that is, professional or graduate degrees or undergraduate degrees with honors—voluntarily dropped out of employment at some point in their lives, compared with 24 percent of similarly qualified men.[33] Among women with one or more children, the proportion rises to 43 percent. The primary reason that these women take time out is for "family time," but for men it is to change careers.

Women who drop out of their careers to stay home to care for their children do not necessarily find this decision easy. The psychological investment in a career that comes from long-term preparation followed by on-the-job success can produce distress when the career is suddenly gone. In the words of one former senior newspaper editor and journalist, "When you give up a successful career to spend more time with your children, it is not just the nice clothes, the car and the holidays that have to go. It is your ego, too."[34]

Dropping out of the labor force has many obvious costs beyond surrendering one's psychological investment in paid work: lost income, impeded career growth, depreciation of skills, and difficulty in reestablishing one's career. The long-term income losses from women's employment breaks are substantial. Over one recent fifteen-year period, U.S. women earned an average of $273,592, compared with $722,693 for men. By this measure, women's earnings were only 38 percent of men's, in large part because of their time away from paid work. In addition, the more time off mothers take, the less experience and seniority they have and the less they earn when they return to employment. Such income losses persist over time. Being employed is like running in a long-distance race: the wages of most women who take significant breaks from employment never catch up to those who do not take breaks.[35]

The costs of leaving employment are exacerbated by the fact that, for women, the prime years for having children typically coincide with the critical years for establishing a successful career. It can be difficult to regain career momentum, even for women with excellent educational credentials. About one-fourth of such women who want to regain employment fail to find jobs, and only a minority of those who regain employment obtain full-time, professional jobs.[36]

Although limiting time away from employment mitigates this loss of income for employed mothers, staying continuously employed does not entirely remove the motherhood penalty. In most studies, motherhood is associated with a loss of income, even when controlling for time out of the workforce, hours worked, and other factors (see chapter 5).[37]

Even though more women than men leave employment for family reasons, most mothers employed full-time do not quit their jobs when they have a child. One study found that the likelihood of a mother remaining in her full-time job after childbirth is 75 percent that of a childless woman remaining in hers during the same time period. In contrast, women employed part-time usually do quit when they have a child.[38]

The fact that a portion of mothers quit their jobs to stay home with their children has created the misperception that women quit jobs more than men do. But in reality, because there are many reasons for quitting, women *do not* quit their jobs more often than men. On the contrary, men and women differ little in quitting, and among managers, men quit somewhat more often than women. In fact, both men and women quit most often for reasons unrelated to family, although among managers and younger workers, women quit because of family obligations more than men do.[39]

In summary, domestic obligations contribute to some women's loss of job tenure and experience and consequently to their lesser workplace advancement. Abandoning employment entirely, even as a temporary expedient, seriously compromises women's advancement and pay. Women who limit their time away from employment can reduce this motherhood penalty, although it is challenging to remain employed full-time after becoming a mother. Nevertheless, most women do not abandon their jobs but instead find various other solutions to manage family responsibilities. We now examine those solutions.

Taking Leaves of Absence and Sick Days

Leaves of absence can help parents accommodate their family responsibilities. For managers, such leaves are rare, although they are more common among women. Career losses for female managers are about the same whether they take family or sick leaves, and about the same as for men taking sick leaves. Because few men take family leaves, it is not possible to test whether they would be penalized even more than women for such actions.[40]

Occasional absences from work are more common than leaves, and women in the United States and most other countries take more sick time than men do. The more young children a woman has, the more sick days she takes, but men's sick days are not affected by how many children they have.[41] So women's absences apparently reflect their family responsibilities, which may in turn reflect their beliefs that mothers should nurture and care for sick children. One mother explained, "I'm the one who stays home when the kids are sick . . . With my husband, it's not a lack of effort, but a lack of insight. He has the best of intentions, but he needs direction . . . Men caring for sick children? Well, mothers mother more."[42]

Seeking Flexible Jobs and Part-Time Jobs

To accommodate family responsibilities, many women, and especially those with children, seek flexible jobs. Despite this preference, women often struggle to find flexibility. Overall, women are slightly less likely than men to have jobs with flexible schedules. In fact, professional, managerial, and executive positions allow more flexibility in setting work hours than clerical and administrative support positions, which are highly female-dominated.[43]

Some women who can't arrange flexible hours on their jobs may instead seek part-year or part-time employment. But in general, women do not obtain part-year employment more than men do, despite the advantages that it might offer. What women find more often is part-time employment. Even women in traditionally male-dominated, high-status professions, such as physicians and lawyers, reduce their work hours more often than their male counterparts.[44]

Although part-time jobs allow more time for domestic work, caring for young children cannot fully explain women's part-time employment. Among employed women with at least one child under age six, 29 percent have part-time jobs, compared with 25 percent of women without children. Among employed men with at least one child under age six, only 4 percent have part-time jobs, compared with 15 percent of men without children.[45] So having young children reduces part-time employment in fathers and slightly increases it in mothers.

Part-time employment has the obvious consequences of lowering income and reducing job benefits such as pension contributions. Even on an hourly basis, part-time workers are paid less than full-time workers. Although part-time employment hinders career advancement, it is more favorable for careers than not being employed at all. Women's current earnings are higher the more years they have been employed either full-time or part-time.[46]

All in all, despite the weakening of the household division of labor, family responsibilities still take a much greater toll on the workplace careers of women than those of men. A minority of mothers quit their jobs, some because they prefer to be full-time homemakers and others because they can't obtain sufficient flexibility in their employment. Other mothers find flexibility through obtaining leaves of absence, taking sick days to meet their children's needs, or arranging part-time schedules. These actions contribute to women's slower advancement to leadership positions, a consequence that many women recognize. In fact, although most women believe that gender discrimination continues to be a problem, most consider the lack of workplace flexibility to be an even greater problem.[47] Because many women adjust their employment to meet family responsibilities, they may seek jobs having different demands than those men seek, or women may be less psychologically committed to their jobs. We now evaluate these possibilities.

Job Preferences and Career Commitment

Some experts on leadership maintain that women may not want to lead as much as men do. Barbara Kellerman, director of the Center for Public Leadership at Harvard University's Kennedy School of Government, argues that, beyond family commitments, one reason there are fewer female than male leaders is that women are deterred by the stress and difficulty of leading:

> Work at the top of the greasy pole takes time, saps energy, and is usually all-consuming. Maybe women's values are different from men's values. Maybe the trade-offs high positions entail are ones that many women do not want to make. Maybe when deciding what matters most, gender matters. One of the least talked about aspects of leadership, of holding a position of considerable authority, is the toll taken. Leading is stressful. Leading is time-consuming. Leading is limiting. Leading is isolating. Leading is tiring.[48]

If leadership is such hard work, perhaps most women don't desire it. Of course, it is also possible that most men don't desire it either. One way to evaluate whether women seek easier work than men is to examine the job attributes that men and women prefer. For example, do men desire exercising leadership and being challenged in their jobs more than women do?

Preferences for Job Attributes and Advancement

The attributes that men and women seek in jobs have been extensively researched for many years and summarized in a meta-analysis of 242 samples of adults, adolescents, and children. Consistent with traditional gender roles, men and boys, more than women and girls, prefer jobs that provide opportunities for solitude, leadership or supervision, good earnings, and autonomy. Also, women and girls, more than men and boys, prefer jobs that provide opportunities to work with people and help others, as well as jobs that provide an easy commute, possibly reflecting their preference for time flexibility. But no evidence supported the idea that women and girls desire easy work. Instead, compared with men and boys, women and girls more often prefer work that provides a feeling of accomplishment and intrinsic stimulation, such as intellectual challenge.[49] And ironically, one of the largest sex differences is young males' greater preference for employment that provides ample leisure time away from the job.[50]

None of these differences was large at any point in time. Women and men are quite similar in their preferences, particularly for traditionally masculine job characteristics such as good earnings. Also, over time many differences have weakened among adults in similar occupations, including the greater male preferences for leadership, promotions, and autonomy. Still, some differences have held up over time, specifically, females' greater preference for good hours and working with and helping people, and young males' greater preference for leisure.[51]

How about ambition to advance in the workplace? Women and men in similar positions who are well established in managerial careers report similar ambition to rise to positions of authority. Even among university students, women and men regard managerial roles as equally attractive, although women believe it is less likely that they will attain such positions.[52]

Another possibility is that employed mothers and wives avoid positions with leadership responsibility because they expect these positions to conflict with their family responsibilities. But there is no support for this idea. If employed women opted out of leadership roles to better manage their family duties, then women with family responsibilities would not appear very often in positions of authority. However, in the United States and elsewhere, employed women who are wives and mothers do not have any less authority in the workplace than do single or childless women. In general, the desire for job advancement in women who are employed does not appear to be undermined by their family responsibilities or domestic work.[53]

Psychological Commitment to Paid Work Versus Family

The overall similarity in the job preferences of males and females suggests that employed men and women would not differ very much in their psychological commitment to their careers or to the organizations where they are employed. In fact, a meta-analysis of twenty-six studies revealed no difference between men and women in feeling committed to their organizations.

In addition, for both sexes, the role of employee is less important and central to their identities than are family roles. And this commitment to family is increasing. Compared with previous generations, a higher percentage of women *and men* report a desire to center their lives on family. And even among those who are college educated, many would prefer to forgo having a highly demanding career.[54]

Still, women continue to be more family focused than men. Somewhat more men than women value paid work over family, although both men and women who value career over family are in the minority. And women report greater willingness to accept a homemaker role than men do. Specifically, when a survey question has forced U.S. respondents to choose between a job and full-time homemaking, women consistently have been about equally divided between these options, and men consistently have preferred paid work over staying home (see figure 4-3). Nevertheless, the difference between men and women in family and career focus is changing. Now, 27 percent of men, the highest percentage ever, report that they would prefer a homemaker role over a paid job, and for more than 3.5 million couples, or 6 percent of all married couples, the wife works and the husband does not. In addition, increasing percentages of women say that they would continue to be employed even if they did not need to work for financial reasons.[55]

Job commitment also shows up in the amount of effort people devote to their jobs. Gary Becker, a well-known economist who has promoted a human capital view of the gender wage gap, made the following claim about women's effort: "Since child care and housework are more effort intensive than leisure and other household activities, married women spend less effort on each hour of market work than married men working the same number of hours. Hence, married women have lower hourly earnings than married men with the same market human capital, and they economize on the effort expended on market work by seeking less demanding jobs."[56]

Becker is wrong in his assertion that women expend less effort than men per hour of market (or paid) work. First, this argument conflicts with women's greater preference for challenge and accomplishment in their jobs and the greater preference of young men for an easy work pace. Second, it also conflicts with the similar level of commitment to organizations and careers that men and women report. Third, sociologists Denise Bielby and William Bielby found that women and men reported comparable work effort overall, but among women and men with similar family and

FIGURE 4-3

Percentage of U.S. female and male poll respondents who preferred having a job outside the home or staying home, 1974–2005

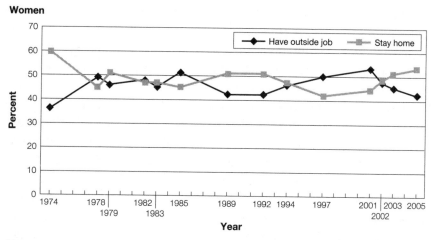

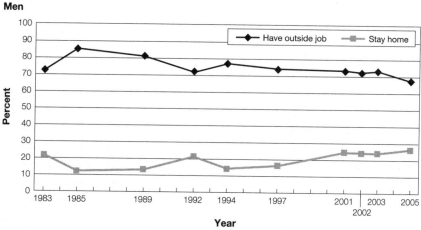

Source: Adapted from D. W. Moore, *Gender Stereotypes Prevail on Working Outside the Home*, tables 1 and 2, August 17, 2005, Gallup Brain.

job conditions, women reported greater effort than men. And fourth, men have more time for breaks during the work day and have more flexibility in scheduling their work hours.[57]

Although employed men put in more hours of paid work than employed women on average, many men as well as women would prefer to reduce these hours to have more time at home. In fact, more fathers than mothers report having too little time with their children.[58] Given the pressures of many managerial and professional jobs, men often feel locked in by jobs with very long hours. One male engineer bemoaned his inability to obtain the eight-hour days of his father's generation: "I hate my job . . . It's a rat race. I would rather have a nine-to-five job thirty minutes from home and be home more with my family."[59] Such sentiments reflect the increasing tendency for family to take precedence over career in personal identity.

In summary, women and men in similar jobs desire leadership equally and report similar levels of commitment to their careers. Women report putting in at least as much effort at their jobs as men and express a greater desire for stimulating work than men do. In the trade-offs between family and career, more women than men would consider forgoing their career. But even in the face of family responsibilities, employed women's desire for career advancement remains high. Nevertheless, the greater percentage of men than women who are focused primarily on their careers likely contributes to the gender gap in advancement.

Conclusion

Raising children and having a career are hard work. Many women worry that success in the workplace comes at the expense of family life.[60] Increasing the number of women who can successfully have children and maintain their employment depends on men becoming more equally involved in the domestic sphere. Currently men do not fully share domestic responsibilities with women, even though they share more of the domestic work than ever before. Therefore, to manage family responsibilities, women continue to be the ones who interrupt their careers, take more days off, and work part-time. These actions result in women's having fewer years of job experience and fewer hours of employment per year, interruptions that slow their career progress and reduce their earnings.

Women with high earnings or other sources of wealth likely do not experience as great an interference between family and employment responsibilities, because they can pay for a substantial amount of domestic help. Such women may delegate a portion of childcare and housework to nannies and housekeepers, and they can afford to send their children to excellent childcare centers. However, because most families find such options financially difficult, women's greater workplace advancement for the most part depends on greater domestic inputs from men.

The routes that women take to leadership in the workplace are not simple or direct but convoluted and frequently obstructed, especially for mothers. Balancing the demands of family and jobs is crucial for women who desire to make their way through the labyrinth. Family considerations do not, of course, account for all the obstacles that women confront. In chapter 5, we explore another source of these obstacles: discrimination against women as leaders.

CHAPTER FIVE

Is Discrimination Still a Problem?

DISCRIMINATION should be a thing of the past in the United States, given the general support for equal opportunity. But this support may falter when it comes to equal access by women to power and authority. Discrimination occurs if women receive fewer leadership opportunities than men even *with equivalent qualifications*. Such discrimination is entirely plausible, given the research we present in chapter 2 showing that women remain underrepresented in leadership, and in chapter 3 showing that this underrepresentation is not a result of sex differences in personality or abilities.

Chapter 4 reveals the toll that family responsibilities take on women's careers. Women's greater family responsibilities, however, can explain only a portion of the gender gap in leadership, as we now show in this chapter. The possibility of sex discrimination in the workplace, therefore, deserves our attention as a cause of women's lesser advancement, and the research does reveal discrimination, which contributes to the barriers and dead ends that women must overcome while navigating the labyrinth. Progress through the labyrinth is difficult when the paths to the goal are constricted by discrimination.

To provide strong tests of discrimination, social scientists go beyond asking people about their personal experiences in the workplace. Instead, they design studies that compare how well women and men fare in hiring, wages, and promotions when they have equal qualifications. First, we review research on wages and promotions that statistically controls for differences between men and women on a wide variety of qualities. Second, we consider experiments in which people evaluate men and women who are presented as identical in all respects other than their sex. Both of these methods yield answers to the question of whether women—or men—suffer discriminatory disadvantage in the workplace.[1]

Correlational Studies of Wages and Promotions

There would be no discrimination if men's higher wages and faster promotions were based entirely on their superior qualifications. Whether this is so is the subject of hundreds of correlational studies, most of them carried out by economists and sociologists. This research is relevant to leadership because both wages and promotions demonstrate workplace advancement—promotions as a direct indicator of advancement, and wages as an indirect but still useful indicator. We first consider studies of wages and then studies of promotions to higher positions.

Studies of Wages

No one would be surprised that simple comparisons of the average wages of women and men show that men earn more. For all U.S. workers in 2005, without taking into account their hours on the job or any other considerations, women earned 73 cents for every dollar that men earned. For full-time workers, women earned 81 cents for every dollar that men earned. This wage gap exists in all races and ethnicities, although it is larger among whites and Asian Americans than among blacks and Hispanics (see figure 5-1). Even so, the current wage gap is much smaller than the 63 cents for every dollar reported for full-time workers in 1979, the first year for which these data were available.[2]

Figure 5-2 shows the changes in earnings of full-time male and female employees for 1979 through 2005. Women's earnings rose while men's earnings fell, especially in the first half of the 1990s.[3] Economists describe the resulting decrease in the wage gap as "dramatic." Still, in recent years, the narrowing of the gap has slowed after the substantial shifts of the 1980s and early 1990s. Economists forecast that the gap will continue to decline but quite slowly and will not disappear in the foreseeable future.[4]

To explain the wage gap, studies ask whether factors that may differ between men and women, such as hours worked per year and type of occupation, account for wage gaps. These studies sometimes pool the male and female data in a regression analysis designed to predict wages from workers' sex, years of education, job experience, and numerous other factors. Such analyses determine whether a wage gap remains even after the

FIGURE 5-1

Median usual weekly earnings of full-time wage and salary workers, displayed by sex and race or ethnicity, 2005 U.S. annual averages

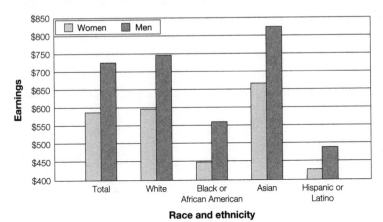

Source: U.S. Bureau of Labor Statistics, 2006a, Highlights of Women's Earnings in 2005, chart 2.

FIGURE 5-2

Median usual weekly earnings of full-time wage and salary workers in constant (2005) dollars, displayed by sex, 1979–2005 U.S. annual averages

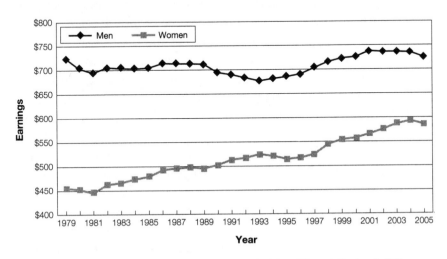

Source: Adapted from U.S. Bureau of Labor Statistics, 2006a, Highlights of Women's Earnings in 2005, table 12.

effects of the other characteristics are controlled—that is, after men and women are made statistically equal on these other variables. The gap that remains provides an estimate of discrimination.

A related method involves analyzing men's and women's wages separately to test whether the gains and losses that people experience for their skills and other personal attributes are different for women and men.[5] For example, it might be that for one sex, wages rise more sharply with each additional year of work experience than for the other sex. This method, like the first one, adjusts wages for sex differences in characteristics such as years of education and work experience; but it goes further, controlling for how strongly wages are associated with these characteristics in men versus women.

Virtually all of the hundreds of studies that have applied these two methods show that after statistically equalizing male and female characteristics, the wage gap shrinks but is not eliminated. The fact that a gap remains suggests that discrimination affects wages.

One of the most comprehensive of these studies was conducted by the staff of the U.S. Government Accountability Office (GAO).[6] The study was based on data from 1983 through 2000 from a representative sample of Americans between the ages of twenty-five and sixty-five. Because the same people responded to the survey repeatedly over the years, the study provided accurate estimates of past work experience, which is important for explaining later wages.

The GAO researchers used both of the statistical methods that we described to test whether individuals' total wages could be predicted by their sex and other characteristics. The researchers included part-time and full-time employees and took into account all the factors that they could estimate and that might affect earnings, such as education and work experience. Without controls for these variables, the data showed that women earned about 44 percent less than men during the entire period 1983 to 2000. With these controls in place, the gap was only about half as large but still substantial. The control factors that had the most effect in reducing the wage gap were the different employment patterns of men and women: men undertook more hours of paid labor per year than women and had more years of job experience.

Although most variables affected the wages of men and women similarly, there were exceptions. A few qualities, especially marriage and parenthood, were associated with higher wages in men but not in women (see chapter 4). In contrast, a few other characteristics, especially years of education, had a more positive effect on the wages of women. Even after adjusting wages for all of these ways in which men and women differ, the GAO study, like similar studies, showed that women's wages remained lower than men's.[7] This unexplained gender gap of around 21 cents on the dollar (averaged over the entire 1983 to 2000 time period) is consistent with the presence of wage discrimination. This gap is substantial.

From studies of this general type, it is not clear whether discrimination has lessened over time. Some researchers, like the authors of the GAO report, have approached this question by following the same group of people over many years. Such studies tend to find little meaningful change in amount of discrimination since the early 1980s. Other methods, which compare wage gaps found in studies conducted at earlier and later time periods, do suggest that discrimination has weakened.[8]

Within any given occupation, men almost always have higher wages than women, even though there are a few occupations in which women have slightly higher wages than men—for example, computer support specialists and bill and account collectors. This *within-occupation* wage gap especially favors men in more highly paid occupations, including management.[9] In addition, there is a *between-occupations* wage gap; that is, male-dominated occupations are more highly paid than female-dominated occupations. The higher the proportion of men in an occupation, the higher the salary of its male and female workers. Therefore, the clustering of women in service, clerical, and administrative support areas as well as in nursing and elementary school teaching contributes to the overall wage gap.[10]

Whether the lower wages that prevail in female-dominated occupations are discriminatory is a contentious issue. Conventional economic theory ascribes this between-occupation wage inequality not to discrimination but to free-market forces, such as differences in men's and women's occupational preferences and work experience. However, most sociologists argue that labor markets are tainted by discriminatory barriers and the cultural devaluation of female work.[11] Whatever the causes of the lower wages in occupations populated mainly by women, legal remedies have proven to be elusive. The courts have increasingly interpreted these between-occupation pay differences as merely reflecting market forces.[12]

All in all, research on wages does provide evidence of discrimination against women, despite some disagreements about the meaning of the lower pay in female-dominated occupations. Discrimination, although not assessed directly, is inferred from the inability of education, employment patterns, type of occupation, and other characteristics to fully explain wage differences between men and women.

Studies of Promotions

Promotions provide a direct index of workplace authority. Most employees enter organizations at lower levels. Some rise to managerial and executive positions within the same organizations, others move to different organizations to gain higher positions, and still others fail to advance at all. Career ladders exist, but not all people climb them.

As chapter 2 indicates, a wealth of research has shown that positions held by women are less likely to entail the authority to make important decisions and to control others' wages and promotions. Even when women have the same job titles as those of men, the female managers often have less decision-making authority than male managers do.[13]

The statistical methods for examining whether promotions are discriminatory are the same as those for examining wages. Researchers test what happens to the disparity in women's and men's job ranks or the speed of their promotions after controlling for human capital variables such as skills, years of education, and work experience. These studies show that a gender gap in authority remains. Promotions come more slowly for women than for equivalent men. After being hired, women wait longer than men to be promoted to supervisors or managers and wait longer between promotions within managerial levels.[14]

One illustrative study followed a nationally representative sample of workers from 1980 to 1992. The study found that white men were more likely to attain managerial positions than white women, black men, and black women. Controlling for other characteristics such as education and hours worked per year, white men were ahead of the other groups when entering the labor market, and their advantage in attaining managerial positions grew throughout the course of their careers. Many other studies have also demonstrated such divergences in career paths.[15]

Do such studies point to the presence of a glass ceiling? Although there is no evidence of a rigid barrier beyond which women cannot ascend at all, it is possible that a looser interpretation of the glass ceiling might receive support. This idea is that it gets increasingly harder for women to rise at the higher levels—in other words, that women's promotions become progressively less likely than those of men at higher levels within organizations. In fact, research typically does *not* support even this less literal interpretation of the glass ceiling. Large-scale surveys of U.S. data have generally not shown such patterns. Instead, after other variables are controlled, a general bias against women appears to operate with approximately equal strength at all levels.[16]

Readers may find it puzzling that discrimination may not become more intense at higher levels. Doesn't the mere fact that there are few female CEOs and corporate officers in the *Fortune* 500 demonstrate that women are particularly blocked from advancing to higher levels of management? The answer is no. In fact, the increasing rarity of women at higher organizational levels can result from a uniform bias against women at all ranks.

To understand how this works, consider a hypothetical firm that has five levels: worker, supervisor, manager, executive, and CEO (see table 5-1). Among the workers, ten thousand are men and ten thousand are women. For purposes of illustration, we introduce discrimination by setting the chances of a man being promoted to the next level at 10 percent, and of a woman being promoted at 5 percent. Thus, two men are promoted for every one woman at each level. Given this discriminatory promotion bias, even though there is one man for every woman at the worker level, there are seventeen men for every woman at the CEO level. This constant bias, 2-to-1 in favor of men at all levels, creates the illusion of greater anti-female discrimination for higher positions. Instead, the same amount of bias operating at all levels produces this dwindling representation of women in higher positions.[17]

Might women actually have a promotion advantage in female-dominated fields? The answer is a resounding no. Even in these fields, men receive

TABLE 5-1

Effects of a uniform bias favoring men on the representation of men and women at differing levels in a hypothetical organization

Hierarchical level	Number of men	Number of women	Percent of men promoted	Percent of women promoted	Number of men for every woman
CEO	1	0.06	—	—	16
Executive	10	1.25	10	5	8
Manager	100	25	10	5	4
Supervisor	1,000	500	10	5	2
Worker	10,000	10,000	10	5	1

quicker promotions than women. Although token women generally suffer especially slow promotion in male-dominated careers, token men advance quickly in female-dominated careers. Sociologist Christine Williams dubbed this phenomenon the *glass escalator*—that is, the faster ascent of token men than women even in fields where women predominate.[18] Williams showed that in four such fields—nursing, librarianship, elementary school teaching, and social work—men attained authority positions faster than women. Other studies have shown similar effects.[19] Still, it isn't clear whether men have a greater promotion advantage in female-dominated than male-dominated fields or merely have a uniform, across-the-board advantage.[20]

Hundreds of studies have examined promotions and wages within single organizations or in specialized samples of managers and professionals. Some of these studies have been carried out for academic research purposes, and others to obtain evidence in legal cases when organizations have been charged with discrimination.[21] In legal contexts, the evidence is often statistical but may include women's accounts of their experiences in seeking promotions.

The most famous recent study of a single organization in the United States emerged from the Wal-Mart sex discrimination case, which has been adjudicated in federal court for several years. In 2004, a U.S. District Court judge ruled that the case would become a class action lawsuit, thereby including more than 1.6 million current and former female employees of Wal-Mart.[22] Statistical evidence of discrimination at Wal-Mart showed that women earned less and received promotions less often than men despite having superior qualifications and records of service. At every level of management, women were promoted less often than would be expected based on their representation in the "feeder pools" of employees having credentials suitable for promotion. Statistical consultant Richard Drogin summarized this quantitative evidence on behalf of the plaintiffs: "Women employees at Wal-Mart are concentrated in the lower paying jobs, are paid less than men in the same job, and are less likely to advance to management positions than men. These gender patterns persist even though women have more seniority, have lower turnover rates, and have higher performance ratings in most jobs."[23]

The case against Wal-Mart is based in part on testimony from women employees concerning their frustrated attempts to obtain equitable access to promotion. Such testimony often recounts blatant instances of discrimination. Women report that, despite their very good performance ratings and their requests to be considered for promotion, men with less experience and inferior qualifications were promoted instead of them. For example, one employee's declaration to a U.S. District Court contained the following statement, which was typical of the women plaintiffs: "I asked for my well-earned promotion to Assistant Manager from everyone that I thought could facilitate it . . . I continued to speak several times with District Manager [name deleted] about my wish for a promotion to Assistant Manager, but he just continued to put me off . . . Finally Store Manager [name deleted] confided in me that District Manager [name deleted] was not in favor of women being in upper management."[24]

In contrast to the Wal-Mart case, management researchers Gary Powell and Anthony Butterfield found a higher rate of promotion for women than men in their research on the Senior Executive Service of a cabinet-level government agency.[25] However, these women were more qualified than their male counterparts in education, performance evaluations, and other attributes. Controlling for these factors, the women and men were equally likely to be promoted.

Despite this encouraging result observed in a single government agency, broader studies of the federal workforce found that women were promoted more slowly than men, controlling for experience, education, and number of relocations. Nevertheless, the Powell and Butterfield study demonstrates that women are not inevitably victims of discrimination in large organizations. Equal opportunity may prevail in some agencies of the federal government because their evaluation procedures require explicit criteria and careful documentation (see chapter 9). Consistent with the smaller gender wage gap in the public than the private sector, governmental positions appear to provide women with better access to leadership.[26]

Other studies have examined promotions and wages in broader samples of managers and professionals from, for example, companies in particular industries, executive search firms, and lists of MBA graduates. These studies have almost always produced findings similar to those reported for nationally representative samples—that women fare less well than men in promotions and wages, controlling for a wide range of other factors.[27]

In summary, men generally have a promotion advantage even when characteristics such as job experience are controlled. This conclusion is especially compelling because it emerges from a wide range of different types of studies.

Limitations of Correlational Methods

These studies by economists and sociologists are consistent with the presence of sex discrimination. Controlling for differences in men's and women's job experience, education, and other factors, studies still show gender gaps in wages and promotions. However, ambiguities remain. It is possible that factors not represented in the studies could account for these gender gaps.

Examples of factors rarely considered in these studies are psychological variables such as workers' preferences for different types of jobs or their intentions to take career breaks for childrearing.[28] Also, researchers possess little of the data often available to firms' personnel departments, such as academic transcripts and information revealing the quality of past job performance. Therefore, research of this type may overestimate discrimination by omitting determinants of wage and promotion gaps that can be non-discriminatory. Conversely, these studies may underestimate discrimination by omitting predictors (such as academic records) that may favor women or by including predictors (such as job experience) that themselves may be tainted by discrimination against women.

Because of these ambiguities, we supplement the correlational research with studies that use a different method. These other studies are experimental, a method that allows stronger conclusions about causality but typically investigates prejudice against hypothetical women and men, not actual discrimination occurring in natural settings.

Experimental Studies of Gender Prejudice

Some researchers, especially in psychology and organizational behavior, have studied prejudice by conducting experiments in which research participants evaluate individual male or female managers or job candidates. In such experiments, all characteristics of these hypothetical individuals are held constant except for their sex. The participants evaluate how suitable the individuals are for hiring or promotion or how competent they are at their jobs.

This experimental method implements the *Goldberg paradigm*, named for a 1968 experiment by Philip Goldberg.[29] This simple, elegant study had student participants evaluate written essays that were identical except for the attached male or female name. The students were unaware that other students received the identical material ascribed to a writer of the other sex. This initial experiment demonstrated an overall bias against women: women received lower evaluations unless the essay was on a feminine topic.

The advantages of this approach follow from the hallmarks of the experimental method. Experiments entail manipulation of a variable (in this instance, the sex of the writer) and random assignment of participants to the resulting conditions. This method circumvents the main ambiguity of correlational studies, which is the impossibility of statistically controlling for all the differences in the job-relevant characteristics of women and men. As a result, experiments allow a stronger causal argument about the effects of sex than do the correlational studies that we have already described.

Researchers quickly applied this Goldberg method to study whether women are disadvantaged as job candidates and leaders. Because this method ensures that the individuals who are evaluated are identical except for their sex, any differences in these evaluations must be due only to research participants' different expectations about men and women. For example, if participants rate a female job candidate as less desirable to hire, they must be basing their judgments on their preconceptions about male and female applicants and not on any differences in the information provided by the experiment.[30]

In an early experiment, male undergraduate business students played the role of consultants hired to evaluate job applicants applying for executive positions.[31] These students received job applications that included standard personal information, a description of the applicant's work history, an interviewer's comments, and either a male or a female name attached to the application materials. The male applicants fared better than the female applicants, especially for positions that were described as more demanding. Many studies of this same general type have accumulated over the years, with students or employees serving as the evaluators.

Based on the meta-analytic methods that we note in chapters 1 and 3, reviews of Goldberg experiments on hiring have yielded clear findings. Organizational scientists Heather Davison and Michael Burke conducted the most recent review, taking forty-nine studies into account. They found that men were preferred over women for masculine jobs such as auto salesperson and sales manager for heavy industry, and women were preferred over men for feminine jobs such as secretary and home economics teacher. For gender-neutral jobs such as psychologist and motel desk clerk, men were also preferred over women, although to a somewhat lesser extent than for masculine jobs.[32]

These data illustrate a common pattern: men have a clear advantage over women in masculine settings but also some advantage in gender-integrated settings. Women have some advantage over men only in feminine settings. The biases revealed by these experiments are not trivial. For example, the bias against women in masculine positions roughly translates into rates of success of 59 percent for men and 42 percent for women, when success is defined as a favorable recommendation for a job.[33]

Given that leadership roles are ordinarily culturally masculine (see chapter 6), this research shows that women are at a disadvantage for such positions, even when they are exactly equivalent to their male counterparts in all characteristics other than sex. Even for management positions that are now more integrated by gender, women are likely to be disadvantaged. Men are at a disadvantage only for female-dominated positions such as receptionist and secretary—positions that they rarely seek.

A few experiments in this tradition are more naturalistic but less controlled. For example, some researchers sent false job applications to companies, and others had research assistants respond by telephone to advertised jobs.[34] In these field experiments, gender bias also depended on the sex-typing of jobs. To illustrate this approach, consider an experiment in which the researchers first located classified advertisements appearing in two Atlanta newspapers for jobs that were male- or female-dominated.[35] Then male and female students posing as job seekers applied for these jobs by calling the telephone numbers that appeared in the ads.

When the students applied for jobs that were atypical for their sex, they usually received discriminatory responses. These responses included outright refusals based on sex—for example, "Honey, I'm sorry, but we need a man to do that" or, "We are just looking for a girl." In other cases, the callers were told that the job was filled when their sex did not match the job, and that it was open when it did match. Many responses to the sex-mismatched callers, although not outright refusals, were skeptical and discouraging—for example, "It's hard to believe that a guy is really qualified for this work" or, "It's pretty dirty work—are you sure you wouldn't want to work somewhere else?"[36]

Other experiments have examined evaluations of leaders, usually by presenting written descriptions of leadership behavior that differ only in the leaders' sex. Some of these experiments presented research participants with actual male and female leaders who had been trained by the researchers to lead laboratory groups in exactly the same style.[37] A meta-analysis of sixty-one experiments using either actual leaders or descriptions of leaders found a small bias against the women compared with the men. Consistent with the research on job candidates, this anti-female bias was stronger for the more male-dominated leadership roles.[38]

Along with biases in evaluating men and women, people show biases in their explanations of successes and failures. Attributing a person's success not to high ability, but to hard work or luck, demonstrates less confidence in that person's competence. Do people come up with different explanations depending on the sex of the person who succeeds or fails? The answer is yes, especially for tasks that are traditionally masculine. As shown in a meta-analysis of fifty-eight relevant experiments, it is the common perception that women do well on masculine tasks because of their hard work but that men do well on them because of their competence. Reactions to failure are different. Here it is the common perception that women fail on masculine tasks because they can't handle the challenges of the work but that men fail on them because they are lazy or merely unlucky.[39]

In summary, experimental studies of hiring biases show anti-female (or pro-male) prejudice in most contexts. Men are advantaged over equivalent women for jobs traditionally held by men as well as for more gender-integrated jobs. Similarly, male leaders receive somewhat more-favorable evaluations than equivalent female leaders, especially in leader roles usually occupied by men. Because leadership is usually perceived as a masculine activity, women are also vulnerable to having their successes ascribed to their hard work rather than their ability, and their failures to their being overwhelmed by the difficulty of the work.

Limitations of Experimental Methods

These experiments have several limitations. Generalization from their findings has some risks, because the experiments were rarely conducted with samples of participants who are representative of the U.S. population. Although employees and job recruiters sometimes have served as participants, students are the more typical participants, and this feature raises questions about generalizing these results to workplaces.[40] Even when large numbers of such experiments are combined meta-analytically, they do not allow generalizations to the society as a whole. Also, in most experiments, only a limited amount of information is presented about each woman or man—less information than would usually be available in natural settings.

It is also true that these experiments do not assess actual discrimination, even in field studies, because no one is actually hired. Instead, the studies assess attitudinal bias, or *prejudice*, which likely contributes to discrimination if the people who hire employees share the same bias. In fact, as chapter 6 shows, gender prejudices are widely shared in the culture and consequently are likely to operate in many settings.

Is There a Discriminatory Male Advantage in Leadership?

The evidence is persuasive that discrimination contributes to men's advantage in wages and promotions. We have demonstrated with two very different methods that it is highly likely that people discriminate against women in authority and leadership. Fortunately, each of the research methods that we have relied on has advantages that compensate for the other's shortcomings. Most of the strengths and the weaknesses of the correlational studies differ from those of the experiments, but the two types of studies yield the same answer. These two traditions of research—one correlational and the other experimental—agree that men have an advantage over objectively equivalent women. Discrimination appears to be responsible for quite a few of the turns and dead ends in the labyrinth.

The correlational studies that make a case for discrimination also identify differences between men and women that explain a portion of the gaps in wages and promotions. These differences are mainly employment patterns, which, as we show in chapter 4, reflect women's greater domestic responsibilities. This correlational research therefore confirms that factors other than outright discrimination account for a portion of gender gaps in leadership. Also, the ambiguities in empirical tests of whether discrimination has decreased over time suggest that women's increasing education and job experience are the main causes of the dramatic increase in the number of female managers and the narrowing of the wage gap.

Despite evidence of female advantage in culturally feminine settings such as clerical work, women do not achieve leadership more readily than men even in these contexts. Regardless of whether fields are populated mainly by women or by men, the men ascend to supervisory and administrative positions more quickly than the women. Because men possess a consistent advantage in promotion, their gains over women in authority and wages grow larger with longer job tenure.

What do Americans think about sex discrimination? Although Gallup polling has shown that Americans increasingly believe that equal job opportunity exists, the issue is viewed somewhat differently by men and women. In Gallup's 2005 poll, 61 percent of men and 45 percent of women endorsed the idea that women have job opportunities that are equal to those of men.[41] However, this belief in equal opportunity held by approximately half of Americans is not supported by the facts of social scientific data.

The growing optimism about workplace fairness probably reflects people's observations of women in many high-visibility leadership roles as well as some lack of insight into the processes that continue to produce discrimination. Nevertheless, the obvious lack of consensus about the presence of equal opportunity is consistent with the ambiguities inherent in the labyrinthine barriers that women encounter—barriers that sometimes can be overcome and that often are not obvious to casual observers. But how does discrimination come about? Biased thinking is one contributor, and it is this psychology of prejudice that we examine in the next chapter.

CHAPTER SIX

What Is the Psychology of Prejudice Toward Female Leaders?

THE DISCRIMINATION against women revealed in chapter 5 has roots in the everyday psychological processes that create prejudice. The psychology that underlies prejudice toward female leaders is driven by conscious and unconscious mental associations about women, men, and leaders. People associate women and men with different traits, linking men with more of the traits that connote leadership. Such beliefs can make people conclude that no woman could have the "right stuff" for powerful jobs. Prejudgments of this sort abound, as in the *Wall Street Journal* statement, "Male directors are simply afraid to take an unnecessary risk by selecting a woman."[1] So what's risky about choosing a woman?

Even in the twenty-first century, these perceived risks follow from thinking that women have the "wrong stuff" for leadership. Understanding how people come to these ideas requires shifting the frame of our analysis to the psychology of prejudice. This psychology is subtle, because currently in the United States, few people actually intend to discriminate. Instead, people spontaneously compare their mental images of men and women with their image of what would make a good leader. They favor the person who strikes them as best qualified. Fair enough?

In truth, there is good reason to question fairness as long as the traits that come to mind in relation to leaders and leadership evoke masculine images. Men have predominated in leadership roles for so long that leadership itself is perceived as a masculine domain. Regardless of their objective qualifications, men have an advantage over women merely because people ascribe mainly masculine qualities to leaders. To explain this phenomenon, we look at how everyday thinking about women, men, and leaders contributes to the male advantage.

Stereotypes as Social Constructions

We all mentally group people based on characteristics that they share, often by relying on observable attributes such as sex, race, nationality, and occupation. We then form expectations about how these groups will behave, and we assume that people in the same group will have certain interests and skills that differentiate them from people in other groups. School teachers, for example, are thought to have the ability to work effectively with children, and professional athletes are assumed to be physically well coordinated.

Ideas about social groups grow from the experiences that people have with these groups, either directly through personal contact or indirectly through media and cultural traditions. These beliefs constitute stereotypes and become part of a society's shared knowledge. They include expectations about what members of a group are *actually* like (*descriptive beliefs*) and what they *should* be like (*prescriptive beliefs*). For example, people think that engineers are good at math and that they should be good at math.[2]

We all use stereotypes as shortcuts to guide our judgments but are generally unaware of their presence. Stereotypes help us make guesses about how others are likely to behave and how best to interact with them. For example, knowledge about a new acquaintance's political affiliation affords some good guesses about that person's attitudes. This stereotype makes it possible to avoid saying things that might immediately offend.

Although stereotypes can be helpful in daily life, they easily lead us astray. They bias the way we process information, because we interpret— or assimilate—new information to fit our stereotypes. In a simple demonstration of assimilation, college student research participants were led to believe that a child was from either a wealthy or a poor family.[3] After watching a videotape of this child taking an academic test, those who believed she came from wealth rated her ability as above her grade level, and those who believed that she was a child of poverty rated her as below her grade level. They assimilated what they saw to their stereotypes about children of differing social backgrounds.

People are especially influenced by stereotypes when they have little other information to go on.[4] Acquiring more information can take effort or time. Even if people acquire information beyond someone's sex or race or social class, that information can be ambiguous. People can also be too busy, distracted, or otherwise mentally occupied to take much additional information into account, so they revert to snap judgments based on stereotypes.

For most of us most of the time, stereotypes operate under the surface, not bubbling up to conscious awareness. To limit their influence, people must recognize that their stereotypes have been activated and must desire to counteract their influence, conditions which are seldom present.[5]

Mental Associations About Women and Men

People instantly categorize individuals as male or female. In the rare cases in which this instant recognition fails, people keep probing until they resolve the ambiguity of an androgynous appearance. In fact, sex provides the strongest basis of classifying people; it trumps race, age, and occupation in the speed and ubiquity of categorizing others.[6] Classifying a person as male or female evokes mental associations, or expectations, about masculine and feminine qualities. These associations are pervasive and influential even when people are not aware of them.

To demonstrate these automatic processes, social psychologist Mahzarin Banaji and her colleagues had participants view stereotypically masculine or feminine words on a computer screen. These words referred to feminine or masculine traits, such as *sensitive* or *logical*. Right after each appearance of a masculine or feminine trait word (called a "prime"), a sex-typed first name such as Jane or John appeared on the computer screen. Participants were instructed to very quickly classify each name by gender by pressing one of two keys on the computer. Although the fast sequencing of each trait word and name gave participants little time to think about the words, they responded more quickly when the names connoted the same gender as the trait word they had just seen. That is, quick presentations of feminine traits such as *sensitive* and *gentle* increased the speed of identifying the gender of feminine first names such as Jane; quick presentations of masculine traits such as *logical* and *strong* increased the speed of identifying the gender of masculine names such as John.[7]

A simple principle explains these results: things that people have experienced as occurring together—bread and butter, women and sensitivity, men and logic—are responded to as a unit. People associate things that co-occur more quickly than things that do not. These faster responses reveal preexisting mental associations—for example, linking women to sensitivity and men to logic. And these associations come automatically to mind, without people necessarily even being aware of them.

Studies such as this one have shown that words or things that are culturally masculine (fireman, catcher's mitt) or feminine (salesgirl, oven mitt) automatically elicit gender-consistent associations. With associations instantly coming to mind, often not consciously, it may merely "feel right," for example, to select a woman as a kindergarten teacher or a man as a prosecuting attorney, because "kindergarten teacher" elicits feminine associations and "prosecuting attorney" elicits masculine associations.[8] As we will demonstrate, to the extent that leadership itself connotes *male*, it can "feel right" to choose a man as a leader, thereby providing men with a straight road to authority and pulling women back into the labyrinth.

Even without any conscious awareness of them, these mental associations guide people's thoughts and behaviors and help maintain traditional arrangements such as men's predominance as leaders. With masculine and feminine associations elicited automatically by cues related to gender, they influence virtually all social interaction.[9]

Content of Mental Associations About Men and Women

Two connotations predominate in people's associations about women and men: the communal and the agentic. *Communal* associations convey a concern with the compassionate treatment of others. Women elicit communal associations of being especially affectionate, helpful, friendly, kind, and sympathetic as well as interpersonally sensitive, gentle, and soft-spoken. In contrast, *agentic* associations convey assertion and control. Men elicit agentic associations of being especially aggressive, ambitious, dominant, self-confident, and forceful as well as self-reliant and individualistic.

These associations about agency and communion form the basis of gender stereotypes. In national polls and in surveys of university students conducted in many nations, people consistently describe women in terms of communion and men in terms of agency.[10] Despite some nuances specific to cultures, these gender stereotypes about communion and agency are quite similar across cultures.

These ideas about communion and agency are prescriptive as well as descriptive. People generally think that it is a good thing for women to be nice, nurturing, and kind, and for men to be strong, assertive, and ambitious. Not only do people encourage others to comply with these prescriptions, but they can also become accepted as personal ideals for one's own behavior.[11] Women's acceptance of the idea that they should be especially "nice," for example, may deter them from assertively claiming leadership and may make them feel awkward when performing managerial behaviors such as reprimanding others. In these ways, the prescriptiveness of stereotypes about women contributes to the labyrinth that slows women's route to authority.

The qualities that are more strongly prescribed for one sex are not necessarily forbidden to the other sex.[12] Feminine qualities such as sensitivity are not undesirable in men, nor are masculine qualities such as ambitiousness undesirable in women. But men are not pushed to be sensitive, and women are not pushed to be ambitious. Also, there *is* forbidden territory for each sex, and it lies in the more negative qualities that are ascribed to the other sex.[13] Undesirable feminine qualities such as being weak and melodramatic are quite unacceptable in men and more tolerable in women. And undesirable masculine qualities such as being controlling and promiscuous are quite unacceptable in women and more tolerable in men. As we show in chapter 7, people especially dislike and resist women leaders who manifest undesirable masculine qualities such as being autocratic or domineering.

Sources of Mental Associations About Women and Men

These associations about men and women are firmly rooted in a society's division of labor between the sexes.[14] What does the division of labor have to do with it? We can't directly observe people's traits, so we form impressions of people by looking at how they behave. We then assume that their behaviors reflect their personality. Caring behavior implies a nice, caring person; aggressive behavior implies a dominant, aggressive person, and so on.

In making these judgments about personality, we tend to overlook the fact that particular behaviors are often required when we fill certain social roles. Merely because women and men typically engage in different activities in the family and workplace, the two sexes are seen as having quite different personality traits. For example, ignoring the influence of role pressures, observers would ascribe a mother's caring behavior to her caring personality rather than to the demands of the mother role.[15]

This psychological process of inferring traits from observations extends easily to perceptions of entire groups of people. Stereotypes consist of the characteristics that seem to underlie what members of groups do in their typical roles. People associate women with the domestic role, which involves childrearing and maintaining family harmony—responsibilities that require nurturance, sensitivity, and warmth. As a result, people expect women to have superior social skills.

In contrast, people associate men with the employment role, especially in occupations that claim authority, in which men often display assertive and self-confident behaviors. So in people's minds, men become linked with agentic traits. Of course, most women are employed, too, but often in female-dominated occupations, many of which are seen as especially requiring communal traits.[16]

Status differences between the sexes also foster expectations that men are controlling, assertive, and directive and that women are supportive, sympathetic, and cooperative.[17] These expectations arise from people's everyday observations of inequalities between individual men and women: men usually interact with women who have less income and less-prestigious jobs than they do—for example, a male executive interacting with female secretaries and clerks. Men interact more rarely with women who are equal or superior to them in income and prestige—for example, a male executive interacting with female executives.[18]

The inequalities that individual men and women commonly experience are transformed into widely shared beliefs, not merely in men's greater status and power but also in their greater know-how and ability. Once people have associated men with high status and women with low status, men more readily exercise influence over women in new encounters, even outside of workplaces, and women more readily accept this influence. These expectations that flow from men's higher status then shape interactions even when a man and a woman are objectively equal in status. Even in equal-status contexts on the job, for example, the women may end up making coffee and doing errands and other low-status tasks. As one woman in an IT company recounted, "It seemed like the Christmas party, birthdays, and holidays always fell to women. While I admired the effort that was made to make the environment more hospitable, the trade-off was that it seemed to marginalize the women in this hard-driving atmosphere."[19] It is easy to recognize such blatant examples of gender affecting workplace behavior. However, more often people are not aware that they are reacting to one another in ways that presume a gender hierarchy.[20]

Because our mental associations about women and men follow from our observation of these groups, they can change with new observations. Social psychologists Nilanjana Dasgupta and Shaki Asgari demonstrated such change by exposing female students to photos and brief biographies of famous women such as Toni Morrison, Meg Whitman, and Marian Wright Edelman. Even these relatively brief exposures somewhat reduced students' gender stereotyping on a measure testing how quickly they associated male names with agentic qualities and female names with communal qualities.

In a related field study, these same researchers compared the gender stereotypes of students at a women's college and at a coeducational college. They found that, by the students' second year, gender stereotypes had become weaker at the women's college but not at the coeducational college. The size of students' reduction of stereotyping at the women's college was correlated with the amount of experience that these students had with female faculty in the classroom. These studies show that, when groups are viewed in new roles, people's spontaneous mental associations about them change to correspond to these roles.[21]

Readers may assume that, because of women's lower status, beliefs about them are generally negative. However, to the contrary, people do not typically have more negative associations about women than men. Because the nice, friendly, caring qualities that predominate in thoughts about women are positive, people tend to regard women more favorably than men.[22] Some women bask in this perception of wonderfulness, savoring the approval that traditionally feminine qualities can reap. But, as sociologist Mary Jackman has argued, this especially positive portrayal of women buttresses their traditional obligations such as childcare and domestic work.[23] And these obligations do not include leadership.

In summary, because gender is a fundamental distinction of human life, categorization of people by sex is instant, automatic, and pervasive. With this categorization come automatic associations of feminine or masculine characteristics—communal qualities linked with women, and agentic qualities with men. This stereotyping is not mysterious but follows from everyday observations and reflects ordinary psychological processes.

Yet stereotyping can be accentuated by emotions. For example, some persons who are angry or frustrated may especially seize on information implying that women are unqualified for leadership. Those who promote the status quo of male–female relations may also evaluate women harshly as leaders.[24] Consequently, the stereotyping of women, sometimes accentuated by emotions, is an important component of the labyrinth in which female leaders and potential leaders try to find their way. But to fully understand why gender stereotypes limit women's leadership opportunities, we must consider how people think about leaders.

Mental Associations About Leaders

The crux of our psychological argument about the importance of gender to leadership opportunities comes from comparing people's typical associations about women and men to their typical associations about leaders. These associations about leaders are what make up leadership roles. Once people categorize someone as a leader, they tend to assimilate that person to their expectations about leaders.[25]

Mental associations about leaders do not cancel out associations about men and women. It might seem that roles should be far more important than gender in work settings, but that is true only in part, because gender spills over onto expectations based on job roles.[26] In the workplace and elsewhere, gender stereotypes still come to mind automatically, triggered by the mere classification of a person as female or male. Consequently, people consider female managers to possess an amalgam of qualities derived from their dual roles as women and managers—for example, nice as well as competent in the case of successful female managers.[27]

Under some circumstances, this amalgam can be weighted strongly toward feminine qualities. For example, gender has a greater influence on people's thinking about physically attractive women because attractiveness heightens perceptions of femininity. Therefore, in the workplace, a woman's beauty or feminine appearance can actually disadvantage her in attaining leadership roles that are thought to require predominantly masculine qualities. In contrast, beauty can advantage a woman in attaining positions (such as secretary or food server) that are thought to require a greater measure of feminine qualities.[28]

Masculine Construal of Leadership

Leadership is ordinarily conflated with men and masculinity, as shown by everyday descriptions of leaders. When journalist Frank Rich reflected on the terrorist attacks of September 11, 2001, in an essay titled "The Father Figure," he described the people of the United States as searching for a father: "When a nation is under siege, it wants someone to tell us what to do, to protect us from bullies, to tell us that everything's O.K., and that it's safe to go home now."[29] Mayor Rudy Giuliani of New York became this positive father figure and then the 2001 Man of the Year for *Time* magazine. Rich's portrayal of this longing for a father in a crisis illustrates the edge that men generally possess in gaining powerful leadership roles and performing well in them.

The masculinity of ideas about leadership also appears in researchers' descriptions of the role of manager. In the 1950s, for example, management scholar John Miner identified six activities that are required of managers in business organizations. The emphasis is on competition and hierarchy: managers are expected to stand out from the group, tell other people what to do, and compete with their peers.[30]

Contemporary descriptions of managers include some stereotypically feminine qualities such as being helpful and understanding as well as gender-neutral qualities such as demonstrating intelligence and dedication. At the same time, culturally masculine qualities have remained well represented.[31] For example, business school students identified numerous managerial behaviors as masculine, including delegating, disciplining, strategic decision making, problem solving, and punishing. They identified some other managerial behaviors as feminine, including recognizing and rewarding, communicating and informing, and supporting.[32]

REQUIREMENTS OF THE MANAGERIAL ROLE ACCORDING TO JOHN MINER

- **Competing with peers:** engaging in competition with peers involving occupational or work-related activities

- **Imposing wishes on subordinates:** telling others what to do and using sanctions in influencing others

- **Behaving assertively:** behaving in an active and assertive manner

- **Standing out from the group:** assuming a distinctive position of a unique and highly visible nature

- **Performing routine administrative functions:** executing activities of a day-to-day administrative nature

- **Maintaining positive relations with authority:** developing positive relationships with superiors

Despite such feminine themes, people usually see managers as more similar to men than women. Industrial/organizational psychologist Virginia Schein demonstrated this "think manager—think male" phenomenon by having people rate either women, men, or successful middle managers on traits that are stereotypical of women or men.[33] Ratings of managers and men were similar on a wide range of agentic characteristics, such as being competitive, self-confident, objective, aggressive, and ambitious, and having leadership ability. Ratings of managers and women were similar on only a few communal qualities, such as being intuitive and helpful. Even in recent studies, leaders in general are viewed as possessing more masculine, agentic characteristics than feminine, communal characteristics.[34] Schein and other investigators have found this "think manager— think male" effect not only in the United States but also in the United Kingdom, Germany, Singapore, Japan, China, and other nations.[35]

Political leadership has a decidedly masculine image. People believe that political offices require agentic characteristics more than communal ones.[36] Because of this perception, which was extraordinarily strong in the past, the few women who attained powerful political positions had little choice except to identify themselves in masculine terms. Elizabeth I of England "invariably referred to herself as a prince, comparing herself with kings and emperors."[37] When she rallied her troops at Tilbury to fight against the armies of the Duchy of Parma, she said, "I know I have the body of a weak and feeble woman, but I have the heart and stomach of a king."[38]

Even in societies in which gender boundaries are more fluid, the first women to occupy powerful political roles sometimes have projected a masculine or androgynous identity. For example, Margaret Thatcher is widely described has having adopted a highly dominating and combative "male" style. One of her biographers wrote that she "discarded most of the significant gender traits and became for all practical purposes, an honorary man."[39] Indira Gandhi declared, "As Prime Minister, I am not a woman. I am a human being."[40] In a similar mode, Jane Byrne, who was elected mayor of Chicago in 1979, said, "I never saw myself as a woman."[41] These women's fulfillment of highly masculine leadership roles led them away from presenting themselves as feminine or womanly.

Many leadership roles still retain strongly masculine images, especially in male-dominated organizations. If in the minds of men—or women— a good woman cannot be a good leader, then leadership presents particular difficulties for women. One senior female British police officer thus acknowledged that it was difficult to cede authority to women. She put it this way: "For me, it's all about the idea that people will follow you, whatever you do or say . . . It's that special thing, very brave, very smart, the heroes of policing, or should I also say heroines, now that we have some women up there, but it doesn't quite sit well in those terms."[42]

So cultural stereotypes give a man a double advantage in being recruited into positions of leadership: he is of course immediately categorized as male. This activates masculine associations, which are similar to beliefs about leaders and thus increase the odds that he is regarded as a leader. Once a man is viewed as a leader, the qualities associated with leadership are further ascribed to him, giving him an additional edge in the competition for leadership roles. No such bolstering occurs for women. In fact, experiments have shown that, even when a woman behaves agentically, people may not recognize her behavior as competitive and assertive. So gender stereotypes aid men on their path to leadership but complicate the labyrinth that women negotiate on their way to positions of authority.[43]

The conflation of ideas about men and leaders can make it difficult to envision women in particularly elite leadership roles. For example, well before Lawrence Summers was chosen as president of Harvard University in 2001, one of Harvard's most prominent and influential administrators remarked to a member of his staff that the next person appointed as president of Harvard could not be a woman. This judgment was rendered in advance of evaluating any candidates for the role.[44] In subsequent years, however, there has been an upsurge in women appointed as presidents of elite universities, and Harvard contributed to this trend by appointing Drew Gilpin Faust in 2007.

Because the cultural stereotype of leaders is relatively masculine, the mere activation of the female stereotype can undermine women's interest in leadership. In an elegant demonstration of this principle, social psychologists Paul Davies, Steven Spencer, and Claude Steele showed a group of male and female college students ads that had appeared on network television. Half of the students viewed ads that contained no images of people— for example, ads for cellular phones. The other students viewed these neutral ads plus ads that depicted women in gender stereotyped ways—for example, a female college student hoping to become a homecoming queen. Then the students were invited to work on a problem-solving task in a small group in which they could function as either a leader or a follower. Compared with the women who had viewed only the neutral ads, the women who had viewed the stereotypical ads indicated less interest in being the group leader and more interest in being a follower. Men were unaffected by the content of the ads. Merely bringing stereotypes about women to mind was enough to lower women's interest in becoming a leader.[45]

This phenomenon, called *stereotype threat*, occurs when individuals are in a situation where they might confirm an unfavorable stereotype about a group to which they belong. Awareness of the stereotype and concern about fulfilling it can interfere with a person's ability to perform a task well, even when that person does not believe the stereotype to be true.[46] Activation of gender stereotypes can be self-fulfilling by reducing women's interest in pursuing leadership roles and undermining their performance as leaders. Associations about femininity make women shy away from leadership. As a result, stereotypes block women's progress through the leadership labyrinth in two ways: by fueling people's doubt about women's leadership abilities and by making women personally anxious about confirming these doubts.

Despite the traditional conflation of leadership and masculinity, change is under way. The propensity to "think manager—think male" has weakened somewhat over time, perhaps particularly among male managers, who once held very traditional views.[47] Researchers have also shown that women who are especially confident about their leadership ability are not disheartened by explicit suggestions that men are more qualified than women for leadership. Instead, such women react by exhibiting even more competence as leaders than they otherwise would.[48] Very confident women can evidently steel themselves to overcome stereotypes, provided that they can recognize their influence. The effects of below-the-surface, unconscious activation of gender stereotypes are far more difficult to counteract.

Differences in Leadership Roles

The ways that people think about leaders depend on the context. People do not hold a rigid mental model of all leaders. Instead, they adjust their thinking for the types of tasks that leaders perform and the context in which they lead. Somewhat different associations come to mind when people think about elementary school principals compared with corporate CEOs or military officers. Although people ascribe some qualities, such as intelligence, to most types of leaders, they view other qualities, such as competitiveness or discipline, as more typical of particular types of leaders.[49]

Rank in organizational hierarchies influences ideas about leaders. At the highest levels, masculine qualities often prevail. For example, male managers consider highly agentic traits to be required for success as an executive (see

"Characteristics Ascribed to Successful Executives").[50] Such qualities are also regarded as especially important for higher political offices. In contrast, the cultural image of middle-level leadership positions incorporates traditionally feminine human relations skills that foster cooperative effort and the development of subordinates.[51]

In some contemporary circumstances, even powerful political roles have acquired a more feminine aura in special situations. The emergence of female presidents in Liberia (Ellen Johnson Sirleaf) and Chile (Michelle Bachelet) in 2006 illustrates this transformation. Both nations had experienced traumatic periods of violence, and both Sirleaf and Bachelet projected the maternal image of a woman who could help heal her country and bring peace and stability. Sirleaf portrayed Liberia as a sick child in need of her loving care, and Bachelet is well known for radiating "empathy and genuine concern for people."[52]

Maternal symbolism also propelled Violetta Chamorro into office as president of Nicaragua in 1990, also after a period of violent civil war. Chamorro conveyed an image "modeled after that of the Virgin Mary, the valiant, self-sacrificing, and suffering mother . . . the maternal savior of the Nicaraguan people."[53] And Ségolène Royal, the Socialist Party candidate for president of France in 2007, "portrayed herself as the mother-protector of the nation."[54] Even in the United States, some powerful female politicians now call attention to their maternal qualities. For example, Senator Patty Murray won her 1992 election campaign with "just a mom in tennis

CHARACTERISTICS ASCRIBED TO SUCCESSFUL EXECUTIVES

- **Change agent:** inspirational, risk taker, energetic, decisive, persuasive

- **Managerial courage:** courageous, learns from adversity, resilient, resourceful

- **Leadership ability:** intelligent, leadership ability, team builder, well-informed, visionary, strategic thinker

- **Results oriented:** proactive, industrious, articulate, politically astute, action oriented, high expectations, achievement oriented

shoes" as her signature slogan, and Nancy Pelosi initiated her role as Speaker of the House by being photographed surrounded by a large group of children that included her own grandchildren.[55]

Leadership roles vary widely. The most elite and powerful roles usually have more agentic definitions, even in fields (such as education and health care) that have culturally "softer" images. Ordinarily, the masculinity of leadership roles mirrors the extent to which they have been in the province of men. As we explain in chapter 9, when women enter these male-dominated situations, they confront a culture that is marked by masculine values and styles.

Prejudice Against Female Leaders

Prejudice against women leaders flows from the usual mismatch between people's mental associations about women and leaders. As we have shown, this inconsistency results from people associating communal qualities predominantly with women, and agentic qualities predominantly with leaders. Thinking about a woman occupying a leadership role can place two sets of expectations in competition—those based on gender and those based on leadership. When people's ideas about leadership do not match their view of women, they evaluate women less favorably as leaders. So although people think that women are nicer, kinder, and generally more wonderful than men, they usually prefer male leaders.

Prejudice against members of other groups is similarly grounded; it results from the mismatch between the stereotyped attributes that people ascribe to a group and those they ascribe to a particular social role.[56] People are thus prejudiced against men as childcare providers as well as against women as leaders, regardless of a given individual's actual qualities. Such prejudice is not necessarily explicit and overt but often implicit and covert. What results is an attitudinal penalty, or lower evaluation, of the person who is stereotypically mismatched to a role.

There are many demonstrations of this type of favoritism toward male over female leaders.[57] For example, polls have asked people to respond to the question: "If you were taking a new job and had your choice of a boss, would you prefer to work for a man or woman?" Figure 6-1 shows the responses obtained from Americans in selected years ranging from 1953 to 2006.[58] Male bosses were preferred in all years. However, this preference for male bosses decreased through the years, with a particularly sharp drop between 2000 and 2002 but some increase from 2002 to 2006. In 2006, 37 percent of

FIGURE 6-1

Percentage of U.S. poll respondents preferring male or female boss, 1953–2006

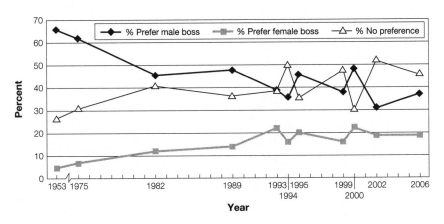

Source: Adapted from J. Carroll, Americans Prefer Male Boss to a Female Boss, September 1, 2005, Gallup Brain.

respondents favored a male boss compared with 19 percent favoring a female boss.[59]

Changes have also occurred in attitudes toward women political leaders. Figure 6-2 shows responses to two questions from a nationally representative survey of Americans. The very conservative statement, "Women should take care of running their homes and leave running the country up to men," had 34 percent agreement in 1974, but only 15 percent by 1998, the last year when this question was included. Another statement, "Most men are better suited emotionally for politics than are most women," elicited 47 percent support in 1974, but 25 percent in 2004.

Since 1937, polls have asked whether people would vote for a well-qualified woman nominated for president by their own party. As shown in figure 6-3, approval increased from only 33 percent of respondents in 1937 to 92 percent in 2006. In contrast, a question about whether America is "ready for a woman president" yielded only 55 percent agreement in 2006, up from 40 percent in 1996 when this question first appeared.[60] The huge majority now indicating personal willingness to vote for a woman may reflect social pressure to give a politically correct answer, in view of the much smaller majority believing that the country is ready for a woman president. And only somewhat more than half of respondents (57 percent)

FIGURE 6-2

Percentage of U.S. poll respondents agreeing with statements included in the General Social Survey

1974–1998

Women should take care of running their homes and leave running the company up to men.

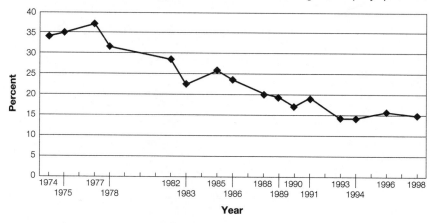

1974–2004

Most men are better suited emotionally for politics than are most women.

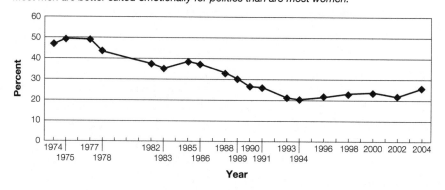

Source: Adapted from J. A. Davis, T. W. Smith, and C. V. Marsden, *General Social Surveys*, 2nd ICPSR version (Chicago: National Opinion Research Center, 2005). Reprinted with permission.

indicate that the country would be governed better if more women were in political office.[61]

All in all, studies of attitudes establish that people evaluate female leaders less favorably than male leaders. But the shift toward greater acceptance of female leaders is at least as impressive as the remaining prejudice. Presi-

FIGURE 6-3

Percentage of U.S. poll respondents willing (yes) or not willing (no) to vote for a woman candidate for president, 1937–2006

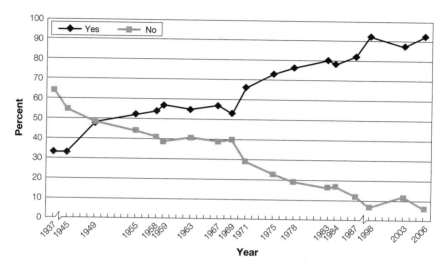

Source: Adapted from D. W. Moore, Little Prejudice Against a Woman, Jewish, Black, or Catholic Presidential Candidate, June 10, 2003. Gallup Brain; CBS News/*New York Times*, 2006. A Woman for President. February 5, 2006.

dent George W. Bush expressed this change in his statement about the presidency that "there is no doubt in my mind that a woman could do the job."[62] Nevertheless, a degree of prejudice remains, and this lingering prejudice produces detours in women's routes to leadership. And gender prejudice can be compounded by prejudice based on other demographic characteristics—in particular, race and sexual orientation. It seems plausible that women of color and of lesbian or bisexual identity may face more intense prejudice, but research is sparse.[63]

Although prejudicial attitudes do not invariably lead to discriminatory behavior, such attitudes, along with other factors, limit women's access to leadership roles. However, the increasing approval of female leaders over time is a sure sign that women's advancement is better described by their navigating a still-present labyrinth than by their being blocked by a glass ceiling. But might it make more sense to claim instead that a shattered glass ceiling now leaves a clear path to the top? Obviously not, because women do not enjoy equal access to leadership. Women face complexities not encountered by men because of continuing uncertainties about their ability to lead. In chapter 7, we present evidence that the increasingly favorable evaluations of women as leaders do not necessarily take the form of unqualified endorsement, but instead an edgier ambivalence reflecting the continuation of many of the traditional beliefs along with the introduction of new, more progressive ideas.[64]

CHAPTER SEVEN

Do People Resist Women's Leadership?

GENDER is the first thing we notice about people, and it automatically evokes gender stereotypes, as discussed in chapter 6. These stereotypes and the prejudice they induce contribute to the workplace discrimination that we document in chapter 5. In this chapter, we explore how people's stereotypes about women and leaders create resistance to women's leadership by placing competing demands on women. On one hand, female leaders are expected to fulfill the female gender role by being warm and selfless, and, on the other hand, they are also expected to fulfill the leadership role by displaying assertiveness and competence.

As a result of these pressures to be nice and friendly, women in leadership roles may have to overcome hostile reactions to their exertion of authority over others. While women follow this detour in the labyrinth, doubts are often raised about their competence as leaders, requiring them to outperform men to be seen as equally competent. Undertaking leadership in the face of these conflicting demands is no easy task. Despite these obstacles, many women can and do lead successfully, as we demonstrate in later chapters.

The Double Bind

Female leaders face a dilemma. The prescriptions for the female gender role stipulate that women be especially communal, and the prescriptions for most leadership roles stipulate that leaders be especially agentic. The communal woman is expected to be helpful and warm. She avoids being overly assertive or dominant, doesn't promote or very prominently display her accomplishments, and makes no overt attempt to influence others. In contrast, the agentic leader is expected to be direct and assertive, exhibit confidence and competence, and exert influence over others.

These expectations create a double bind for women. Highly communal female leaders may be criticized for not being agentic enough. But female leaders who are highly agentic may be criticized for lacking communion.

Given the double bind, it is hardly surprising that people are more resistant to women's influence than men's. This resistance creates obstacles within the labyrinth to women seeking leadership.[1] Influence—the ability to affect the beliefs or behaviors of others—is required for effective leadership. Because of the double bind, people may resist a woman's influence, particularly in masculine settings. Sometimes they resist because they think she lacks communion, so they don't like her. Sometimes they resist because they think she lacks competence, so they don't respect her. Yet people have greater influence when they appear both competent and warm—when they elicit both liking and respect.[2]

So for women to gain influence, the double bind requires a difficult balancing act. Kim Campbell, who briefly served as Canadian prime minister in 1993, acknowledged precisely this problem:

> *I don't have a traditionally female way of speaking. I don't end my sentences with a question mark. I'm quite assertive. If I didn't speak the way I do, I wouldn't have been seen as a leader. But my way of speaking may have grated on people who were not used to hearing it from a woman. It was the right way for a leader to speak, but it wasn't the right way for a woman to speak. It goes against type.*[3]

Expectations That Women Will Be Communal

One way the double bind penalizes women is by denying them the full benefits of being warm and considerate. As chapter 6 explains, people believe that women are self-sacrificing, helpful, and supportive and consider these traits particularly desirable in women. Although such traits bring approval, they do not produce respect for women as authorities and leaders. On the contrary, people consider warmth and selflessness to be ideally suited for women's traditional roles, such as homemaker, nurse, and teacher of children. And because people expect women to be wonderful in these traditional ways, nice behavior that seems noteworthy in men seems unimpressive in women. For example, in one study, helpful men reaped a lot of approval, but helpful women did not. And the men got away with being unhelpful when women did not. In an organizational study, male employees received more promotions when they reported helping their organizations above and beyond the requirements of their jobs. But female employees' promotions were not related to their helpfulness.[4]

Resisting Assertive, Directive, or Dominant Women. The double bind requires women to be communal and to avoid directive and assertive behavior. So a dominant manner places women at risk of being disliked and can undermine their ability to wield influence. For instance, managers in a large financial institution reported providing more mentoring and support to their male subordinates who used direct and assertive influence tactics, but more support to female subordinates who used weak and indirect tactics.[5]

Women risk not getting a job or promotion when they are too direct. For example, research has established that people regard women who ask for a raise in salary as overly demanding and therefore less hirable than women who do not make such demands.[6] So instead, women often exert influence in a less direct manner. One female Wall Street executive explained how she used this strategy: "You have to be strong and assertive without offending people. So you push a little and then back off, push a little and back off. You're always testing the waters to see how far you can go, trying not to get angry, trying not to be confrontative, trying to think of other ways to say, 'You're not right,' without attacking the person. It's getting more and more difficult the higher I go."[7]

This ambivalence about women's assertiveness may pose even more obstructions in the labyrinth for black women than white women, to the extent that black women are more assertive. There is limited evidence that black women and girls may have a more direct style of interaction than white women and girls. For example, in one survey, black women reported having an especially "sassy" style.[8] Consistent with the possibility of stronger resistance to black women's influence, in the survey black female managers, compared with their white counterparts, reported more challenges to their authority by their supervisors, subordinates, and peers.

Studies have presented men and women engaging in various types of dominant behaviors and gauged people's reactions to them. The findings are quite consistent. Nonverbal dominance, such as staring at others while speaking to them or pointing at others, is more damaging for women than men. Verbally intimidating others can undermine a woman's chances of getting a job or advancing in her career. Even disagreeing can sometimes get women into trouble, undermining their appeal and influence. Men who disagree get away with it more often than women. So women may cope by expressing disagreement more subtly. For example, one female executive and corporate board member used this tempered approach to express disagreement with her male boss: "My relationship with my boss, the CEO, is a good strong relationship. I've learned a style or adopted a style of disagreeing with him that was accepted. That didn't mean that he always changed his mind and agreed with me. But, it was a way of putting my opinion in front of him without offending him—without implying he was wrong."[9]

Although women are better liked and more influential when they moderate their style as this woman did, men have more freedom. Several experiments and organizational studies have assessed reactions to behavior that is warm and friendly versus dominant and assertive. The findings show that men can communicate in either a warm or a dominant manner, with little consequence. People like men equally well and are equally influenced by them regardless of their warmth.[10] So dominant men usually don't experience a likability penalty, but dominant women often do. Given such reactions, women feel pressure to smile and be nice, as one female manager noted: "Early in my career, I ran into the stereotype of the woman who always needs to be the nice one, smiling and accepting and nurturing. And I was that stereotype. I really was. I had this tape that said, 'No matter what somebody says to you, just smile and take it.' So when I'd be giving a speech, I'd be smiling. I could be talking about the most serious thing in the world, and you wouldn't know it from my body language and posture."[11]

Resisting Self-Promoting Women. Self-promotion can be risky for women. Although self-promotion can convey status and competence, it is not at all communal and so is not compatible with the demands of the double bind. In contrast, men can get away with bluster, which can get them noticed. One woman leader remarked on this: "I've noticed a lot of strutting with the guys, you know. It doesn't matter what they say as long as everybody looks. And they're trying to sound profound, but they need to be noticed."[12]

People may accept boastfulness in men, but, as demonstrated by several researchers, they more often dislike boastful women and consider them less deserving of recognition or support than more-modest women. As a result, self-promoting women risk having less influence than women who are more modest, even though people who self-promote are considered more competent than their more-modest counterparts.[13] Modesty is expected even in highly accomplished women, as linguistics professor Deborah Tannen observed: "This [need for modesty] was evident, for example, at a faculty meeting devoted to promotions, at which a woman professor's success was described: She was extremely well published and well known in the field. A man commented with approval, 'She wears it well.' In other words, she was praised for not acting as successful as she was."[14]

Because of pressures on women to avoid self-promotion, many women present themselves modestly. And, at least under some circumstances, a leader's modesty can motivate subordinates to contribute to the group effort. For example, one CEO compared her behavior to the behaviors she had observed in male leaders: "Leadership is not about strutting about . . . Men like to win the point, whereas I was fairly humble from the outset. So if someone says to me in a meeting, 'Why don't we try it this way?' and it makes sense to me, as it frequently does, then. . . I'm not threatened . . ."[15]

Resisting Women in Masculine Domains and Leadership Roles. The double bind is particularly strong in masculine domains, where the contrast is most apparent between expectations of female communion and of masculine agency. Masculine domains often call for highly dominant and aggressive behavior, and so people suspect that women who succeed in such domains probably are not very communal. For example, in athletics, penalties are more likely to be called against female than male athletes for excessive aggression.[16] Similarly, as one study found, when people hear about a woman succeeding in a male-dominated occupation such as electrical engineering, they assume that the woman is less likable, less attractive, less happy, and less socially desirable than a woman who succeeds in a typically feminine career. In another study, people characterized the group "successful female managers" as more deceitful, pushy, selfish, and abrasive than "successful male managers."[17] In the absence of any evidence to the contrary, people suspect that such highly effective women are not very likable or nice. In the words of one female leader, "I think that there is a real penalty for a woman who behaves like a man. The men don't like her and the women don't either."[18]

Because leaders are expected to be agentic, as we explain more fully in chapter 6, women leaders, like women in masculine domains, can experience particular resistance. Research suggests that male leaders can show their warm, feminine side without penalty, but female leaders who show their strong, masculine side are resented.[19] Jean Hollands, founder of an executive coaching company, unflatteringly calls such female executives "bully broads." These exceptionally competent women "deal the deals, win the wars, sell the contracts, and run the institutions" but derail when their assertiveness offends others. Hollands acknowledges that many male executives bully people and can get away with it:

> In the name of ascending the corporate ladder, some men have succeeded by grabbing power with both hands and doing whatever it takes to hold on, using intimidation, impatience and aggression as their tools. Maybe they are disliked by their subordinates and colleagues, but they can also be the darlings of management and richly rewarded for their behavior. On the other hand, very few women can succeed with such heavy handed tactics.[20]

Sometimes women leaders can provoke ire in their subordinates without being bullies, merely by doing their jobs and giving others clear direction. Caitlin Friedman, author of an advice book for women, reported that she's heard many complaints about female bosses: "[People say] 'I loved my woman boss until she started telling me what to do.' But that is what a boss does! It's okay coming from a man, but very often—still, even in these supposedly enlightened times—not from a woman."[21]

Men's Resistance to Agentic Women. Men, in particular, resist female leadership because men possess higher societal status than women and view women who attempt to wield influence as competing with them for power and authority. As experiments have demonstrated, on average, men disapprove of high levels of competence and authority more in women than in other men and resist women's influence more than women do.[22] For example, in meetings at a global retail company, people responded more favorably to men's overt attempts to influence than to women's. In the words of one of this company's female executives, "People often had to speak up to defend their turf, but when women did so, they were vilified. They were labeled 'control freaks'; men acting the same way were called 'passionate.'"[23]

Similarly, a female executive in the entertainment industry described how men maintain their authority in meetings: "Men who conduct meetings usually act like a pitcher, throwing lots of questions at various batters. It's a way of maintaining the dominant position. It's a game that's played: 'Look how smart I am!' . . . If you can lob it back he sits up in his chair."[24]

Some men sit up in response to female assertiveness because they don't like it. In fact, male resistance is such that women can sometimes increase their influence with men by communicating in ways that both sexes consider less competent than regular speech, such as by speaking in a tentative or indirect manner.[25] For example, one study found that a female executive used this less direct approach to get a male subordinate to attend a meeting he did not want to attend. Instead of issuing a direct order, she said, "I do think you should go. I can't and I think we should be represented . . . But this is something we have to get involved in. Let me put it this way, John. I invite you to go. But feel free to leave at any time."[26] After some additional subtle prompts by the executive, the man attended the meeting.

Male resistance to female influence also affects the hiring of women for traditionally masculine jobs. In experiments, men have shown a stronger preference than women for hiring male applicants over female applicants, even when the professional records of the women match or surpass those of the men.[27] Experiencing such reactions, Katherine Hudson, former CEO and president of Brady Corporation, described how men reacted to her hiring at Brady: "I came to Milwaukee to run the Brady Corporation in January 1994 . . . I went to meet my management team . . . As I walked down the hall, I could see a half dozen men waiting, trying to determine who was coming. I saw the strange look on their faces as they realized, 'My God, it's a woman.'"[28]

Men may feel competitive toward women especially in higher-level leadership positions traditionally held by men, where men have more to lose from women's advancement. Female leaders, particularly in areas such as business, engineering, and science, are likely to experience intense male resistance. Cornelia Dean, science editor for the *New York Times* from 1997 to 2003, noted the challenges of being a woman in this influential role, particularly in her interactions with male scientists:

> I went to the annual meeting of the American Association for the Advancement of Science, a convention that attracts thousands of researchers and teachers. My name tag listed my new position, and the scientists at the meeting all seemed to have the same reaction when they read it: "You're the new science editor of The New York Times!?" At first I was deluded enough to think they meant I was much too delightful a person for such a heavy-duty job. In fact, they were shocked it had been given to a woman. This point was driven home a few weeks later when, at a dinner for scientific eminences, a colleague introduced me to one of the nation's leading neuroscientists. "Oh yes," the scientist

murmured, as he scanned the room clearly ignoring me. "Who is the new sci-
ence editor of The New York Times, *that twerpy little girl in short skirts?"*
Dumbfounded, I replied, "That would be me."[29]

Women are also at a particular disadvantage when they are in the minority or are the sole woman in a group of men, as shown in several studies.
Under such circumstances, the women's ideas tend to be ignored by the
men.[30] Women are at less of a disadvantage in integrated groups, where the
presence of other women helps ease their way through the labyrinth. Yet
women in positions of higher power and authority seldom find themselves
in gender-balanced groups and therefore often face increased resistance to
their leadership.

One manifestation of male resistance to women's leadership and authority is the prevalence of sexual harassment. Legally, sexual harassment
occurs in the workplace when a person is offered rewards for sexual favors,
punished for refusing to provide such favors, or subjected to unwanted sexual behavior that interferes with his or her job or creates an intimidating or
offensive working environment.[31]

On average, 58 percent of employed women have experienced treatment at their jobs that meets the definition of sexual harassment.[32] As
shown in figure 7-1, the incidence is highest for the most male-dominated
environment: the military. Here, 69 percent of women had been harassed.
Furthermore, surveys show that when harassment occurs it usually is committed by men and directed at women.[33] Most complaints received by the
Equal Employment Opportunity Commission—the U.S. agency responsible for enforcing laws against employment discrimination—are from women
(see figure 7-2).

Women's risk of harassment increases when they are particularly well
educated or are in supervisory positions, even though young, unmarried
women and women in entry-level or trainee positions are also especially
vulnerable. Women's risk also increases in traditionally masculine occupations and in environments with a high percentage of men, consistent with
the high rate of harassment in the military.[34] Such harassment may be triggered by threats to some men's masculinity when men are confronted with
women who are expert in traditionally masculine domains.[35] The presence
of upwardly mobile women in otherwise masculine settings creates prime
conditions for male resentment. Neurosurgeon Frances Conley described
some of her experiences of sexual harassment by colleagues at Stanford
Medical School: "I was asked to go to bed, but it was always in jest, for

FIGURE 7-1

Percentage of U.S. women experiencing sexual harassment on the job in different types of organizations

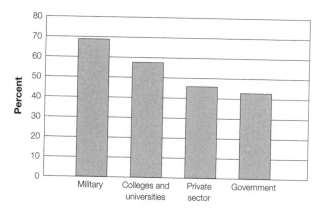

Source: Adapted from R. N. Ilies et al., "Reported Incidence Rates of Work-Related Sexual Harassment in the United States: Using Meta-analysis to Explain Reported Rate Disparities," table 2, *Personnel Psychology* 56 (2003): 607–631.

FIGURE 7-2

Percentage of sexual harassment complaints by women and by men to the U.S. Equal Opportunity Employment Commission, 1992–2006

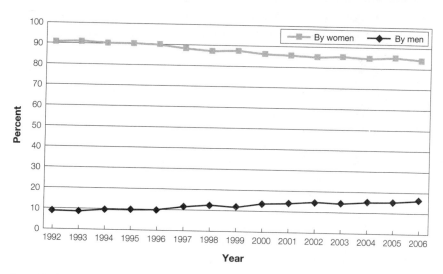

Source: Adapted from U.S. Equal Opportunity Employment Commission, 2007, Sex-Based Discrimination, table "Sexual harassment charges."

effect . . . If I had a different opinion than my male colleagues, they said it was because I was suffering from premenstrual syndrome or 'on the rag.'"[36]

Women who are harassed on the job can face a serious threat to their careers. If they do nothing, they can be intimidated and demeaned in the eyes of their colleagues. Yet most women take no formal action against their harassers.[37] Although doing nothing may seem counterproductive, assertive objections often worsen a woman's conditions on the job and reduce her opportunities for promotion.[38] Thus, harassment can be a potent means of male resistance to women's leadership. Given the difficulties of crafting a satisfactory response to this type of resistance, harassment forms yet another stumbling block on many women's paths through the labyrinth.[39]

Concerns That Women Lack Agency

The belief that leaders should be assertive and should confidently display their competence, coupled with disapproval of such behavior in women, produces half of the double bind for female leaders. The other half follows from the belief that women should be selfless and modest but that such individuals lack agency. So the dangers that slow women's paths through the labyrinth include being regarded as an abrasive dragon lady or a soft pushover. Carly Fiorina experienced the double bind as CEO of Hewlett-Packard: "In the chat rooms around Silicon Valley, from the time I arrived and until long after I left HP, I was routinely referred to as a 'bimbo,' or a 'bitch'—too soft or too hard, and presumptuous, besides."[40]

Doubts About Female Leadership Competence. Concerns about women's agency place additional demands on women to perform exceptionally well. Women are held to a higher standard of leadership competence than men, consistent with the evidence in chapter 4 that people evaluate female leaders somewhat less favorably than objectively equivalent male leaders. And to be influential, men do not have to avoid assertive forms of influence to be liked, nor do they have to be as concerned with proving their abilities as women do.[41]

This double standard impedes women's ability to obtain desirable jobs, influence others, and attain leadership. In response to these pressures, female leaders succeed by performing extraordinarily well. For example, Katherine Hudson overcame resistance to her hiring at Brady Corporation by creating an enviable track record. She remarked, "Since I've been here, we have doubled the size of the company, tripled the market cap, and have done eleven acquisitions . . . I've passed their test, and now they're passing mine."[42]

Women are well aware that their influence is diminished by doubts about their competence. If a man has something important to say, people are likely to pay attention, but if a woman does, people may discount or ignore her.[43] A female vice president of a manufacturing company described how her ideas and those of other women are ignored in meetings: "It immediately gets lost in the conversation. Then two minutes later, a man makes the same suggestion and it's 'Wow! What a great idea!' And you sit there and think, 'What just happened?'"[44]

In a study that vividly documents this tendency to overlook women's ideas, research psychologist Kathleen Propp studied four-person groups assigned the task of determining who should get custody of a child in a divorce case. Specific case information was given to one or more members of the group, and then the entire group discussed and reached consensus on the case. The group used the supplied information in reaching its decision more often when it was presented by a man. This trend was most pronounced when the information was known to only one person; in that condition, the information was used 72 percent of the time when it was presented by a man, but only 13 percent of the time when it was presented by a woman.[45] An everyday example comes from one female attorney's difficulty with being heard in the courtroom: "I was half way through my theory when the judge interrupted me and said 'Oh, come on now, shut up. Let's hear what the men have to say.'"[46]

Women who have difficulty being heard sometimes cope by being persistent and using humor to their advantage. For example, when one woman failed to bring a meeting to order, she tried again, saying, "As difficult as it may be to believe, this group of folks is coming to order." And then when one male holdout continued to ignore her, she added, "Tom, you come to order, too," which provoked laughter and brought the meeting to order.[47]

Women confront concerns about their competence especially in masculine domains. As chapter 4 notes in relation to hiring, men are somewhat advantaged in neutral contexts not associated with either sex, but they are especially favored in masculine settings.[48] In such settings, people may assume that the rare woman benefited from preferential hiring and discount her merit on that basis.[49] And in masculine domains, people hold women to a higher standard of performance to be seen as the equal of men. For example, in a study of military cadets, men and women gave their male peers higher ratings for motivation and leadership than their female peers, even though the men and women were equal on objective measures, such as grades and rank. Such outcomes occur because women often need to outperform men to be seen as their equals.[50]

Such was the case with Ann Hopkins, who sued Price Waterhouse (now PricewaterhouseCoopers) for denying her a partnership even though she had performed better than men who had been promoted to partner. Before being denied partnership, Hopkins had successfully secured a $25 million contract with the Department of State, which the partners in her office judged "an outstanding performance" that Hopkins had carried out "virtually at the partner level." Her evaluators praised her as "an outstanding professional" with "strong character, independence and integrity." Her clients characterized her as "extremely competent, intelligent," "strong and forthright, very productive, energetic and creative." At the discrimination trial, it was established that "none of the other partnership candidates at Price Waterhouse that year had a comparable record in terms of successfully securing major contracts for the partnership."[51] Yet Hopkins's performance was not good enough.

Even if people credit a man and a woman with equal credentials, they may still prefer the man for the position because the same credentials just seem more impressive in a man. In a study illustrating this phenomenon, participants evaluated either a man or a woman for a position as a police chief, a male-dominated leadership role. The candidate was described either as highly educated with administrative experience or as streetwise but lacking higher education and administrative experience. When evaluating the male candidate, the participants considered education a more important criterion of job success when he was well educated, and street smarts as more important when he was not. Whatever credential the male applicant offered seemed desirable in a police chief, thereby justifying his hiring. But for the female candidate, participants did not bend the hiring criteria to fit the qualities that she possessed.[52] So people may creatively redefine job criteria to fit the qualifications of the candidate whose gender seems to fit the job.

Ironically, some experimental evidence shows that women who display unusual competence in masculine settings can sometimes even *increase* doubts about their competence. How could female experts appear incompetent? Apparently, it is often difficult for people to determine who has the best ideas, particularly in situations involving complex problems that do not have obvious solutions.[53] Under such conditions, which are common for real-world problems, people rely on stereotypes to evaluate performance. In traditionally masculine settings, with their skepticism about female expertise, expert women are often discredited, but expert men are given the benefit of the doubt.

With this difficulty of recognizing excellence in women, any imperfections become magnified. Carly Fiorina learned this when she was summarily dismissed from her role as CEO of Hewlett-Packard. Although the company enjoyed increasing success soon after Fiorina's departure, she received little credit for it. In a television interview, Fiorina expressed her view about the way she was treated: "A transformation takes a lot of time and a lot of work and the success that HP enjoys today is in no small measure due to the work of tens of thousands of employees that were working hard as well as myself, head down under the hood for 5½ years . . . I was the first outsider. I wasn't an engineer. I came from big east coast companies, not small Silicon Valley startups. I didn't come from the computer industry and I was a woman."[54]

The double standard reverses direction in feminine domains, as chapter 4 explains in relation to hiring decisions.[55] People more often doubt men's competence in domains such as childcare work. As a result, women are more influential in traditionally feminine domains, and men wield more influence in traditionally masculine domains such as the military.[56] To the extent that leadership is itself perceived as a masculine domain, women leaders therefore face challenges in wielding influence.

These findings may seem fair, with each sex favored in its own domain. What's the harm in thinking that men are more skilled as firefighters and business executives, and that women are more skilled as secretaries and elementary school teachers? The problem is that if people act on such stereotypical perceptions, they confine women to jobs with lower pay, ignore real differences in individuals' skills, and deny women leadership opportunities merely because leaders are thought to have more masculine than feminine characteristics.

Because women's excellent performance can be overlooked and setbacks can slow progress, successful women persist, redouble their efforts, and continue to excel. Astronaut Cady Coleman recounted how she learned from the challenges that she had faced when rowing on the crew team at MIT: "The only way to get through the race is not to think 206 strokes ahead because you just give up. Instead, you think, 'This stroke, and then the next stroke, and then the next stroke' . . . What I learned to do is concentrate on the part I can bite off, and then bite off one piece at a time . . . You have to have the ability to persevere."[57]

Shifting Standards of Competence. The double standard is complicated by the fact that people spontaneously compare individuals to similar others—women to other women, and men to other men. As social psychologist Monica Biernat and her colleagues have demonstrated, comparing a person to similar others causes standards for evaluation to shift, depending on whether a man or a woman is evaluated. To demonstrate shifting standards, consider a woman who is five feet ten inches in height and universally regarded as "tall." In contrast, a man of this same stature is regarded as "fairly average." Expectations for height thus shift, depending on the sex of the person who is judged.

Similarly, when people describe a woman and a man as "competent," they may not necessarily mean that the woman and man are equal in ability but rather that the woman is competent *for a woman* and the man *for a man.* So even when men and women receive comparable evaluations of their competence, those evaluations can have different meanings on a so-called *common standard* that forces people to use the same judgment standard for both sexes.[58]

Because common standards have a fixed meaning, they readily reveal group stereotypes. For example, asking people to judge the heights of men and women on the common standard of feet and inches would reveal the (accurate) belief that men are taller. However, asking people to judge these same heights on a *subjective scale* extending from "very short" to "very tall" would obscure this belief. On this scale, men of average height (five feet nine inches in the United States) and women of average height (five feet four inches) would be judged about "average," thereby hiding the fact that men as a group are taller than women.[59]

A study of U.S. Army officers illustrates these shifting standards. The officers, who attended a leadership training course, evaluated the leadership competence of each member of their training group. Given the military setting, it is not surprising that the women received lower evaluations than the men overall. Yet the women did fairly well when the ratings were made on subjective scales, ranging from "needs improvement" to "outstanding," because these scales allowed standards to shift to accommodate the officers' lower expectations for women. The women were rated more poorly when the officers ranked each person in the group relative to every other person, a procedure that forced a common standard.[60] So when it came down to identifying the better leaders from among the women and men, a very strong pro-male bias emerged.

If they are not aware of shifting standards, women making their way through the labyrinth can be misled about what others think of them. Especially in masculine contexts, people often assume that women have lower competence, even while they appear to evaluate them favorably. Common standards can reveal a devaluation of women's competence that does not show up in the more ordinary subjective evaluations of competence.

Consistent with several experiments on judgments of competence, people must receive clear and unambiguous evidence of a woman's substantial superiority over available men before judging the woman to be better than a man at a task.[61] So when a woman succeeds at meeting this high expectation, people may view her performance as extraordinary and credit her with even more competence than an objectively equivalent man. People think that only extreme individual competence could allow women to surmount the challenges that they have had to overcome.[62] And because white people often have lower expectations for black than for white people, an accomplished black woman may be seen as especially remarkable.[63] One black female manager noted this reaction: "They were surprised that I was smart, competent, and capable because they didn't expect that . . . I get high praise sometimes because I think they didn't expect anything. When I can speak English and do whatever I'm supposed to do, people are just overwhelmed. I then become the exception."[64]

Such reactions may exist only on the surface—that is, in relation to shifting standards whereby this woman is regarded as excellent *for a black woman*. However, when she is judged for promotion in comparison to her colleagues, gender and racial stereotypes are likely to prevail, placing additional pressures on black women to establish themselves as especially competent.[65] One way women respond to such pressures is to perform extremely well and to recognize that others may underestimate their worth. One black female neurosurgeon remarked, "We can't expect to be validated as individuals, but we can make the field different for those who come behind us. We must do good work and eventually the work will speak for itself . . . I learned every day not to count on others' acceptance as a measure of my worth."[66]

Because the bar is set higher for women, the old adage that a women must be "twice as good as a man" to get a job holds true, at least for jobs that are traditionally male dominated, including most leadership positions. Yet when people have low expectations for a particular group, research shows that they usually set a lower minimum standard of competence for that group.[67] Because of this lower minimum standard, it may be easier for a woman to get into the pool of candidates. Being chosen from that field of candidates is quite another matter. Given the higher requirements for excellence in women, an individual woman would have to show that she was exceptional to be selected.

The trouble that women have in getting beyond the short list emerged for an investment company that intended to increase the number of women it hired by interviewing more women candidates. The strategy failed to work because "the 30 minutes allotted for each interview—the standard practice at most business schools—was not long enough for middle-aged male managers, who were conducting the vast majority of the interviews, to connect with young female candidates . . . [The women] hadn't had enough time to impress their interviewer."[68] To the extent that these interviewers held an implicit higher standard for women, these female candidates had a very difficult task to perform in a short interview.

Given doubts about female competence, it not surprising that women executives often report that having an extraordinary track record was important to their career success, an issue we revisit in chapter 10.[69] One woman, a senior vice president in a Wall Street firm, experienced the high requirements imposed on women in this way: "We have to know everything before we take action. A guy can be more brazen. If he gets caught with his pants down, he just laughs and says, 'No big deal,' whereas a woman looks like an utter fool. If you ever show any weakness in nuts-and-bolts knowledge, you really are never forgiven."[70]

Doubts about female agency are especially pronounced in higher-level leadership positions, where to be seen as excellent means much more than performing one's job impeccably. Consider, for example, this description of female managers by *BusinessWeek* journalist Michelle Conlin: "She has Everest-size ambitions, a flawless track record, and an uncanny knack for strategy. 'I'd love to promote her,' the CEO says. 'But she just doesn't have "it."' . . . 'It' refers to that ability to take hold of a room by making a polished entrance, immediately shaking people's hands and forging quick, personal connections instead of defaulting to robotic formalism and shrinking into a chair." Conlin thus argued that women lack *executive presence* because they are hampered by their "nice girl, seen-not-heard communication styles."[71]

Concerns about women's lack of agency also include worries that women are too weak to be effective leaders at very high levels. The criticism of not being "tough enough," is rarely directed at comparable men, even though there are successful male leaders who are modest and unassuming. In fact, in his analysis of the most consistently successful companies in the *Fortune* 1000, management scholar Jim Collins found that they had excellent male CEOs who were humble and not self-aggrandizing, such as Darwin Smith of Kimberly-Clark and Coleman M. Mockler of Gillette. Similarly, American presidents such as Abraham Lincoln and Gerald Ford were humble and yet effective political leaders.[72] But women are not allowed such latitude.

Conclusion

In everyday behavior on the job, women encounter more obstacles to their leadership and authority than men do. Women who are too assertive, competitive, or even competent can at times threaten others, who then resist female influence and leadership. This resistance to their leadership can lower evaluations of women's personalities and skills, obscure women's contributions to group tasks, undermine their performance, and even subject them to sexual harassment. At the same time, women can be criticized for being too nice.

Men, unlike women, do not bear the burden of having to be especially likable to be influential or to be accepted as leaders, nor do they have to establish themselves as clearly superior in ability. People presume that men are agentically competent, even for behavior that might be seen as not so competent when exhibited by women. Dominance is accepted in men, allowing them—with little, if any, penalty—to be relatively self-serving and noncommunal in their interactions with others. Because men generally receive the benefit of the doubt, they are relatively less affected by how much they establish themselves as competent or communal. They enjoy considerable leeway in how they lead and influence others. Thus, their path to leadership is relatively clear and direct.

Women are not so fortunate. For them, the route to leadership wends through a labyrinth, where they find themselves diverted—sometimes by doubts about their competence, sometimes by doubts about their warmth, and sometimes by resentment of their very presence. However, throughout our analysis, we indicate that these problems are more intense in some leadership roles than others, particularly in roles ordinarily held by men and at higher levels in organizations. Where women have become more numerous as managers, as they have in many areas (see chapter 2), women and men are treated more equivalently. In these circumstances, the double bind loosens. Especially in more culturally feminine occupations, such as those in education and social services, the resistance we have documented is no doubt less extreme.[73]

For women in other leadership roles, the double bind remains a greater problem. However, as we discuss in chapters 8 and 10, in response to the challenges presented by the double bind, female leaders often cultivate a style that overcomes the hazards that they encounter in the labyrinth.

CHAPTER EIGHT

Do Women Lead Differently from Men?

IT IS A COMMON BELIEF that women lead in a more collaborative and democratic manner than men. If that is true, how can some experts on leadership maintain that male and female leaders do not differ at all as long as they have the same leadership positions? In fact, both of these ideas have an element of truth: many women lead with behaviors that are tinged with culturally feminine qualities. But male and female leaders differ only in some respects and some circumstances and, on the whole, do not differ by much. The good news for women is that their somewhat less masculine ways of leading have come into greater fashion: their styles approximate the now valued model of a leader who acts as a *good-coach* or *good-teacher* rather than a traditional *command-and-control* boss.

These issues pertain to *leadership style*—leaders' characteristic ways of behaving that have a consistent meaning or function. A leader regarded as having a collaborative style, for example, emphasizes collaborative behaviors (consulting, encouraging, discussing, negotiating) that vary depending on the circumstances. All leaders have their typical modes of acting—their own distinctive styles. This chapter addresses two questions about style: do women differ from men in leadership style, and, if so, do these differences work to the advantage or the disadvantage of women?[1]

Leaders' styles are important: people often blame leaders' failures on faulty styles. For example, when Howell Raines, former executive editor of the *New York Times*, resigned under pressure in 2003, his management style was faulted even more than the precipitating event of journalistic fraud by one of the *Times*'s favored writers. This event caused "long-simmering complaints" about a "top-down management style" to surface.[2] Similarly, when Lawrence Summers, then president of Harvard University, made statements suggesting that women might be intrinsically less qualified than men for high achievement in science, he became the target of a wide-ranging critique of his leadership style as well as his views on women. These criticisms were instrumental in causing his subsequent resignation.[3]

Journalists scrutinize women's leadership styles and personalities with a thoroughness that is rarely expended on men unless male leaders face serious problems, as did Raines and Summers. This focus on women's style occurs because people who defy expectations—the *male* nurse, the *female* surgeon, the *male* secretary, the *female* CEO—attract attention.[4] When observing leaders, people wonder, "How does *she* do it?" more often than, "How does *he* do it?"[5]

Women leaders generally find this type of attention unwelcome. In the words of corporate executive Elaine La Roche, "Issues of style with respect to women can unfortunately often be more important than issues of substance."[6] Carly Fiorina, former CEO of Hewlett-Packard, complained, "When I finally reached the top, after striving my entire career to be judged by results and accomplishments, the coverage of my gender, my appearance and the perceptions of my personality would vastly outweigh anything else."[7]

Female politicians often complain that they must worry not only about their hairstyles but also about "projecting gravitas," as former U.S. Representative Patricia Schroeder put it.[8] As a 1999 presidential candidate, Elizabeth Dole thus received disproportionate media attention to her leadership style as well as her personality traits, appearance, family life, and gender—types of scrutiny not directed nearly as much to the male candidates.[9]

Why are perceptions of powerful women so biased? Because men have long held such roles, people have based their notions of leadership on men. Therefore, men rarely have to worry about being too masculine or too feminine or about tailoring their leadership style so that they can be taken seriously. Women leaders worry a lot about these things, complicating the labyrinth that they negotiate.

Debates About Leadership Style

Even broaching the issue that men and women differ in leadership style incites debate among social scientists.[10] Those who prefer to avoid discussing the matter often argue that portraying women as nicer, kinder, collaborative leaders promotes gender stereotypes. Those who prefer to address the issue argue that portraying women and men as the same promotes masculine leadership styles, which female leaders can find uncomfortable and inauthentic.

But what is the basis of any of the claims made about leadership styles? The most prominent claims about difference come from authors of books and articles written for management audiences and the general public.[11] The best known of these authors is management professor Judy Rosener. In a 1990 article in *Harvard Business Review*, she wrote that an *interactive style* is typical of female leaders:

> *The women leaders made frequent reference to their efforts to encourage participation and share power and information . . . In describing nearly every aspect of management, the women interviewees made reference to trying to make people feel part of the organization. They try to instill this group identity in a variety of ways, including encouraging others to have a say in almost every aspect of work . . . To facilitate inclusion, they create mechanisms that get people to participate and they use a conversational style that sends signals inviting people to get involved.[12]*

Rosener based her conclusions on a survey of women who belonged to an organization that promotes women's career success and included a comparison group of men in the survey. To obtain the comparison group, each woman nominated a man who held a position similar to her own. Using qualitative methods, Rosener summarized the descriptions that these women and men gave of their leadership.[13]

Many leadership researchers have disagreed with such generalizations about women's distinctive leadership styles. For example, Bernard Bass, a well-known scholar of leadership, wrote, "The preponderance of available evidence is that no consistently clear pattern of differences can be discerned in the supervisory style of female as compared to male leaders."[14] Management researcher Gary Powell expressed similar views in a widely read article.[15]

Other researchers have argued that seemingly different male and female styles are an illusion because any difference in style is really a reflection of the typically different roles that men and women occupy.[16] It's surely true that different roles can foster different styles. For example, if more women are in human resources management and more men in line management, apparent sex differences might really be role differences. But the real issue, and the one that we address, is whether men and women differ when they occupy the *same* role.

Which Is More Plausible—Similarities or Differences in Leadership Style?

There are good reasons for thinking that men and women who are in the same role lead in similar ways. Male and female leaders are ordinarily selected by the same criteria and are required to have the same types of background, such as an MBA degree. Also, leaders' behavior is influenced by the roles that they occupy: certain ways of doing things are expected in certain roles. Therefore, women are under pressure to carry out tasks in the same ways as their male colleagues.[17] Here is how Marietta Nien-hwa Cheng described her transition to the role of symphony conductor: "I used to speak more softly, with a higher pitch. Sometimes my vocal cadences went up instead of down. I realized that these mannerisms lack the sense of authority. I strengthened my voice. The pitch has dropped . . . I have stopped trying to be everyone's friend. Leadership is not synonymous with socializing."[18]

Cheng's comments reflect the highly authoritative character of the conductor role. Conductors rarely negotiate the interpretation of passages with the violin section or the flute player. People who succeed as conductors have their own unique behaviors and eccentricities but adapt to a model of relatively autocratic leadership.

The idea that leadership roles suppress any sex differences in leadership styles, despite its tempting logic, is not the whole story. As chapters 6 and 7 show, leaders are constrained by gender. People expect male leaders to speak assertively, compete for attention, influence others, and initiate activity. In contrast, people expect female leaders to speak more tentatively, not draw so much attention to themselves, accept others' suggestions, support others, and solve interpersonal problems. As a woman executive observed, "There's a basic expectation that a woman is going to be the comfortable, team-building, soft, forgiving type."[19]

Expectations based on gender also influence how leaders think about themselves. Consider that 98 percent of a group of female executives chose, from a long list of leadership qualities, the terms *collaborative, flexible, inclusive,* and *participative* to describe themselves. It is doubtful that such a high proportion of male executives would have chosen these communal attributes. Yet, only slightly smaller percentages of these women also described themselves as *assertive, decisive,* and *strong.*[20]

Why do people have these expectations about female leaders being communal? The answer is that these women have the burden of negotiating two roles: woman and leader. They have to reconcile the communal qualities that people prefer in women with the agentic qualities that people think leaders need to exhibit to succeed. Finding an appropriate and effective leadership style is therefore a delicate task, and women know this. Catalyst's study of *Fortune* 1000 female executives thus found that 96 percent rated as *critical* or *fairly important* that they develop "a style with which male managers are comfortable."[21]

As chapter 7 explains, female leaders are buffeted by cross pressures that complicate their route through the labyrinth. They are constrained by negative reactions to strong assertions of their authority over others. Then the idea that they are acting "just like a man" brings the sting of dislike. On the other side of this dilemma, hints of being soft or tentative bring disrespect. Then the "not tough enough" charge quickly emerges, as French presidential candidate Ségolène Royal complained.[22]

Women generally split the difference between these masculine and feminine demands by finding a middle way that is neither unacceptably masculine nor unacceptably feminine. Consider, for example, a Canadian study of on-the-job behavior. Showing the influence of gender, friendly, people-oriented, and expressive behaviors were more common in women than men, regardless of their job status.[23] Showing the influence of workplace roles, assertive, confident, and competent behaviors were more common in people who had higher-status jobs, regardless of their gender. Women in managerial roles—being both female and higher-status—blended assertive competence with supportive friendliness. However, as we will demonstrate, women also modulate their style to meet the demands of their particular leadership roles.

Gender is able to exert its effects on leadership because leaders have some latitude in fulfilling their roles. They have some freedom, for example, to lead in a style that is friendly or more remote. They may exhibit much or little excitement about future goals, consult many or few colleagues, provide extensive or limited mentoring of subordinates, and so forth. These discretionary aspects of leadership are susceptible to shaping by gender norms because they are not closely regulated by leader roles.[24] But do men and women really differ in how they lead? To prove that they do, at least to some extent, we turn to research on leadership styles.

Task-Oriented and Interpersonally Oriented Leadership

As many studies have shown, some leaders have a relatively *task-oriented* style—emphasizing behavior that accomplishes assigned tasks—and others have a more *interpersonally oriented* style—emphasizing behavior that maintains positive interpersonal relationships. Task leadership includes activities such as requiring subordinates to follow rules and procedures, setting high standards for performance, and clarifying leader and subordinate roles. Interpersonal leadership includes activities such as helping and doing favors for subordinates, looking out for their welfare, and being friendly and available.[25] Gender norms tend to steer male leaders toward a task-oriented style, and female leaders toward an interpersonally oriented style. However, leaders' jobs typically require some attention to both task and interpersonal concerns.

To assess these leadership styles, researchers generally have observers judge how often leaders engage in behaviors of each type. These observers often are leaders' subordinates, and sometimes their supervisors or peers. In some research, leaders report on their own behaviors. Studies using such measures have established that both task and interpersonal behaviors contribute to leaders' effectiveness and that interpersonal behaviors especially promote followers' satisfaction with leaders.[26]

A meta-analysis of studies of leadership style showed equal task orientation of men and women but slightly greater interpersonal orientation in women.[27] A closer look at the data, however, reveals some complexities. Women's greater interpersonal orientation was present mainly among nonmanagers, as we would expect if men and women lead similarly when they are in the same managerial role.[28] And among managers, a somewhat greater interpersonal orientation of women than men was present only in more gender-integrated roles and absent in more male-dominated roles.[29] When women are rare in a leadership role, they likely lose authority if they try to lead in a culturally feminine style. Where there are very few women, the only legitimate styles may be those that are typical of men.

One female executive in the financial industry clearly expressed this pressure to conform to a masculine style of leadership: "I don't know exactly when it happened, but I learned that you had to be slightly less warm, slightly less good-natured, slightly less laughing, carefree, and happy. You have to put on a more serious demeanor, to establish credibility more quickly. I don't advocate trying to be nasty, but you stop trying to be warm, wonderful, and nice. It works better."[30]

The meta-analysis also found that both men and women were more task oriented when leading in roles that are more congruent with their gender. Leaders in roles less aligned with their gender (for example, a *female* athletic director or a *male* nursing supervisor) were perceived as less task oriented—that is, they did not get as much recognition for competently executing the task aspects of their jobs. This finding reveals one of the ways that nontraditional roles can put leaders at somewhat of a disadvantage (see chapter 6).[31]

Democratic and Autocratic Leadership

Another way of describing leadership styles contrasts *democratic* with *autocratic* styles, or *participative* with *directive* styles. A democratic or participative leader takes others' opinions into account in making decisions, but autocratic or directive leaders seldom do.[32] Although a democratic approach may seem inherently superior because of its consistency with American values, the effectiveness of these styles depends on the circumstances. Autocratic leadership can provide efficient decision making. Such a style can be desirable when a very quick decision is needed or when subordinates lack relevant competence or interest in helping make decisions. In such situations, leaders who fail to be directive would be at a disadvantage. On the other hand, an autocratic leader can make subordinates dissatisfied, damage their morale, and even cause them to exit a group or organization.[33]

Stereotypically, women are more participative and collaborative than men, and there is in fact some empirical evidence that groups having more women tend to be more egalitarian than groups having fewer women.[34] A preference on the part of women for democratic leadership makes sense, given that people are particularly discontented with autocratic leaders who are women (see chapter 7).[35] Such women are often viewed as acting too masculine and are generally disliked more than autocratic men.[36] Women may therefore seek ways to soften their leadership styles by bringing others into decision making. Here is how one woman leader described her progress toward a more collaborative style:

> I can be abrasive at times, and I have had to be over the years, and there have been stages in our development when I've been very tough—but basically, my style is collaborative and to try to pull people in, and I have grown even more sophisticated at it over the years because I'm more sensitive to what's causing the problem. I certainly in the early years didn't understand as much about

human nature as I do now, so when I meet impediments now I am more able to work it in a calmer and supportive style to help people come around to something that I need to do.[37]

Because of the potential for harsh reactions, it makes sense for women to avoid a highly directive leadership style. That is exactly what has emerged from the leadership style meta-analysis: in general, women adopt a somewhat more democratic or participative style than men.[38] Similar findings emerged in a study of committee chairs in state legislatures. The female chairs, more than their male counterparts, acted as facilitators rather than traditional "take charge," directive leaders. As an example of this type of political leadership, consider a colleague's description of Christine Quinn, Speaker of the New York City Council: "She has injected more democracy, with a little 'd,' into the Council. Every single council member has a say in the budget. Every single council member has the ability to fight for their constituents."[39]

Also, in their inaugural addresses, female governors express collaborative themes more often than male governors do. For example, New Hampshire's Jeanne Shaheen closed her 1997 inaugural address by saying, "After all, history is not only comprised of epic events, but also of the quiet, steady work of people striving together to make tomorrow a little better than today . . . let us do it together. Then, we will truly make history."[40]

Even though women lean toward a democratic style, this style can disappear in situations where there are few women, as also shown in the leadership style meta-analysis. Without a critical mass of other women to affirm the legitimacy of a participative style, women leaders usually opt for whatever style is typical of the men—and that is sometimes autocratic. World leaders who were the "firsts" of their sex—Margaret Thatcher, Golda Meier, Indira Gandhi—led in ways that were as commanding as those of men, if not more so. Highly masculine settings can demand a top-down style from women as well as men.

Illustrating such pressures, the father of a Canadian military recruit shared the following description of his daughter's experience: "I sent my seventeen-year-old daughter to boot camp this summer in the Canadian military as the first step in her training to become an officer. She passed all aspects of the course except leadership. Because of poor leadership skills she failed the course and she is being released from the military . . . The only advice she got from her sergeants was she needed to take aggression pills and be more of a bitch."[41]

An instructive example of a female manager with a highly directive style in a male-dominated organization is Linda Ham, who was head of a mission management team of the National Aeronautics and Space Administration (NASA). This team directed the ill-fated *Columbia* space shuttle, which self-destructed during reentry in 2003. Ms. Ham had a particularly directive and autocratic style: "She was an intimidating figure, a youngish, attractive woman given to wearing revealing clothes, yet also known for a tough and domineering management style. Among the lower ranks she had a reputation for brooking no nonsense and being a little hard to talk to. She was not smooth. She was a woman struggling upward in a man's world. She was said to have a difficult personality."[42]

Autocratic leadership at NASA may have contributed to this and other shuttle mission disasters. Had higher-level managers been more receptive to the troubling information coming from lower-level employees, they might have reacted more appropriately to the developing signs that the shuttle mission was endangered.

In summary, many thoughtful women leaders sense that others accept them more when they lead in a relatively collaborative way and thereby share power. In some settings, women's democratic, collaborative style may be pronounced. However, differences in men's and women's styles generally appear as a mild shading, with considerable overlap. And in roles rarely occupied by women, many women leaders are just as autocratic as their male colleagues.

Transformational, Transactional, and Laissez-Faire Leadership

In the 1980s and 1990s, leadership scholars began to think about the complexities of good leadership in contemporary contexts. In large organizations, many having a global reach, leadership does not come merely from one or a few individuals located at the tops of hierarchies but from people who are spread throughout the organization. Such leadership is sometimes referred to as *postheroic* because it places less emphasis on all-powerful and all-knowing individuals and more emphasis on shared influence.[43] Although this postheroic theme incorporates aspects of democratic and participative leadership, it has many other elements.

Political scientist James MacGregor Burns is an influential early proponent of this contemporary model of leadership. He proposed a type of leadership that he labeled *transformational*.[44] Such leadership involves establishing oneself as a role model by gaining followers' trust and confidence. Transformational leaders state future goals, develop plans to achieve them, and innovate, even when their organization is generally successful. They mentor and empower followers, encouraging them to develop their full potential and thus to contribute more effectively to their organization.[45]

Epitomizing such a style is Rose Marie Bravo, former CEO and now vice chairman of Burberry, who describes her leadership style with these words: "We have teams of people, creative people, and it is about keeping them motivated, keeping them on track, making sure that they are following the vision. I am observing, watching and encouraging and motivating . . . We try to set an agenda throughout the company where everyone's opinion counts, and it's nice to be asked."[46]

Transformational leaders differ from *transactional* leaders, who establish give-and-take relationships that appeal to subordinates' self-interest. Such leaders manage in the conventional manner of clarifying subordinates' responsibilities, rewarding them for meeting objectives, and correcting them for failing to meet objectives. Although transformational and transactional leadership are different, most leaders adopt at least some behaviors of both types.

In addition to these two styles, researchers also have identified a *laissez-faire* style, which is marked by a general failure to take responsibility for managing. Researchers typically assess all of these styles by obtaining ratings of leaders on the Multifactor Leadership Questionnaire (or MLQ). As shown in table 8-1, this approach identifies five specific aspects of transformational leadership and three aspects of transactional leadership, along with laissez-faire leadership.[47]

Researchers intended that transformational leadership capture the essence of effective leadership under modern conditions. Is there evidence that transformational leadership really is effective? The answer is yes. A meta-analysis of studies relating these styles to measures of leaders' effectiveness revealed higher effectiveness overall for transformational leaders.[48]

The findings for transactional leadership are more complex. Leaders' effectiveness related positively to its "contingent reward" component, which features rewarding subordinates for appropriate behavior. Rewarding good performance was also strongly associated with subordinates' satisfaction with their leaders. Effectiveness was enhanced only slightly by leaders' drawing attention to subordinates' flaws and otherwise punishing them (the style aspect known as "active management by exception"). As expected, intervening only when situations become extreme (the style

TABLE 8-1

Definitions of transformational, transactional, and laissez-faire leadership styles in the Multifactor Leadership Questionnaire (MLQ) and mean effect sizes comparing men and women

MLQ scales	Description of leadership style	Effect size
TRANSFORMATIONAL		−0.10
Idealized influence (attribute)	Demonstrates qualities that motivate respect and pride from association with him or her	−0.09
Idealized influence (behavior)	Communicates values, purpose, and importance of organization's mission	−0.12
Inspirational motivation	Exhibits optimism and excitement about goals and future states	−0.02
Intellectual stimulation	Examines new perspectives for solving problems and completing tasks	−0.05
Individualized consideration	Focuses on development and mentoring of followers and attends to their individual needs	−0.19
TRANSACTIONAL		
Contingent reward	Provides rewards for satisfactory performance by followers	−0.13
Active management-by-exception	Attends to followers' mistakes and failures to meet standards	0.12
Passive management-by-exception	Waits until problems become severe before attending to them and intervening	0.27
LAISSEZ-FAIRE		
	Exhibits frequent absence and lack of involvement during critical junctures	0.16

Source: Eagly, Johannesen-Schmidt, and van Engen. 2003. Transformational, transactional, and laissez-faire leadership styles: A meta-analysis comparing women and men. *Psychological Bulletin* 129: 569–591, tables 1 and 3.

Effect sizes are means of all available studies. Positive values indicate that men had higher scores than women, and negative values indicate that women had higher scores than men. No effect size appears for overall transactional leadership because its component subscales did not show a consistent male or female direction.

aspect known as "passive management-by-exception") proved to be ineffective, as did laissez-faire, hands-off leadership.

How do male and female managers compare in these leadership styles? A meta-analysis integrated the results of forty-five studies addressing this question.[49] It included some large studies assessing thousands of managers as well as many smaller studies. As shown in table 8-1, female leaders were somewhat more transformational than male leaders, especially when it comes to giving support and encouragement to subordinates. Women also engaged in more of the rewarding behaviors that are one aspect of transactional leadership. On the other two aspects of transactional leadership (active and passive management-by-exception), men exceeded women. And men were also more likely than women to be laissez-faire leaders, who take little responsibility for managing.[50]

The startling conclusions from this project are the following: women, more than men, have generally effective leadership styles, and men, more than women, have styles that are only somewhat effective or that actually hinder effectiveness. What accounts for the fact that women favor transformational leadership and the reward aspect of transactional leadership? The answer may be that these leader behaviors are effective and yet do not seem particularly masculine.[51] In fact, at least one aspect of transformational leadership is culturally feminine—*individualized consideration*, which is consistent with the cultural norm that women be caring, supportive, and considerate. It is in this aspect of leadership style that women most exceed men.

Being a caring and supportive leader brings advantages but can present pitfalls. If helpful behaviors are expected of women leaders (see chapters 6 and 7), people may assume that helpful women are merely acting in a "natural," maternal way. Moreover, such behavior is typically considered to be less essential for promotion to the most senior levels of leadership than the more charismatic behaviors such as inspiring others and articulating a vision. Therefore, helpful, considerate behavior may make a manager likable without doing much to foster promotion to top positions.[52]

A related pitfall is that sometimes a relational, considerate style is not in the best interest of the organization. Consider this comment by a woman business entrepreneur: "I go the second and third mile and men won't do that. Because I want someone to succeed so much, I often find myself being too lenient. And I have found this to be a serious problem. I recently let an employee go after 2 months. In the past I would have kept him at least 6 months. I consider this a major milestone for me."[53]

There probably is another reason women have a favorable profile on transformational and transactional leadership. These sex differences in style may reflect the operation of a double standard in attaining leadership roles. As chapter 7 establishes, women often have to be more qualified than men to attain these roles at all, and if their performance falters they may be jettisoned more quickly. When this happens, easier standards for men would result in a greater number of skilled women than men in leader roles. This greater skill may show up in women specializing in more-effective leader behaviors and avoiding less-effective ones.

The Importance of Culture

The effects of gender on leadership style may vary depending on the cultural context. Ideally, there would be many cross-cultural studies to explore this issue, but such studies are rare.[54] There are also few studies that have taken subcultures into account by considering race and ethnicity along with gender. Therefore, it remains an open question whether the gender effects on leadership style that we have described are consistent across cultures and subcultures.[55]

Although data are sparse, it is clear that women of color who have careers in organizations that are dominated by white men can face the dual challenges of racism and sexism. Some have argued that this situation fosters especially creative and flexible leadership styles among black women.[56] As we report in chapter 7, black women may tend to have a dominant style of interaction, contributing to *executive presence*. However, it is unlikely that white male executives, who predominate in many organizations, would react more favorably to dominant black women than to dominant women of other races. On the contrary, as we also indicate in chapter 7, there is some evidence that black women elicit even more resistance to their influence than white women do. These issues deserve greater attention.

Asian cultures can exert other pressures by emphasizing personal modesty, deference toward others, consensus building, and collective decision making. In the words of one Asian American man, "The Asian personality tends to be low-key, quiet. We'll talk when there is a requirement to talk. White males will pound the table." Self-promotion can also be uncomfortable for Asian Americans. As one white manager noted, "Most of them [Asian Americans] . . . do not know how to boast." These cultural demands can make it more complex for Asian American women and men to negotiate advancement in managerial hierarchies, perhaps especially at the upper levels.[57]

Organizational culture also affects leadership style. Although people generally prefer leaders with transformational and collaborative styles, it would be a mistake to assume that such styles fit the traditions of all organizations. Some organizations continue to promote highly directive styles. Consider, for example, the following statement from the *Wall Street Journal*:

"Most of the time, hard-charging managers like to take command of a meeting going badly. They redefine the agenda around what they believe are the key issues. They argue their case so passionately that skeptics rally to their side. And if necessary, they overpower opponents with logic, humor or steely eyed toughness. Such techniques help leaders rocket up the organization."[58] In fact, there is little direct evidence that democratic and transformational management predominates in U.S. organizations, despite what some organizational experts perceive as its ethical advantages and potential to build employee loyalty and commitment.[59]

Preferred leadership styles also change over time within cultures. In fact, at least for political leadership, the preference for softer styles weakened in the United States with the terrorist attacks of September 11, 2001. Tough, masculine political leadership gained new currency when Americans felt threatened by terrorism. The 2004 national presidential nominating conventions of both Democrats and Republicans featured militaristic, macho posturing, as presidential candidates John Kerry and George W. Bush both portrayed themselves as masculine and tough. As Frank Rich wrote in the *New York Times*, "Both parties built their weeklong infotainments on militarism and masculinity."[60] At the Republican convention, Arnold Schwarzenegger, governor of California, labeled the Democratic opposition as *girlie-men*. Whether this masculinized posturing portends a longer-term shift in favor of command-and-control political leadership is an open question.

The events of 9/11 produced widespread fear and apprehension—emotions that may foster attraction to leaders with authoritative styles and visionary plans for solving collective problems.[61] The idea that people's fears increase their preference for strong, heroic leadership received empirical support in a study conducted by social psychologist Florette Cohen and her colleagues. This experiment showed that inducing university students to contemplate their own deaths increased their approval of a political leader portrayed as bold and masterful and decreased their approval of a leader portrayed as relationship oriented. Traumatic events may thus influence preferences for leadership styles.[62]

Will a threatened nation's attraction to tough-seeming, masculine leaders compromise women's chances for political leadership? As we indicated in chapter 6, conflict-torn nations such as Liberia have sometimes turned to women leaders, but nations confronting imminent threats may turn to male leaders. Men have consistently been viewed as more competent than women to deal with national security and military issues and with the war on terror.[63] An associated preference for top-down, authoritative variants of leadership could disadvantage women, because ostentatiously self-assured leadership has been a male specialty. In fact, in the 2006 congressional election, U.S. voters elected a disproportionate number of Democratic men noted for "their carefully cultivated masculinity—the Macho dems."[64] And despite the overall surge of support for Democrats, female Democratic candidates fared poorly in general. Whether this election portends a longer-term trend is unknown. Given the evidence we have presented, it seems unlikely that highly bold, heroic female leaders can emerge in the near term and be as successful as men who have this style.

Reprise: Do Women and Men Differ in Leadership Style?

The demands of leadership roles promote similarity in male and female leaders. Still, even among managers in the same role, some sex differences have been detected. Women, more than men, have a democratic, participative, collaborative style. However, this tendency erodes somewhat when women are in male-dominated roles. Because women in senior management are rare, particularly in large corporations, they very often lead in much the same way as their male counterparts do.[65] It is when leader roles are more integrated that women are more likely to exceed men in displaying democratic, participative styles as well as interpersonally oriented styles.

It is also true that female managers are slightly more likely to have a transformational style than male managers. This trend emerges most strongly in the attention and mentoring that women managers provide to their subordinates. Also, women, more than men, use rewards to encourage appropriate behaviors. In contrast, men, more than women, attend to subordinates' failures to meet standards and adopt more problematic behaviors of avoiding solving problems until they become acute and being absent or uninvolved at critical times.[66]

When women display transformational leadership, it may be blended with participative, democratic behaviors. An example of this amalgam comes from Janet Holmes à Court, owner and chairman of Heytesbury Limited, the Australian company that she successfully led after her husband's death: "The company was quite hierarchical. I often think it was like a pyramid with Robert [her husband] at the top and lots of us paying homage to him. I try to turn the pyramid upside down so that I'm at the bottom and bubbling away and encouraging people and energizing them so that they are all empowered so that they can do what they need to do, now that's the dream."[67]

The differences in leadership style that we have described are merely average differences. Despite women's tendency toward democratic leadership, for example, some women are extremely autocratic, and some men are extremely democratic. Also, average differences tend to be small and do not necessarily appear in all types of leadership roles or in all nations. Whether small differences are important is open to some debate. Effects that seem quite small can have considerable practical importance.[68] For example, the relation between taking aspirin and preventing heart attacks is statistically quite weak—in fact, weaker than most findings that we discuss in this book—but it justifies the routine use of aspirin to treat heart disease.[69] Of course, because the outcomes of leadership styles are far more diffuse than life or death, it is hard to say how important these differences are. Yet when subtle differences occur repeatedly over long periods, their implications are magnified. If female leaders are, for example, slightly more encouraging and rewarding to followers than male leaders are, people notice this difference and come to expect women to act in this way.[70]

Research on leadership style surely provides no basis for denying women leadership opportunities on the grounds that they favor inappropriate styles. For many years, leadership researchers have urged managers to adopt transformational and collaborative styles to manage the complexities of contemporary organizations.[71] In fact, the cultural wave seems to be moving toward greater appreciation of leadership styles of this general type. And, despite the post–9/11 pressures on American political leaders to display tough leadership, many men may be relinquishing autocratic and top-down styles in other contexts.

This possibility is consistent with journalist Michael Sokolove's insightful description of the leadership style of Mike Krzyzewski, head coach of the highly successful Duke University basketball team. As Sokolove put it, "So what is the secret to Krzyzewski's success? For starters, he coaches the way a woman would. Really."[72] Sokolove proceeded to describe Krzyzewski's mentoring, interpersonally sensitive, and highly effective coaching style. Similarly, the 2007 Super Bowl matchup of the Chicago Bears and the Indianapolis Colts brought attention to the "self-controlled, self-effacing" leadership styles of Bears' coach Lovie Smith and Colts' coach Tony Dungy. Such a coach supports his players and keeps "a step back from the personal prominence he could command, the better to let others shine. And he understands that you cannot scare anyone into being excellent."[73] So if male leaders are discovering the advantages of transformational leadership even as coaches of sports teams, men may indeed be changing.

To better understand the implications of the leadership styles of women and men, we need to take into account the organizations within which leadership typically takes place. Could it be that twists and turns in the labyrinth are put there by organizations themselves and have little to do with how women lead? We answer this question in chapter 9.

CHAPTER NINE

Do Organizations Compromise Women's Leadership?

MOST LEADERS ARE MEN. Predictably, people think about leadership mainly in masculine terms. These mental associations about leadership not only shape stereotypes about leaders but also influence organizational norms and practices. As managers follow precedents set by their colleagues, informal norms develop, consensus emerges about what is appropriate, and guidelines become hardened into bureaucratic rules. Over time, organizational leadership inevitably has come to embody the preferences, lifestyles, and responsibilities of the men who usually have held these leadership roles.[1] In this chapter, we demonstrate that many of these organizational traditions disadvantage women.

Each organization has its own social structure—regular and predictable patterns of behavior—and its own culture—shared beliefs, values, symbols, and goals. Leadership is an important part of this social structure and culture. Because of both structural and cultural barriers, women generally have had less access than men to leadership roles in organizations. To attain these roles, women negotiate labyrinthine arrangements that present various kinds of obstructions, few of which were expressly designed to discriminate against women although they have this effect.

To reveal this portion of the labyrinth, we analyze those aspects of organizational structure and culture that disadvantage women. We show that considerable change would have to take place in organizations before women would enjoy equal access to leadership. This conclusion holds even though women have already gained much greater access than at any other period in history.[2]

To gain some initial insight into organizational practices that disadvantage women, consider the experiences of a woman attorney in a large law firm that serves corporate clients. This organization's work practices included legal work interspersed with long lunches with other attorneys and considerable chitchatting in one another's offices. These side activities, together with heavy task demands, prevented the associate attorneys from meeting the firm's normative requirements for *billable hours*, the time spent working on clients' cases, during the conventional 9-to-5 schedule. Therefore, most of the associate attorneys stayed very late at the office virtually every evening and also worked most of the weekend.

As a mother, this woman found that the system interfered with her family responsibilities. She instead focused on the legal work that had to be accomplished. Long lunches were infrequent, and casual socializing was kept short. Although her legal work received kudos all around and she turned in an above-average number of billable hours, she was told that, to achieve partner status, she should "get to know" more of the partners in the firm. Getting to know them presumably involved not only working on their cases but also devoting more time to the lunches and chitchatting that give associate attorneys opportunities to assure partners that their career goals are in harmony with the culture of the firm.

Almost all of the women associate attorneys who were or became mothers, including this particular woman, exited the firm's partner track. Some dropped out to become full-time homemakers. Others moved to part-time legal positions that provided considerably less income and virtually no possibility for advancement. The woman in our example, like many other female associates, found a full-time attorney position in the public sector. Even some of the firm's women partners abandoned their positions when they had a child. Although these exits might suggest that the women merely preferred less demanding work or a homemaker role, the fact remains that the firm's own culture undermined its explicit policy of increasing gender diversity.

Research on the careers of lawyers confirms these informal observations. A study of Chicago lawyers showed that women were no less likely than men to begin their careers at large firms but more likely to leave these firms for positions in the public sector or as counsels for corporations. Consequently, women were much less likely than men to hold the leadership positions in large law firms—the positions that are most highly paid and that confer (arguably) the highest prestige. The problems for the women were concentrated in work–family trade-offs. Among those relatively few women who did become partner, 60 percent had no children, and the minority who had children generally had delayed childbearing until after they attained partner status.[3]

It might seem that this outcome of fewer women attaining partner status is entirely fair, because it rewards those who devote themselves most fully to their law firms. However, any such conclusion is wrong. Research by sociologists Fiona Kay and John Hagan showed that higher standards were applied to female than male candidates for partner. Women had to demonstrate higher work commitment as well as especially enthusiastic advocacy of firm culture—that is, "to embody standards that are an exaggerated form of a partnership ideal."[4] Here is yet another demonstration of the double standard discussed in chapter 7.

Women attorneys in law firms, like women in corporate and other executive positions, face at least two types of problems in achieving positions of authority. One barrier is that extreme time demands can make it difficult to combine employment obligations with a family life that involves more than minimal responsibility for children. The other barrier is that, to convince her colleagues that she is worthy of advancement, a woman is often held to standards that are set higher for women than men.[5]

Organizational Barriers to Women's Advancement

When newcomers enter an established organization, its structure and culture are already in place, invented in the past and modified during the life of the organization. Organizational practices are held in place by their repeated implementation. Such practices evolve slowly, in a dynamic exchange with the beliefs of the individuals who inhabit these organizations. Organizational practices and individuals' beliefs continually shape one another. However, because most employees begin near the bottom of organizational hierarchies, it is much easier for them to accept existing practices than to lobby for change.

To many people who inhabit organizations, workplaces may not seem to be biased in favor of either sex. However, underlying this veneer of fairness there is often an implicit model of an ideal employee. Such an individual is continuously on call to work long hours and make other personal sacrifices for the good of the organization. Because this ideal presumes minimal outside encumbrances, the person who best matches this model is someone who has only limited family obligations. Men, even if married with children, can fit this model if they delegate most domestic responsibilities to their wives. Women typically fit the model less well because they are less able to shift family obligations to their spouses (see chapter 4). Even those women who have no children do not fit the ideal employee model if they are seen as potential mothers.[6]

Demands for Long Hours, Travel, and Relocation

Organizations have become greedy in claiming employees' time in higher-level managerial positions as well as in many professional positions. Sociologist Lewis Coser wrote prophetically in the 1970s about the growing demands that organizations placed on managerial workers, requiring "exclusive and undivided loyalty" in addition to long hours.[7] The situation has only become more extreme in the intervening years. As one female executive noted, "The big problem is that when you get to an executive level, the company does own you. I don't think that one of our senior officers takes a family vacation without its being interrupted with a call from the president or an emergency."[8]

Whether workers' hours in the United States have actually increased over the years has been a matter of some debate among social scientists. Starting this debate was economist Juliet Schor's 1991 book *The Overworked American*. Schor argued that Americans are working more than at any time since World War II and are therefore harried and overworked. Other social scientists disagreed, maintaining that work hours have not changed.[9] Subsequent research has resolved this disagreement by showing that the average workweek has not changed in recent years in the United States, but variation around the average has increased. Some workers have gained shorter workweeks, and others have gained longer ones. In general, the more educated men and women are, the longer their workweeks. Managerial, professional, and technical workers have longer-than-average workweeks.[10]

At the highest job levels, hours can become very long and therefore difficult to reconcile with family responsibilities. A study of women who had quit their high-level managerial and professional jobs found that 86 percent cited work-related factors as coercing their decision, especially norms dictating extremely long hours. In the words of one study participant, a former marketing manager in a high-technology company, "The high-tech workweek is really sixty hours, not forty. Nobody works 9 to 5 anymore."[11]

Sometimes the expectation for long hours is implicit and learned merely by observing the habits of workplace colleagues. In other situations, the pressures are explicit. As one employee in the federal workforce put the matter, "In my division, [the boss] would come through and he would say, 'I expect to see all your faces when I come here in the morning, and I expect to see you here when I leave at night. And only the people who do that will be promoted.'"[12]

Higher-level executives are expected to be especially devoted and available to their organizations. They can be called on to work late into the evening and on weekends. Cell phones and BlackBerry communication devices have blurred the division between home and office, making many executives accessible to their organizations on virtually a 24/7 basis. Executives are expected to remain continuously employed, not requesting leaves for childbirth or childcare. They rarely take vacations.

Very long hours can be a prerequisite to achieving a higher managerial position. Working nights and weekends can serve as an indicator of managers' commitment to the organization, even when such efforts are superfluous.[13] Hours spent working have become a prime indicator of one's worth to the organization. Such systems can ignore employees' productivity and focus on the quantity of work hours rather than the quality of work products.

True enough, high achievers work longer hours than those who achieve less. Among highly educated, high-achieving women, more-successful women spend more time on the job. Also, for executives in general, those who work longer hours, work more evenings, and report themselves willing to work still more hours have higher salaries and win more promotions.[14] As one female executive put the matter, "I had the opportunity to close a business deal once, and I was the only woman at the table. It was a table full of men, and they all said that they never see their kids. One man said, 'I see my kids two hours a week.' If women were running businesses we wouldn't have that kind of life. It's just not acceptable."[15]

The demand for long hours affects women differently from men. Because of anticipated conflict of such work with childcare responsibilities, women in high-status careers tend to forgo or delay childbearing.[16] Men with wives who accept most domestic responsibilities are far less conflicted. Although work–family conflict should have eased for women because husbands have increased their domestic work, this gain has been offset by increasing time demands of most high-level careers as well as escalating pressures for intensive parenting (see chapter 4). Both changes make it difficult for women in demanding careers to manage a family life that includes children. A former associate attorney at a corporate law firm explained,

> In order to make partner, I'd say you'd need to bill about twenty-three hundred hours at least some years. Assuming one took ten days off a year (including holidays), you'd have to bill forty-six hours a week. That's 9.2 hours a day if you don't work weekends. So, assuming you don't even go to the bathroom, you'd have to work from nine to just past six every day. Now, subtract time for the bathroom, transitioning between projects, lunch, etc., and travel—to court, or across the country for a deposition—because travel typically doesn't count as billable hours. So clearly the career choice does require relinquishing any other interests, like family.[17]

These norms about employment became entrenched when a far larger proportion of women were full-time homemakers. Among the dual-earner couples who now predominate, these norms create stresses for wives, who, more often than husbands, transport children to and from childcare or school, take children to doctors' appointments, participate in teacher conferences, stay home with sick children, and provide care for aging relatives. Of course, extreme commitment to paid work can be feasible for female employees who have few of these family responsibilities—mainly childless women or older women whose children are no longer at home.

The long-hours lifestyle is possible for women with children at home if they are willing and able to share childcare with husbands, other family members, or paid workers. However, decision makers often merely assume that mothers have domestic responsibilities that make it inappropriate to promote them to demanding positions. As one participant in a study of the federal workforce explained, "I mean, there were 2 or 3 names [of women] in the hat and they said, 'I don't want to talk about her because she has children who are still home in these [evening] hours.' Now they don't pose that thing about men on the list, many of whom also have children in that age group."[18]

This system is certainly not free of costs for men. With very long hours, men participate minimally in childrearing and may lack time to develop or sustain a strong relationship with their wives or partners. Men with time-intensive careers can be largely cut off from the relational aspects of family that lend everyday life much of its emotional resonance. They also fail to contribute much of the care that fosters their children's development, instead contributing indirectly by providing economic resources.

Requiring very long hours may benefit organizations by minimizing the number of highly paid workers that they employ. When competitive pressures force organizations to downsize, they generally demand more work from their remaining employees. However, long hours can also reflect managers' lack of planning and discipline concerning what work really needs to be done and how to allocate their staff to accomplish these tasks efficiently. Merely requiring constant availability creates stressed employees and can actually reduce organizational performance.[19] As management scholar Lotte Bailyn wrote, "Problems are dealt with by people working harder and longer, and the organization is in a continuous crisis mode."[20]

Many elite workers, especially in management, face demands not only to travel frequently but also to relocate. Even a high-performing manager may have little possibility of advancement in his or her local office because no higher-level positions exist or are unfilled. When positions open up in other locations, fast-track employees may have to relocate or step off the fast track. This system of requiring employees to "move to get ahead" characterized the Sears organization, as revealed in the 1980s discrimination case of *EEOC v. Sears, Roebuck & Co.* Some employees relocated three or four times during a ten-year period, and such relocations resulted in promotions and significant salary increases.[21]

Men face less disruption in moving to a new location if their wives are homemakers or have careers that are secondary to their husbands' careers. Because most employed women have employed husbands who are co-breadwinners or primary breadwinners, a move for the wife's career could unacceptably compromise the husband's career or require that the couple live apart. For employed mothers, the complexities of moving may also involve terminating arrangements with trusted childcare providers. As a result, mothers can face great disruption when career advancement requires a move to a new city. At Sears, for example, the "move to get ahead" system tended to close women out of opportunities for promotion.[22] Demands for relocation as well as long hours extend the labyrinth that women negotiate as they attempt to rise in organizational hierarchies.

All in all, many executive positions have become hard on family life.[23] The people at the tops of these organizations have themselves made these life choices, and they expect aspiring executives to do so as well. The result is a system that is roundly disliked, not only by women but also by many men. As columnist and radio host Matt Miller noted in a *New York Times* op-ed, "There is something telling (if not downright dysfunctional) when a society's most talented people feel they have to sacrifice the meaningful relationships every human craves as the price of exercising their talent."[24]

Challenges of Building Social Capital

The earlier example of the lawyer who was expected to spend time chatting and having long lunches may seem to lack bureaucratic rationality. However, such activities can serve organizations by building social relationships. The fact that managers and professionals spend considerable time in informal interactions coheres with social scientists' understanding of *social capital*, the relationships between people and the feelings of mutual obligation and support that these relationships create.[25] These informal ties are as essential to organizations as the human capital that allows competent work in the narrower, technical sense. Relationships build knowledge, trust, cooperation, and shared understanding.

People bond through networks both within their organizations and beyond them. Good relationships make it possible to call on others for support, ranging from getting advice and information to setting up deals and transactions. Empirical evidence has shown that managers' social capital, especially their relationships with people in other organizations, fosters their advancement.[26] Such relationships can yield valuable information, access to help and resources, and career sponsorship.

In a demonstration of the importance of social capital, one study yielded the following description of managers who advance rapidly in hierarchies: fast-track managers "spent relatively more time and effort socializing, politicking, and interacting with outsiders than did their less successful counterparts . . . [and] did not give much time or attention to the traditional management activities of planning, decision making, and controlling or to the human resource management activities of motivating/reinforcing, staffing, training/developing, and managing conflict."[27] It thus appears that social capital can be even more essential to managers' advancement than skillful performance of traditional managerial tasks.

Gender affects social capital: women usually have less of it. One interpretation is that men excel at strategically building crucial professional relationships. In the words of one female banking executive, "Women talk about competence all the time. They miss the dynamics of relationships. Some men have more personality than brains, but those are usually the ones who 'get it.'"[28] Despite this perception that women don't "get it," women as well as men are generally aware of the importance of social capital. For example, in a study of senior women in business and professions in the Boston area, 78 percent viewed informal networking as "helping to a great extent" in their development as leaders, and 70 percent cited informal mentoring relationships.[29]

The perception that women are not as effectively networked as men is often accurate but mainly reflects causes other than women's lack of understanding of how organizations really work. One difficulty is that networking exacerbates the long work hours that present obstacles to women (and men) with family responsibilities. Managers with significant family responsibilities may fully realize the value of networking but merely decide not to "play the game." Consider a mother who is a manager or professional. Rather than go out for drinks after work, she picks up her child and often prepares a family dinner. She rarely joins a golf outing on the weekend.

Even during ordinary work hours, informal networking can be difficult if women are a small minority. As business journalist and former CEO Margaret Heffernan wrote, "It's still hard to resist the feeling that at meetings, at conferences, on golf courses, women are gatecrashers."[30] When women are a small minority, most networks, especially influential networks, are composed entirely or almost entirely of men. In these male-dominated networks, women usually have less legitimacy and influence and thus may benefit less than men from participation. In such contexts, women can gain from a strong and supportive mentoring relationship with a well-placed individual who possesses greater legitimacy—typically a man.[31]

Breaking into these male networks can be difficult, especially when men center their networks on masculine activities. As one woman in corporate finance remarked, "Sunday night was basketball night where everybody in the department goes and plays basketball. I don't play basketball . . . so there was a big social network there that revolved around men's sports and men's activities, and to be on the outside of that really impacted my ability to develop relationships with people."[32] At a motion picture production company, wheeling and dealing took place on a yearly raft trip—no "girls" allowed.[33]

In organizations that are more integrated by gender, women do not necessarily have fewer relationships than men. However, networks are often largely segregated, with women joining with other women and men with other men. All-women networks are limiting for women. Greater influence would follow from participating in networks with the generally more powerful group of men.

Women also can benefit from relationships with other women. They may gain social support, role modeling, and information about overcoming discriminatory obstacles. In the words of one female *Fortune* 500 manager, "I found it useful [to network with other women], because I learn a lot of techniques for dealing with difficult situations . . . I'm the only woman manager in my organization. Since I don't see [other women] daily, I have to take deliberate steps to stay in touch."[34]

Where there are few female executives, they often reach out beyond their own unit or organization to form helpful relationships with like-minded women. To some extent, relationships that bridge outward may compensate for women's difficulties in building social capital within their own organizations.[35]

Women of color can face even greater challenges than white women in gaining social capital, because both their gender and their race set them apart from the typical white male power holders. These women's strategies for networking are twofold: while attempting to join influential, mainly white male networks, they also network with others who share their race and gender. These strategies thus resemble those used by white women, except for the special effort to connect with women of their own race. This approach makes sense in terms of finding role models and sharing advice about advancing in the presence of barriers that can stem from both race and gender.[36]

Challenges of Fitting In with Organizational Culture

Related to the difficulties that women often experience in building social capital at work are challenges in fitting in with organizational culture.[37] In the survey of the Boston women in executive and professional positions, the barrier to advancement cited most frequently was "a male-dominated work culture." In the words of one of the participants in this study, "While men create the culture, women adapt to it."[38]

The culture of organizations involves shared, sometimes unspoken, values, meaning, and understanding. Culture is expressed through dress and office arrangements as well as through the symbols that represent organizations and the language that employees use to describe their work.[39] Many organizations are imbued with masculine values, sometimes including displays of competitive masculinity, especially among executives. The fun and games that lighten executives' work might involve, for example, late-night racing of rental cars around hotel parking lots.[40] One egregious example of especially negative aspects of masculine culture involved financial services corporation Smith Barney:

> Three women in the Garden City, N.Y., office of Smith Barney sued that firm in 1996, in what became known as the "Boom-Boom Room" case. Their male colleagues had set up a party room in the basement of what was otherwise a business office, hanging a toilet seat from the ceiling and mixing Bloody Marys and other drinks in a big plastic garbage bin. The men called it the Boom-Boom Room, but the women called it an example of frat-house behavior in a request for class action status in federal court.[41]

Enron, the failed energy company implicated in an extraordinary level of corporate scandal, provides other examples of masculine culture. Jeff Skilling, president and chief operating officer, was a key player in establishing an extremely competitive culture. He said that he liked to hire "guys with spikes" who had a unique talent:

> If an executive had a singular narrow talent—a spike—[Skilling] was willing to bring him into Enron and lavish him with money, no matter what his other shortcomings. Egomaniacs, social misfits, backstabbers, devotees of strip clubs . . . Jeff could care less whether people got along with each other," says one of his early hires. "In many cases, he felt it was better if they didn't get along, since it created a level of tension that he believed was good for helping people come up with new ideas." A former trading executive adds: "Jeff always believed pitting three people against each other would be the quickest way to assure the best ideas bubbled to the top. He wanted them to fight.[42]

Skilling also organized Enron executives and important customers for daredevil athletic exploits that included long road races with Jeeps and dirt bikes—for example, the Enron Baja Off-Road Rally.[43] Such activities defined the company's hypermasculine culture.

Wal-Mart has provided additional examples of masculine managerial culture. For example, an executive retreat took the form of a quail hunting expedition at Sam Walton's ranch in Texas. To make the masculine culture message clear, one executive received feedback that she probably would not advance in the company because she didn't hunt or fish. Middle managers' meetings included visits to strip clubs and Hooters restaurants, and a sales conference attended by thousands of store managers featured a football theme.[44]

Masculine culture can also be manifested in taking fast action and being outwardly decisive rather than consulting and working out issues behind the scenes. One female senior British police officer understood this issue and learned to package her work in language that satisfied her male colleagues:

Men see a problem and tackle it straight on and sort out all the other bits after, whereas a woman's approach is to look at all the issues . . . so you may end up in the same timeframe but you will have gone about it differently. This may not be as attractive to men because they feel nothing is happening and in this organization there is a requirement for action very early on; it can be difficult as they feel nothing is going on, although things are of course happening. I know that unless I constantly keep telling them that something is happening, battling on about it, they think nothing is happening.[45]

Consistent with men's emphasis on action, masculine organizational culture is often expressed in language replete with sports and military terminology. Successful activity is termed a *slam-dunk* or *home run* or *batting a thousand*, and good behavior involves *being a team player*. Militaristic language includes phrases such as *uphill battle*, *getting flak*, and *killing the competition*. Women can surely learn such vocabulary, facilitated by their increasing participation in athletics, but this language no doubt has remained more effortless for men.

If men are more enthusiastic about masculine culture than women are, and there is evidence that this is the case, a masculine organizational culture can at least make many women uncomfortable and thus form part of the labyrinth that women negotiate.[46] Of course, sometimes women may merely figure out aspects of a masculine culture and accommodate to it. Dawn Steel, who became president of Columbia Pictures, exemplified this approach: "By habit, these guys wandered in and out of each other's offices. By the time they got to the weekly production meeting, all the really important decisions had already been made . . . I did not participate in these ad hoc meetings because I was not part of this herd of roaming men. The lesson here . . . Join the roamers." And that's exactly what Dawn Steel did.[47]

Challenges of Obtaining Desirable Assignments

Female managers frequently report difficulty in obtaining appropriately demanding assignments. Lack of access to such assignments, known as *developmental job experiences*, can disqualify women for promotions.[48] Meeting the challenges inherent in tough assignments and becoming recognized for having overcome these challenges are prerequisites to advancement to upper-level management, but social capital is a prerequisite for winning the chance to take on such projects.[49]

Demonstrating that women often lack opportunities for appropriately demanding work, organizational psychologists Karen Lyness and Donna Thompson surveyed women and men who were in similar midlevel and senior executive positions in a large multinational financial services corporation. They found that the women had fewer international assignments and were less likely than men to have roles that gave them authority over others. In addition, the women encountered greater difficulty in obtaining demanding and important assignments and opportunities to relocate to a new location for a better position. They also performed fewer complex activities encompassing multiple functions, products, customers, and markets.[50]

More than one process may contribute to women's difficulties in obtaining challenging assignments. Under some circumstances, women apparently choose, or at least agree to perform, work that is not especially challenging, perhaps reacting to implicit expectations in their workplaces. Also, bosses are apparently less likely to assign challenging work to women, perhaps because they hold sexist but chivalrous attitudes that women should receive less stressful forms of work and men the "tougher" assignments.[51] For example, one woman noted how a colleague of hers was impeded from advancement by being denied travel opportunities: "She should have been the director of the office in about 1985 but what happened was that they brought some man in from another place and put him above her. They gave as a reason that she didn't travel. They never let her travel."[52]

Whatever the causes of women's lesser access to challenging work, the low-stakes assignments that they often receive do little to foster their careers. Working hard at routine assignments is not a route to advancement. Lois Frankel, president of Corporate Coaching International, had this to say:

> People aren't hired and promoted simply because they work hard. It happens because the decision maker knows the character of the person and feels confident about his or her ability not only to do the job but also to do it in a way that promotes collegial team relationships. By keeping her nose to the grindstone, the woman [featured in a vignette] was actually acting in a way detrimental to getting what she most wanted—more interesting work and an opportunity to show she was capable of doing more.[53]

Or, as a prominent female executive told one of us, "You don't want to be 'Jane the Drudge,' sitting in your office and just working all the time. You have to gain visibility and recognition for your work."[54]

Women's difficulties in obtaining developmental job experiences are compounded by their occupancy of managerial roles that serve staff functions, such as human resources and public relations, rather than line functions, which are more critical to the success of organizations. Women are usually aware that their chances for advancement are limited by placement in staff positions. For example, a large multinational study of executives from major corporations found that women, more than men, complained about their limited opportunities for line management.[55] As stated by Ann Fudge, chairman and CEO of Young & Rubicam Brands, "A woman who really wants to attain a high-level office in the corporate world must be strong and outspoken enough to say she wants to run the business and be a bottom line employee. That means thinking more in terms of finance and less in terms of the jobs women have historically migrated to, like support staff."[56]

Why are women more confined than men to staff management roles? The most likely explanation is that women's stereotypical abilities and interests match staff positions more than line positions. As chapter 6 shows, women are thought to be well endowed with qualities such as social sensitivity and interest in people, attributes that are seen as prerequisites to success in staff managerial roles. Men, in turn, are thought to be well endowed with qualities such as assertiveness and decisiveness, attributes that are seen as prerequisites to success in line managerial roles. When organizations develop stereotypical norms about which sex is optimal for various types of management, men are more often channeled into line management, with its better opportunities to ascend into senior leadership.[57]

Given these twists and turns in the corporate labyrinth, women, more often than men, feel that they have to leave their organizations to have an opportunity to advance.[58] Changing jobs to advance may also reflect the greater importance that women place on the intrinsic satisfaction provided by their jobs (see chapter 4). So women may leave organizations not only because they end up with unexciting work but also because they are less satisfied than men would be with such assignments.

Companies can stem losses of women managers by giving them more-demanding assignments. For example, journalist Claudia Deutsch reported in the *New York Times* that Procter & Gamble had experienced an executive attrition rate that was twice as high for women as men. Among high-performing women who left, many disclosed feeling that they were not valued by the company. Some of these women reported having to move between companies to land jobs that provided challenging work.[59] Subsequently, Procter & Gamble made a greater effort to attract women into line management. This change improved the retention of women and increased the number of women in senior management.

Despite women's difficulties in obtaining demanding assignments, there is also evidence that some women are placed, more often than comparable men, in highly risky positions. Organizational psychologists Michelle Ryan and Alexander Haslam refer to this phenomenon as the *glass cliff*.[60] They showed that companies in the United Kingdom are more likely to place women in high-level executive positions when the companies are experiencing financial downturns and declines in performance.

A U.S. example is the appointment of Anne Mulcahy as CEO of Xerox when the company was on the brink of bankruptcy and under investigation by the Securities and Exchange Commission for irregular accounting methods. In such especially precarious circumstances, executives face a fairly high likelihood of failing, although Mulcahy proved to be outstandingly successful. The reasons for this glass cliff phenomenon may include companies' greater willingness to risk sacrificing their female executives and women's greater willingness to take these positions, given their poorer prospects for obtaining more-desirable positions.

Ironically, then, women apparently have special access to managerial tasks that are virtually impossible as well as to tasks that are especially easy. The glass cliff and the lack of developmental job experiences are cut from the same cloth: both deny women access to the "good" assignments that offer reasonable opportunities for showing oneself as a high-potential manager.[61]

Organizational Innovations to Foster Gender Equality

There are many ways to remove barriers to women's advancement. However, attaining greater fairness is no simple matter. Who gets hired and promoted is a complex outcome of organizational practices interacting with market forces. Nonetheless, specific policies and practices that have a discriminatory impact on women, such as the requirement that managers relocate to advance, can be changed.[62]

A solution that is often proposed is for governments to implement and enforce antidiscrimination legislation and thereby require organizations to eliminate inequitable and discriminatory practices. However, legal remedies can be elusive when gender inequality results from norms that are embedded in organizational structure and culture. The courts often decide that such practices do not violate antidiscrimination legislation despite their adverse impact on women.[63]

Some of the most important organizational changes would confront the ways that the differing life situations of women and men interface with the characteristics of organizations. As chapter 4 details, women's lifestyles are in general different from men's, especially in their greater domestic responsibility.

Flexible Work

To address the disadvantage that women face from their larger share of domestic work, various proposals have been made to design jobs differently. For instance, managers (and professionals) might have positions that consume fewer hours per week, perhaps having a part-time schedule or even sharing a job with another manager. Also, some managers might work from home for at least a portion of the workweek.

The most famous proposal of this type appeared in *Harvard Business Review* in 1989 in an article written by Felice Schwartz. She was the founder and first president of Catalyst. Schwartz argued that most women in management careers are not "career-primary women" but "career-and-family women," who want both good careers and a family life that involves substantial participation in childrearing. Schwartz proposed that corporations provide flexible jobs for such women even though these jobs would have lower pay and slower advancement. In her view, this strategy would allow companies to retain valuable female executives who could at later points give greater priority to their careers.[64]

Schwartz's article ignited a firestorm of criticism. Although Schwartz did not term her proposal a "mommy track," it was so labeled by its critics, thus trivializing the career path that she described. The main objection was to Schwartz's assumption that women and companies have the burden of adjusting to the typically unequal division of labor between wives and husbands. A *New York Times* editorial castigated Schwartz for accepting this status quo:

> And where . . . is that new world in which male and female were to work side by side, not only on the job but in the home? It's not here yet, nor will it ever be while women are required to make a choice that is never asked of men—and

not until society acknowledges that men can be as ambivalent as women about what they owe their jobs and what they owe their families. The challenge is to give women, and men, maximum help and flexibility as they try to achieve that equilibrium.[65]

Schwartz responded that young women are unrealistic in thinking that they can have excellent career growth and yet take generous time off to care for their children.[66] When big-time careers prove too inflexible, Schwartz warned, women drop out. Indeed, women with professional degrees (law, MBA, MD) or doctorates are approximately three times as likely as their male counterparts to be out of the labor force ten years after receiving these degrees, with family responsibilities being women's usual reason for their exit.[67] The dropout women, although a minority of the women in these samples, evidently preferred a career break to pursuing their careers through a labyrinth of cross pressures from family and jobs.

Despite the brouhaha that followed Schwartz's proposal, reactions to suggestions for flexible work have become more positive. Proposals include upgrading part-time work with greater responsibility and better wages. Full-time jobs could offer flexible hours. Allowing employees having significant parental responsibility more time to prove themselves worthy of promotion is another widely discussed option. Such parents (most often mothers) may need extra time to build their credentials, in many cases only an additional year or two. Their potential is thrown away if they are forced off the promotion path by lockstep rules about when they must be evaluated for higher-level positions. It is also important to allow high-performing women who step off the fast track an opportunity to return to responsible positions after a period out of the workforce.[68]

Family-friendly practices can allow women to stay in their jobs during the most demanding years of childrearing, build social capital, keep up-to-date in their fields, and eventually compete for higher positions. A study of seventy-two large U.S. firms thus showed that family-friendly human resource practices increased the proportion of women in senior management five years later, controlling for other organizational variables.[69]

Many organizations are incorporating such practices, which may encompass flexitime, job sharing, telecommuting, elder care provisions, adoption benefits, and dependent childcare options, sometimes including employee-sponsored on-site childcare. Although some people claim that such reforms are costly and inefficient, systematic analyses suggest that firms as well as employees can gain from such policies. The gains to individuals are obvious, and the gains to firms can include retaining and recruiting talented employees, increasing employee motivation, reducing turnover, and gaining a favorable public image as a "good place to work."[70]

Despite these advantages, dangers lurk in family-friendly benefits that are taken only by women, as Schwartz's critics correctly discerned. The exercise of options such as generous parental leave and part-time work slows the careers of those women who take such benefits. More profoundly, having many more women than men take such benefits can harm the careers of women in general because of the expectation that they may well exercise such options. A system of family friendliness directed only to women can make it harder for women to gain access to essential managerial roles.[71]

More-profound changes would challenge the long-hours norm of many higher managerial and professional jobs. Critics of these practices point out that it is not necessarily true that the best employees are those who spend the longest hours at work. Face time and constant availability are not the same thing as excellence of performance. Organizations can change the emphasis on long hours by placing more value on the quality of work and by planning for efficient use of employees' time. Reasonable work hours can improve employees' morale and family life, reduce their stress, and enhance their performance. Such reforms have the potential for increasing organizations' competitiveness.[72]

Other Progressive Innovations

There are many innovations, in addition to changing the long-hours norm, that would facilitate women's advancement in organizations. All of these proposals involve making organizations fairer, so that they reward individuals' merit and accomplishment.

Reforming Performance Evaluations and Recruitment. To ensure fairness, the evaluation of candidates for promotion should become less subjective than it has traditionally been. Promotions should be based on explicit, valid performance evaluations that limit the influence of decision makers' conscious and unconscious biases. In addition, recruitment from outside of organizations should involve open processes such as advertising and using employment agencies rather than informal social networks and referrals. Recruitment from within organizations also should be transparent, with posting of open positions in appropriate venues. Research has shown that these open personnel practices increase the numbers of women in managerial roles.[73]

Without objective evaluations and open recruiting, biases very likely contaminate personnel decisions. One such bias is the tendency of people to like and associate with others who are similar to themselves.[74] People feel more comfortable with those who share their demographic character-istics, social background, personality, and attitudes. Because similarity promotes liking, discrimination in organizations can derive from men's in-group preference to work with other men more than any antipathy they may feel to working with women.

In-group loyalty can cause people in authority positions to fill positions with individuals who are similar to themselves, especially in characteristics such as gender, race, and religion. Also, other factors being equal, supervi-sors give more-favorable evaluations to subordinates who are similar to themselves in gender and race.[75] Therefore, it is hardly surprising that the presence of larger proportions of men in higher positions leads to larger numbers of men subsequently hired to fill such positions. These processes, labeled *homosocial reproduction* by management scholar Rosabeth Moss Kanter, perpetuate traditional elites at the tops of organizations.[76]

In the absence of clear standards applied to all candidates, people mak-ing hiring or promotion decisions are free to rely on their stereotypes or personal preferences. To ensure fairer evaluations, organizations must in-corporate oversight and accountability, but that often doesn't happen. In the Wal-Mart sex discrimination case, for example, advisers for the prose-cution have ascribed an apparently discriminatory pattern in promotions to lax human resources practices. Although Wal-Mart had written guidelines for promotions, managers were allowed to exercise considerable discretion in their promotion decisions.

In an analysis of Wal-Mart's personnel policies, sociologist William Bielby wrote, "In contrast to the centralized coordination and control that characterizes the operations side of Wal-Mart's operations, its human resources practices regarding equal employment opportunities are too dif-fuse to establish meaningful oversight and accountability."[77] The door is wide open to discrimination if managers have free rein to follow whatever hiring and promotion principles that they personally think are appropriate.

These problems are exacerbated by the tendency for people in authority to be especially likely to stereotype those who are subject to their power, per-haps because their feeling of entitlement leads them to be inappropriately confident of simple beliefs about others.[78] Further compounding this problem is people's typical lack of awareness of the influence of stereotypes on their judgments (see chapter 6).

For these reasons, it makes sense to hold managers accountable for basing their evaluations on valid evidence of abilities and accomplishments.[79] To ensure fairness, monitoring of personnel decisions is generally necessary. Therefore, many organizations have established structures that assign responsibility for opening up positions to all groups; for example, they create affirmative action plans, diversity committees, and staff positions designed specifically to monitor diversity. Research shows that such organizational structures can be effective in increasing the number of women in management.[80]

Programs for ensuring equal access to hiring and promotion are far easier to implement at lower managerial levels, where selection is traditionally based at least in part on objective qualifications that include educational credentials, training, and experience. At the executive levels, selection is based more on subjectively evaluated performances, including, for example, presentations in front of committees and boards and impressions made on others in negotiations and informal networking.[81] Compounding the difficulties of such selection for women are the norms encouraging modest self-presentation on the part of women that we note in chapter 7.

Legitimizing Women's Contributions as Leaders. By conveying respect for and confidence in women as leaders, organizations can lessen the resistance to female leadership that we document in chapter 7. An initial step is to emphasize the promotion and development of female as well as male employees and to make sure that women are included among those who are given training opportunities. In fact, a general emphasis on development of all employees can yield larger numbers of women in top management positions.[82]

Once a woman is chosen for a leadership position, it is important to convey that she was selected on the basis of her demonstrated ability and not on some other basis such as demands to fulfill diversity goals.[83] Still, some suspicion often remains that she does not really have what it takes for an important leadership position. Underlying this suspicion is the role incongruity that we explain in chapter 6—the ascription to women of qualities that are different from those typical of leaders.

To allay these suspicions, executives can signal their confidence in women's effectiveness as leaders. In an experiment testing this proposition, participants received information that for the tasks their group was assigned, women often serve as leaders because they are particularly effective. In groups that received this information, female leaders overcame the disadvantage they otherwise suffered and became as influential and effective as male leaders.[84] In organizations, too, legitimizing women's authority is helpful because women can lack the built-in legitimacy that men more often possess.

Along with legitimizing women's contributions as good leaders, organizations can develop norms that diversity is good for the organization, and, indeed, as we show in chapter 11, gender diversity can enhance organizations' effectiveness. If members of an organization accept the idea that diversity fosters success, they become more likely to accept women as decision makers.

Reducing Tokenism. In many settings, it is a breakthrough to appoint even one woman, and such first steps are important. However, because token women receive extra scrutiny, it is essential to move beyond token representation. Token women are often subjected to intense performance pressures. As Katharine Graham, former CEO of the *Washington Post*, wrote, "Each time I was the only woman in a room full of men, I suffered lest I appear stupid or ignorant."[85] In addition, token women tend to end up in narrow stereotypical roles such as "seductress," "mother," "pet," or "Iron Maiden." As one woman banker remarked, "When you start out in banking, you are a slut or a geisha. The pretty young things fresh off of the college campus. And you get all kinds of attention because you are fit and cute."[86]

Such treatment of women limits their options and makes it difficult for them to rise to positions of responsibility. Having a critical mass of women in executive positions—not just one or two women—can lessen this problem. When women are not a small minority, their identities as women become less salient, and colleagues are more likely to react to them in terms of their individual competencies.[87]

Some research suggests that on corporate boards of directors three or more women constitute an effective critical mass that often enhances board performance.[88] As stated by Albert J. Wilson, vice president, chief counsel, and corporate secretary of TIAA-CREF, "I don't think having a minority or a woman means anything if you have a board of 12 to 15 people and you only have one woman or one minority. But if you have more than that, and if they are on the significant committees, and if this policy filters down into the executive branch of the company, then there is change. Then you can start to equate diversity with performance, because these people are now part of decision-making and part of carrying out policy."[89]

Changes in Organizational Norms of Good Leadership

As we argue throughout this book, a major component of the labyrinth that women must negotiate to become leaders derives from the fact that leadership has long been associated with men and masculine characteristics. Therefore, women can be regarded with suspicion when they occupy leadership roles. However, the qualities that constitute good leadership have changed in ways that lessen this role incongruity for women.[90] Consider the following confident assertion by journalist, author, and political adviser David Gergen:

> *Women leaders, it turns out, seem perfectly tailored for this new style . . .*
> *When we describe the new leadership, we employ terms like* consensual, rela-
> tional, web-based, caring, inclusive, open, transparent—*all qualities that*
> *we associate with the "feminine" style of leadership. One can argue whether*
> *this feminine style is in women's genes or is created by socialization. It doesn't*
> *matter much . . . The key point . . . is that women are knocking at the door of*
> *leadership at the very moment when their talents are especially well matched*
> *with the requirements of the day.*[91]

These changes in what is considered to be desirable leadership reflect underlying socioeconomic changes. Primary influences in these changes are accelerated technological growth, faster social change, and increased complexity of organizations' missions. Compounding these changes are increasing workforce diversity, intense competitive pressures, and the fading of geopolitical boundaries. Executives, especially CEOs, must function in a landscape of increasing complexity: on the pages of the *Wall Street Journal*, the job of CEO is described as increasingly demanding social and political skill: "[The CEO interacts with] a widening array of shareholder advocates, hedge funds, private-equity deal makers, legislators, regulators, attorneys general, nongovernmental organizations and countless others who want a say in how public companies manage their affairs. Today's CEO, in effect has to play the role of a politician, answering to varied constituents."[92] Therefore, as one business journalist noted, "Boards are increasingly looking for CEOs who can demonstrate superb people skills in dealing with employees or other stakeholders while delivering consistent results."[93] Executives in other domains—for example, presidents of universities—also must deal with multiple stakeholders.

In such environments, autocratic managers, especially bosses who show they are in charge by being overbearing and domineering, are handicapped in negotiating the complex relationships that come with the modern managerial job. Because of this changed environment, the current generation of managerial experts has increasingly emphasized democratic relationships, political skills, participatory decision making, delegation, and team-based leadership skills that are more androgynous than masculine.[94]

New models of good leadership make sense, given that many managers no longer focus mainly on the traditional functions of planning, organizing, directing, and controlling. Instead, they primarily support teams of employees who execute tasks. Facilitating the work of a team demands solving many interpersonal as well as technical problems and dealing with the details of performance reviews and sometimes with budgetary issues. "Command and control" has little place in many of these positions, but instead managers' days are filled with communicating, listening, monitoring, teaching, and encouraging.

Leadership roles have taken on important elements of teaching and coaching. In the words of sociologist Mary Waters, "A strong leader is not just someone who can name a goal or force a change, but someone who can bring out the best in people and find ways to encourage teamwork."[95] It is in this environment that Mike Krzyzewski, Duke University basketball coach, has become a leadership guru in the United States.[96]

These changes have produced new pressures on male leaders to learn culturally feminine skills, or to "release your inner woman," as journalist Michael Sokolove put the matter when discussing Krzyzewski.[97] A similar message emerged in the *Wall Street Journal*'s 2005 poll of recruiters of MBA recipients. These recruiters reported that they encountered gender stereotypical qualities in both male and female MBAs: "Men are perceived as forceful, if sometimes overly pushy leaders, as well as more adept in math. Women, recruiters agreed, tend to interact more effectively with clients and colleagues and excel in strategy and communications."

These recruiters recommended that men and women take on the qualities of the other sex: "Women are encouraged to 'toot their own horns,' take more risks, develop a stronger handshake and dress more professionally. As for men, recruiters strongly urged them to be more humble and collaborative, listen better to other points of view and stop taking credit for other people's accomplishments."[98]

So this stereotype-laden advice is not only for women to become more like men but also for men to become more like women. In many contemporary organizational environments, the best managers manifest both traditionally masculine and traditionally feminine qualities.

Conclusion

Critical components of the labyrinth that women encounter in trying to advance derive from organizational traditions and practices, which in turn reflect the traditional family division of labor. The extremely long hours on the job that are normative for many managers and professionals conflict with women's domestic responsibilities (and sometimes those of men). Aside from these work-life issues, organizations often embody a many-sided masculine culture that can hinder women from accumulating the social capital they need to advance. In these settings, preferences of executives to work with people similar to themselves, along with beliefs that executive positions require masculine qualities, compound women's difficulties in advancing.

Managerial roles are in flux because of broader changes in the economy and society, so now is an excellent time to propose and try out innovations that may make organizations more hospitable to female managers and executives. In addition, many men are becoming receptive to family-friendly changes in workplaces, because they have accepted more domestic responsibility than in the past. We have provided many suggestions for reforming organizations so that they become as welcoming to women as to men. Implementing such suggestions requires thoughtful analysis by the women and men who hold positions in organizations. Moving forward with progressive proposals requires activism on the part of those who desire organizations with greater gender integration and families with more equal male and female roles.[99]

CHAPTER TEN

How Do Some Women Find Their Way Through the Labyrinth?

TO BECOME LEADERS, women must navigate through the labyrinth, overcoming barriers and dead ends along the way. Ideally, there would be no labyrinth, and women and men would have the same paths to leadership. But currently, the male path is more direct, and the female one more labyrinthine.

Clearly, women cannot resolve the problems presented by the labyrinth on their own. In chapter 9 we analyze how organizations create some of these barriers and explain how organizations can work to break them down and help women advance. In this chapter we provide advice to women who want to chart a successful path through the labyrinth, given current conditions. Our advice is not a set of one-size-fits-all rules but rather provides two general suggestions for coping at the workplace, along with cautions about when these suggestions would work less well: first, women should demonstrate that they are both agentic and communal, and, second, they should create social capital. Beyond the workplace, women who advance in their careers find ways to negotiate the detours that can follow from family responsibilities. We address these concerns by providing evidence of the benefits of undertaking multiple roles—employment as well as family responsibilities.

Numerous books offer advice on how women can advance in their careers, but that advice is often contradictory. Typically, authors recommend one of two strategies: to act masculine or to act feminine. Both of these one-sided approaches fail to account for the dilemmas posed by the double bind that we describe in chapter 7.

Authors in the act-masculine camp urge women to be aggressive, confident, strong, bold, and fearless. Kate White's advice in *Why Good Girls Don't Get Ahead But Gutsy Girls Do: 9 Secrets Every Working Woman Must Know* is to reject feminine niceness and to attack the career world head on.[1] Her chapter titles include "A gutsy girl breaks the rules" and "A gutsy girl doesn't worry whether people like her." White cautions women not to take a mothering approach to managing because it produces lazy employees who lower their standards. In *How Men Think: The Seven Essential Rules for Making It in a Man's World*, Andrienne Mendell coaches women to be aggressive and "always try to take control and be in control."[2] Mendell advocates learning masculine skills such as verbal combat. The overall message is that women lead best by becoming male clones.

A further search of bookstore shelves yields authors who are in the act-feminine camp. In *How To Succeed in Business Without a Penis: Secrets and Strategies for the Working Woman*, Karen Salmansohn argues that because corporations are like families, women can "silently rule with their innate mommy-nurturing skills."[3] Similarly, Ann Crittenden, in *If You've Raised Kids, You Can Manage Anything: Leadership Begins at Home*, tells ambitious women to embrace the communal skills of effective parents, noting that the *"enlightened parent* model of leadership has become the most fashionable approach to management."[4]

The act-masculine advice speaks to managerial women who feel themselves in alien territory. Women may marvel at men's brash self-confidence and intense competitiveness. As a woman executive in the New York financial industry observed, "We're all supposed to act like we know *exactly* what will happen next and can predict it."[5] Another woman in finance commented, "In many public forums, men are trying to find a weakness, trying to make you display a weakness. And that's done not only to women, the men do this to each other. This is the standard mode of operation."[6] To make inroads into such territory, women might try to blend in by emulating their male colleagues.

The contrasting act-feminine approach assumes that women don't need to emulate men because leadership roles change to accommodate women. Any tendency of women to be nurturing or collaborative leaders would be not only acceptable but also advantageous. By this logic, women embracing their feminine side are welcomed into the ranks of leaders. As Bella

Abzug, feminist activist and former congressional representative, wrote, "In my heart, I believe women will change the nature of power rather than power changing the nature of women."[7]

The authors in these act-feminine and act-masculine camps are correct in that effective leadership poses particular challenges for women. However, their advice is invariably simplistic. Optimal ways of plotting a course through the labyrinth are more subtle and multifaceted.

Leadership Behavior: Pitfalls and Opportunities

Women confront numerous obstacles in their path to leadership. What behavioral strategies might they apply to ease their route through the labyrinth?

First Principle: Blend Agency with Communion

To overcome resistance to their leadership under current conditions, women must quell two types of doubts: suspicion that they are not sufficiently agentic and that they are not sufficiently communal. People think that leaders should be agentic, but they doubt women's agency because they consider men to be inherently more agentic than women. They suspect that women might be too soft, not tough enough in negotiations, and not decisive enough in crises. So women are pressured to establish themselves as agentically competent. People also doubt women's communion when they take charge without conveying obvious warmth and friendliness. These suspicions can create resistance because people think that all women should be nice.

These two types of doubts about women leaders create the double bind that we discuss in chapter 7. Nice, friendly female leaders may be criticized for not being assertive and decisive enough unless they temper their communion with agency. But strong, decisive female leaders may be criticized for not being warm and nice enough unless they temper their agency with communion. Also, some behaviors that clearly convey agency, such as self-promotion or aggressiveness, are seen as incompatible with communion. Establishing both agency and communion can be challenging, as film executive Dawn Steel explained: "It was a tough balancing act, being a woman in that place, and gauging how to juggle my masculine side and my feminine side. And it's interesting to see where the lines had to be drawn. In your dress, in your talk, in your body language, for starters."[8]

To surmount these dual demands of her leadership role and her gender, a woman has to first establish an exceptional level of competence as a leader because, as we show in chapter 7, this level of competence is needed to convince others that she is equal to men. Women can demonstrate this competence by, for example, mastering job-relevant knowledge and being exceptionally well prepared for meetings and negotiations. It isn't fair, but women often need to be exceptionally good to be credited with the abilities of less-competent men. Sheila Wellington, former president of Catalyst, pointed to the importance of demonstrating competence to women's career success: "The best isn't good enough. Successful women tell Catalyst over and over, 'Perform beyond expectations' . . . Deliver more than people expect. Impress them over and over again. This is how you build a track record that will serve you well both with your immediate boss and with the organization at large. This is how you counter the 'competency barrier' that women tell us they face when working with men."[9]

Establishing competence involves far more than gaining superior task knowledge and working hard. Leaders' competence derives from a confluence of tasks involving monitoring, advising, encouraging, directing, sanctioning, and solving both interpersonal and technical problems. Establishing a record of competence in such activities requires the cooperation of followers.

Competence should also be established on reasonably difficult tasks. As chapter 9 explains, advancement in organizations requires that women stand out from the crowd by achieving success at challenging work. In addition, rising to the highest executive positions in business settings generally requires obtaining line management roles involving responsibility for the operations that produce profits and losses. But because women may not be offered tough assignments or line management opportunities, they often have to put themselves forward and actively seek experiences that can qualify them for promotions. Yet putting oneself forward is complicated by the widely shared cultural expectation that women ought to be unselfish and deploy their knowledge and skills to benefit others within the organization. So grabbing on to the best assignments can seem ungenerous and selfish when a woman does it.

As a rule, a woman can finesse the double bind to some extent by combining assertive task behavior with kindness, niceness, and helpfulness. Communal actions are also desirable in men, and many of the best male leaders are quite communal.[10] Nevertheless, given the labyrinthine complexities encountered by female leaders, they have more to gain from being warm and nice.

To integrate communion and agency, a woman can direct others while also being verbally supportive and expressing warmth nonverbally through behaviors such as smiling and looking at people who are speaking rather than looking away. Although it is wise to avoid seeming shy and tentative, assertive women can seem harsh and self-interested unless they also expresses warmth. A woman who communicates in a highly competent but warm manner quells doubts simultaneously about her ability and her likableness, and this approach can increase her influence, even with men.[11] Therefore, women who are already viewed as highly agentic sometimes try to fend off concerns about their lack of warmth by presenting their softer side. For example, children were visibly in attendance at Hillary Clinton's kick-off event for her presidential campaign. Most Americans already perceive Clinton as a strong leader, so for her, achieving a blended image of agency and warmth is an appropriate goal.[12]

As these examples indicate, the communal qualities that serve women well as mothers and in many female-dominated occupations can increase their influence and contribute to their success as leaders.[13] However, the leadership skills that enhance family life do not transfer directly to organizations. Workplace colleagues are not surrogate children. But good leaders, whether in organizations or in families, encourage subordinates and reward them for their positive contributions. Many women have experience with such behaviors because in conventional families they are the ones who provide daily encouragement, support, and mentoring to their children.

Not surprisingly, then, outstanding women leaders are often recognized for their "good mother" behaviors, as was Anne Mulcahy, CEO of Xerox: "Since May 2000 when Xerox ousted G. Richard Thoman as chief executive and named Ms. Mulcahy, then in her 24th year with the company, as president, she has been like a mother glued to the bedside of a child in intensive care, often in the office as early as 6 a.m., rarely out before 7 p.m., and continuing to make phone calls from home . . . What emerged was a portrait of an executive who is equal parts hard-nosed chief and sensitive mom."[14]

Incorporating explicitly communal behaviors in one's leadership does not mean being a pushover or attempting to be liked by everyone. Oprah Winfrey, who epitomizes warmth in her role as television talk show host, makes this point clear: "I didn't want to say 'No' because I didn't want people to think I'm not nice. And that, to me, has been the greatest lesson of my life: to recognize that I am solely responsible for it, and not trying to please other people, and not living my life to please other people, but doing what my heart says all the time."[15] Winfrey continues to convey warmth but has learned to add assertiveness and decisiveness to her behavioral mix.

Acting aggressively presents risks for female leaders. As chapter 7 points out, people often resist women's leadership more than men's, especially when women behave aggressively or autocratically. Men may get away with this type of leadership, but women seldom do. Debra Brittain Davenport, CEO of a consulting firm, noted the consequences of an autocratic style of leadership and the importance of developing a more nuanced style:

> In my very first management position, I ruled with tight-fisted authority. I was a true dictatorial maven and so proud to have my people scampering at my slightest command. Little did I know that these bright talented and hard-working people probably wished me dead (or at least comatose) . . . It was not until later in my career that I acquired a modicum of leadership wisdom . . . I wanted to have a company that valued people, nurtured them and fostered their development as human beings.[16]

Mary Minnick, president of marketing, strategy, and innovation at Coke, also described her escape from her earlier reputation as a tough, abrasive boss: "It's not so much about softening as it is about being less intense and more balanced in my sense of urgency."[17]

Blending agency with warmth can counteract resistance to women's leadership. Many experienced female leaders recognize the value of this approach. For example, film executive Dawn Steel wrote, "Women have begun to forge a style that combines the best of men and women—tough and compassionate, aggressive and morally and emotionally responsible, decisive and creative."[18] This blended style often involves aspects of transformational leadership, the amalgam of effective leadership behaviors that we describe in chapter 8. One exemplar is Meg Whitman, the highly successful CEO of eBay, who is known for listening to her company's customers and employees and thereby running a flexible and responsive organization.[19]

Similarly, Cynthia Carroll, CEO of Anglo Mining, received the accolade of having an exceptional record of "improving operational performance and transforming culture" and displaying the ability to be "a leader and a warm and friendly person."[20] New York City Planning Commissioner Amanda Burden is another instance, given that her "soft-spoken demeanor is a terrific foil for a will of steel."[21] Such women's actions can reconfigure conventional ideas about leaders to a more inclusive model of ideal leadership, thus fulfilling Bella Abzug's wish that women change the nature of power.

Limits to the Effectiveness of the Blended Style in Highly Masculine Settings. Resistance to women's leadership is strongest in highly masculine domains and in leadership positions that have rarely been occupied by women. In such contexts, where perceptions of women can be particularly harsh, our first principle of blending agency with communion has limitations. Some environments may allow few deviations from traditionally masculine leadership because there have been few, if any, leaders who have acted in other ways. Breakthrough women—the first female occupants of highly male-dominated roles—would rarely win approval for using a new and different leadership style. They would risk being condemned as weak if a hyperagentic style is typical of their male counterparts.

Consider an article appearing in the *Financial Times* recounting a meeting between Angela Merkel, chancellor of Germany, and a prominent business executive who had taken actions unfriendly to her initiatives a few months into her term.[22] This man reportedly was "stunned by the chancellor's lack of bombast," and an informant noted, "So much passivity makes you wonder whether she will be able to make decisions quickly when the going gets tough." Yet the article further acknowledged that Merkel "has brought a dose of discussion, discretion and collegiality to the government." Obviously, some observers did not welcome what appeared to be a more female-typical, collaborative leadership style, given that the expectations for the chancellor role were set by what the *Financial Times* labeled "Gerhard Schroeder's testosterone-fuelled reign." Consistent with this stereotype-laden example, being regarded as not tough enough is a clear and present danger for women in highly male-dominated leadership roles.

As this reaction to Merkel shows, people scrutinize women's behavior in very masculine environments, searching for any weakness. Even communal behavior that is ordinarily desirable and effective may signal weakness for some observers. Therefore, as chapter 8 also indicates, women leaders' reliance on a relatively democratic and interpersonally oriented leadership style diminishes in extremely male-dominated roles.

Given the demands of masculine environments, emotional displays can suggest weakness, and women are advised to avoid crying when upset. For example, professional development advice offered to women engineers made this point: "While crying is expected for extreme situations (i.e. breaking an arm, or a death in the family), it is considered taboo for professional women in response to normal work situations. We have all seen men lose their temper at work (remember that anger is an emotion)[;] however, nothing reinforces the negative stereotype of women being ruled by emotions rather than professionalism like a crying woman professional."[23]

The paradox for women in roles usually occupied by men is that they may be condemned for crying or otherwise seeming not tough enough, but also disliked for any toughness they do show. An equal opportunity manager for the Goddard Space Flight Center described the disapproval that female employees can face for the behavior that is required for success in their jobs: "These women have had to be quite aggressive to get to where they are in the technical field. Their behavior is no different from their male peers, yet the prevailing attitude is that they shouldn't behave this way."[24]

Men, in particular, may be threatened by women who exhibit dominance, lead in an autocratic manner, or show exceptional skill in masculine domains. But communal behaviors aren't the solution to the extent that they compromise a woman's authority in such environments. Faced with such problems, women should recognize that not every good leader is universally liked. They should lead in an assertive, competent manner, accompanied by especially nice, friendly behavior only to the extent that it does not undermine their authority.

In male-dominated roles, encountering obviously sexist or harassing behavior can pose additional difficulties for women. There is no simple strategy for eliminating such behavior. Firmly explaining that such actions are unacceptable is sometimes effective, especially if the offending party has exhibited the behaviors unwittingly. Although, as we note in chapter 7, formal complaints and other direct actions often have unfavorable outcomes, such action can be successful under some circumstances—for example, when the organizational climate does not tolerate harassment and the harasser has relatively less status within the organization.[25]

Taking Credit for Accomplishments. One way to advance in the agentic mode is to consistently tell others how competent you are. But many women feel uncomfortable blowing their own horn. This discomfort is not surprising because, as chapter 7 reports, women who engage in self-promoting behavior risk being seen as lacking feminine niceness. People penalize women for immodesty more than they penalize men, and women respond by displaying modesty. Men can be less concerned about negative reactions to their self-promotion because they are not under as much pressure to be nice.

Even when women believe themselves equal to men in ability, they generally use fewer superlatives to describe themselves publicly than men do. Research shows that women are especially modest when interacting with someone less accomplished than they are, to avoid making the person feel inadequate. Illustrating this behavior, a female managing director at an investment company explained how she initiated her classes in modern portfolio theory for predominantly male stockbrokers. She would say, "You know more about this than I'll ever know, but let me share with you the secrets of other successful brokers."[26] Now that's modesty.

In part, women's modesty reflects their lower confidence. Women often underestimate how well they actually perform, and men more often overestimate their performance.[27] Charlotte Otto, a senior vice president of Procter & Gamble, illustrated this tendency in describing her unfounded doubts about her ability to land a job after business school: "I recall worrying whether I was going to have any job offers, and I had fifteen of them when I graduated from business school . . . The only job offer I didn't get was the very first one I tried for, at AT&T."[28]

How can women handle the dilemma inherent in self-promotion—its advantages for advancement but incompatibility with traditional femininity? One way to avert hostile reactions is to promote oneself in a friendly and collaborative manner.[29] For example, a woman might call attention to her excellent proposal by inviting others to react to her suggestion and help her develop it further. Or in response to accolades for achievements, a woman might be careful to acknowledge the help of her collaborators while also taking personal credit.

Other routes for women to highlight their accomplishments without eliciting a backlash rely on supportive colleagues. For example, a group of professors at a major university devised a stratagem to solve the problem of male colleagues taking credit for their proposals at department meetings: When it happened, another women would say, "John, I see that you agree with Emily's suggestion. Emily, can you tell us more about your idea?"[30] This approach obviates the need for Emily to draw attention to the slight and thereby seem to be defensive, aggressive, or selfish.

Negotiating Effectively. Negotiating often makes people anxious, although effective negotiation is important in obtaining a good starting salary and other career advantages. Yet, research has shown that women reap fewer profits from negotiating than men do. The effects on salaries are notable. For example, in a survey of Ivy League MBA graduates, equal percentages of men and women reported negotiating for higher salary after receiving an initial salary offer, but men obtained better offers.[31]

Men's greater success in negotiating their salaries partly reflects discrimination on the part of those who set wages. Research indicates that people view women who initiate salary negotiations as more demanding and less nice than women who accept the salaries they are offered.[32] But men's success also likely reflects women's reluctance to promote themselves and their underestimation of their value. And as we have noted, women are penalized for self-promotion more than men are, and negotiation requires some degree of self-promotion. So negotiation is another challenge typically encountered in the labyrinth.

In a demonstration of women's reluctance to recognize and promote their value, researcher Lisa Barron had MBA students simulate a job interview and then asked them about the experience. She found striking differences between the men and the women: 85 percent of the men reported that they knew their worth in the negotiation, but 83 percent of the women reported feeling unsure of their worth. Among the men, 70 percent felt entitled to be paid above-average compensation, but among the women, only 30 percent did. One of these men reported to Barron, "I honestly think that my value is greater than the package . . . that was offered me out there."[33] Most of the men also felt that they could use self-promotion to justify a higher salary, but women were more reluctant to highlight their accomplishments in this manner. In explaining this, one woman noted, "It's hard to talk about yourself and say great things about yourself . . . You tend to just be humble and hope that people can see that you're a great person."[34] As a result of these different levels of entitlement, the men requested higher salaries and got them.

In general, studies show that women are more satisfied with lower levels of reward than men are. Also, female and male managers in comparable positions indicate equal satisfaction with the conditions of their jobs, even when the men have higher salaries.[35]

Why are women satisfied with inferior salaries? It appears that women base their judgments of fair compensation on people like themselves—namely, on other women, who in general are less well compensated than men. Women therefore feel less entitled to high pay than men do. As a result, women often fail to recognize that they are personally discriminated against when they receive lower pay and fewer other benefits than comparable men.[36] Despite this failure to perceive personal discrimination, women often recognize that women in general are discriminated against.

Comparison standards are at work again: when judging whether women in general suffer discrimination, women compare women to men and suspect discrimination.[37]

To avoid the pitfalls of undervaluing themselves, women should obtain as much information as possible about typical salaries and benefits and compare themselves to similarly qualified men. If it is not possible to obtain such information, women should just up their requests somewhat to avoid undervaluing themselves. Also, in negotiating for salary or rank, female managers should present a balanced picture of themselves by displaying both task competence and social skills, thereby quelling doubts about their agency and communion. And women must also overcome any reluctance to initiate negotiations: those who negotiate obtain higher salaries than those who do not.[38]

Feeling Authentic in Leader Roles. In addition to other challenges presented by the labyrinth, women can feel out of place and inauthentic in traditionally masculine organizational settings. Female leaders may find that their leadership styles and values are not in harmony with masculine organizational cultures, as chapter 9 demonstrates. Such might be the case, for example, when women emphasize high ethical standards and fair and compassionate treatment of others, values more generally characteristic of women than men (see chapter 3). In the words of one female managing director of a large bank, "I've gotten close to the top of the organization, and I'm not sure I like what I see. Nothing grossly illegal, but immoral . . . My boss . . . is one of five men at the top. They are all incredibly ambitious. My boss would go to bat for me as long as he didn't put himself at risk. I have a hard time with that from a moral perspective. I don't always see them doing the right thing. They rationalize it."[39]

A female former vice president in a *Fortune* 500 company cited the organization's extremely aggressive culture as a principal reason for leaving the organization: "After you get to a certain level, it's not developing the best strategic plan, it's the sheer competitiveness of it—who can kill everyone else."[40]

How do women executives who experience such sentiments achieve a feeling of authenticity in their jobs? Experts on leadership typically advise that authenticity follows from being open and transparent. In the words of leadership scholars Bruce Avolio and his colleagues, authentic leaders "know who they are, what they believe and value, and . . . act upon those values and beliefs while transparently interacting with others."[41] Presumably, such leaders inspire trust in others and thereby boost their subordinates' job attitudes and performance.

But this advice, however reasonable it may seem, is more useful for men than women. A woman who transparently reveals her values places herself at risk if those values are not shared by her male colleagues. In addition, people may view a woman as having less legitimacy to represent an organization's values.[42] As a result, women who express and act on their values may undermine their own influence and find themselves facing increased resistance and rejection. On the other hand, women who lead by emulating the behaviors and values of their male colleagues may feel personally inauthentic, as if they are putting on a mask and acting in an unnatural way. For example, Jane Rosenthal, a producer and founder of a film production company, said, "Sometimes I feel I have to be tougher, to show authority . . . I have a little girl's voice, so sometimes I will say certain things to get a point across. I feel as if I were being difficult, at times. And then I find myself saying, 'But this isn't me.'"[43]

The pressure to accept values and exhibit behaviors that are not one's own can create discomfort that goes beyond the challenges of learning a new role. Instead, genuine dilemmas can arise. Women (and men) in such situations surely should attempt to create more acceptance of their behavioral styles and values. The question is how to do this while still remaining loyal to the organization and not surrendering career success.

In an insightful book that deals with these challenges, Debra Meyerson introduced the concept of *tempered radicals*, defined as "people who want to succeed in their organizations yet want to live by their values or identities, even if they are somehow at odds with the dominant culture of their organizations."[44] Tempered radicals often take seemingly small actions that gain support when noticed by others. Individuals with the courage to take such steps can foster progressive change in organizations.

Some of Meyerson's tempered radicals resisted efforts to change their leadership style to the more autocratic style that was normative in their organizations. Even in the role of head surgeon, which is ordinarily enacted autocratically, one of the women Meyerson featured proceeded collaboratively in a manner that valued input from all members of the surgical team. This woman provided an alternative model of excellent performance and succeeded in changing some doctors' and nurses' ideas about how surgical teams should be run.

Once more, men have a clearer, straighter path to leadership than women. Men, more often than women, can succeed merely by "being themselves" because they match other people's concepts of what leaders are like. Women face more complexity because they initially don't seem as leader-like to others and may also have somewhat different values and attitudes than most of their male colleagues. Coping with these complexities tests female leaders' intelligence, interpersonal skills, and personal maturity.

Second Principle: Build Social Capital

As we show in chapter 9, those who create social capital through good relationships with colleagues, both within and outside their organization, are more likely to rise to positions of authority. Employees can amass social capital by interacting with colleagues and establishing positive relationships with them. Parties in such relationships should anticipate offering help and advice as much as they obtain such benefits. Workplace advancement flows from supporting one's colleagues and not merely from expecting help from them.

Joining and participating in networks create social capital. Networks can provide emotional support, contacts with clients, leads about job prospects, inside information, advice on work-related problems, and information about a wide range of job-related issues.[45] One way that women in male-dominated fields can reduce feelings of isolation is by networking with other women. Such networks can be useful, even though they sometimes risk eliciting the suspicion of male colleagues. In the words of one senior British police officer, "When three of us [women] had lunch together last week, people were commenting about it, you know 'what's going on' . . . The boss of one of the women walked in and said 'I have obviously interrupted something.'"[46]

But women should also network with men, given that the more-powerful networks are usually dominated by men, as we indicate in chapter 9. Even though women often have difficulty joining these networks, cultivating them is a useful strategy for women leaders.[47] As one female executive remarked, "I rarely felt included in networks. I usually had to initiate my own contacts and did not experience others coming to me, even though I was in a very high position in my organization. I really had to do it myself, almost all of the time."[48] This woman's assertive approach allowed her to develop valuable relationships despite others' reluctance to reach out to her.

Leaders also often credit their advancement in part to having had a mentor.[49] Hospital executive Sandra Labas Fenwick acknowledged the importance of a mentor to her career: "I looked at the person I'd be working with and tried to determine whether he could help me grow, provide me with new opportunities, open doors for me, and teach me as a mentor. He did. I was promoted as the first woman administrator the hospital ever had. Finding a good mentor to help you is as important as your title or salary."[50]

Mentors can teach their protégés about their organizations or professions and help them to obtain good assignments. Mentors can also offer encouragement, acceptance, and friendship. Protégés benefit from both the coaching and the personal support that mentoring provides. Higher compensation and speedier promotions can follow, along with greater job satisfaction and career commitment. Black female managers, in particular, report that having a mentor can lead to corporate success and that not having a mentor is a major barrier to advancement.[51]

Individuals who are new to an organization are well advised to seek out mentors both informally and formally through established organizational channels. Although women and men appear to be about equally likely to have a mentor, men are more likely to have male mentors. In fact, protégés with male mentors tend to receive more financial compensation, regardless of their own gender.[52]

Relationships with more-powerful associates can be especially advantageous, but it is wise to form positive relationships with coworkers of all statuses. As Libby Sartain, senior vice president of human resources at Yahoo! noted, "Forming good relationships above you, on the same level with you, and below you is how people succeed in the workplace."[53] It would be a mistake to assume that certain people are not important enough to warrant bothering with them. For example, one of us knows a professor whose office is rarely cleaned and who must wait a long time to have equipment repaired, all because he has been uncivil to the maintenance staff at his institution. Coworkers at every level can have much to offer, including inside information that is shared only in the context of positive, trusting relationships.

Balancing Employment and Family

Now we address a crucial matter: balancing employment and family responsibilities. We do not presume to provide basic principles for finding this balance, because there is a wide range of satisfactory (and unsatisfactory) resolutions. Women who marry, and especially those who become mothers, should keep in mind that even though discrimination remains a serious obstacle, a major portion of the labyrinth derives from their family responsibilities. Although female leaders and managers may remain single or childless or may delay childbearing until their careers are established, most are or have been married and have one or more children. Domestic responsibilities then present most of these women with challenges that men do not face to the same degree.

Women who have delayed childbearing and have established managerial careers generally have better-than-average earnings, and sometimes stratospheric ones. Women with excellent incomes have easier options for balancing career and family demands. Such women can delegate housework and can rely on babysitters, nannies, and excellent childcare centers to reduce some of their childcare duties. Still, given contemporary expectations for intensive parenting, even for these women caring for children usually remains a major responsibility. As chapter 5 shows, men continue to devote less time than women to childcare, even though men in general contribute substantially more than they did in the past.

Challenges and Benefits of Having It All

"Having it all" is a divisive phrase, because no woman wants to admit that she has accepted half a loaf or half a life. The phrase generally refers to achieving a successful career and a successful family life that includes children. Without a doubt, that life situation is appealing to many women. More women would aspire to demanding careers if they did not believe that this choice would unacceptably compromise their family lives. And women with career aspirations would be greatly aided by husbands or partners who accepted half of the domestic responsibilities.

Some talented women choose careers that they hope will allow some flexibility to handle family obligations while staying employed. However, as chapter 5 demonstrates, this flexibility may not be forthcoming. Fast-track positions in management, law, and other professional fields require a large time commitment. Often, highly educated and talented women who want both career and family must choose between fast-track career paths that provide limited time for family and less-prestigious careers that may allow part-time employment or breaks from employment—not an easy choice.

Many mothers, including some who have superb career credentials, choose part-time employment, take lengthy leaves of absence, or even leave employment entirely while raising children. However, as chapter 5 shows, women who take such actions do so very likely at the expense of their long-term careers. Many women may not realize the magnitude of the costs they may incur. And many women may not fully understand the advantages of maintaining employment despite substantial family responsibility.

What are these advantages? Because people want a healthy and satisfying life, we ask whether the combination of employment, marriage, and parenthood is the best way to achieve such a life. The answer isn't obvious. In fact, there are two very different ways that social scientists have theorized about multiple roles. According to one view, having multiple life roles creates stress, strain, and overload because multiple demands quickly become excessive. According to an alternative view, having multiple roles enhances well-being and health because each additional role creates opportunities for learning and mastery. Also, each new role generally affords some increase in social support and builds social capital. In this view, a life full of challenges does not wear people down but instead strengthens them.[54]

Women who consider having a family and a demanding career should be skeptical about informal advice concerning the costs and benefits of multiple roles. Such advice is common. For example, Patricia Woertz, CEO of Archer Daniels Midland, disclosed that one of her first bosses assured her that children would ruin her career: "Get yourself fixed," he said, "and put it on your expense report." She went on to have three children and an extraordinarily successful business career.[55]

In fact, many studies have compared the health and well-being of people who have more or fewer significant life roles. Although people can experience stress from multiple roles, it is clear that, for both sexes, a life involving both paid work and family responsibilities is associated overall with better mental and physical health and superior feelings of well-being.

There are several reasons for these benefits. One reason is that satisfaction from the work role and satisfaction from the family role add up to produce a larger total amount of satisfaction. In addition, problems in one role can be buffered by successes in the other. Moreover, the skills and resources acquired in one role can also enhance the other role. For example, time-management skills acquired at a job or in the home can be used in the other setting. As a result, both men and women who possess a variety of important life roles are better off than people who reply on only one important life role.[56] They may experience higher self-esteem, a more interesting life, more shared experiences with their partners, and improved physical and mental health.

But what about the more targeted question of whether women, especially those who have children, benefit specifically from paid employment? Here, too, correlational studies show benefits. In general, across a substantial number of studies, women's employment is linked to less psychological distress, fewer physical ailments, and lower mortality rates, whether or not the women have children. These findings seem to refute the idea that having multiple roles increases stress and to confirm the idea that roles expand individuals' capacities. However, because these data are correlational, it is unclear whether multiple roles lead to these positive effects or whether good mental and physical health increases the chances that people will undertake multiple roles in the first place.[57] Both possibilities are plausible.

To determine whether employment enhances health and well-being, social scientists conduct longitudinal research by following people over time. They see whether those who were employed at an earlier time subsequently have better or worse health than those who were not employed. Studies of this sort yield less ambiguous results but are far more difficult to conduct and consequently are relatively rare. Yet these studies also show that women have better physical and mental health when they have jobs than when they don't. Studies showing adverse effects are rare. So the consensus of research argues against the role stress hypothesis.[58]

Having both a fulfilling career and a good family life can be gratifying, as Cathleen Black, president of Hearst Magazines, attests: "I have fulfilled my dreams and more. Who thought that a young girl from the South Side of Chicago could . . . become president of a large division of a corporation? I get up in the morning and get excited about what I'm going to do that day. I have a wonderful marriage, two great kids, and a very interesting career. I feel like I have it all."[59]

Well-being and health are influenced by all important life roles. Parenthood usually brings great satisfaction and pleasure, but at the same time it can be a major source of stress. Mothers and fathers experience higher levels of depression than those who do not have children, and long-term stay-at-home mothers are generally less healthy than other women. Caring for infants can be particularly stressful and even precipitate depression, especially for mothers who are solely responsible for their children's care. And parents report somewhat less marital satisfaction than nonparents.[60]

The feelings of accomplishment and challenge provided by jobs can act as a buffer to reduce the stresses that mothers can experience in their parental role. In fact, success in any major life role, such as partner, paid worker, or parent, can buffer difficulties in other life roles.[61] As noted by one female vice president of a *Fortune* 500 company, "It is really a positive thing in my life to have an intellectually engaging and challenging job, to have children and to have a strong partnership at home. Anything I can do to keep one makes me better at the other two."[62]

Research shows that, in general, children do equally well whether their mothers have jobs or are homemakers. As we indicate in chapter 4, studies have shown that employed mothers compensate for their time away from their children by giving up leisure and personal time to nurture them. They spend considerable time interacting with their children, although they typically do share childcare with other caretakers. What really matters to children's development is that they are cared for by skilled and nurturing adults, whether that care comes from a mother, a father, another relative or caretaker, or the staff of a high-quality childcare center.[63]

Clearly, on average multiple roles enhance mental and physical health. Given the evidence of these benefits for both sexes, it is striking that journalists and popular writers confine their discussions of "having it all" to the situations faced by women. People generally assume that it's the responsibility of women to resolve the dilemma of having it all. But without men's cooperation, this dilemma cannot be resolved.

Moving Toward Equality

Successful women leaders often acknowledge their spouses as helping them advance. Sheila Wellington, past president of Catalyst, and her husband, Harry, supported each other in their careers and reaped the benefits. She noted, "I don't see why anyone can't do very well in lots of different spheres . . . Harry and I would have been totally bored if either of us came home to someone who just wanted to know about our day."[64] Law partner Martha Lindner remarked, "My husband was . . . very supportive throughout law school and my career . . . together we took care of the children."[65] And corporate executive Connie Matsui, executive vice president, corporate strategy and communications at Biogen Idec, said of her husband, "We've been partners in everything, especially in raising our children."[66] Spouses who share domestic work can be especially helpful to women seeking leadership roles.

As we point out in chapter 4, more men than ever are involved in caring for their children and more than ever would consider staying home full-time. In fact, of the women on *Fortune's* 2002 list of the most powerful women in business, about one-third had husbands who were at home either full-time or part-time.[67]

As men commit themselves more fully to children and family, they have the same conflicts as employed women and may even encounter more intolerance for these commitments. According to Todd Greck, a radio advertising sales executive, few of the employed involved fathers he knew were honest about their commitment to family while at their jobs. "'If someone wanted to go at 4 p.m. and meet clients for beers, it would be OK,' he explains. Not so if they want to see their kid in a school play, he says . . . 'They would say they have an appointment and sneak out[;] otherwise the perception would be that they are loafing.'"[68] Norms may change as men devote more time to their children. In fact, among employed married parents, men now express more concern about insufficient time with their children than women do.[69]

Both men and women can benefit from active involvement in family roles as well as paid work roles. Paternal involvement in childcare not only would reduce women's work load but also would enrich men's lives. And a greater sharing of employment and family responsibilities can also benefit men by reducing their burden as breadwinners. Journalist Michael Elliot acknowledged the costs of the traditional division of labor for men:

> I allowed work to take over my life, spending nights or weekends working on books or TV films. I've spent nothing close to the time I wanted to with my two daughters . . . It's not just women who are disappointed that modern life has not accommodated their various needs. So are the millions of baby-boomer men who wanted their marriage to be a genuine partnership of equals . . . So long as they [women] stay out of the marketplace, their husbands are trapped in it—otherwise family incomes would fall.[70]

Further benefits of couples' shared family and employment responsibilities include more similar life experiences and therefore greater mutual understanding.[71]

There are other advantages of women's continued employment. Divorce rates remain high, and widowhood is also common. By maintaining their careers at a high level, women protect themselves from the financial disaster that can follow from divorce or widowhood as well as from a husband's or partner's job loss or underemployment.[72]

The direction of social change is toward increased equality between men and women in domestic responsibilities. Still, obstacles remain in the competitive nature of the contemporary workplace, which in many professions makes advancement contingent on the person's accepting extremely long workplace hours. Also, given that men often earn more than women, when couples decide that one parent should take major responsibility for childcare, they typically select the mother, in part because of her lesser earning power. However, as figure 10-1 shows, it has become far more common than before for wives to have higher incomes than husbands: in about one-fourth of families in which both spouses are employed, the wife now earns more. This situation changes the calculus of career versus family toward more equal contribution by mothers and fathers in both domains.

Conclusion

Women confront a labyrinth that poses many challenges to their leadership. Clearly, women can't tear down the labyrinth on their own. Employment discrimination, organizational policies that favor men, and inequities in domestic responsibilities all contribute to women's lesser advancement. So organizations, men, and society in general must do their part to enable women and men to attain true equality and gain the same paths to leadership. Our advice in this chapter, then, is not intended to burden women

FIGURE 10-1

Percentage of U.S. employed, married women who earn more than their husbands, 1987–2004

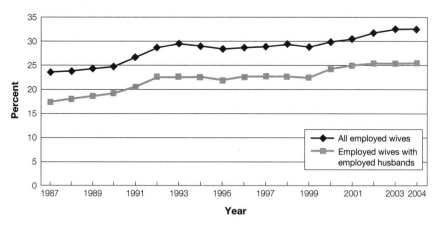

Source: Adapted from U.S. Bureau of Labor Statistics, 2006c, Employment Characteristics of Families, table 25.

with further demands. Rather, we offer suggestions to empower women who wish to navigate a path through the labyrinth that currently exists.

Some readers may object to some of our advice, because it implies that women must accommodate themselves to existing cultural and organizational norms rather than the other way around. Our point is that women should not wait to seek leadership until organizational and cultural changes have created a level playing field. Women who initially break into male-dominated roles face special challenges, but when they are successful, they can foster progressive organizational change that creates greater fairness for the women who follow in their footsteps.

A woman who heads a branch of a brokerage firm reflected on the importance of such efforts: "Although I'd like it to be a perfect world where gender had nothing to do with professionalism, I think we have to live and work in a male-dominated society. Since I can't change that, I adapt . . . I don't want to go home every day thinking I've failed because I'm trying to change something that is beyond my power to change . . . If only we each do a little something in our own way, that can be more revolutionary than if we try to change the world overnight."[73]

In this chapter, we eschew specific "rules for success" because such rules seldom reflect the complexity of women's lives. It is more effective for women to consider the general principles we have offered and to figure out how to apply them in their own situations. These principles are to combine exceptional competence with warmth and friendliness and to build social capital on the job.

Breakthrough women in masculine settings should carefully monitor whether communal behavior undermines or enhances their effectiveness. They can also forge connections with others in multiple networks and seek the guidance and support of male and female mentors. Women can remind themselves of their worth, assertively seek demanding assignments, expect more rewards for their work, and learn to negotiate well. In addition, they can rely on husbands and partners to share childcare and other domestic work, and those with enough income can pay for help with household chores and childcare. Women should remember too that staying in a career and negotiating its labyrinth generally benefit long-run health and happiness more than dropping out, as shown by the extensive research on the positive effects of multiple roles.

As we consistently argue, leadership roles are changing toward the model of a *good coach* or *good teacher*, and this model is more congenial to women than earlier models. This type of leadership allows women to combine competence and warmth and to be, as one woman publisher described it, "smart, driven, aggressive, strong, and tough, but also fair and openhearted."[74] This cultural shift eases women's paths to leadership. And simultaneously women have already changed substantially in personality, abilities, education, career ambition, labor force participation, and job preferences. These changes reflect women's accommodation to their new roles and opportunities.

Women will continue to change. And the actions of women leaders will in turn change organizations and the culture, helping to remove barriers that obstruct women's path through the labyrinth.

CHAPTER ELEVEN

How Good Are Women Leaders and What Does Their Future Hold?

THE GLASS CEILING has been cracked and shattered so many times and in so many contexts that it no longer makes sense to use this metaphor to portray the barriers that women encounter in the workplace. Women no longer face monolithic roadblocks that obstruct all access to high-level positions. Yet impediments still exist, producing the sometimes confusing and often indirect paths that women travel. Astute pathfinders maneuver through this labyrinth.

One indicator of these changes is the serious attention that Hillary Clinton is receiving as a candidate for president, the most powerful position in the United States. This emergence of a viable female presidential candidate was impossible until very recently. Only a few years ago, highly qualified female candidates such as Elizabeth Dole emerged and were quickly rejected. However, the glass ceiling in political leadership has not been replaced by a thoroughfare. Consider Bob Herbert's words in a *New York Times* editorial: "When the crunch comes, the toughest issue for Clinton may be the one that so far as been talked about least. If she runs, she'll be handicapped by her gender. Anyone who thinks it won't be difficult for a woman to get elected president of the United States should go home, take a nap, wake up refreshed and think again."[1] Another article in the *New York Times*, appearing under the discouraging headline "How suite it isn't: A dearth of female bosses," carried a similar message for corporate leadership.[2]

These negative statements show that women have a long way to go before achieving equality with men in access to power and authority. Those who see the glass as half full ask, How have so many women gained access to leadership? And those who see it as half empty ask, What is holding women back? We have answered both questions in this book. In this chapter, we summarize our answers and then discuss how women's rise can increase the effectiveness of leadership and the success of organizations. We also evaluate the implications of the slowing pace of change evident on some indicators of women's access to leadership.

The questions we have addressed are thoroughly contemporary. Until recently, the question of why women are rare in higher-level leadership positions would not have been asked, let alone been taken seriously. Men's social dominance outside the domestic sphere was so complete that it seemed an indication of the natural order or, as some people put it, a consequence of "biological necessity." Aside from historical rarities such as a few queens, women had no access to national leadership or to other positions of significant authority. The concrete wall prevailed for centuries, to be replaced in the 1970s and 1980s by a transitional glass ceiling that allowed women entry into lower-level leadership roles but blocked their ascent to higher levels.

It was only very late in the twentieth century that more than a few women began to gain access to positions of substantial authority, a shift so recent that many inequalities remain. Women still have much less power than men in the public sphere. As a corollary of this inequality, women retain more domestic responsibility than men. Changing this situation to reach gender equality is no simple matter. It is true that a dramatic worldwide shift toward gender equality has accompanied societal modernization, with its transition from agrarian to industrial to postindustrial economies.[3] Complete equality, however, eludes even the most progressive of these societies.

In the United States, only a small percentage of corporate and political leaders are women. Although many other nations have a much greater proportion of women in political offices, including in their national parliaments, women's small representation in the ranks of corporate executives is a global phenomenon. However, exclusive focus on corporate statistics diverts attention from women's enormous progress in a wide range of other leadership roles. In fact, 23 percent of the chief executives of U.S. organizations are women, as are the majority of managers in domains such as human resources and education.

Is the pace of change fast or slow? The answer depends on where you look. In a widely read book published in 1998, psychologist Virginia Valian labeled this advancement as decidedly slow.[4] We hesitate to label women's advancement as slow—or fast, for that matter. In daily life, it is impossible to miss the substantial increase in women's access to an ever-widening range of leadership positions. Still, the rate of women's advancement varies in different sectors of society. It is this unevenness that makes some changes seem rapid and momentous, and others snail-like and small.

The Causes of Women's Partial Ascent to Leadership

In trying to explain the situation of women as leaders, most people point to only one piece of the causal picture. The media and public often embrace only certain explanations, temporarily lending them popular appeal. Social scientists focus on the causes studied within their own disciplines. Psychologists emphasize personality traits and stereotypes, political scientists focus on political attitudes and officeholding, sociologists study the family division of labor and occupational segregation, management and organizational scientists examine the norms and practices of organizations, and economists study human capital and labor markets. But focusing on a single type of explanation, however appealing, is limiting. *All* types of explanations should be considered.

But not all explanations are valid. In fact, we rejected one explanation for gender inequality in leadership that, if valid, would trump all others. This idea, advanced by some evolutionary psychologists, is that evolution has endowed men—and not women—with a natural ability and desire to lead. Assumptions about evolved dispositions may provide a plausible explanation for one sex difference: the greater physical aggressiveness of men, especially of young men toward other young men. But instead of enhancing men's suitability for leadership in the modern era, physical violence disqualifies them—except in gangs, criminal groups, some types of athletic teams, and some military settings.

Some psychological dispositions do predict leadership. People with certain types of personalities and abilities have a greater chance of becoming leaders and functioning effectively in leader roles. What types? Sociable, assertive individuals who are open to new ideas and who are conscientious, honest, and trustworthy tend to become effective leaders. And general intelligence enhances leadership, just as it enhances job performance in general.

Neither the contribution of general intelligence nor of this set of personality traits, however, gives men the edge over women as leaders. A mix of traits—some culturally feminine, others masculine, and still others androgynous—contributes to leadership. In addition, sex differences in this profile's culturally masculine traits such as assertiveness have been shrinking over time. This change has occurred because masculine qualities have increased in women, and not because they have decreased in men. If women's opportunities may have been limited in the past by a lack of certain masculine traits, this situation has changed.

Another fundamental argument about women's lesser power and authority is that their greater family responsibilities limit their careers. Despite a marked weakening of the traditional family division of labor, having children reduces labor force participation for women and increases it for men. Women's less-consistent labor force participation and fewer hours of employment contribute to their lower wages and lesser workplace authority. So there is validity to the argument that on average men have more on-the-job experience, which increases their chances for promotion to higher ranks.

Although in general men have more job experience than women, discrimination also takes its toll on women's opportunities. When we gave human capital variables, including job experience, a chance to trump discrimination, they didn't. Because such factors account only partially for gender gaps in earnings and promotions, women's lesser job experience does not fully explain the greater number of male leaders. The unexplained gender gap that remains provides evidence that discrimination contributes to women's exclusion from leadership.

This claim that workplace discrimination is alive and well also emerges from experiments that compare the evaluations of identical job applications from women and men. These experiments demonstrate gender bias: men receive more-favorable evaluations than equivalent women in all but markedly feminine contexts, such as clerical work. The conclusion that prejudice and discrimination hamper women's access to leadership roles thus rests on the corroborating evidence from experiments and correlational studies.

Prejudice and discrimination are a consequence of the ways people observe and interpret everyday social interaction. Social psychologists have shown that gender stereotypes come to mind automatically when people encounter cues related to gender. These associations form a constant backdrop, coloring the judgments made about people in organizations and other contexts. Because leadership predominantly evokes masculine associations, it conflicts with associations about women.

This conflict leaves women vulnerable to prejudice. Sometimes women are considered unqualified because they are perceived to lack the stereotypical attributes of good leaders, and other times women are criticized because they display those very attributes. Women leaders who embrace traditional femininity can thus be rejected for seeming to be insufficiently masculine (not tough, decisive, or competent enough) and too feminine (weak, uncertain, or ineffectual). Women leaders who embrace the agentic demands of leadership can be rejected for seeming to be too masculine (dominant, highly competent, or self-promoting) and insufficiently feminine (not warm, selfless, or supportive enough). This is the double bind that we have emphasized. A woman who does not carefully walk the line between these conflicting expectations can find herself labeled a bitch or a bimbo, as Carly Fiorina put the matter.[5]

Resisting the authority of women can involve negative evaluations of women's qualifications and performance, rejection of their efforts to take charge, and sometimes outright sexual harassment. Given some resistance to women's leadership, it would be astonishing if their leadership styles were exactly the same as men's. Women do lead differently from men, but these differences are more subtle than is often claimed. Close study of leadership by women shows that the labyrinth they negotiated has not channeled them into inferior leadership styles. Instead, the leadership styles that women manifest slightly more than men are generally effective in contemporary organizations. Ironically, the penalties that women incur when exhibiting a dominating, command-and-control style apparently have led them to adopt leadership styles that work well in a wide range of contemporary settings.

Organizational processes also slow women's progress toward workplace equality. Stereotypes and beliefs held by individuals within organizations give rise to organizational norms that take on a life of their own and can be difficult to change. Even when individuals question practices that are unfriendly to women and families, those practices can still prevail. Some of this unfriendliness reflects the unequal family division of labor that enables many fathers to work very long hours and yet maintain their (admittedly limited) family lives. These work patterns are difficult or even impossible for mothers who have the bulk of the family responsibilities.

In organizations, limited access to male networks and other sources of social capital can also hold women back. In addition, women often confront an inhospitable masculine organizational culture and male executives who prefer to work with other men rather than with someone less similar to themselves. Although these features of organizations do not change easily, we have described many sensible innovations that can foster progressive change.

Our analysis speaks to the twenty-first-century woman charting her way through the labyrinth. To advance herself and foster progressive organizational change under the conditions that now prevail, this woman should consider two general principles that can guide workplace behavior: blending agency with communion and building social capital.

Women who blend agency with communion address both sides of the double bind by demonstrating that they are sufficiently directive and assertive to be good leaders but that this agency does not undermine the warmth that women are expected to display. Women who achieve this amalgam of assertiveness and sociability should find it easier to maneuver skillfully in organizations—in other words, to follow our second principle of building social capital, despite its challenges for women. People like working with friendly, assertive leaders and appreciate their goal-directed energy. Women leaders who have such qualities usually have the best chance of being welcomed in networks and included in relationships that foster workplace advancement. However, the advice to incorporate a good measure of warmth and friendliness in one's behavior has limits in extremely masculine environments, where this approach can sometimes undermine women's authority. Therefore, women need to proceed with eyes wide open, noticing the effects of their behaviors on workplace colleagues.

Women should also think carefully about the work–life front. Research has shown that women experience long-term advantages in life satisfaction and well-being from retaining a career, despite parenting responsibilities. As journalist Carol Hymowitz wrote, "Reach for the top—and don't eliminate choices too soon or worry about the myth of balance."[6] Attaining the advantages of a successful career and a successful family life requires negotiation of the demanding "rush hour of life," when the pressures of career growth and children's needs coincide.[7] For many women, this period of life is the main detour in the labyrinth.

The Consequences of Women Attaining More Equal Access to Leadership Roles

Does it really matter whether women have equal access to leadership in society? Legal and moral arguments, of course, favor equal opportunity.

Exclusion on the basis of demographic characteristics such as sex and race violates American values and receives very little support in U.S. public opinion and no explicit support in the law. But is there any gain beyond fairness?

There are obvious gains. Having a larger candidate pool increases organizations' opportunity to obtain excellent leadership. Hiring and promoting the most qualified individuals increase chances for success. But what if women really don't have the "right stuff" to lead? As we have shown, there is no defensible argument that men are naturally, inherently, or actually better suited to leadership than women are. Furthermore, at least in the United States, blatant sex discrimination increases the likelihood of legal penalties and expensive litigation. Organizations also lose because the image that all-white, all-male leadership groups present to the public is no longer favorable. Therefore, some corporate stakeholders, including large institutional investors, have pressured for diversification of boards of directors.[8] And selection for Fortune's list of "best companies to work for" entails scrutiny of companies' fairness in hiring and promotion and its diversity practices.[9]

Another reason that organizations may benefit from women leaders is that their leadership styles appear to be somewhat more attuned to most contemporary conditions. Although this consideration could give an advantage to women, leadership style is only part of the story of effectiveness. Women's favorable ways of leading can be undermined by prejudice and resistance and by a hostile organizational culture.

These complexities are reflected in the mix of opinions that journalists offer concerning women leaders. Sometimes they heap praise on women: "After years of analyzing what makes leaders most effective and figuring out who's got the Right Stuff, management gurus know how to boost the odds of getting a great executive: Hire a female."[10] On the other hand, sometimes they belittle women's accomplishments, as did editorial writer Maureen Dowd in commenting on Katie Couric's ascension as the first female anchor of a network evening news program: "The sad truth is, women only get to the top of places like the network evening news and Hollywood after those places are devalued."[11]

Given these considerations, the bottom-line question remains: are women leaders as effective as men leaders? The answer is not a simple yes or no.

One type of answer emerges from research that compares male and female leaders on how well they have actually performed as leaders. Such studies exist in abundance and have been combined in a meta-analysis that integrated ninety-six of them.[12] These studies examined managers in organizations and, in a few instances, leaders of small laboratory groups. The male and female leaders who were compared held the same or generally comparable roles. Researchers typically determined leaders' effectiveness by having people rate how well the leaders performed. These evaluations are not necessarily unbiased and may well be contaminated by prejudice against women leaders, especially in male-dominated settings. But because leaders cannot be effective unless others accept their leadership, these evaluations, however biased, serve as a relevant measure of how well a person leads.[13]

Given the importance of the fit between expectations about men and women and the requirements of leadership roles (see chapter 6), the success of male and female leaders should depend on context. In male-dominated settings, ideas about leadership and women diverge most sharply, causing more people to doubt women's qualifications for leadership and to resist the authority of women who do hold leadership positions.[14]

As anticipated, the meta-analysis of leaders' effectiveness reveals that men surpass women in male-dominated leadership roles or culturally masculine settings. However, women surpass men in settings that are less male dominated or less culturally masculine. Consistent with these findings, women are judged substantially less effective than men in the military, one of the most traditionally masculine environments. However, women are somewhat more effective than men in educational, governmental, and social service organizations, which have higher concentrations of women.

Also according to the meta-analysis, female managers fare particularly well in effectiveness, relative to male managers, in middle-level leadership positions. Middle management generally requires complex interpersonal skills, a domain in which women typically excel.[15] In general, women exceed men in leadership roles that people perceive as attractive to women and as rewarding such stereotypically female characteristics as cooperativeness and the ability to get along well with others. Men exceed women in roles that people perceive as attractive to men and as rewarding such stereotypically male characteristics as directiveness and the ability to control others. Overall, leaders' effectiveness appears to track gender stereotyping quite closely.[16]

It is not surprising that female leaders encounter more difficulties in masculine settings, given the organizational impediments that we detail in chapter 9. The unwelcoming practices of long hours and masculine cultures are typically more intense in such settings. And women employed in highly masculine domains often contend with traditional suspicions that they lack the toughness, competitiveness, and competence needed to succeed. In such settings, it is challenging for women to build needed relationships and to gain acceptance in influential networks.

Given these difficulties, advancing up a highly male-dominated hierarchy requires an especially strong, skillful, and persistent woman who can avoid the wavering of confidence that colleagues' doubts can instill. Such a woman is likely to be truly excellent but also truly vulnerable. Her gender, highly salient to others, can be quickly blamed for any failings.[17] But exceptional women do succeed. It is unfair that these women must be exceptional, but such is the burden of the trailblazers of social change. Their achievements break down barriers and erode prejudices for the women who come after them.

So far, our discussion of effectiveness has relied mainly on people's subjective evaluations of individual leaders. But effectiveness should also be evaluated by how well a leader's team or organization performs. Although it can be difficult to assess performance, businesses can be evaluated by the standard of their financial success—their bottom line. As corporate executive Joanne Griffin stated, "We need to demonstrate to businesses that it is in their interest, in a dollars and cents way, to treat women fairly. Unfair gaps and unnecessary barriers are awful in their own right, but once businesses realize it's to their benefit to be fair, change will occur very quickly."[18]

Abstract arguments about the economic advantages of nondiscrimination have occasionally been put to the test by relating companies' financial success to the gender diversity of their executives and boards of directors. One such effort, appearing repeatedly in USA Today, compared the yearly stock performance of the Fortune 500 companies led by women CEOs with the performance of those led by men. This approach, which has revealed good years and bad years for the companies led by women, is hardly a reliable guide, given that so few large corporations are led by women.[19]

A better test—one that relates gender diversity of top management groups to financial performance—was conducted by Catalyst on the Fortune 500. This study found that, for the period 1996–2000, the companies with the highest representation of women (the top 25 percent on representation) fared substantially better than the companies with the lowest representation (the bottom 25 percent).[20]

A more sophisticated study related the percentage of women in top management teams of companies in the Fortune 1000 to the companies' financial performance for the period 1998–2000, taking into account factors such as company size and industry performance. This study found that companies with a larger proportion of women in their top management groups had better financial performance.[21] Similar research on large U.S. companies in the 1990s revealed that superior financial performance was associated with higher percentages of women on boards of directors.[22]

Another investigation showed that firms' stock prices dropped with the announcement of the appointment of a female CEO, a result not observed with the announcement of male CEOs.[23] This reaction, suggesting shareholder prejudice, was weaker if the female CEO was a firm insider. The rarity of female CEOs in large corporations apparently produces uncertainty in investors' minds. However, in the long run it is firm performance that determines share value.

In summary, studies on corporate executives and boards of directors in U.S. firms find that the inclusion of women is associated with stronger financial performance. Despite the considerable ambiguity of such correlational findings, these studies demonstrate that women's participation as business leaders can coincide with economic gains for business. For many people, this good performance of organizations that integrate women into their leadership groups provides a more compelling argument for nondiscrimination than the legal argument that discrimination violates laws or the moral argument that it is inconsistent with American values. As Karin Curtin, executive vice president of Bank of America, stated, "There is real debate between those who think we should be more diverse because it is the right thing to do and those who think we should be more diverse because it actually enhances shareholder value. Unless we get the second point across, and people believe it, we're only going to have tokenism."[24]

Why might female executives and board members benefit organizations' bottom lines? In addition to the advantages of a larger candidate pool, a more favorable public image, and desirable leadership styles, gender diversity provides a wider range of perspectives and points of view on many issues, including product selection, advertising, public relations, and labor relations. Also, organizations that serve women as clients, customers, and employees can have better relationships with these groups when women are among those who hold leadership positions. Robert Campbell, CEO of Sun Oil, put the matter this way in a letter to the editor of the *Wall Street Journal*: "Often, what a woman or minority person can bring to the board is some perspective a company has not had before—adding some modern-day reality to the deliberation process. These perspectives are of great value, and often missing from an all-white, male gathering. They can also be an inspiration to the company's diverse workforce."[25]

Another reason why women's perspective can be especially valuable is that, as the less traditional occupants of executive roles, they may be more receptive to innovation and change, as some empirical evidence suggests.[26] Other evidence suggests that women executives may be less likely to cross over into fraudulent and illegal business dealings (see chapter 3). All in all, equal opportunity can allow organizations not only to be fair to women but also to become more successful.

Despite the advantages that may come to organizations from equal opportunity, increasing women's representation in leadership roles can be stressful for some people, at least in the short run, especially for men. Some men feel threatened by the entry of women. They may be uncomfortable with female colleagues or may fear that the presence of women will drag down their own wages. Some men may find it difficult to identify with a female boss and may not display as much cooperation and loyalty to her as to a male boss.[27]

So the positive effects of gender diversity are not the whole story. In fact, research on diversity in teams and organizations has sometimes yielded negative effects. For example, a study of symphony orchestras in the United States, the United Kingdom, and Germany in the early 1990s observed increased organizational problems and reduced player motivation and satisfaction after blind auditions enabled more women to join the orchestras. In general, these negative effects were larger among men than women, and these declines flattened or reversed when the proportion of women approached 50 percent.[28]

Although there is evidence that salaries are *not* depressed by the entry of women into occupations once closed to them, gender diversity brings challenges, especially when men feel threatened by the entry of women.[29] Successful gender integration, like successful racial integration, requires patience and good planning to avoid and mitigate the resistance, miscommunication, and frictions that can occur. Managing diversity to reap its potential advantages is one of the most important challenges faced by modern organizations.[30]

Societal Pressures Favoring Gender Equality

In contemporary highly industrialized societies, discrimination is irrational—a distortion of democratic values and free markets.[31] It is not in the interest of organizations to maintain gender inequality for its own sake. To maximize efficiency and profitability, employees must be chosen based on their abilities and retained based on their performance. Discrimination distorts labor markets and undermines organizational performance, because it allows employees to be hired and promoted on bases other than job-relevant skills. Therefore, the removal of discriminatory barriers enhances competitiveness.

These arguments about competitiveness do not imply that modern economic institutions are motivated per se to advance women.[32] Instead, at least in the United States, strong support exists for equal opportunity and rewarding individuals based on the merit of their performance. The cultural support that exists for equal opportunity and meritocracy should benefit women especially, given their increasing educational advantage over men. However, the unspoken model of what a manager should be like often assumes few, if any, constraints from child-rearing responsibilities.

This model of employees totally devoted to their organizations does not resemble the real-world experiences of most women, who often meet demanding family obligations in addition to career obligations. Increasingly, however, as men accept more responsibility for childrearing and other domestic work, the model of the totally devoted employee also fits them less well. Time constraints faced by fast-track men married to fast-track women can prompt both groups to resist careers that severely curtail their participation in family life. It will take activism by men as well as women to induce organizations to revise practices that compromise family life and thwart gender equality.

The state also has no interest in maintaining gender inequality for its own sake. Women vote and support political candidates, just as men do. Significantly, the disparity in the voter turnout of women and men has become steadily larger in the United States, with 60 percent of women voting in the 2004 presidential election, compared with 56 percent of men. Because women are slightly more than half of the population, the numerical predominance of female voters has become stunning: 67.3 million women voted in the 2004 presidential election, and only 58.5 million men.[33] Given this substantial difference, politicians increasingly pursue the support of women.

In yielding more to women, if only for reasons of political expediency, politicians must take into account differences in the attitudes of men and women on social and political issues. Although women hold a wide range of attitudes, on average their attitudes differ from those of men. Women more often favor policies that advance women's social position and that prescribe increased resources and rights for women, children, and disadvantaged groups.[34]

The presence of more women in political offices advances policies that reflect women's values and attitudes. Compared with male legislators, female legislators vote more often for policies such as family leave, birth control education, and improved public education. Women in state legislatures and local councils advocate, with some success, on behalf of women, children, and families. As the political power of women gradually increases, both as voters and political officeholders, policies unfriendly to women and families should recede.[35]

Despite the potential for women's family responsibilities to foster progressive social policies, overall the family remains a conservative influence because it typically maintains a somewhat traditional division of labor. According to sociologist Robert Max Jackson, the engines of gender equality lie outside the family, in the economy and polity, which inherently favor nondiscrimination and thereby indirectly affect the division of labor in the family.[36] We agree that family roles change in response to external shifts in the status of women and men. For example, women's increasing access to well-paid, high-status employment has implications for couples' decisions about how their paid work should accommodate childcare. It is now not so unusual that a wife has a larger income than her husband, as chapter 10 shows, and this situation can induce greater role equality within the family.

Family roles have yielded considerably to equality pressures. Still, this shift is only partial. The contemporary family, with its greater domestic responsibilities for women, continues to present obstacles to women's leadership. However, as changes in the economy continue to erode traditional family roles, a new equilibrium may gradually emerge in postindustrial societies in which men and women are very similar to one another in their devotion to family and career.[37]

Dynamics of the Psychology of Prejudice

In explaining the gender gap in leadership, we have placed some emphasis on the gender stereotypes that portray men as more leaderlike than women. This psychology, in and of itself, slows the advancement of women. Psychologists have long regarded these shared beliefs as restraints that hold women back through stereotypical thinking that is deeply embedded in cultures and therefore difficult to eradicate. However, stereotypes and attitudes adjust to the realities of social change. In recent decades, attitudes toward women leaders have become markedly more favorable in economically advanced societies such as the United States, Canada, and the nations of Western Europe.[38]

Accompanying these attitudinal shifts are changes in the commonsense psychology of sex differences. As research by social psychologist Amanda Diekman and her colleagues has shown, people know that the gender system has changed. They believe that today's women are different from women of the past and that women of the future will be different from women of the present. People view women as acquiring a greater measure of masculine personality traits, masculine cognitive skills, and even masculine physical strength as they increasingly occupy roles outside the home. In other words, it is the common perception that women have become and will continue to become more assertive, ambitious, and confident as well as more rational, mathematical, and analytical and physically strong and robust. For the most part, people do not think that women have lost culturally feminine qualities such as warmth and sensitivity, and they generally find it acceptable that women have added relatively masculine qualities.[39] In contrast to this perception of change in women, people regard men as changing very little.

What produces these ideas that women are changing? The answer is simple: the changes are based on our observations of women and men, especially women's increasing presence and success in a wide range of paid employment, including jobs with high status and wages. We assume that people usually have the characteristics needed to perform their roles. We are correct, because most people in fact deliver what is demanded by their roles. Therefore, the ideas that have produced prejudice against female leaders—beliefs that women don't resemble leaders—are slowly being updated as we observe more women in leadership roles as well as the increasing similarity of men's and women's family roles.

The Male Perspective

The ambivalence that some men express about women's rise into positions of authority emerges repeatedly in this book. Men, more than women, ascribe the rarity of women in high places to women's lack of human capital, and not to discrimination. Men, more than women, believe that a good leader possesses mainly masculine attributes. Men also resist women's authority more than women do and are more likely to implement a double standard that penalizes women. Some men display overt hostility to women through sexual harassment.

Men's misgivings about women's rise also emerges in the laments of male social critics. For example, Benjamin DeMott in *Killer Woman Blues: Why Americans Can't Think Straight About Gender & Power* complains about "women-becoming-men" and assimilating a masculine "kickbutt culture."[40] Political scientist Harvey Mansfield writes nostalgically about *manliness*, which he defines as "the *confidence* of manly men and their ability to *command*."[41] Anthropologist Lionel Tiger, in *The Decline of Males*, instead views men as objects of pity, increasingly made weak and irrelevant by the rise of women.[42] Law professor Kinsley Browne, in *Biology at Work: Rethinking Sexual Equality*, shows head-in-the-sand obliviousness to women's rise as he assures his readers that women will never gain substantial power because male dominance is built in through evolution.[43]

Despite such signs of many men's reluctance to accept gender equality, men are not immune to the contemporary economic and political forces propelling women's advancement. In industrialized societies, men have in general increased their acceptance of gender equality, even though they typically show less acceptance than women.[44] The exclusion of talented, ambitious women from leadership positions no longer has widespread approval even among men. Encouraging employed wives to quit their jobs to stay home as child caretakers has become less straightforward. And many men have daughters with talent and ambition who win their fathers' support in furthering their career aspirations. Given such changes, men today are less inclined than men of their fathers' generation to support discriminatory practices.

Of course, men's collective self-interest encourages them to thwart gender equality even while social and economic pressures encourage them to accept it. Few elite positions exist, and the advancement of women means that fewer still are available for men. Therefore, women are to some extent men's competitors for limited power and rewards. Also, some men undoubtedly take comfort in thinking of themselves as superior to women and as rightly deserving higher status.

Belief in male superiority is difficult to maintain when women are competently functioning as university presidents, secretaries of state, symphony conductors, and chief executive officers. As more women assume positions of authority, men can no longer regard such women as mere exceptions. Still, at least for some men, women's rise seems to diminish men. Nevertheless, given that men could have mobilized themselves into a social movement dedicated to blocking women's rise, their reactions to gender-equality pressures have been more supportive than might have been anticipated.[45] The usual alliance of men and women in families makes it difficult for men to regard women mainly as competitors. Instead, in daily life men and women are partners in their efforts to attain shared goals.

The Future

It is unlikely that the future will bring continuous, even progress toward gender equality, with women steadily rising into leadership positions in a more or less linear progression. Yet it is a common perception that women will steadily gain greater access to leadership, including to elite positions of power. Polls have shown that most Americans expect a women to be elected president or vice president within their lifetimes.[46] Also, university students queried about the future power of men and women indicate that women's power will increase; they are less certain about any changes in men's power.[47] These students extend women's gains in power and authority into the future, as if our society is on an expressway to gender equality.

What's the flaw in this image of a continuous march toward equality? Social change does not proceed easily or without struggle and conflict. As women gain greater equality, a portion of people react against these changes, thereby producing some backlash. They long for traditional roles and distrust change in anything as fundamental as the relations between women and men.

In fact, signs of a pause in changes toward gender equality have appeared on many fronts. Readers who have looked carefully at some of the data we have presented no doubt have noticed, for example, that some trends moved up sharply in the 1970s and 1980s but slowed and flattened out in the past few years. This pause in change is evident in women's shift toward male rates of labor force participation and male wages, and in the percentage of managers who are women (chapters 2 and 5). The pause also is evident in some attitudinal data—for example, in approval of male and female bosses and of the notion that men are better suited than women for politics (chapter 6).

This pause has not gone unnoticed. Recent reports in the media have been trumpeting women's supposed retreat from the workplace, claiming that female advancement has stalled because women are choosing not to pursue high-level careers.[48] Social scientists have taken up this debate and point to the various forces of resistance to gender equality. Some, such as social psychologist Cecilia Ridgeway, point to changing gender beliefs as activating "people's deep seated interests in maintaining clear cultural understandings of gender difference."[49] Others emphasize the continuing organization of family life by gender, coupled with employer policies that favor those who are not hampered by primary responsibility for childrearing.

Despite some resistance to further change, these forces of cultural inertia and the traditional family division of labor have failed to stop the enormous changes in women's status that have occurred in the past century. It is unclear why such forces would now gain new strength and erode the dynamic of change. Nevertheless, on some fronts change is proceeding more slowly than it did from the 1970s through the first half of the 1990s.

What accounts for this slowing of change? Perhaps men need time to adjust more fully to changes in women's roles. Women may be merely catching their breath before pressing for more change, or women may be starting to retreat somewhat. However, we believe that retreat is unlikely. The forces that have maintained gender inequality will continue to be subverted by women's resistance to their subordination and by the inspiration that flows from media images of competent female leaders. Change should also continue to be fueled by women's increasing educational qualifications, by low birthrates, and by organizations' and communities' needs for quality leadership.[50]

In the twentieth century, feminist activism fueled change toward gender equality. This activism arose when women came to view themselves as collectively subjected to illegitimate and unfair treatment. Recent polls show less conviction about the presence of discrimination, and feminism does not have the cultural relevance it once had.[51] This lessening of activism on behalf of women puts pressure on individual women to find their own way without the ideological guidance that feminism provided to an earlier generation of ambitious women.

Contemporary women still face many challenges, especially in relation to male-dominated leadership roles. They must be brave, resourceful, creative, and smart to be successful, because they can face the most elaborate of labyrinths on their path to leadership. The women who find their way are the pathbreakers of social change, and they usually have figured out how to negotiate the labyrinth more or less on their own. We have written this book to ease the task of such women. Their successes, in turn, will help chart paths for those women who come after them.

Chapter 1

1. Price, 1997.
2. "Coeds," 2007.
3. Clymer, 2001, p. A16.
4. Milwid, 1990, p. 13.
5. Ibid., p. 15.
6. Bowman, Worthy, and Greyser, 1965, p. 14.
7. Hymowitz and Schellhardt, 1986, p. 1.
8. Federal Glass Ceiling Commission, 1995a, 1995b.
9. See F. N. Schwartz and Zimmerman, 1992, p. 17.
10. Berkeley, 1989, p. 1.
11. F. N. Schwartz and Zimmerman, 1992, described the removal of wedding rings by female MBAs.
12. Federal Glass Ceiling Commission, 1995a, p. 33.
13. Hymowitz, 2004. The quote appeared on p. R1.
14. Klenke, 1997, used the term *leadership and information labyrinth* in discussing the challenges that women leaders face, especially in the field of information technology.
15. For the Boston study, see Manuel, Shefte, and Swiss, 1999, p. 22. For the survey of global executives, see Galinsky et al., 2003. For Fiorina's statement, see Markoff, 1999, p. C1.
16. J. Black, 2003. Petersen, Saporta, and Seidel, 2000, provided some evidence of lack of discrimination against women in high-tech organizations.
17. For evidence of increasing approval of gender equality, see C. Brooks and Bolzendahl, 2004; Inglehart and Norris, 2003; Twenge, 1997a.
18. Whitman, 1999, p. 272.
19. For definitions of leader and leadership, see Chemers, 1997; Heifetz, 1994; Hogan and Kaiser, 2005; Hunt, 2004; Northouse, 2004; Rost, 1991; Yukl, 2006.
20. For a distinction between leadership and management, see, for example, Bennis, 1989, and Zaleznik, 1977.
21. On meta-analysis, see Lipsey and Wilson, 2001; B. T. Johnson and Eagly, 2000.
22. MacCoun, 1998, provided an interesting discussion of bias in research.

Chapter 2

1. This phrase was associated with Clinton from his first presidential campaign onward. For example, in one of the debates, Clinton said, "I think I owe the American people a White House staff, a Cabinet and appointments that look like America but that meet high standards of excellence." See Third Clinton-Bush-Perot Presidential Debate, 1992.
2. M. Hill, 2003, pp. 100–101.
3. U.S. Bureau of Labor Statistics, 2007c, table 11.
4. U.S. Equal Employment Opportunity Commission, 2006.

5. For U.S. data, see U.S. Bureau of Labor Statistics, 2007c, table 2; U.S. Census Bureau, 2007, tables 11, 575, and 578. Women's rate of full-time and part-time employment is 81 percent of men's rate in the United States, compared with 87 percent in Sweden, 83 percent in Canada, 79 percent in France, 79 percent in the United Kingdom, 76 percent in Germany, 68 percent in Argentina, 65 percent in Japan, and 61 percent in Italy (United Nations Development Programme, 2006, table 27).

6. U.S. Bureau of Labor Statistics, 2006d, table 20. The age distribution of part-time employees differs between men and women, with midlife women (ages 35–54) and older men (55 and older) especially well represented (Hirsch, 2004).

7. U.S. National Center for Education Statistics, 2005, table 246. For analysis of these data, see Peter and Horn, 2005.

8. U.S. National Center for Education Statistics, 2005, tables 246, 265, 268, and 271. In general, the greater number of degrees among women than men is intact within all racial and ethnic groups, although this difference is larger among African Americans. For example, for bachelor's degrees classified by race and ethnicity, see ibid., table 261.

9. In the United States, 29 percent of men and 27 percent of women possess at least a bachelor's degree. U.S. Census Bureau, 2007, table 215.

10. United Nations Development Programme, 2006, table 26. For discussion of this increase in the education of women relative to men, see Goldin, Katz, and Kuziemko, 2006.

11. Wootton, 1997.

12. The 18 percent statistic is for a similar, but not identical, grouping of managerial occupations (U.S. Census Bureau, 1973, table 372). Before 2003, the U.S. Bureau of Labor Statistics defined the management category as "executive, administrative, and managerial," and data from this category are not strictly comparable to the current data. However, the Bureau projected occupational data in the new classifications back to 1983, and we report these data for "management, business, and financial operations" occupations in figure 2-3. For clarification, see U.S. Bureau of Labor Statistics, 2007a; Bowler et al., 2003.

13. United Nations Development Programme, 2006, table 25.

14. For percentages of employed women and men who are managers, see U.S. Bureau of Labor Statistics, 2007c, table 10. The two types of supervisors are the seventh and fourteenth most common occupations for women in terms of total employment (see U.S. Department of Labor, Women's Bureau, 2006). The six most common occupations among women, beginning with the largest, are (a) secretaries and administrative assistants, (b) cashiers, (c) registered nurses, (d) elementary and middle school teachers, (e) retail salespersons, and (f) nursing, psychiatric, and home health aides. For variation in the United States by race and ethnicity as well as by region, see Caiazza, Shaw, and Werschkul, 2004; U.S. Bureau of Labor Statistics, 2006d, tables 10, 11, 12; 2007c, tables 10 and 11.

15. These statistics on corporate officers in the *Fortune* 500 are from the 2005 Catalyst census; see Catalyst, 2006c.

16. Helfat, Harris, and Wolfson, 2006. This study was based only on the executives that companies listed in their official reports and filings. In contrast, Catalyst submits its preliminary counts to the companies, which are allowed to add the names of female corporate executives who do not appear in their official lists. This method may somewhat inflate the numbers of female executives reported by Catalyst. See also Cappelli and Hamori, 2005, for data on the *Fortune* 100.

17. Committee of 200, 2002, p. 17. The executive is Connie K. Duckworth, partner in 8Wings Enterprises.

18. For statistics on line and staff positions, see Catalyst, 2006c; Helfat, Harris, and Wolfson, 2006. For comparison of women and men in comparable positions, see Lyness and Thompson, 1997, and R. A. Smith, 2002, for overall review.

19. Catalyst, 2006c. As this book goes to press, ten women hold CEO positions in *Fortune* 500 companies. For 1970s CEOs, see Mineham, 2005. Marion Sandler was co-CEO with her husband, Herbert Sandler.

20. The Catalyst statistics are from a 2005 census; see Catalyst, 2006b. For other statistics on boards of directors, see Bilimoria, 2000; Singh, Vinnicombe, and Terjesen, 2007.

21. International comparisons are not precise because of differing definitions of what constitutes an executive position. See R. J. Burke and Mattis, 2000; Davidson and Burke, 2004; Wirth, 2001, 2004.

22. For Canadian data, see Catalyst, 2002, 2005a. For European Union data, see European Commission, 2006. Norway's statistics are changing rapidly because its government has mandated that 40 percent of the seats on corporate boards must be held by women; Sweden has instituted a 25 percent quota (Singh, Vinnicombe, and Terjesen, 2007).

23. The 2006 Global 500, 2006.

24. See analysis and review by J. S. Goodman, Fields, and Blum, 2003, and R. A. Smith, 2002.

25. Center for Women's Business Research, 2007. Women of color owned approximately 2.4 million privately held firms, employing nearly 1.6 million people and generating nearly $230 billion in sales. Klein, 2006, reported on the size of women-owned firms.

26. For educational administration, see U.S. Bureau of Labor Statistics, 2007c, table 11. For presidents of colleges and universities, see King and Gomez, 2007. For presidential salaries, see *Chronicle of Higher Education*, 2006.

27. For Senior Executive Service, see U.S. Office of Personnel Management, 2005, p. 72. For law firms and judgeships, see American Bar Association Commission on Women in the Profession, 2006. For the military, see U.S. Department of Defense, 2005.

28. Council on Foundations, 2006.

29. Hass, 2005, section 2, p. 1.

30. Gehrke, 2006; Wakin, 2005, p. 10. Wakin noted in addition that several women now hold the once entirely male-dominated role of concertmaster in U.S. symphony orchestras. For the effects of blind auditions, see Goldin and Rouse, 2000.

31. U.S. Bureau of Labor Statistics, 2007c, table 11.

32. "The best and worst managers of the year," 2005.

33. Colvin, 2004.

34. Driscoll and Goldberg, 1993, p. 96.

35. See D. P. Moore and Buttner, 1997, p. 23, for information on top reasons for starting new firms and p. 42 for the quote about discrimination.

36. See, for example, claims by political scientist Andrew Hacker in interview by Vogl, 2003.

37. U.S. National Center for Education Statistics, 2005, table 277.

38. Zweigenhaft and Domhoff, 1998, reviewed earlier predictions about women executives and CEOs. Helfat, Harris, and Wolfson, 2006, provided quantitative forecasts for women CEOs in the *Fortune* 1000.

39. Mero and Sellers, 2003, p. 82. Also in *Fortune* see Yang, 2005b, for discussion of women's reasons for dropping out and in many cases subsequently returning to a top job.

40. For the *New York Times* article, see Belkin, 2003; the quote appeared on the cover page. For *Fast Company*, see Tischler, 2004. For *Time*, see Wallis, 2004. See chapter 4 for discussion of the continuity of women's labor force participation. See also Dunn-Jensen and Stroh, 2007, for discussion of the validity of media claims about women in the workforce.

41. In the *Wall Street Journal*, see Hymowitz, 2004, p. R1; 2006a, p. R1.

42. In *Fortune*, see Yang, 2005a; "Fortune 50 most powerful women in business," 2006.

43. Center for American Women and Politics, 2007a. Of the women serving in Congress, 24 percent are women of color, all in the House of Representatives (Center for American Women and Politics, 2007b).

44. Inter-Parliamentary Union, 2007. In this organization's first report, published in 1997, the world average representation of women in parliaments was 12 percent.

45. For a listing of quota systems by nation, see International Institute for Democracy and Electoral Assistance and Stockholm University, 2007. For general discussion, see Dahlerup, 2006.

46. E. Goodman, 2004, p. A11.

47. Adler, 2007; de Zárate, 2007. The nations with female presidents are Ireland, Latvia, Finland, the Philippines, Liberia, Chile, and Switzerland; the nations with female prime ministers are Germany, New Zealand, Bangladesh, Jamaica, and Mozambique. It is notable that women have served as heads of government in some countries in which the overall status of women is generally low, but not in countries (such as the United States) where gender equality is greater. Particularly in Asia and Latin America, these women's family ties have provided a route to political power, with many women leaders serving as symbolic representatives of husbands or fathers who previously held office. See Jalalzai, 2004, for discussion.

48. Center for American Women and Politics, 2006.

49. See Center for American Women and Politics, 2007a. Among women holding statewide elective executive offices, only 5 percent are women of color; among women in state legislatures, 20 percent are women of color (Center for American Women and Politics, 2007b).

50. G. Collins, 1998, p. 54.

51. In the 1992 elections, the number of female senators increased from two to six, and the representatives from twenty-nine to forty-eight. For discussion, see Delli Carpini and Fuchs, 1993.

52. Eagly and Karau, 1991. This meta-analysis, like others, represented the effect of interest in each study in terms of an effect size. This effect size is a difference score (known as d), which represents the

difference in the amount of leadership shown by the men and the women in the groups examined in each study. The difference is divided by the standard deviation to produce a "standardized" difference, which provides a common metric for examining the values across studies. (Because different studies have different types of measures—e.g., a 1 to 5 scale, a 1 to 100 scale—their data cannot be meaningfully compared without establishing a common standard.) Effect sizes of 0.00 reflect exactly no difference. Differences in one direction receive a positive sign, and differences in the other direction receive a negative sign. These effect sizes are averaged across the available studies to determine how large the difference is in the male or the female direction. In Eagly and Karau's meta-analysis, the mean effect size, or d, representing greater male than female leadership, was 0.32 for overall leadership and 0.41 for strictly task-oriented leadership. The mean effect size for social leadership was smaller, with an effect size of –0.18 showing greater leadership by women than men (although only a small number of studies had assessed social leadership). For descriptions of meta-analysis, see B. T. Johnson and Eagly, 2000; Lipsey and Wilson, 2001.

53. See Eagly and Karau, 1991.

54. See Beckham and Aronson, 1978, for the earlier study, and Foley and Pigott, 1997, for the more recent study. See also D. J. Devine et al., 2000.

55. See Weinberger, 2006, for analysis of these data. Sample sizes ranged from 3,500–4,000 for each of the eight groups of white students, and from 350–390 for each group of black students. For information on these nationally representative surveys of high school seniors, go to http://nces.ed.gov/surveys/SurveyGroups.asp?Group=1. The relevant surveys include ELS, NELS, HSB, and NLS-72.

56. Evidence for the greater overall career success of men than women as well as a decline in this gender gap emerged in a meta-analysis of 140 research articles carried out by Ng et al., 2005. For discussion of the implications of social class and racial or ethnic differences within gender groups, see Caiazza, Shaw, and Werschkul, 2004; L. McCall, 2001.

Chapter 3

1. By the term *evolutionary psychology*, we refer to the most visible subgroup of psychologists who address the evolutionary origins of behavior. For overviews of evolutionary psychology, see D. M. Buss, 2005; D. M. Buss and Kenrick, 1998; Geary, 1998; Laland and Brown, 2002; and Low, 2000. For consideration of the aspects of evolutionary psychology most relevant to leadership, see Browne, 1999, 2002; Kenrick, Trost, and Sundie, 2004. See also S. Goldberg, 1993, for an earlier statement.

2. Browne, 2002, p. 117. Kingsley Browne, a law professor at Wayne State University, although not an evolutionary psychologist by disciplinary specialization, has adopted this theory. His work provides the most detailed analysis of the implications of evolutionary psychology for leadership and management. On the book jacket of Browne's 2002 book, the following endorsement by noted evolutionary psychologist David Buss appears: "An absolutely first-rate, even-handed, and scientifically sound book that takes a clear-headed look at the evolution of sex differences and how they play out in the modern workplace."

3. Browne, 1999, p. 57.

4. Although these ideas derive from Charles Darwin's analyses of sexual selection in nonhuman species, he expressed skepticism about the applicability of this aspect of evolutionary theory to modern human societies. See Darwin, 1871, especially p. 178. Trivers, 1972, first proposed this elaboration of Darwin's theory. In general, the inheritance of relevant genes is assumed to transmit behavioral traits such as dominance and competitiveness between generations. Genes are regarded as providing psychological predispositions that are then played out in response to environmental conditions. See, for example, Dawkins, 1989. For an alternative view emphasizing pair-bonding instead of competition between men, see Hazan and Diamond, 2000.

5. A. Campbell, 1999, 2004.

6. D. M. Buss and Kenrick, 1998, p. 983.

7. Fukuyama, 1998, p. 27.

8. For other critical discussion, see Buller, 2005; Laland and Brown, 2002; Richerson and Boyd, 2005; H. Rose and Rose, 2000.

9. See review of anthropological research by W. Wood and Eagly, 2002.

10. For example, D. M. Buss, 1995, and Browne, 1999, 2002.

11. Boehm, 1999; Hayden et al., 1986; Knauft, 1991; Salzman, 1999; Sanday, 1981. For a review of anthropological discussions on patriarchy and social hierarchy, see W. Wood and Eagly, 2002.

12. Lepowsky, 1993, p. viii. This source provides a detailed ethnographic study of the Vanatinai.

13. D. M. Buss and Kenrick, 1998; Geary, 1998.

14. See, for example, Ember, 1978; Kaplan et al., 2000. W. Wood and Eagly, 2002, reviewed relevant evidence. See Wrangham et al., 1999, for a related argument.

15. Another basis of evolutionary psychologists' claim of universal male dominance is that men evolved to experience sexual jealousy and to control women's sexuality. See Smuts, 1995; M. Wilson and Daly, 1992. For a critique of this claim, see Harris, 2003; W. Wood and Eagly, 2002.

16. W. Wood and Eagly, 2002; see also Eagly and Wood, 1999; Eagly, Wood, and Johannesen-Schmidt, 2004.

17. See Inglehart and Norris, 2003, for discussion of societal modernization and its implications for the status of women.

18. See Eagly, 1987; Eagly, Wood, and Diekman, 2000; Eagly, Wood, and Johannesen-Schmidt, 2004.

19. Evidence of biological mediation, where it exists, can be ambiguous because biological processes themselves reflect interactions between genetic endowments and the environment. In relation to testosterone, see Archer, 2004, 2006b; D. Cohen et al., 1996. For evidence of a possible mechanism, some psychologists argue that prenatal hormones that vary between the sexes affect children's subsequent behavior. Girls exposed prenatally to high levels of male hormones have a more active style of play than other girls and also may be more aggressive. However, given the lack of evidence of effects on adult personality, the relevance of such findings to leadership is, at best, unclear. For review and discussion, see Hines, 2004.

20. Meta-analyses of aggression research include Archer, 2004; Bettencourt and Miller, 1996; Eagly and Steffen, 1986; Hyde, 1984. See Daly and Wilson, 1988, on homicide and violent crime. A. Campbell, 2004, has analyzed female aggressiveness toward other females.

21. Federal Bureau of Investigation, 2004, table 42. In some contexts, women are as physically aggressive as men. As Archer, 2000, 2002, has shown, women are slightly more aggressive than men in heterosexual partner relationships if all aggressive acts are taken into account. However, men inflict greater injury. See also M. P. Johnson and Ferraro, 2000. As Archer, 2006a, has also shown, these trends are responsive to the status of women, with lesser female victimization and greater male victimization in nations having greater gender equality.

22. Psychologists refer to this type of aggression as indirect, relational, or social. For indirect aggression, see Björkqvist, 1994; for relational aggression, see Crick and Grotpeter, 1995, and Crick, Casas, and Nelson, 2002; for social aggression, see Underwood, 2003. See also a review by Archer and Coyne, 2005. See A. Campbell, 2005, for discussion of these sex differences from an evolutionary psychology perspective.

23. See Archer, 2004, and Archer and Coyne, 2005, for meta-analytic evidence and discussion.

24. For discussion of workplace aggression and related dysfunctional behaviors, see Griffen and Lopez, 2005; Hepworth and Towler, 2004; Neuman and Baron, 1998. See Baron, Neuman, and Geddes, 1999, and Rutter and Hine, 2005, for reports of sex differences.

25. Feingold, 1994; see also Costa, Terracciano, and McCrae, 2001.

26. See Carli, 2001a, on assertiveness, and D. M. Buss, 1981, on dominance.

27. See meta-analysis by Eagly et al., 1994, for motivation to manage, and Sidanius and Pratto, 1999, for social dominance.

28. The studies involve mainly student participants. These sex differences are somewhat greater in team competitions and face-to-face interaction. See Walters, Stuhlmacher, and Meyer, 1998. The mean effect size in d, or standardized difference terms, was 0.07 overall, 0.16 in explicit or face-to-face bargaining, and 0.03 in matrix games such as the prisoner's dilemma, which involve little or no direct contact with the other player. In another meta-analysis, Carli and Fung, 1997, produced an overall nearly zero effect size of 0.005, an extremely small effect, in the direction of greater male competition.

29. See Gneezy and Rustichini, 2004. Also, in an earlier study (Gneezy, Niederle, and Rustichini, 2003) involving computer maze problems presented to university students, competitive incentives produced increased performance only among men. Of course, computer games are also more engaging to men than women. Later research by Niederle and Vesterlund, 2005, demonstrated greater male competitiveness in a laboratory experiment involving mental arithmetic. However, quantitative skills are another domain in which males are more confident than females.

30. Federal Bureau of Investigation, 2004, table 33. See also Lynch, 2002.

31. For discussion of these cultural trends, see DeMott, 2000. Trends over time in psychological research on aggressiveness have been disputed. See Hyde, 1984; Knight, Fabes, and Higgins, 1996.

32. See meta-analysis by Twenge, 1997b.

33. Twenge, 2001.

34. Bass, 1990; Van Vugt, 2006. See also Lord, De Vader, and Alliger, 1986, for the meta-analytic finding that dominance correlated 0.10 with leader emergence.

35. Dorning, 2005, section 1, p. 24. For experimental evidence of the negative effects of dominance on perceptions of competence and leadership, see Driskell and Salas, 2005. See also McCauley, 2004, for general discussion of this point.

36. For analysis of the managerial qualities recommended in trade books, see Fondas, 1997. For recommendations of feminine qualities, see for example, Crittenden, 2004; Grzelakowski, 2005.

37. Kuhn and Weinberger, 2005. This study included data only about males.

38. Arvey et al., 2006. This study on the determinants of occupying leadership roles compared identical male twins to fraternal male twins to estimate the genetic contribution to leadership.

39. Weinberger, 2006. For discussion of the reasons that some degree of genetic determination of traits does not necessarily explain group differences, including sex differences, see Richerson and Boyd, 2005.

40. See reviews by McCauley, 2004; Zaccaro, 2007; Zaccaro, Kemp, and Bader, 2004. The question of why most leaders are male is addressed more directly by research on leaders' emergence than on their effectiveness. If women have fewer of the personality traits that underlie emergence, these differences would contribute to the deficit of female leaders. In contrast, the application of the same criteria to select men and women for leadership roles would favor similarity in the personalities of female and male leaders (see Fagenson, 1990; Melamed and Bozionelos, 1992).

41. Judge, Colbert, and Ilies, 2004. Specifically, the correlations of intelligence with measures of the extent to which people act as leaders ranged between 0.15 and 0.25. See also earlier meta-analysis by Lord, De Vader, and Alliger, 1986. For a broader meta-analysis relating intelligence to occupational attainment and job performance, see Schmidt and Hunter, 2004. For discussion of the subtleties of the relations between intellectual abilities and effective leadership, see Sternberg, 2007.

42. Judge et al., 2002. For general discussion of the Big Five personality traits, see McCrae and Costa, 2003.

43. We report these relationships in regression coefficients, which control each variable for the effects of the other four. Statistical controls of this kind are often used when variables overlap, such as would occur if extroverts are also less neurotic. The controls allow researchers to establish how much each variable is related to leadership, independent of the other variables. For the uncorrected statistics (correlations), see Judge et al., 2002. Also, Bono and Judge, 2004, meta-analyzed the relations between the Big Five personality traits and a type of prototypically good leadership known as transformational leadership (see chapter 8). These relationships were similar but somewhat smaller than those for overall leadership that we display in figure 3-1. In addition, a meta-analysis on career success by Ng et al. (2005) found similar, but weaker, relationships between the Big Five personality traits and success, with extraversion emerging as the most consistent predictor of success.

44. On the need for power, see McClelland, 1985; McClelland and Boyatzis, 1982; Spangler and House, 1991. For political skill, see Semadar, Robins, and Ferris, 2006. For emotional intelligence, see Mayer, Salovey, and Caruso, 2004; Van Rooy and Viswesvaran, 2004. For critiques of emotional intelligence, see Antonakis, 2004; Zeidner, Matthews, and Roberts, 2004. For empathy, see Kellett, Humphrey, and Sleeth, 2002.

45. McCauley, 2004, argued that in addition to the relationship-building qualities that produce success in lower levels of organizational hierarchies, at the executive level leaders need skill in strategic decision making. See also Van Velsor and Leslie, 1995.

46. "It wasn't so easy for Roosevelt, either," 2005, p. 36.

47. Sullivan, 2005, p. T03.

48. For a discussion of the presence of some introverts among successful CEOs, see D. Jones, 2006a.

49. The idea that entrepreneurs have a higher propensity to take risks than other managers is in dispute; see Miner and Raju, 2004.

50. Ciulla, 2004. Lipman-Blumen, 2005, analyzed the moral deficiencies of "toxic" leaders. See Dirks and Ferrin, 2002, for relations between trust in leadership and individual and organizational outcomes, and Simons, 2002, for relations between managerial integrity and organizational outcomes. Turner et al., 2002, found that managers with more mature moral reasoning were more likely to have a transformational leadership style (see chapter 8).

51. This discussion raises the question of whether the marked increase in females' athletic participation in the United States has enhanced their potential for leadership. The answer to this question is not clear (Ewing et al., 2002), although athletics surely provides one domain in which leadership skills may be

acquired. Findings showing that female athletes are more assertive, achievement oriented, dominant, self-sufficient, independent, aggressive, and intelligent than other females may reflect the qualities needed to participate in athletics in the first place rather than the effects of athletic experience (J. M. Williams, 1980). Surveys showing that a high percentage of women executives retrospectively report having played team sports (for example, Oppenheimer Funds and Mass Mutual Financial Group, 2002) are of uncertain meaning without base rates of athletic participation for women in general and comparison groups of women who excel in other types of careers.

52. For sex differences and similarities in intelligence and cognitive abilities more generally, see Halpern, 2000, 2001. Some specific cognitive abilities are higher in one sex; for example, some types of spatial ability are greater in males. For personality, see Costa, Terracciano, and McCrae, 2001, and Feingold, 1994. We report Costa and colleagues' personality data for U.S. adults; their report for college-age and adult samples in twenty-five other cultures shows similar findings.

53. Costa, Terracciano, and McCrae, 2001, table 2. The meaning of each of the components, or facets, is apparent from its name, with the possible exception of activity (an extraversion facet), which refers to the tendency to lead a fast-paced life rather than a more leisurely and relaxed one. Also, with respect to social skills more generally, particularly the ability to communicate nonverbally, women have the advantage. See Knapp and Hall, 2002; Hall, 2006; McClure, 2000; Riggio, 1986.

54. Feingold, 1994; see also Costa, Terracciano, and McCrae, 2001.

55. For comparisons of women and men on emotional intelligence, see Brackett et al., 2006; Guastello and Guastello, 2003; Mandell and Pherwani, 2003; Petrides and Furnham, 2000; Schutte et al., 1998; Van Rooy, Alonso, and Viswesvaran, 2005. Although the skills that make up empathy appear to be complex, women are superior to men at least with respect to sensitivity to nonverbal cues. See Hall, 2006, for review.

56. See Winter, 1988; R. L. Jacobs and McClelland, 1994. See also Gardner and Gabriel, 2004, for related research on different types of self-construals in men and women. S. H. Schwartz and Rubel, 2005, demonstrated greater emphasis by men than women on power as a personal value ($d = -0.31$ in an international adult sample).

57. See meta-analysis by Byrnes, Miller, and Schafer, 1999. Experimental economists continue to investigate risk-taking in women and men in relation to financial decision making and experimental games. See Cadsby and Maynes, 2005; Schubert et al., 1999.

58. Vinnicombe and Bank, 2003, p. 78.

59. For women's greater moral traditionalism and social compassion expressed in attitudes on social and political issues, see Eagly et al., 2004. For religiosity, see J. Kelley and DeGraaf, 1997; Walter and Davie, 1998. Feingold's meta-analysis of sex differences in personality traits (1994) demonstrated women's greater nurturant concern with others. See Jaffee and Hyde, 2000, for a meta-analysis of studies of moral reasoning showing a sex difference in care orientation favoring females ($d = -0.28$). Also, a smaller sex difference in justice orientation, which expresses concern with equity and fairness, favored men ($d = 0.19$). For women's greater endorsement of benevolent values ($d = 0.25$ in international adult sample), see S. H. Schwartz and Rubel, 2005. For evidence of a compassion theme in the values of young women, see Beutel and Marini, 1995.

60. On questionable business tactics, see meta-analysis by Franke, Crown, and Spake, 1997; see also Borkowski and Ugras, 1998, and Roxas and Stoneback, 2004, for similar findings. For ethicality of negotiation behaviors, see Volkema, 2004, for a nine-country analysis. For tolerance of dishonest or illegal behavior, see Swamy et al., 2001. There is some disagreement about whether this attitudinal difference between women and men is responsible for the lower level of government corruption in nations with larger proportions of women in parliaments and senior government bureaucratic positions. See Dollar, Fisman, and Gatti, 2001; Sung, 2003.

61. Ones and Viswesvaran, 1998; $d = 0.16$ in these data. See this article for a review of research showing that these tests have satisfactory predictive validity in relation to a range of criteria. See also Ones, Viswesvaran, and Schmidt, 1993.

62. On criminal behavior, see Federal Bureau of Investigation, 2004, table 42; U.S. Bureau of Justice Statistics, 2005. On resistance to temptation, see meta-analysis by Silverman, 2003b. Perhaps related to this greater ability of girls and women to resist temptation is their greater ability (a) to delay gratification (see meta-analysis by Silverman, 2003a), and (b) to exert effortful control by controlling their behavior, focusing their attention, and persisting at tasks (see meta-analysis by Else-Quest et al., 2006). However, it is not clear that males cheat more than females: Silverman, 2003b, found no sex difference, although Whitley, Nelson, and Jones, 1999, claimed greater cheating by males.

63. *Time* magazine featured noted female whistle-blowers as its "Persons of the Year" of 2002. See Morse and Bower, 2002.

64. Milwid, 1990, p. 157.

65. See Zahra, Priem, and Rasheed, 2005, for analysis of fraud by top management.

66. Burns, 2006, p. 29.

67. MacDonald and Schoenberger, 2006. Also see Rynecki, 2003, for discussion of Krawcheck.

68. Browne, 2002, p. 38.

69. Colvin, 2006.

70. Gergen, 2005, p. xix.

71. See Sargent, 1981, for an early statement that effective leaders draw from stereotypically masculine and feminine behavioral repertoires.

72. Brescoll and LaFrance, 2004.

Chapter 4

1. Di Leonardo, 1992.

2. The 2005 sample included a relatively small number of married teenagers, and the other samples included only married adults. In addition, race affects the domestic division of labor among married and unmarried individuals. Women's hours per week of housework exceeded men's hours by 6.7 among whites, 4.8 among blacks, and 11.2 among Hispanics (U.S. Bureau of Labor Statistics, 2006b, table 3). See also J. P. Robinson and Godbey, 1997. For further discussion of the time diary data, see Bianchi, 2000. For related survey results see J. T. Bond et al., 2002. For comparisons of the drop in housework among employed women and women without jobs, see Bianchi et al., 2000. For discussion of possible factors contributing to the decline in housework, see Artis and Pavalko, 2003; Cowan, 1983; J. P. Robinson and Milkie, 1998; Strasser, 1982.

3. U.S. Bureau of Labor Statistics, 2005a, table 8-A. Results are for adults between 25 and 54 years of age.

4. See S. Gupta, 1999; J. P. Robinson and Godbey, 1997; and South and Spitze, 1994, for the relation of marital status and housework. See Bittman et al., 2003, for evidence that in the United States and Australia women's income has relatively little effect on men's housework. Some research shows fairly constant amounts of housework by men, regardless of the earnings of their wives or female partners (Bittman et al., 2003), whereas other research shows that men do less housework when their female partners either earn a great deal or very little of the family income (Greenstein, 2000).

5. Martinez et al., 2006.

6. Singleton and Maher, 2004, p. 238.

7. Bianchi, Robinson, and Milkie, 2006. See also J. T. Bond et al., 2002, for survey data showing increases in men's childcare. See Families and Work Institute, 2005, for comparisons of generations. Participants who were born between 1945 and 1964 were classified as Baby Boomers, those born between 1965 and 1979 as Generation X, and those born between 1980 and 1984 as Generation Y. The increase in childcare among more recent generations was found regardless of the age of the children. See U.S. Bureau of Labor Statistics, 2005a, table 8-A, for comparisons of married men's and women's childcare. See G. Moore, 2004, for research on childcare by executives and government leaders.

8. In a large international survey of executives, 75 percent of the men had spouses without jobs and 74 percent of the women had spouses employed full-time. The women were three times as likely as the men to have delayed having children, and 90 percent of the men had children compared with 65 percent of the women (Galinsky et al., 2003). See M. W. Walsh, 2001, for discussion of executive women with stay-at-home husbands.

9. In a nationally representative U.S. sample, the percentages of men and women, respectively, who endorsed equal responsibility for various parental tasks were 70 percent and 71 percent for childcare, 97 percent and 93 percent for discipline, 95 percent and 97 percent for play, and 61 percent and 66 percent for financial support (Milkie et al., 2002). For effects of education on attitudes, see Martinez et al., 2006. This study also found more-traditional views among Hispanic than non-Hispanic whites and blacks. Changes in attitudes about women's and mothers' employment were found in polls taken between 1988 and 2002; see Davis, Smith, and Marsden, 2005.

10. For evidence of satisfaction with the division of domestic labor, see Wilkie, Ferree, and Ratcliff, 1998. See also B. A. Shelton and John, 1996, for evidence that men's attitudes have a greater influence than women's attitudes on the division of domestic work.

11. Hochschild, 1997, p. 38.

12. For changes in time devoted to childcare, see Families and Work Institute, 2005; Sandberg and Hofferth, 2001; Sayer, Cohen, and Casper, 2004. Bianchi, Robinson, and Milkie, 2006, reported about primary childcare, where the child was the focus of parental activity. See also Bryant and Zick, 1996a, and J. T. Bond et al., 2002.

13. Bianchi, 2000.

14. Personal communication to Linda Carli, January 2006.

15. See Bianchi, Robinson, and Milkie, 2006, for a discussion of increasing pressures on parents to spend more time with their children. Some commentators have argued that the media and other influences have fueled the beliefs that women are not fulfilled unless they have children, that women are better primary caretakers of children than men, and that good mothers fully devote themselves to their children. See Douglas and Michaels, 2004; Pear, 2006; Warner, 2005.

16. Cowan, 1976.

17. Brazelton, 1988; Spock, 1946. See Hays, 1996, for discussion. Concerns about child safety and potential victimization have also increased mothers' time with their children (Jenkins, 1998; Warr and Ellison, 2000).

18. See Arendell, 2000; Bianchi, Robinson, and Milkie, 2006; Hays, 1996, for attitudes about mothering. However, anthropological evidence indicates that other forms of parenting, including "multiple mothering" or "multiple parenting," occur in non-Western cultures (Ambert, 1994; W. Wood and Eagly, 2002). See Bianchi, Robinson, and Milkie, 2006, for evidence that mothers feel they spend too little time with their children and for a comparison of time spent with children by employed mothers in 2000 and mothers without jobs in 1975.

19. Hays, 1996, p. 116.

20. Pew Research Center for the People and the Press, 1997. See also Hays, 1996.

21. Spragins, 2001, section 3, p. 10.

22. Bianchi, Robinson, and Milkie, 2006.

23. See Bianchi, Robinson, and Milkie, 2006, for the representative national time diary study. Comparisons of mothers who were employed with those who were not employed controlled for a number of family characteristics, such as the age of the mothers and children, and refer to primary childcare. The reduction in time devoted to childcare by employed mothers occurs mainly for older children. See Zick and Bryant, 1996a, for similar findings from survey data, and Bryant and Zick, 1996b, for the effects of children's age on childcare.

24. See Bianchi, Robinson, and Milkie, 2006. These results were based on time diaries from a national sample of Americans in 1998–1999 and 2000, with hours extrapolated from single-day reports. However, these researchers, using a nonrepresentative sample of married, dual-career parents' time diaries taken over a full week, obtained slightly fewer total work hours among mothers than fathers. Additional analyses are needed to resolve ambiguities about the division of labor among dual-career couples.

25. See Bryant and Zick, 1996b, for combining household activities with interactions with children; Huston and Aronson, 2005, for mothers' loss of leisure and social time; and Mattingly and Bianchi, 2003, for effects of marital status on leisure. See also Bianchi, Robinson, and Milkie, 2006, for evidence that married mothers' leisure time has shown some decline since 1965, whereas married fathers' leisure time has remained about the same.

26. Married men averaged 35.3 hours of leisure per week compared with 31.2 for married women in a nationally representative time diary study (U.S. Bureau of Labor Statistics, 2006b, table 3). See also Bittman and Wajcman, 2000, and Mattingly and Bianchi, 2003, for reports of comparable results for white, black, and Hispanic participants. Men more often have pure leisure, whereas women combine their leisure with unpaid work—for example, watching TV while also folding laundry. When fathers spend their free time with their children, they more often do so in the company of other adults, who presumably share responsibility for watching the children, but women spend more of their leisure time alone with children. So women's leisure more often includes unpaid work or sole responsibility for the care of children.

27. For feelings of being time-crunched in representative surveys of Americans, see Bianchi, Robinson, and Milkie, 2006; J. P. Robinson and Godbey, 1997. For effects of job hours on time pressure, see Maume and Houston, 2001; Phipps, Burton, and Osberg, 2001.

28. See J. A. Jacobs and Gerson, 2004, table 1.2, for data on hours on the job. The data on weekend job-related work are based on Presser's analysis of the 1997 Current Population Survey (cited in J. A. Jacobs and Gerson, 2004). See J. T. Bond et al., 2002, for phone calls and other intrusions outside usual employment hours.

29. Kay and Hagan, 1999, p. 546.

30. Angrist and Evans, 1998; Corrigall and Konrad, 2006; Kaufman and Uhlenberg, 2000. In nonindustrialized countries, children are often cared for by someone other than their mother, and mothers, regardless of employment status, spend considerably less time in childcare than women in industrialized countries (see Bianchi, 2000).

31. Corrigall and Konrad, 2006.

32. Sayer, Cohen, and Casper, 2004. Single mothers more often work part-time than single fathers or work fewer hours when they work full-time.

33. Hewlett and Luce, 2005.

34. Mallabar, 2006.

35. For the study comparing male and female salaries cumulatively over fifteen years (between 1983 and 1998), see S. J. Rose and Hartmann, 2004. For effects of time off on experience, seniority, and pay, see Jacobsen and Levin, 1995, and also Budig and England, 2001; Waldfogel, 1997, 1998. Career breaks for childcare produce a greater drop in annual income after women return to work than breaks for other reasons (Arun, Arun, and Boroaah, 2004). Even highly qualified women experience a lowering of income when returning to work (Hewlett and Luce, 2005). For data on the persistence of losses over time, see D. J. Anderson, Binder, and Krause, 2003; Jacobsen and Levin, 1995; Spivey, 2005.

36. Hewlett and Luce, 2005.

37. U.S. Government Accountability Office, 2003. See also Budig and England, 2001, and England, 2006. But see also the report in Lundberg and Rose, 2000, of a nationally representative study of married dual-career couples, showing that continuous employment removed the motherhood penalty. For comparisons of women with differing levels of education, see D. J. Anderson, Binder, and Krause, 2003.

38. See Klerman and Leibowitz, 1999. Only 8 percent of women employed part-time prior to giving birth returned to their old jobs, compared with 61 percent of women employed full-time.

39. Based on a meta-analysis of forty-two organizational studies, men quit very slightly more than women ($d = .06$; Griffeth, Hom, and Gaertner, 2000). Unlike an earlier study by Cotton and Tuttle, 1986, which did not distinguish between quitting and being fired or laid off, this meta-analysis focused solely on quitting. Also, a study of 25,000 managers revealed that men quit more than women (Lyness and Judiesch, 2001). In addition, studies probably overestimate women's quitting because quitting is higher among those with a poor salary, low status, or little opportunity for advancement, conditions more common among women (Gronau, 1988; Sicherman, 1996). See Almer, Hopper, and Kaplan, 1998, for a study showing that managers expected female job applicants to quit more often than male job applicants. For evidence that women quit for family reasons more than men, see Keith and McWilliams, 1997, 1999; Lyness and Judiesch, 2001.

40. In a study of leaves taken by managers, 10 percent of the women took leaves compared with less than 1 percent of the men (Judiesch and Lyness, 1999). For experimental research showing less-favorable reactions to men than women for taking family leaves, see Allen and Russell, 1999; Butler and Skattebo, 2004; and J. H. Wayne, 2003. For example, Butler and Skattebo found that employees rated a male supervisor (but not a female supervisor) less favorably for missing work to care for a sick child. Men may have less latitude to adjust employment demands to family demands.

41. See Barmby, Ercolani, and Treble, 2002, for cross-national comparisons. Absences were higher in single than married men, and in married than single women. Overall, women were absent more than men, but this difference in absenteeism was eliminated when age and marital status were controlled. For effects of children on sick days for men and women, see Boise and Neal, 1996; S. Bridges and Mumford, 2001; and Vistnes, 1997. Studies that partition sick days into those taken for workers' own sicknesses and for other reasons show that the greater use of sick days by women is not for their own sicknesses; see Mastekaasa, 2000; S. Bridges and Mumford, 2001.

42. Personal communication to Linda Carli, December 2005.

43. In a nationally representative 1995 poll, 44 percent of women versus 38 percent of men reported that they would be more satisfied with jobs providing flexible hours (Roper Starch Worldwide, 1995, p. 37). See Corrigall and Konrad, 2006, for the effect of parental status on the desire for flexibility. See Glass and Camarigg, 1992, and Glass, 1990, for lack of flexibility in female-dominated jobs, and U.S. Bureau of Labor Statistics, 2005b, table 2, for flexibility in managerial, professional, and office and administrative support occupations. However, the proportions of women and men who do job-related work at home are approximately equal (U.S. Census Bureau, 2007, table 592). See Shapiro, Ingols, and Blake-Beard, 2007, for a survey of upper-level female managers showing that women in such positions can use flexible job options to remain fully employed. Over all occupations, slightly more white women have flexible occupa-

tions than Asian, Hispanic, or black women, with 27.8 percent, 22.4 percent, 21.2 percent, and 20.9 percent, respectively (U.S. Bureau of Labor Statistics, 2005b, table 1).

44. In 2005, men and women sixteen years old and older had similar rates of part-year employment when employed full-time (15 percent for men and 18 percent for women) or part-time (52 percent for men and 48 percent for women) (U.S. Bureau of Labor Statistics, 2007b, table 1). In 2006, 25 percent of employed women usually worked part-time compared with 11 percent of employed men; the percentages of women and men who worked part-time were, respectively, 27 percent and 11 percent among whites, 17 percent and 11 percent among blacks, 21 percent and 9 percent among Asians, and 22 percent and 8 percent among Hispanics (U.S. Bureau of Labor Statistics, 2007c, table 8). For evidence of greater part-time employment in mothers and married women, see Corrigall and Konrad, 2006. In general, the more female-dominated an occupation is, the larger its proportion of part-time workers and the smaller its proportion of overtime workers (Jacobsen, 1998, table 6.11). Nevertheless, women in male-dominated professions more often work part-time than men do (Boulis, 2004; Lundgren et al., 2001; Noonan and Corcoran, 2004).

45. U.S. Bureau of Labor Statistics, 2006c, table 5.

46. For the effects of part-time employment, see, for example, Prowse, 2005, for advancement, and Hirsch, 2004, and Manning and Petrongolo, 2006, for pay. Compared with prior nonemployment, prior part-time employment is associated with increased income but only if this employment status is voluntary (Green and Ferber, 2005).

47. Lifetime Women's Pulse Poll, 2006. In this nationally representative poll of women, 53 percent considered discrimination to be a serious or very serious problem, and 68 percent considered lack of flexibility to be a more serious problem than discrimination.

48. Kellerman, 2003, p. 55. Kellerman's argument is related to the idea that people who take on difficult responsibilities are rewarded with promotions as well as higher wages. See Kilbourne et al., 1994, for discussion of the *theory of compensating differentials* in relation to wage gaps.

49. Political scientist Warren Farrell (2005) claimed that women's greater desire for "fulfilling" as opposed to well-paying careers contributes to the gender wage gap. He cited as evidence a study of full-time employed college graduates from the United Kingdom showing that men preferred financial rewards more than women and that women preferred intrinsic job rewards more than men (Chevalier, 2004). Desiring financial rewards was associated with higher income in men and women, and desiring intrinsic rewards was associated with lower salaries in men. But women's desire for intrinsic rewards was unrelated to their income. Therefore, men's desire for financial rewards, and not women's desire for fulfilling jobs, most accounted for the income gap.

50. The meta-analysis by Konrad et al., 2000, was based on U.S. data from 1970 through the 1990s. Overall, males expressed a greater desire for leisure, as did male high school and college students. Only five studies examined the preference for leisure among adult men and women in the same occupation, and these had inconsistent results. For additional findings on a desire for leisure, see also a representative U.S. poll, which asked how important it is to have "enough free time to do the things you want to do." The percentages of women and men, respectively, who indicated that it was very important were 57 percent and 65 percent for whites, and 64 percent and 68 percent for blacks (*Washington Post*, Kaiser Family Foundation, and Harvard University, 2006).

51. By the 1990s, among adults in similar occupations, women expressed a greater preference for job security, prestige, responsibility, challenge, accomplishment, and recognition, and women and girls expressed greater preference for task enjoyment and the use of their education and skills. See Greene and DeBacker, 2004, for related findings. See also *The American freshman: Forty-year trends*, 2007, for university students' career preferences, and Marini et al., 1996, for a representative U.S. sample of high school seniors between 1976 and 1991. In addition, see Lippa, 1998a, for evidence that women prefer people-oriented occupations and that men prefer thing-oriented occupations, and see Eddleston, Veiga, and Powell, 2006, for evidence that among managers men desire status and women desire good relationships. These sex-typed occupational preferences reflect many influences, including the expectations of parents and teachers, which in turn affect children's ideas about their competencies (Correll, 2001, 2004; Eccles, 2001).

52. For evidence of men's and women's ambition, see Catalyst 2004c. See also Merrill-Sands, Kickul, and Ingols, 2005; Cassirer and Reskin, 2000. However, in a study of global executives by Galinsky et al., 2003, men more than women aspired to roles as CEOs or managing partners. Because the men in this sample had somewhat higher-status jobs and higher salaries, men and women in comparable situations might not differ. For research on university students, see Killeen, López-Zafra, and Eagly, 2006, and Lips, 2000, 2001.

53. A large study of the United States, Canada, the United Kingdom, Australia, Sweden, Norway, and Japan did not show a relation between workplace authority and marital or parental status, except to some degree in Canada (Wright, Baxter, and Birkelund, 1995). See Families and Work Institute, 2005, and Corrigall and Konrad, 2006, for evidence that women's family responsibilities do not reduce their desire for advancement. See also Elliott and Smith, 2004; R. A. Smith, 2002.

54. See Aven, Parker, McEvoy, 1993, for the meta-analysis on organizational commitment. See D. D. Bielby and Bielby, 1984; W. T. Bielby and Bielby, 1989; Eddleston, Veiga, and Powell, 2006; Families and Work Institute, 2005; and Thoits, 1992, for the relative importance of family and employee roles. See Families and Work Institute, 2005, for evidence that recent generations of men and women are more family centered and less career oriented.

55. For evidence of somewhat more career-focused men than women, see W. T. Bielby and Bielby, 1989, and Families and Work Institute, 2005. The more similar men and women are in their family responsibilities and employee status, the more similar they are in career and family commitment (W. T. Bielby and Bielby, 1989). See D. W. Moore, 2005, for evidence of men's willingness to remain at home. See U. S. Census Bureau, 2007, table 586, for numbers of couples with stay-at-home-husbands and working wives. In the Lifetime Women's Pulse Poll, 2006, the percentage of women reporting that they would not work if they didn't have to for financial reasons was 54 percent for Baby Boomers, 47 percent for Generation X, and 42 percent for Generation Y.

56. Becker, 1985, p. S35.

57. In the meta-analysis on job preferences, among adults in similar occupations, women showed a very slightly higher preference for challenge ($d = -0.09$; Konrad et al., 2000). D. D. Bielby and Bielby, 1988, assessed job effort in a nationally representative survey of employed adults, statistically equating men and women on family responsibilities, job conditions, experience and education. For work breaks, see Glass, 1990.

58. Based on representative U.S. survey data, 33 percent of men and 40 percent of women would prefer to be employed fewer hours (Reynolds, 2003). See Milkie et al., 2004, for opinions about time with children.

59. Personal communication to Linda Carli, January 2006.

60. In the Lifetime Women's Pulse Poll, 2006, 71 percent of the women agreed with a statement that business success would come at the expense of personal life.

Chapter 5

1. For discussion of different types of discrimination, see Elliott and Smith, 2004; Jacobsen, 1998.

2. U.S. Bureau of Labor Statistics, 2006a, tables 1 and 5.

3. At least a portion of the growth in women's earnings beginning in the 1980s appears to reflect their increased education and work experience. The decline in men's wages reflects the pressures of economic restructuring and globalization. For discussion, see O'Neill and Polachek, 1993; M. Morris and Western, 1999; Weinberger and Kuhn, 2006.

4. For example, Blau and Kahn, 2007, p. 7, described the decrease in the gender wage gap as "dramatic," "significant," and "remarkable." See also Blau and Kahn, 2006a, 2006b. Also, the gender wage gap has shrunk over time particularly for entry-level positions (see Weinberger and Kuhn, 2006). For discussion of longer-term historical trends, see Goldin, 2006, and for predictions about the future, see Blau and Kahn, 2007.

5. See Jacobsen, 1998, pp. 292–297, for an explanation of this method, which was introduced by Blinder, 1973, and Oaxaca, 1973.

6. U.S. Government Accountability Office, 2003. The data in this GAO study are from the Panel Study of Income Dynamics. These percentages, of course, differ from those that we cited for 2005 because they are from an earlier time period.

7. B. A. Jacobs's, 2002, analyses of the National Educational Longitudinal Study also showed that women have benefited more than men from increased education. The GAO study found that parenthood was associated with higher wages for men and lower wages for women, controlling for all other variables. This finding is consistent with the motherhood penalty that we discussed in Chapter 4. For other evidence of the wage gap, see, for example, Bayard et al., 2003; Blau and Kahn, 2006a, 2006b, 2007.

8. For evidence of a decrease over time when earlier and later studies are compared, see meta-analyses by Jarrell and Stanley, 2004; Solberg, 1999; Stanley and Jarrell, 1998. For evidence of little or no decrease, see U.S. Government Accountability Office, 2003, and Weichselbaumer and Winter-Ebmer, 2005, in an international data set. See also Nelson and Bridges, 1999, especially pp. 85–87, for relevant methodological issues.

9. U.S. Bureau of Labor Statistics, 2006a, table 2. In *Why Men Earn More*, Farrell, 2005, presented a list of thirty-nine occupations in which women earn at least 5 percent more than men. Most of these occupations are absent from the standard tables of the U.S. Bureau of Labor Statistics because the occupations have fewer than fifty thousand men or women. Huffman, 2004, showed that the wage gap is larger for higher-status occupations. However, wage differences between women and men are generally smaller the more narrowly the occupational category is defined. For example, within the same firm, these gaps are small. See Blau and Kahn, 2007.

10. U.S. Census Bureau, 2007, table 602. See also Boraas and Rodgers, 2003, and O'Neill, 2003, for discussion. On average, women are employed in occupations that are 68 percent female, and men in occupations that are 70 percent male. Although occupational sex segregation in the United States is considerable, it has declined over time (Tomaskovic-Devey et al., 2006) and is less pronounced than in most industrialized countries (W. P. Bridges, 2003).

11. See, for example, England, 1992, and Kilbourne et al., 1994, for analysis of negative effects on wages of being in an occupation that has a higher proportion of women or that requires nurturing skills. See Nelson and Bridges, 1999, for analysis of organizational practices that foster wage inequity and review of debates about whether between-job wage disparities are discriminatory.

12. Nelson and Bridges, 1999. Consequently, in the United States, there has been little progress toward *comparable worth* equity, whereby wages reflect the demands of jobs based on the skill level, education, and responsibility that they require.

13. See, for example, Mitra, 2003. For review, see R. A. Smith, 2002. Research also establishes that female managers tend to be concentrated in sex-segregated jobs having higher proportions of female bosses and subordinates.

14. L. E. Cohen, Broschak, and Haveman, 1998; J. A. Jacobs, 1992; L. Kramer and Lambert, 2001. See review by R. A. Smith, 2002.

15. For the study examining sex and race effects, see Maume, 2004. The data are from the Panel Study of Income Dynamics. For additional studies on managers, see Cox and Harquail, 1991; Schneer and Reitman, 1994; Stroh, Brett, and Reilly, 1992. For studies on lawyers, see Hull and Nelson, 2000; Kay and Hagan, 1998; Spurr, 1990; R. G. Wood, Corcoran, and Courant, 1993.

16. An occasional small-scale study has substantiated the presence of greater bias at higher levels. See Lyness and Judiesch, 1999, for example, for such an organizational study. In contrast, Baxter and Wright's large-scale study (2000) found no evidence that the gap in promotions increased at higher levels in the United States, but weak evidence for such an effect in Australia and Sweden. See also Elliott and Smith, 2004; Meyersson Milgrom and Petersen, 2006; Tharenou, 1999; Wright, Baxter, and Birkelund, 1995.

17. The disappearance of women from higher levels would have to be even more extreme than this type of model allows to show that anti-female selection is more stringent at higher levels. See Martell, Lane, and Emrich, 1996, for simulations of the effects of various types and amounts of anti-female bias.

18. C. Williams, 1992, 1995. See Yoder, 2002, for a review of tokenism findings.

19. For example, Hultin, 2003; Ott, 1989; Maume, 1999a, for white men; Yoder and Sinnett, 1985.

20. Studies have produced mixed findings on this issue. See, for example, Budig, 2002; G. B. Goldberg et al., 2004; Maume, 1999a, 1999b. Although men's promotion advantage appears to be quite general, the processes by which women are deselected may differ depending on the context (see chapter 9).

21. Nelson and Bridges, 1999, described four major court cases (two public sector, two private sector) involving discrimination charges against organizations.

22. Featherstone, 2004; Wal-Mart Class Web site, 2004.

23. *Betty Dukes et al. v. Wal-Mart Stores, Inc.*, 2003b, p. 46.

24. *Betty Dukes et al. v. Wal-Mart Stores, Inc.*, 2003c, pp. 3–4.

25. Powell and Butterfield, 1994.

26. For the study on promotions in the federal workforce, see Naff, 1994. See also Lewis, 1998, for a study of wage disparities in the federal workforce. For evidence of smaller wage gaps in the public than the private sector, see D. Robinson, 1998. See also R. A. Smith, 2002, for general review.

27. For example, Brett and Stroh, 1997; Dreher and Cox, 2000; Judge et al., 1995; Lam and Dreher, 2004; Stroh, Brett, and Reilly, 1992.

28. See Chevalier, 2004. In this study of university graduates in the United Kingdom, expectations of taking career breaks for family reasons, which were greater among women, accounted for a portion of the gender wage gap.

29. P. Goldberg, 1968.

30. At least in early Goldberg experiments, there was a small defect that compromised the equivalence of the male and female candidates, as shown by Kasof, 1993: researchers had inadvertently chosen slightly more positive names for the men than the women portrayed in these experiments.

31. Rosen and Jerdee, 1974.

32. Davison and Burke, 2000. The effects sizes were $d = 0.34$ for the masculine jobs, $d = -0.26$ for the feminine jobs, and $d = 0.24$ for the gender-neutral jobs (Davison, 2005, personal communication). We thank Heather Davison for providing this analysis on the gender-neutral jobs. For earlier meta-analyses of this research, see Olian, Schwab, and Haberfeld, 1988; Swim et al., 1989; Tosi and Einbender, 1985.

33. This estimate of success rates is based on the binomial effect size display (or BESD); see R. Rosenthal and Rubin, 1982.

34. Firth, 1982; McIntyre, Moberg, and Posner, 1980.

35. Levinson, 1982.

36. Some field experiments, known as *audit studies* or *paired testing studies*, involve comparing the experiences of pairs of actual job applicants who are matched on characteristics other than those that are expected to lead to discrimination (see Darity and Mason, 1998; Fix and Turner, 1998; Heckman, 1998). Most studies have compared minority and majority men. Economist David Neumark, 1996, applied this method to study sex discrimination in restaurant server jobs and found discrimination against women, but only in high-priced restaurants.

37. For the studies that initiated this tradition, see Rosen and Jerdee's experiment (1973) involving vignettes describing managerial behavior, and D. M. Lee and Alvares's experiment (1977) involving confederates who role-played leaders.

38. Eagly, Makhijani, and Klonsky, 1992. The overall bias against women corresponded to $d = 0.05$; male-dominated leadership roles yielded $d = 0.09$. See also Swim et al., 1989.

39. Swim and Sanna, 1996. Findings for feminine tasks were weaker except for tendencies to ascribe men's failures to their lack of ability and women's failures to the difficulty of the task. Because most of these experiments pertained to laboratory or academic tasks, there is reason for caution in extrapolating these findings to the workplace.

40. See Olian, Schwab, and Haberfeld, 1988, however, for meta-analytic evidence that student research participants yield similar data to employee research participants.

41. J. M. Jones, 2005a. Political ideology has strong effects on these beliefs, with liberal respondents, especially liberal women, perceiving more sex discrimination than conservative respondents. For similar results in a poll of female respondents, see Lifetime Women's Pulse Poll, 2006. A Gallup poll also reported that 22 percent of women and 9 percent of men indicated that they had been victims of workplace discrimination (D. C. Wilson, 2006). Although attributing one's personal lack of success to discrimination can have self-protective effects (Crocker and Major, 1989), belief in pervasive discrimination against women on the whole appears to decrease women's well-being (e.g., Schmitt, Branscombe, and Postmes, 2003).

Chapter 6

1. Dobryznyski, 2006, p. A16.

2. For discussion of descriptive and prescriptive stereotypes about men and women, see Burgess and Borgida, 1999; S. T. Fiske and Stevens, 1993; Heilman, 2001. Eagly and Karau, 2002, stated similar ideas in terms of role expectations.

3. Darley and Gross, 1983. For discussion of assimilation to stereotypes, see Dunning and Sherman, 1997; S. T. Fiske, 1998; von Hippel, Sekaquaptewa, and Vargas, 1995.

4. For discussion of how gender and other stereotypes vary in the presence of additional information, see Kunda and Thagard, 1996, and Kunda and Spencer, 2003.

5. Social psychologists have examined the extent to which people correct for the effects of their stereotypical expectancies. See Blair and Banaji, 1996; P. G. Devine et al., 1991; Kunda and Sinclair, 1999; Plant and Devine, 1998. See Kunda and Spencer, 2003, for an integrative review.

6. On categorization by sex and other attributes, see A. P. Fiske, Haslam, and Fiske, 1991; Stangor et al., 1992; A. van Knippenberg, van Twuyver, and Pepels, 1994.

7. Blair and Banaji, 1996; see also Banaji, Hardin, and Rothman, 1993; Banaji and Hardin, 1996. See Fazio and Olson, 2003, for general discussion of this "priming" method.

8. See Lemm, Dabady, and Banaji, 2005.

9. For additional evidence of automaticity, see, for example, Ito and Urland, 2003. For an overview of research on automaticity and unconscious processes, including their importance in gender stereotyping, see Banaji, Lemm, and Carpenter, 2001. Gladwell provided a popular treatment in *Blink: The Power of Thinking Without Thinking*, 2005.

10. See, for example, J. E. Williams and Best, 1990. For poll data, see Newport, 2001. Many researchers have used the statistical procedure of factor analysis to show that the communal and agentic dimensions account for the majority of the meaning in gender stereotypes. Yet gender stereotypes contain other information—for example, about cognitive and physical characteristics. And, as Prentice and Miller, 2006, showed, any observed difference between a man and a woman is likely to be incorporated into beliefs about men and women in general. See Deaux and Kite, 1993, for review of research on gender stereotypes.

11. Hall and Carter (1999b) showed that behaviors are judged appropriate for one sex to the extent that they are believed to be performed more by that sex. For research on beliefs that men and women hold about their ideal selves, see W. Wood et al., 1997.

12. Prentice and Carranza, 2002.

13. Diekman and Eagly, 2000, and Spence, Helmreich, and Holahan, 1979, examined negative traits ascribed to each sex.

14. For this social role theory of the origins of gender stereotypes, see Eagly, 1987; Eagly, Wood, and Diekman, 2000. For relevant studies, see Eagly and Steffen, 1984; Koenig and Eagly, 2007.

15. Psychologists refer to this process of inferring traits from behaviors as *correspondent inference*. See Gilbert, 1998; Ross, Amabile, and Steinmetz, 1977; Schaller and O'Brien, 1992. See Gawronski, 2003, for research on the specific psychological processes underlying correspondent inference. Uleman, Newman, and Moskowitz, 1996, reviewed evidence that people spontaneously infer traits from observations of behavior.

16. Although these processes create inaccuracy in people's ideas about groups, there can be some truth to stereotypes, because, to fulfill their family and employment roles, most people acquire role-related skills. Women no doubt learn domestic skills, and men learn skills that are useful in the occupations they pursue. For evidence of the overall accuracy of gender stereotypes, see Hall and Carter, 1999a; Swim, 1994. For discussion of the accuracy of cultural stereotypes in general, see Y. Lee, Jussim, and McCauley, 1995; C. S. Ryan, 2002.

17. Cejka and Eagly, 1999; Glick, 1991.

18. For evidence that status differences between the sexes contribute to gender stereotyping, see Conway, Pizzamiglio, and Mount, 1996; Eagly, 1983; Eagly and Wood, 1982; Koenig and Eagly, 2007.

19. Heffernan, 2004, p. 37.

20. See Ridgeway and Bourg, 2004, and Ridgeway, 2006b, for theory about how inequality in everyday interaction creates widely shared beliefs about men and women. See also Berger and Fisek, 2006; Ridgeway, 2001.

21. Dasgupta and Asgari, 2004.

22. For this "women are wonderful" effect, see Eagly and Mladinic, 1994; Hosoda and Stone, 2000. On implicit measures that assess associations that come more automatically to mind, it is women who are particularly more favorable to women than men. See Rudman and Goodwin, 2004.

23. Jackman, 1994.

24. See Spencer et al., 1998, for an example of how negative states exacerbate stereotyping. See Sidanius and Pratto, 1999, for discussion of how stereotypical beliefs maintain the status quo of relationships between groups in society.

25. For research describing leader stereotypes and their effects on information processing, see Phillips and Lord, 1982; Kenney, Schwartz-Kenney, and Blascovich, 1996.

26. Gutek and Morasch, 1982, introduced the term *sex-role spillover* to capture the idea that expectations based on gender are important in the workplace. See also Ridgeway, 1997, 2001.

27. Heilman et al., 1989; Heilman, Block, and Martel, 1995.

28. For evidence that attractive women are perceived as more feminine, see Lippa, 1998b. For the workplace implications of physical appearance, see Cash, Gillen, and Burns, 1977; Heilman and Saruwatari, 1979; Sczesny and Kühnen, 2004.

29. Rich, 2001, p. 23.

30. See Miner, 1993. For other classic descriptions of managerial roles, see Mintzberg, 1979; Tornow and Pinto, 1976.

31. Such studies involve asking people to list traits or qualities of leaders and subsequently having other people rate how characteristic the most commonly named traits are of leaders. Statistical procedures involving factor analysis then reduce the traits to a smaller number by grouping the traits that have a similar meaning. See Epitropaki and Martin, 2004; Offermann, Kennedy, and Wirtz, 1994.

32. Atwater et al., 2004.

33. For review of this research, see Schein, 2001.

34. Sczesny, 2003a.

35. For replications, see Schein, 2001. Other investigators established the masculinity of leadership roles by having respondents indicate what qualities typify a "good manager." See Powell, Butterfield, and Parent, 2002.

36. Rosenwasser and Dean, 1989.

37. Weir, 1998, p. 222.

38. Ibid., p. 393.

39. Young, 1990, p. 304.

40. Carras, 1979, p. 48.

41. Warren, 2004, p. 16.

42. Silvestri, 2003, p. 95. This quote is from an interview study of thirty senior policewomen in Britain, whose ranks extended from inspector to chief officer.

43. See Phillips and Lord, 1982; Kenney, Schwartz-Kenney, and Blascovich, 1996. For evidence that stereotypes obstruct perceivers' correspondent inferences of traits inconsistent with these stereotypes, see Wigboldus, Dijksterhuis, and van Knippenberg, 2003. For the experiment on the difficulties of perceiving (i.e., encoding) female leaders' agentic behaviors as agentic, see Scott and Brown, 2006.

44. Personal communication to Alice Eagly from Harvard staffperson, April 1999.

45. Davies, Spencer, and Steele, 2005. In an additional study, assuring participants that women perform as well as men as leaders mitigated this effect on the female students.

46. Stereotype threat can undermine performance by invoking gender or racial stereotypes. For example, stereotype threat can lower women's performance in mathematics when women are reminded of men's superior math ability or are made aware of gender stereotypes. For a review, see Steele, Spencer, and Aronson, 2002. There is evidence that stereotype threat often interferes with performance by reducing working memory capacity, as shown by Schmader and Johns, 2005.

47. See Duehr and Bono, 2006, for evidence of change among male managers. Schein, 2001, found more change in the United States and Canada than in other nations. However, researchers have detected change in Germany, Australia, and India (Koch, Luft, and Kruse, 2005; Sczesny, 2003a, 2003b; Sczesny et al., 2004). Although gender stereotypes have considerable cross-cultural generality (J. E. Williams and Best, 1990), the cultural shaping of the interface between gender and leadership warrants more attention (Dorfman and House, 2004; Emrich, Denmark, and Den Hartog, 2004).

48. Hoyt and Blascovich, in press.

49. Lord et al., 2001. See also Lord and Maher, 1993. For discussion of how manager roles differ depending on their areas of responsibility within organizations, see Gomez-Mejia, McCann, and Page, 1985; Fondas, 1992; Pavett and Lau, 1983.

50. Martell et al., 1998.

51. See Huddy and Terkildsen, 1993, on political leaders. Studies of how managers at various levels perceive their work include Gomez-Mejia, McCann, and Page, 1985; Paolillo, 1981; Pavett and Lau, 1983. See also Lord and Maher, 1993; Hunt, Boal, and Sorenson, 1990.

52. Polgreen and Rohter, 2006.

53. E. S. Mann, 2005, p. 19; see also Saint-Germain, 1993, pp. 85–86; Bayard de Volo, 2000, 157.

54. Sciolino, 2006b.

55. Toner, 2007.

56. Eagly and Karau, 2002, presented this role incongruity theory of prejudice toward female leaders. See also two related theories: Heilman's "lack of fit" theory (1983) and Burgess and Borgida's theory of workplace discrimination (1999). For discussion of this role incongruity approach to understanding prejudice in general, see Eagly and Diekman, 2005.

57. A limited amount of research has used implicit measures of attitudes based on speed of association between male and female leader concepts and positive and negative words. See Rudman and Kilianski, 2000.

58. J. Carroll, 2006. The "no preference" response must be volunteered by the respondent. Male and female respondents differed somewhat, especially in terms of men's more sharply increasing tendency to

volunteer that they have no preference for one sex over the other, although women showed a clear increase in this response in 2002.

59. When people indicate whether they would prefer a male or a female boss, they may usually think about organizations in which male bosses have more-powerful positions than female bosses. Therefore, images of male and female bosses differ by more than just sex (Liden, 1985). See also Bowman, Worthy, and Greyser, 1965, and Sutton and Moore, 1985, for surveys of executives' attitudes toward women in management.

60. For willingness to vote for a female candidate, see D. W. Moore, 2003; CBS News/*New York Times*, 2006. Other polls have yielded similar results. For readiness for a female president, see CBS News/*New York Times*, 2006. Warner, 2007, provided discussion of these somewhat disparate poll results.

61. See C. Brooks and Bolzendahl, 2004, for an analysis of the causes and patterning of these attitudinal changes. See also Inglehart and Norris, 2003.

62. "George and Laura Bush: The *People* interview," 2006, p. 2.

63. On relations between race or ethnicity and gender, see Ferdman, 1999. For consideration of sexual orientation, see Ragins, Cornwell, and Miller, 2003.

64. For the relation of attitudes to behavior, see Ajzen and Fishbein, 2005.

Chapter 7

1. Carli, 2001b; Lockheed, 1985.

2. See Carli, 2006a, for a discussion of the double bind. See Driskell, Olmstead, and Salas, 1993; Holt-graves and Lasky, 1999; and Rhoads and Cialdini, 2002, for the link between competence and influence. See Carli, 1989; Cialdini, 2001; and W. Wood and Kallgren, 1988, for the link between likableness and influence.

3. Clift and Brazaitis, 2000, p. 128.

4. See Heilman and Chen, 2005, for the experimental study with graduate and undergraduate students showing different reactions to male and female helpfulness and unhelpfulness. See Allen, 2006, for the organizational study.

5. Tepper, Brown, and Hunt, 1993.

6. In an experiment, managers and other adults considered a woman less desirable to hire or work with when she asserted herself by asking for a bigger salary while applying for promotion (Bowles, Babcock, and Lei, 2007). Participants considered such women to be too demanding and not as nice as women who did not ask for more. Similarly, in job interviews simulated in an experiment with marketing and accounting executives, male job applicants showing initiative and directness were better able to persuade corporate executives to hire them (Buttner and McEnally, 1996). Female applicants obtained the jobs more often when they avoided showing the same degree of initiative and directness.

7. McBroom, 1986, p. 120.

8. See Bell and Nkomo, 2001, for the survey. On leadership by African American women and men, see Parker and ogilvie, 1996, for general discussion, and Filardo, 1996, for an empirical study. Also, in students' interracial interactions, whites expressed concern about appearing prejudiced and blacks about being targets of prejudice (J. N. Shelton and Richeson, 2006).

9. Zelechowski and Bilimoria, 2003, pp. 377–378. See Hall, Coats, and LeBeau, 2005, for examples of nonverbal dominance. For reactions to dominant and nondominant women, see Driskell, Olmstead, and Salas, 1993, and Ridgeway, 1987. For reactions to dominant and nondominant men and women, see Copeland, Driskell, and Salas, 1995; Ellyson, Dovidio, and Brown, 1992. See Bolino and Turnley, 2003, for a correlational field survey in which supervisors rated female subordinates as less likable when the subordinates acted intimidating toward their coworkers than when they didn't, but male subordinates were rated as equally likable, no matter how intimidating they were. See also Carli, 2006b, for an experiment with college students showing that women were less well liked and less influential when they disagreed openly than when they did not. Men were equally likable and influential whether or not they openly disagreed.

10. See Carli, 1999, for a discussion of factors that affect men's and women's influence. For other studies on communication style and influence, see Burgoon, Birk, and Hall, 1991; Burgoon, Dillard, and Doran, 1983; Shackelford, Wood, and Worchel, 1996. For example, in a study by Perse, Nathanson, and McLeod, 1996, university students reacted less favorably to a woman communicating in an emotional and threatening manner than in a calm and nonthreatening manner, but reactions to male speakers were unaffected by their style of speech. But see Driskell and Salas, 2005, for evidence that men are sometimes less well liked than women for dominating others.

11. Milwid, 1990, p. 47.

12. Manuel, Shefte, and Swiss, 1999, p. 9.

13. On self-promotion and likability, see Carli, 2006b; L. C. Miller et al., 1992; Giacalone and Riordan, 1990; Rudman, 1998; Wosinska et al., 1996. However, Rudman and Glick, 1999, 2001, showed that self-promoting women are rated as less communal than self-promoting men but can be rated as equally hirable for jobs requiring masculine personality traits. For effects of self-promotion on influence, see Carli, 2006b; L. C. Miller et al., 1992; Rudman, 1998.

14. Tannen, 1990, p. 224.

15. Olsson, 2006, pp. 204–205.

16. See Heilman and Okimoto, 2007, for evidence that agentic women in masculine domains are thought to lack communion. For reactions to agentic female athletes, see Souchon et al., 2004. Referees penalized female handball players for violations involving aggressive contact more than male handball players.

17. See experiments by Yoder and Schleicher, 1996, for reactions to female engineers and electricians, and Heilman, Block, and Martell, 1995, and Heilman et al., 2004, for reactions to female managers.

18. Manuel, Shefte, and Swiss, 1999, p. 8.

19. Such findings emerged in Eagly, Makhijani, and Klonsky, 1992, a meta-analysis of evaluations of leaders who manifested masculine versus feminine styles. See also chapter 4.

20. Quotes are from Hollands, 2002, p. xii and p. xi.

21. A. Fisher, 2006.

22. See Carli, 2004, for male reactions to female competence and authority.

23. Meyerson and Fletcher, 2000, p. 129.

24. Auletta, 1998, p. 77.

25. See Carli, 1990, for tentative speech. See also Matschiner and Murnen, 1999.

26. Troemel-Ploetz, 1994, p. 201.

27. For example, see Foschi, Lai, and Sigerson, 1994; Uhlmann and Cohen, 2005. See also Gill, 2004, for evidence that men's endorsement of prescriptive stereotypes is associated with their negative reaction to women applying for masculine jobs.

28. Hudson, 2001, p. 121.

29. Dean, 2005, p. F3.

30. For effects of minority and majority status on influence, see experiments by Craig and Sherif, 1986, on a masculine task, and Taps and Martin, 1990, on a gender-neutral task. See also Izraeli, 1983, 1984, for surveys of male and female officers on committees of trade unions: female officers reported less influence when in the minority than the majority, and less influence than men in the minority. Being in the minority can be beneficial to men because they stand out in the group and as a result receive more attention and exert a disproportionate amount of influence. However, Chatman et al., 2005, found that being in the minority can also undermine male influence, but only when the task is feminine. See also Yoder, 2002, for a review of reactions to token men and women.

31. U.S. Equal Employment Opportunity Commission, 2006. In addition to the more overt quid pro quo forms of harassment, where job benefits are contingent on providing sex, sexual harassment can include less-extreme behaviors, such as being repeatedly assailed with sexist humor, jokes, pornography or other sexual material, requests for dates, or inappropriate touching. Most incidents of sexual harassment are milder than quid pro quo harassment (see Ilies et al., 2003). For discussion of how women and men perceive and label harassing behaviors, see Magley et al., 1999; Munson, Miner, and Hulin, 2001; Rotundo, Nguyen, and Sackett, 2001.

32. See meta-analysis by Ilies et al., 2003. Berdahl and Moore, 2006, found that women of color experienced the same amount of sexual harassment as white women but also experienced ethnic harassment.

33. See M. A. Bond et al., 2004, and Gutek, 2001, for evidence of the gender of the perpetrators and victims of sexual harassment. In the most recent large-scale representative survey of federal employees, 44 percent of women and 19 percent of men reported that they had been harassed; men were the perpetrators in virtually all of the cases directed at women and one-fourth of the cases directed at men (U.S. Merit Systems Protection Board, 1995).

34. See Gruber, 1998; R. A. Jackson and Newman, 2004; Newman, Jackson, and Baker, 2003; and Uggen and Blackstone, 2004, for effects of education and supervisory position. See Berdahl and Moore, 2006; Gruber, 1998; Fitzgerald et al., 1997; Jackson and Newman, 2004; U.S. Merit Systems Protection Board, 1995; and Welsh, 1999, for masculine and male-dominated organizations. See also Pryor, 1987, and Pryor,

LaVite, and Stoller, 1993, for experimental studies showing relations between male authority and harassment. In general, men who sexually harass women tend to be aggressive and hypermasculine (Bargh et al., 1995; Pryor, Giedd, and Williams, 1995; Pryor and Stoller, 1994).

35. For experimental evidence, see Maass et al., 2003, for effects of expertise in a masculine domain, and Dall'Ara and Maass, 1999, and Maass et al., 2003, for research on feminist women and threats to masculinity.

36. "A surgeon cuts to the heart of the matter," 1991, p. 50.

37. For effects of sexual harassment, see Pryor, 1995, for research on military women; Murrell, Olson, and Frieze, 1995, for research on MBAs; K. T. Schneider, Swan, and Fitzgerald, 1997, for research on women in private sector and academic jobs; and Lim and Cortina, 2005, for research on women in public sector positions in the court system. Sexual harassment reduces motivation, impairs performance, increases stress, lowers feelings of well-being and satisfaction, and increases the likelihood of quitting one's job. Individuals do not have to recognize that they were harassed to experience those costs. Whether or not women labeled their experience as harassment, women from a wide variety of organizational settings reported the same emotional, physical, and career-related costs from sexual harassment (Magley et al., 1999; Munson, Miner, and Hulin, 2001). For research on reporting and other reactions to harassment, see U.S. Merit Systems Protection Board, 1995. See also Bergman et al., 2002, and Cortina and Wasti, 2005, who found similar coping styles among white American, Hispanic American, and Turkish women.

38. For example, see Adams-Roy and Barling, 1998; Bergman et al., 2002; Stockdale, 1998. A survey by the U.S. Merit Systems Protection Board, 1995, found that respondents who confronted or reported the harasser felt that doing so made things better. However, Stockdale's analysis of the same data (1998) revealed that the more that federal employees confronted the harasser, the worse they fared, experiencing increases in sick and unpaid leaves of absence, poorer job conditions, fewer promotions, and a greater likelihood of being fired, transferred, or quitting.

39. See Sims, Drasgow, and Fitzgerald, 2005, for example, for effects on job satisfaction and turnover. Sometimes sexual banter in the workplace is welcomed by both women and men. For discussion of consensual sexual behaviors in work settings, see C. L. Williams, Giuffre, and Dellinger, 1999.

40. Fiorina, 2006, p. 173.

41. For leadership research, see Eagly, Makhijani, and Klonsky, 1992. For influence research, see Carli, LaFleur, and Loeber, 1995; DiBerardinis, Ramage, and Levitt, 1984; J. Schneider and Cook, 1995; Wagner, Ford, and Ford, 1986.

42. Hudson, 2001, p. 121.

43. Because men have higher overall societal status (see chapter 6), people give them more opportunities to express their opinions. As a result, men more often contribute suggestions and opinions, direct the interaction, and obtain the support of others. Such behaviors further increase men's status and emergence as leaders. See James and Drakich, 1993, for speaking; Carli and Olm-Shipman, 2004, and L. R. Anderson and Blanchard, 1982, for task contributions.

44. Swiss, 1996, p. 17.

45. Propp, 1995. See also Thomas-Hunt and Phillips, 2004, who found that group members perceived female experts as having less ability than male experts, despite their objective equality, and that male experts exerted more influence over decisions than female experts did.

46. Lillie, 2003, p. 104.

47. Troemel-Ploetz, 1994, p. 206.

48. Davison and Burke, 2000. Experiments not included in this review continue to show the same pattern of male advantage in hiring, except in traditionally feminine domains. See, for example, Steinpreis, Anders, and Ritzke, 1999.

49. Heilman and Blader, 2001.

50. See Boldry, Wood, and Kashy, 2001, for the cadet study, and Foschi, 1996, 2000, and Heilman, 2001, for further evidence of higher standards applied to women. A double standard exists not only for evaluating women in comparison to men but also for evaluating mothers in comparison to fathers (Correll, Benard, and Paik, 2007; Cuddy, Fiske, and Glick, 2004; Fuegen et al., 2004).

51. *Price Waterhouse v. Hopkins*, 1989, p. 9. The quoted material comes from the court case, which ultimately was won by Hopkins. See S. T. Fiske et al., 1991, for discussion. Consistent with our double bind analysis, the complaints against Hopkins alleged that she failed to conform to norms of femininity.

52. Uhlmann and Cohen, 2005. See Foschi, Sigerson, and Lembesis, 1995, for an experiment showing that women can overcome the double standard in traditionally masculine jobs by demonstrating their clear superiority to men.

53. Thomas-Hunt and Phillips, 2004. In this study, mixed groups of men and women were given the relatively masculine task of deciding how to survive a wildfire. The researchers identified an expert in each group—a participant whose ideas surpassed those of the rest of the group. About half the time the expert was a woman. After the discussion, when group members rated each other's expertise, they rated female experts as having *less* expertise than female nonexperts, but rated the male experts and nonexperts equally. See also Littlepage, Robison, and Reddington, 1997.

54. Harmon, 2006.

55. Davison and Burke, 2000.

56. For example, see Gerrard, Breda, and Gibbons, 1990; Falbo, Hazen, and Linimon, 1982; Feldman-Summers et al., 1980.

57. Coleman, 2001, p. 162.

58. For an overview, see Biernat, 2003.

59. National Center for Health Statistics, 2006. See Biernat, Manis, and Nelson, 1991, for experiments on height judgments.

60. Biernat et al., 1998. In these two studies, some of these shifting standards effects differed depending on the race of the officers and the point in time when they were evaluated. See also Biernat and Vescio, 2002, for evidence of shifting standards in athletics.

61. For experimental evidence, see Shackelford, Wood, and Worchel, 1996; Wagner, Ford, and Ford, 1986; W. Wood and Karten, 1986.

62. Heilman, Martell, and Simon, 1988. Whether these findings reflect shifts to within-sex standards has yet to be evaluated. See Biernat, 2003.

63. See Biernat and Kobrynowicz, 1997, for evidence that black men are subject to shifting standards when applying for an executive position.

64. Bell and Nkomo, 2001, pp. 145–146.

65. A higher percentage of women of color than white women reported the need to work harder than their male counterparts (Manuel, Shefte, and Swiss, 1999).

66. Canady, 2001, p. 168.

67. See Biernat, 2003.

68. Meyerson and Fletcher, 2000, p. 129.

69. Lyness and Thompson, 2000.

70. Swiss, 1996, p. 57.

71. Conlin, 2002. In support of Conlin's observations, women have softer communication styles and talk less than men in more formal settings. See review in Knapp and Hall, 2002. For additional discussion of the effects of gender and power on communication styles, see chapters in Dindia and Canary, 2006.

72. J. C. Collins, 2001. Whether CEO charisma fosters more-successful organizations is in doubt because causation can be the reverse; that is, good organizational performance can foster the perception that a CEO is charismatic. See Agle et al., 2006.

73. See Eagly and Karau, 2002, for review of these context effects in the qualities thought to be necessary for leadership.

Chapter 8

1. For general discussion of leadership style, see Bass, 1990; Howell and Costley, 2006; Yukl, 2006.

2. Steinberg, 2003, p. A1. See also Mnookin, 2004.

3. Finder, Healy, and Zernike, 2006; Rimer, 2005. See also Bradley, 2005, for general discussion of Summers' management style.

4. See D. T. Miller, Taylor, and Buck, 1991, for discussion of this principle and relevant empirical data. See also Pratto, Korchmaros, and Hegarty, 2007, for explanation of why people often designate atypical race and gender features of individuals.

5. See, for example, a novel by Pearson, 2002, about a manager who is a mother, titled *I don't know how she does it: The life of Kate Reddy, working mother.*

6. Truell, 1996, p. D1. La Roche is president and CEO of Salisbury Pharmacy Group.

7. Fiorina, 2006, p. 173.

8. Schroeder, 1999, p. A17.

9. For description of media coverage of the Dole campaign, see Heldman, Carroll, and Olson, 2005.

10. For discussion of the cultural and scholarly debates on sex differences and similarities, see Kimball, 1995.

11. Helgesen, 1990, offered a "web of inclusion" metaphor that characterized women leaders as leveling workplace hierarchies, collaborating with employees, and connecting in a personal way with clients and customers. Helgesen and feminist organizational theorists such as Ely and Meyerson, 2000, have argued that women's distinctive leadership styles are especially effective. Kark, 2004, reviewed a wide range of feminist perspectives on leadership style. For earlier statements, see Loden, 1985; Sargent, 1981.

12. Rosener, 1990, p. 120. These provocative conclusions prompted an exchange in the *Harvard Business Review* between various experts who disagreed or agreed with her claims. See Fuchs Epstein et al., 1991. See also Rosener's subsequent book (1995).

13. In contrast, to produce a quantitative analysis, such responses would be coded according to a set of rules developed by the researchers. Two coders would work independently, and their codings would be compared to establish their reliability. These procedures ensure that there is agreement about the meaning of the responses.

14. Bass, 1981, p. 499.

15. Powell, 1990. Powell's views changed in response to the newer research that we present in this chapter (for example, Powell and Graves, 2003, 2006). For other "no difference" views, see Kanter, 1977; Morrison and von Glinow, 1990; Nieva and Gutek, 1981; van Engen, van der Leeden, and Willemsen, 2001. Also, a 1986 meta-analysis by Dobbins and Platz claimed an absence of sex differences in leaders' style and effectiveness. However, 41 percent of the included studies had deliberately ensured that male and female behavior would be identical by artificially holding it constant in experiments. See Eagly and Carli, 2003a, 2003b, for further discussion of this meta-analysis. See also Vecchio, 2002.

16. For example, Kanter, 1977; Nieva and Gutek, 1981; van Engen, van der Leeden, and Willemsen, 2001.

17. See Bauer, Morrison, and Callister, 1998, and Moreland and Levine, 2001, for discussion of organizational socialization.

18. Cheng, 1998.

19. Manuel, Shefte, and Swiss, 1999, p. 8. For evidence of this stereotyping by U.S. business leaders, see Catalyst, 2005b.

20. Manuel, Shefte, and Swiss, 1999, conducted the study of executives, which lacked a comparison group of men. For a related study, see Lauterbach and Weiner, 1996. See Ely, 1995, for an elaboration of this argument about self-concepts. For general discussion of the implications of women's and men's self-concepts, see Cross and Madson, 1997; Deaux and Major, 1987; Gardner and Gabriel, 2004; W. Wood et al., 1997.

21. Catalyst, 2001. Similar findings emerged in Catalyst surveys in Canada and the United Kingdom. See also Ragins, Townsend, and Mattis, 1998.

22. Sciolino, 2006a.

23. Moskowitz, Suh, and Desaulniers, 1994. In this study, employees reported on their interpersonal behavior for twenty days at various times during the workday. Similar patterns are apparent in physicians' interactions with their patients: female physicians are more likely than male physicians to display communal behaviors, including more friendly talk, more smiling and nodding, more questioning of patients, and more psychosocial counseling. However, male and female physicians do not differ in their medical advice. See meta-analyses by Roter, Hall, and Aoki, 2002, and Roter and Hall, 2004.

24. For example, see Borman, 2004, and Podsakoff et al., 2000, for descriptions of *organizational citizenship behavior*, which involves going beyond the requirements of one's organizational role. Examples of such behavior include helping others with their work and volunteering for work that is not part of one's job.

25. Bales, 1950, introduced this task versus interpersonal distinction in the 1940s in his studies of small groups. Later researchers, such as Hemphill and Coons, 1957, referred to task-oriented behaviors as *initiation of structure*, and interpersonally oriented behaviors as *consideration*. In a related tradition, Likert, 1961, and other researchers identified employee-centered leadership and production-centered leadership. Also, Fiedler, 1967, distinguished between task-oriented and interpersonally oriented leaders, considered as two ends of a single continuum.

26. Judge, Piccolo, and Ilies, 2004, produced a meta-analysis of leadership style research that supported these generalizations. For related meta-analytic findings pertaining only to leadership in teams, see C. S. Burke et al., 2006.

27. Eagly and Johnson, 1990, based these conclusions on 139 comparisons of men and women.

28. These nonmanagers consisted of students and nonmanagerial employees, depending on the study. See also van Engen and Willemsen, 2004, for related findings encompassing studies appearing after Eagly and Johnson's search (1990).

29. Also, Gardiner and Tiggemann's study of Australian managers (1999) found that the men and women did not differ in their interpersonal orientation in male-dominated industries, but in female-dominated industries the women were more interpersonally oriented than the men.

30. McBroom, 1986, p. 72.

31. This finding was based on ratings of how traditionally masculine or feminine leaders' roles were (see Eagly and Johnson, 1990). Also, a small tendency for men to be more task-oriented than women did appear among nonmanagers—that is, in experimental studies and studies of nonmanagerial employees and business school students. As with the findings for interpersonal orientation, the managerial role appeared to reduce this stereotypical sex difference in task orientation.

32. These aspects of style first captured researchers' attention in the 1930s in research by Lewin, Lippitt, and White, 1939, and continued to receive attention in organizational and small-group studies (e.g., Vroom and Yetton, 1973).

33. For reviews of the effectiveness of autocratic and democratic leadership, see Foels et al., 2000; Gastil, 1994. For discussion of factors that affect the outcomes of these aspects of leadership, see Ayman, 2004; Yukl, 2006. Van Vugt et al., 2004, showed that autocratic leadership fosters group members exiting their group. However, subordinates' dissatisfaction with autocratic leadership would not necessarily lower productivity. Although there is a positive relationship between job satisfaction and job performance (Judge et al., 2001), job satisfaction is a much broader variable than satisfaction with one's boss.

34. Schmid Mast, 2004, demonstrated that stereotypically men are associated with hierarchies and women with egalitarian structures. See Berdahl and Anderson, 2005, for a study of student groups showing less hierarchy when women are in the majority in groups, and Schmid Mast, 2001, for evidence that all-male groups formed hierarchical structures more quickly than all-female groups.

35. Feminist writers have often critiqued hierarchical arrangements, in which women generally end up in less powerful roles. See review of feminist writing on leadership and group structure by Bartunek, Walsh, and Lacey, 2000; see also Acker, 1995; P. Y. Martin, 1990; Reinelt, 1994; Riger, 1994. Therefore, it is not surprising that Chin's (2004) study of feminist psychologists found that almost all answered the question "How do feminist women lead?" by describing collaborative styles.

36. See, for example, Jago and Vroom, 1982.

37. The quotation is from a study of female leaders by Astin and Leland, 1991, p. 115.

38. This difference was based on twenty-three studies and various measures of these leadership styles (Eagly and Johnson, 1990). Van Engen and Willemsen, 2004, produced similar findings in a meta-analysis of studies from the 1990s.

39. Cave, 2006, p. B10. For the study of committee chairs, see Kathlene, 1994, p. 561.

40. See Barth and Ferguson, 2002, for discussion of governors' inaugural addresses and p. 75 for the Shaheen statement. Yet female governors, like male governors, also included conventionally top-down expressions of leadership.

41. Personal communication to Alice Eagly, September 2005.

42. The quotation is from Langewiesche, 2003, who analyzed the causes of the *Columbia* disaster.

43. See Fletcher, 2004, for discussion of postheroic leadership.

44. Burns, 1978.

45. Bass, 1985, 1998. See also Avolio, 1999. Some of these same qualities are reflected in Conger and Kanungo's concept of *charismatic leadership* (1998) and political scientist C. S. Rosenthal's concept of *integrative leadership* (1998). Also, Rosenthal's contrasting leadership style, named *aggressive leadership*, emphasizes bargaining and brokered exchanges and bears more than a passing resemblance to transactional leadership.

46. Beatty, 2004, p. B1.

47. For discussion and validation of this nine subscale model, see Antonakis, Avolio, and Sivasubramaniam, 2003; Avolio, Bass, and Jung, 1999.

48. See Judge and Piccolo's meta-analysis (2004) of eighty-seven studies and earlier meta-analysis by Lowe, Kroeck, and Sivasubramaniam, 1996. Measures of effectiveness were varied and included group and organizational performance, leader job performance, and ratings of effectiveness. Additional research has revealed some of the reasons for the positive effects of transformational leadership, including its link to followers' positive organizational citizenship behaviors (Purvanova, Bono, and Dzieweczynski, 2006) and transformational leaders' centrality in networks of influence (Bono and Anderson, 2005).

49. Eagly, Johannesen-Schmidt, and van Engen, 2003. The meta-analysis summarized forty-five studies, many from business and educational organizations; 53 percent of the studies reported U.S. data, and 47 percent reported data from other nations or global samples. The managers assessed had a mean age of

forty-five and held positions at differing managerial levels. Managers' styles were assessed by subordinates, superiors, peers, or the managers themselves. Corroborating the results of this meta-analysis, Antonakis, Avolio, and Sivasubramaniam, 2003, produced similar findings in a large-scale study primarily of business managers. See also C. S. Rosenthal's study (1998) of committee chairs in state legislatures.

50. Eagly, Johannesen-Schmidt, and van Engen, 2003, argued that these results are not due to artifacts such as a bias concerning which studies get published or a tendency of female and male managers to occupy different roles. Researchers have also found women higher than men on charismatic leadership, which encompasses some of the qualities that make up transformational leadership (Groves, 2005).

51. See Yoder, 2001, for this argument. Also see Hackman et al., 1992, for evidence of the cultural femininity of the individualized consideration aspect of transformational leadership. See also Vinkenburg et al., 2007, for evidence that women are perceived to emphasize transformational and contingent reward leadership more than men.

52. On the failure to reward women's considerate, relational behaviors, see Fletcher, 1999, 2004. On the perceived relevance of such behavior for promotion to higher ranks, see Vinkenburg et al., 2007.

53. D. P. Moore and Buttner, 1997, p. 108.

54. A global study of sixty-two cultures reported men's and women's preferences for different types of leaders. In general, women showed stronger preferences for participative and charismatic styles than men, especially in cultures that were more egalitarian regarding gender. See House et al., 2004; Paris et al., 2007. For general discussion of cultural influences on organizational leadership, see Dorfman and House, 2004.

55. See, for example, LaFrance, Paluck, and Brescoll, 2004, on the desirability of studying gender along with other characteristics such as race.

56. Parker and ogilvie, 1996.

57. For discussion of Asian American culture in relation to management, see Woo and Khoo, 2006. Quotations appear on p. 87.

58. Anders, 2005, p. A8. See also R. M. Kramer, 2006.

59. See D. Collins, 1997, for discussion of this issue.

60. Rich, 2004, section 2, p. 1.

61. A national survey by Silver et al., 2002, demonstrated these fearful reactions after 9/11. Weber, 1968/1925, argued that in situations of widespread distress, citizens are attracted to the radical visions of charismatic leaders.

62. F. Cohen et al., 2004. These effects are relative to a control condition in which participants contemplated their next important exam. See also Landau et al., 2004, for experiments showing that reminders of one's mortality and of 9/11 increased support for President Bush.

63. Lawless, 2004, examined gender stereotyping of political leaders in the post–9/11 world. See J. M. Jones, 2005b, for survey data showing that Americans think that a male president would be better qualified to handle national security issues and a female president to handle domestic policy issues.

64. Lizza, 2007, Week in Review, p. 1.

65. See Wajcman's study (1998) of British managers for discussion of leadership style and evidence of the similarity of the leadership styles of female and male senior managers.

66. Also relevant to the leadership styles of men and women are studies by management consultant groups that are sometimes reported in online summaries or excerpted in business publications. For example, Caliper, a global management consultant group, announced a study based on its proprietary battery of personality traits and leadership abilities. Such studies are difficult to evaluate because they are unpublished and may not take into account various potential confounding variables. In addition, it is unknown whether the measures used in these studies are valid or reliable. See Aurora and Caliper, 2005; Caliper, 2005.

67. The quotation is from Woopidoo!, 2006b.

68. For elaborations on the importance of small effects, see Abelson, 1985; Bushman and Anderson, 2001; and R. Rosenthal, 1990. For a cogent statement of the view that small sex differences become inappropriately exaggerated by observers, see Hyde, 2005.

69. Rosnow and Rosenthal, 1989. The relation between taking aspirin and preventing heart attacks is expressed by a correlation of 0.03 (equivalent to a d effect size of 0.06).

70. See Hall and Carter, 1999a, and Swim, 1994, for demonstrations of the overall accuracy of beliefs about women and men.

71. See, for example, Lipman-Blumen, 1996.

72. Sokolove, 2006, p. 98.

73. Fuller, 2007, section 1, p. 19.

Chapter 9

1. Although this analysis often refers to organizational norms and practices, related processes can occur in smaller units such as groups or teams and in larger units such as governments and nations.

2. For wide-ranging discussions of organizational factors relevant to the advancement of women as leaders, see Ely, Scully, and Foldy, 2003; Powell and Graves, 2003, 2006; Ragins and Sundstrom, 1989; Reskin and McBrier, 2000.

3. Hull and Nelson, 2000. The sample consisted of 788 randomly sampled lawyers practicing in Chicago in 1995. See also Noonan and Corcoran, 2004, for a study of differences in the promotion of men and women to partnership among University of Michigan Law School graduates.

4. Kay and Hagan, 1998, p. 741. This study was based on a sample of 905 Canadian lawyers in firm practice. See also Kay and Hagan, 1999; Spurr, 1990.

5. See P. Y. Martin, 2003, for observations of similar corporate work patterns that disadvantage women.

6. J. Williams, 2000, provided extensive analysis of ideal worker norms. See also Acker, 1990.

7. Coser, 1974; see also Maier, 1999.

8. Milwid, 1990, p. 194.

9. J. Schor, 1991. For dissent with Schor, see Rones, Ilg, and Gardner, 1997.

10. J. A. Jacobs and Gerson, 2004. In analyzing U.S. men's hours and wages, Kuhn and Lozano, 2005, found that the escalation of hours worked in recent decades has been concentrated in highly educated, high-wage, salaried older men and reflects increases in marginal wage incentives to supply work hours beyond the normative forty.

11. Stone and Lovejoy, 2004, p. 68.

12. Naff, 1994, p. 511.

13. Rapoport et al., 2002, provided an insightful analysis of this aspect of managerial careers. In a survey of MBA graduates, Brett and Stroh, 2003, documented managers' long hours and outlined some of the causes of this pattern.

14. See Hewlett, 2002, for a survey of high-achieving women. See Judge et al., 1995, for predictors of executives' career success. See also Brett and Stroh, 2003.

15. Brady and Salvatore, 2005, p. 153.

16. Among the younger cohort of women surveyed by Hewlett, 2002, only 45 percent had a child by age thirty-five. For related studies, see Catalyst, 2003; Fagenson and Jackson, 1994; Goldin, 1997; Swiss, 1996.

17. Personal communication to Alice Eagly, September 2005.

18. Naff, 1994, p. 511.

19. See, for example, Armstrong-Stassen, 2005, for effects on stress, and McElroy, Morrow, and Rude, 2001, for effects on performance.

20. Bailyn, 2002, p. 266. See also Meyerson and Fletcher, 2000.

21. For discussion of the Sears discrimination case, see Nelson and Bridges, 1999.

22. Nelson and Bridges, 1999.

23. See Wajcman, 1998, for discussion of long hours and relocation demands in a British managerial context. See also Hewlett and Luce, 2005.

24. M. Miller, 2005, p. A25.

25. See Putnam's book, *Bowling Alone* (2000), which provides extensive discussion of social capital. For the implications of social capital in organizations, see Brass, 2001.

26. See Burt, 1992; Seibert, Kraimer, and Liden, 2001.

27. Luthans, 1988, p. 130. For this study, see Luthans, Hodgetts, and Rosenkrantz, 1988. See also Ellemers, de Gilder, and van den Heuvel, 1998, for distinctions between three types of work commitment: career oriented, team oriented, and organizational.

28. Driscoll and Goldberg, 1993, p. 145.

29. Manuel, Shefte, and Swiss, 1999, p. 11; see Ragins, Townsend, and Mattis, 1998, for similar data.

30. Heffernan, 2004, p. 62. For general discussion of gender and social capital, see Tharenou, 1999; Timberlake, 2005.

31. See G. Moore, 1988, for evidence that women are excluded from powerful networks, and G. Moore, 1990, for evidence that women have smaller job networks than men. See also Davies-Netzley, 1998.

32. Roth, 2006, p. 85.

33. Steel, 1993, p. 133.

34. Ibarra, 1997, p. 97.

35. For research supporting these generalizations about women's networks, see Brass, 1985; Burt, 1998; Forret and Dougherty, 2004; Ibarra, 1997.

36. Catalyst, 2006a.

37. Lyness and Thompson, 2000.

38. Manuel, Shefte, and Swiss, 1999, p. 9.

39. See Alvesson and Billing, 1992, for discussion of gender and organizational culture.

40. Heffernan, 2002.

41. Antilla, 2004.

42. McLean and Elkind, 2004, pp. 55–56.

43. McLean and Elkind, 2004, unnumbered photographic section appearing after p. 200.

44. Featherstone, 2004. Hooters restaurants, designed for male customers, emphasize the sex appeal of scantily clad female servers, called Hooters girls.

45. Silvestri, 2003, p. 129.

46. See van Vianen and Fischer, 2002, for evidence of greater preference for masculine culture among men than women.

47. Steel, 1993, p. 141.

48. See Kelleher, Finestone, and Lowy, 1986; M. W. McCall, Lombardo, and Morrison, 1988; Morrison, 1992.

49. For discussion of the importance of challenging work experiences to managerial development, see M. W. McCall, Lombardo, and Morrison, 1988; McCauley et al., 1994.

50. Lyness and Thompson, 2000. Other studies showing similar effects include de Pater and Van Vianen, 2006; Ohlott, Ruderman, and McCauley, 1994.

51. See de Pater, 2005, for studies giving some evidence that women may choose or accept less-challenging work, and de Pater and van Vianen, 2006, for evidence that supervisors assign women less-challenging work. For discussion of the sexism that could underlie such supervisor behavior, see Glick and Fiske, 1996, 2001a, 2001b.

52. Erkut, 2001, p. 26.

53. Frankel, 2004, pp. 24–25.

54. Personal communication to Alice Eagly, March 2004.

55. Galinsky et al., 2003; Ibarra, 1997; Nadis, 1999.

56. Committee of 200, 2002, p. 11.

57. See Ragins and Sundstrom, 1989, for further discussion of this point; and Lyness and Heilman, 2006, for empirical evidence.

58. Tharenou, 1999. However, among MBA graduates, changing one's employer appears to increase compensation only for white men and not for white women or minority men or women (Brett and Stroh, 1997; Dreher and Cox, 2000).

59. Deutsch, 2005.

60. M. K. Ryan and Haslam, 2005a, 2005b, 2007. These researchers have documented this glass cliff phenomenon in controlled experiments as well as studies of organizations.

61. For discussion of the barriers that prevent women from achieving elective political office, see Fox and Lawless, 2004.

62. See Nelson and Bridges, 1999, for analysis of wage setting in organizations. Consideration of job evaluation and affirmative action is beyond the scope of this book. For review of job evaluation and comparable worth, see England, 1992. For review of affirmative action, see Crosby, 2004; Crosby, Iyer, and Sincharoen, 2006; Harper and Reskin, 2005.

63. See Nelson and Bridges, 1999, for evidence that litigation has proven to be decreasingly effective for remedying organizational discrimination.

64. F. N. Schwartz, 1989.

65. "Why not many mommy tracks?" 1989, p. A18.

66. F. N. Schwartz and Zimmerman, 1992, elaborated Schwartz's proposals in their book, *Breaking With Tradition: Women and Work, the New Facts of Life.*

67. See survey reported by Baker, 2002, tables 2 and 3. For example, in law, 12 percent of the women and 4 percent of the men were out of the labor force. The great majority of women as well as men remained employed in all these professional fields. See also Hewlett and Luce, 2005.

68. See, for example, Crittenden, 2004; Hewlett, 2002; Hewlett and Luce, 2005; J. Williams, 2000. Lawrence and Corwin, 2003, discuss integrating part-time professionals into organizations.

69. Dreher, 2003.

70. See Wax, 2004, for discussion of firms' potential to adopt and maintain family-friendly reforms. See also Crosby, Iyer, and Sincharoen, 2006; Kossek and Lee, 2005; Roehling, Roehling, and Moen, 2001. Osterman, 1995, presented data on the prevalence of various work–family options in private sector establishments. Flexitime was most common, and childcare options such as on-site childcare were relatively rare.

71. For a cross-national study suggesting that mother-friendly employment policies exacerbate occupational gender inequality, see Mandel and Semyonov, 2005. See also D. Gupta, Oaxaca, and Smith, 2006.

72. For discussion, see Meyerson and Fletcher, 2000; Rapoport et al., 2002. See also Brett and Stroh, 2003.

73. Reskin and McBrier, 2000. See also Bernardin et al., 1998; Gelfand et al., 2005.

74. For the implications of this *similarity-attraction principle* to organizational issues, see Byrne and Neuman, 1992.

75. For an empirical demonstration of such in-group preference, see Elliott and Smith, 2004. See also Chambliss and Uggen, 2000, and Gorman, 2005, for evidence that male decision makers in law firms fill fewer openings by hiring women than female decision makers do. For research on supervisors' evaluations, see, for example, S. J. Wayne and Liden, 1995. For a broader discussion of demographic homogeneity in social networks, see McPherson, Smith-Lovin, and Cook, 2001.

76. Kanter, 1977. For empirical evidence, see Konrad and Pfeffer, 1991. But see Graves and Powell, 1996, for a study of recruiters at a university campus showing that female recruiters favored women as job candidates and male recruiters manifested no bias. Powell, 1999, provided some general review of these issues.

77. *Betty Dukes et al. v. Wal-Mart Stores, Inc.*, 2003a, p. 21.

78. See S. T. Fiske and Stevens, 1993; Goodwin and Fiske, 2001. For a general discussion of the effects of social power on information processing and affect, see Keltner, Gruenfeld, and Anderson, 2003.

79. See Goodwin and Fiske, 2001; Rudman, 1998; and Shackelford, Wood, and Worchel, 1996, for experimental evidence that people's outcomes can be constrained in ways that foster less stereotyping and greater equity in decision making.

80. Kalev, Dobbin, and Kelly, 2006.

81. Ishida, Su, and Spilerman, 2002.

82. J. S. Goodman, Fields, and Blum, 2003, reported data consistent with this principle in a study of 228 private sector establishments in Georgia.

83. Beliefs that an individual was hired or promoted to fulfill affirmative action or diversity goals can increase the perception that the individual lacks competence. See Heilman, 1996.

84. Lucas, 2003. This experiment had undergraduate research participants. See also Yoder, Schleicher, and McDonald, 1998.

85. Graham, 1997, p. 420.

86. Heffernan, 2004, p. 28. See Kanter, 1977, for discussion of stereotypical female work roles.

87. For discussion, see Elsass and Graves, 1997; Kanter, 1977; Reskin, McBrier, and Kmec, 1999; Yoder, 2002. See Taylor and Fiske, 1978, for experimental evidence. See also Ely, 1995, for evidence that gender is construed more traditionally in organizations with few senior women, and Bell and Nkomo, 2001, for evidence of different stereotypical roles applied to black women than white women.

88. V. W. Kramer, Konrad, and Erkut, 2006.

89. Brancato and Patterson, 1999, p. 7.

90. Not all experts agree with this view. See, for example, Fletcher, 2004; R. M. Kramer, 2006; Wajcman, 1998, for alternative claims.

91. Gergen, 2005, p. xxi.

92. Murray, 2007, p. A3.

93. Tischler, 2005.

94. For such claims about changes in managerial roles, see Kanter, 1997; Lipman-Blumen, 1996. Also, see A. Martin, 2005, for evidence that managers expect leadership to change even more in these directions. For typical views of managerial experts, see Avolio, 1999; Garvin, 1993; Juran, 1988. See also Fondas, 1997, for analysis of themes in several popular management books.

95. Finder, Healy, and Zernike, 2006. Waters made this statement in reaction to the resignation of Lawrence Summers as president of Harvard University.

96. Sokolove, 2006.

97. Ibid., p. 96.

98. Alsop, 2005, p. R5.

99. See Meyerson and Fletcher, 2000. Also, Madden, 2005, discussed the importance of managers' active agency in promoting change.

Chapter 10

1. White, 1995.
2. Mendell, 1996, p. 69.
3. Salmansohn, 1996, p. 161.
4. Crittenden, 2004, p. 192. For a similar emphasis on mothering, see Grzelakowski, 2005.
5. McBroom, 1986, p. 169.
6. Milwid, 1990, pp. 142–143.
7. Abzug, 1996.
8. Steel, 1993, p. 125.
9. Wellington, 2001, pp. 47–48.
10. J. C. Collins, 2001.
11. See Carli, LaFleur, and Loeber, 1995. In this experiment with undergraduates, men were less influenced by a female speaker and liked her less when she spoke in a competent manner (using fluent, articulate, and fairly rapid speech) than a competent plus warm manner (adding smiling and nodding to such speech). See also Heilman and Okimoto, 2007, for additional evidence that female managers are better liked and receive more-favorable evaluations when they show competence combined with caring and concern. In both studies, men received similar ratings, regardless of their behavior. See also Flynn and Ames, 2006, for evidence that women who monitor their behavior and alter it in response to men's reactions influence the men more than women who do not.
12. Toner, 2007, p. A14. In an ABC News/*Washington Post* poll (2006), 68 percent of those surveyed considered Hillary Clinton to be a strong leader, a higher percentage than those who rated her as friendly and open.
13. For research on influence, see Ridgeway, 1982; Shackelford, Wood, and Worchel, 1996. Burgoon, Birk, and Hall, 1991, for example, found that female physicians were considered more effective in influencing patients when expressing concern for the patient, and male physicians could be directive and still be influential. See also Carli, 1999, for a discussion of women's use of interpersonal forms of power to exert influence.
14. Deutsch, 2002, section 3, pp. 1, 12.
15. Oprah Winfrey as quoted by Woopidoo!, 2006a.
16. Davenport, 2003, pp. 113–114.
17. Sellers, 2006a, p. 61.
18. Steel, 1993, p. 280.
19. Myers, 2005, and Tarsala, 2003.
20. Timmons, 2006, p. C10.
21. Cardwell, 2006, p. A16.
22. Benoit, 2006. The businessman in question, however, denied these comments in a later letter to the editor, perhaps reflecting that some observers were overly eager to find Merkel insufficiently assertive. See Mehdorn, 2006.
23. Atwood, 2006.
24. Swiss, 1996, p. 59.
25. Bergman et al., 2002; Hanisch, 1996.
26. Rapp, 2003, p. 11. See Heatherington, Burns, and Gustafson, 1998, and Heatherington et al., 1993, for research on sex differences in modesty. See also Daubman and Sigall, 1997, for perceptions of the effects of modesty on others.
27. Beyer, 1990; Pallier, 2003. See also Gmelch, Wilke, and Lovrich, 1986; Landino and Owen, 1988, for research on female professors' lesser confidence in their research and administrative performance, compared with their male colleagues'. In a multinational study of employees in business settings, P. B. Smith, Dugan, and Trompenaars, 1997, found that women felt less personal control than men over events in their lives and that managers and professional employees felt more personal control than lower-status employees. In a survey study of British managers by P. Rosenthal, Guest, and Peccei, 1996, men attributed a successful experience at work more to their ability than women did. See also Kling et al., 1999, and Sahlstein and Allen, 2002, for meta-analyses comparing the self-esteem of women and men.
28. Otto, 2001, p. 102.
29. Carli, 2004.
30. Personal communication to Alice Eagly, March 1999.
31. Gerhart and Rynes, 1991. In a meta-analysis by Stuhlmacher and Walters, 1999, men had a slight overall advantage compared with women in gaining money, points, or other benefits in experiments on negotiation.

32. See Bowles, Babcock and Lai, 2007, for evidence that women are penalized for negotiating, and Babcock et al., 2006, for evidence that women initiate negotiations less often than men do.

33. Barron, 2003, p. 644.

34. Ibid., p. 648.

35. For reviews, see Babcock and Laschever, 2003, and Major, 1994. In a meta-analysis of studies on satisfaction with pay, researchers M. L. Williams, McDaniel, and Nguyen, 2006, found that women are slightly more satisfied than men with the same level of pay. This difference has been shrinking over time, however, so that men and women now report more similar levels of satisfaction.

36. Bylsma and Major, 1994; D. Moore, 1992. Further evidence of women's low sense of entitlement comes from a simulated salary negotiation with senior executives. The women obtained higher salaries when negotiating for someone else than for themselves, whereas men obtained comparable salaries when negotiating for themselves or someone else (Bowles, Babcock, and McGinn, 2005).

37. This phenomenon is known as the *personal/group discrimination discrepancy*. See Crosby, 1982, 1984. For a review and evidence of the importance of judgment standards in explaining the effect, see Quinn et al., 1999.

38. Bowles, Babcock, and McGinn, 2005, surveyed MBAs and found that the gender wage gap was higher in industries where job candidates were less certain about what salaries were normative. Women who know the salaries of comparable men expect higher salaries (Bylsma and Major, 1994) and earn more (Zanna, Crosby, and Lowenstein, 1987). See Kolb and Williams, 2000, for further discussion of tactics for employment negotiations, and Hogue and Yoder, 2003, for evidence that informing women of their strengths increases their feeling entitled to greater pay. For evidence that negotiating increases salaries, see Babcock, 2002, cited in Babcock and Laschever, 2003; Barron, 2003. Also, Kray, Galinsky, and Thompson, 2002, showed that when the value of women's stereotypically feminine qualities were made salient, women outperformed men in negotiations. See R. Fisher, Patton, and Ury, 1991, for a general discussion of effective negotiation tactics.

39. Blair-Loy, 2003, p. 38.

40. Ibid.

41. Avolio et al., 2004, p. 803.

42. Eagly, 2005. These problems also surface among members of other groups not traditionally included in higher-level leadership roles in most organizations—for example, people of color and gays and lesbians.

43. Auletta, 1998, p. 76.

44. Meyerson, 2001, p. xi. An extreme version of people feeling inauthentic in a role is known as the *imposter phenomenon*, which occurs when individuals think that they do not deserve their success. Although this phenomenon has usually been discussed in relation to women, research with managers and students suggests that women and men are equally likely to view themselves as imposters. See Fried-Buchalter, 1997; Leary et al., 2000.

45. Wellington, 2001.

46. Silvestri, 2003, p. 156.

47. Davies-Netzley, 1998; Huffman and Torres, 2002; G. Moore, 1988; S. M. Schor, 1997.

48. S. M. Schor, 1997, p. 54.

49. See Rosser, 2005, and Morrill, 1995.

50. Fenwick, 2001, p. 144.

51. See also a meta-analysis by Allen et al., 2004, for the benefits of having a mentor, and a review by Rosser and Egan, 2003, for the types and functions of mentoring relationships. See Catalyst, 2004a, for reports of benefits of mentoring for black women. However, see Bell and Nkomo, 2001, for evidence that black women receive relatively little mentoring.

52. R. J. Burke and McKeen, 1996; Dreher and Cox, 1996; Ragins and Cotton, 1999. Dreher and Cox, 1996, found that having a white male mentor, in particular, was associated with the greatest gains in income. For a review see Ragins, 1999.

53. C. Friedman and Yorio, 2006, p. 33.

54. For the role strain hypothesis, see Goode, 1960, and for the role enhancement or expansion hypothesis, see Marks, 1977, and Sieber, 1974.

55. "From one male bastion to the other," 2006.

56. For reviews assessing the overall effects of multiple roles, see Barnett and Hyde, 2001; Greenhaus and Powell, 2006; Klumb and Lampert, 2004; Repetti, Matthews, and Waldron, 1989. In addition to roles of paid worker, romantic partner, and parent, there are many other meaningful life roles—for example,

involving volunteering, the arts, athletics, and the extended family. See Allen et al., 2000, for a meta-analysis of work–family conflict.

57. For effects of women's employment, see review by Klumb and Lampert, 2004. For a recent study not included in the review, see Lahelma et al., 2002. A number of studies have found that women experience greater benefits than men do from having both work and family roles See, for example, Grzywacz and Marks, 2000, and Van Steenbergen, Ellemers, and Mooijaart, in press. Some researchers have argued that healthy individuals are more likely to be employed, accounting for the superior mental and physical health of employed people, a phenomenon known as the *healthy worker effect* (Repetti, Matthews, and Waldron, 1989).

58. Klumb and Lampert, 2004. Studies completed too recently to be included in the Klumb and Lampert review continue to reveal the benefits of multiple roles for women (for example, Janzen and Muhajarine, 2003; McMunn et al., 2006). Longitudinal studies can also control for how healthy a person was at the earlier time period and measure the effect on health of how much people were employed over time. See Klumb and Lampert, 2004, for discussion of longitudinal designs.

59. C. Black, 2001, p. 83.

60. See Bianchi, Robinson, and Milkie, 2006, for attitudes associated with parenting. In this 2000 U.S. nationally representative sample, most fathers and mothers reported that spending time with their children rated a "10," the highest score for personal satisfaction. See Evenson and Simon, 2005, for a nationally representative U.S. study linking parenthood and depression, and McMunn et al., 2006, for evidence of worse health in married stay-at-home mothers. See also Ramchandani et al., 2005, for depression among parents in Scotland. See NICHD Early Child Care Research Network, 2006, for correlational evidence that mothers who are exclusively responsible for care of their children have higher levels of depression than women who share childcare with others. See meta-analysis by Twenge, Campbell, and Foster, 2003, for evidence that parenthood reduces marital satisfaction.

61. Barnett and Hyde, 2001; McMunn et al., 2006.

62. Blair-Loy, 2003, pp. 110–111.

63. For the effects of maternal employment on children, see J. L. Hill et al., 2005; NICHD Early Child Care Research Network, 2006.

64. Deutsch, 2004, section 3, p. 1.

65. Lindner, 2001, p. 72

66. Matsui, 2001, p. 127. Connie Matsui is executive vice president for corporate strategy and communications at Biogen IDEC.

67. B. Morris, 2002. Some top executive women who have had stay-at-home husbands include Carly Fiorina, Ellen Hancock, Donna L. Dubinsky, Safra Catz, Anne M. Mulcahy, Dawn G. Lepore, Karen M. Garrison, and Deborah C. Hopkins (M. W. Walsh, 2001).

68. C. K. Goodman, 2005, p. C3.

69. Milkie et al., 2004.

70. M. Elliot, 2004, p. 59.

71. Barnett and Hyde, 2001.

72. See Schoen et al., 2002, for a nationally representative study showing that women's full-time employment does not increase the likelihood of divorce in marriages in which both partners are happy or only one is happy. Only when both the husband and the wife are unhappy with the marriage is the wife's full-time employment associated with increased divorce rates. Women's income was also unrelated to divorce in this study. These results indicate that women with high-paying jobs are no less committed to their marriages than other women, but that having such employment gives women the economic resources to leave unhappy marriages.

73. S. A. Friedman, 1996, p. 27.

74. LaFarge, 2001, p. 116.

Chapter 11

1. Herbert, 2006, p. 9.

2. Creswell, 2006, business section, p. 1.

3. See Inglehart and Norris, 2003, for discussion of these transitions. See also Emrich, Denmark, and Den Hartog, 2004.

4. Valian, 1998.

5. Fiorina, 2006, p. 173.

6. Hymowitz, 2006b, p. B1. Hymowitz also presents informal evidence that many successful executive women do not regret the trade-offs that they have made.

7. Frissen, 2000.

8. See Bilimoria, 2000, for discussion of pressures to diversify boards of directors.

9. Levering and Moskowitz, 2006.

10. Sharpe, 2000, p. 74.

11. Dowd, 2006, p. A21.

12. Eagly, Karau, and Makhijani, 1995. See also a related meta-analysis by Bowen, Swim, and Jacobs, 2000. Also, management consulting groups have compared male and female managers on a wide range of measures of leadership skills and effectiveness. Such research is difficult to evaluate, because it did not take into account variables (such as type of leadership role) that probably affect the size and direction of any sex differences. Moreover, the measures used by consultants generally differ from those that appear in the scientific literature and may not meet the same psychometric standards. See Kabacoff, 1998; Merrill-Sands and Kolb, 2001.

13. In the Eagly, Karau, and Makhijani, 1995, meta-analysis, sometimes researchers defined these roles quite broadly—for example, "middle managers in one or more industries." At other times they defined them much more specifically—for example, "elementary school principals" in a particular city. In the majority of studies in the meta-analysis, leaders' subordinates, superiors, or peers rated their effectiveness. In some studies, leaders rated their own performance. A small number of studies included more-objective indicators of performance based on group or organizational productivity.

14. Eagly and Karau, 2002; Heilman, 2001.

15. See, for example, Paolillo, 1981, for this characterization of middle management.

16. The meta-analysis described is the Eagly, Karau, and Makhijani, 1995, project. A panel of judges rated how stereotypically masculine or feminine the various leadership roles were.

17. Contributing to women's vulnerability is an information-processing bias whereby people overestimate the associations between the members of small, distinctive groups and distinctive behaviors. For example, if a law firm had 5 percent female and 95 percent male attorneys and if both groups committed legal errors on 5 percent of possible occasions, the perceived association between women and such errors would likely be exaggerated. For discussion of this bias, known as *illusory correlation*, see Hamilton and Gifford, 1976.

18. Committee of 200, 2002, p. 19. Griffin is vice president of Enterprise Rent-A-Car Company,

19. For example, see D. Jones, 2006b.

20. Catalyst, 2004b. Specifically, in the top quartile compared with the bottom quartile, return on equity was 35 percent greater, and total return to shareholders was 34 percent greater.

21. Krishnan and Park, 2005. See also Dwyer, Richard, and Chadwick, 2003; Richard et al., 2004, for small (nonsignificant) positive relationships of management gender diversity to productivity and return on equity in more limited samples using U.S. banks (and evidence of some moderating conditions).

22. See Carter, Simkins, and Simpson, 2003, for firm value and Erhardt, Werbel, and Shrader, 2003, for financial performance. Earlier U.S. studies produced more ambiguous outcomes—for example, Shrader, Blackburn, and Iles, 1997. Also, a British study produced a small positive relation between board gender diversity and financial performance in the FTSE 100 firms (Singh, Vinnicombe, and Terjesen, 2006).

23. P. M. Lee and James, 2007.

24. Brancato and Patterson, 1999, p. 7.

25. R. Campbell, 1996, p. A11.

26. Musteen, Barker, and Baeten, 2006.

27. For elaboration of this point, see Ellemers, de Gilder, and Haslam, 2004.

28. Allmendinger and Hackman, 1995. The extensive research on gender diversity and other forms of diversity shows many inconsistent effects. This outcome is not surprising, given that multiple processes can underlie these effects. For review, see Finkelstein and Hambrick, 1996; D. van Knippenberg and Schippers, 2007; K. Y. Williams and O'Reilly, 1998.

29. Studies such as Pfeffer and Davis-Blake, 1987, are often cited as showing that wages fall when women enter occupations. However, analyses by England, Allison, and Wu, in press, of longitudinal data from 1983 through 2001 refute this explanation. Scheepers, Ellemers, and Sintemaartensdijk, 2007, have shown that threats to group members' high status can elicit stress reactions; see also Scheepers and Ellemers, 2005.

30. For helpful discussion of managing diversity, see Ely, Meyerson, and Davidson, 2006; Jayne and Dipboye, 2004.

31. See R. M. Jackson, 1998, for discussion of broader economic and political forces that have produced movement toward gender equality.

32. Connell, 2003, 2005.

33. Center for American Women and Politics, 2005.

34. See Eagly et al., 2004, for an empirical study and discussion of sex differences in sociopolitical attitudes (see also Eagly and Diekman, 2006). See Inglehart and Norris, 2003, for a cross-national study of gender gaps in public opinion.

35. See S. J. Carroll, 2001; Kathlene, 2001; Panczer, 2002; C. S. Rosenthal, 2002; K. C. Walsh, 2002. Lovenduski and Norris, 2003, discussed these issues in relation to the British Parliament.

36. R. M. Jackson, 1998.

37. See Giele, 2004, for discussion of changing male identity.

38. Glick and Fiske, 2001a; Inglehart and Norris, 2003.

39. Diekman and Eagly, 2000; Diekman and Goodfriend, 2006. See also Diekman et al., 2005, and Wilde and Diekman, 2005, for data from Latin America and Germany.

40. DeMott, 2000, p. 3.

41. Mansfield, 2006, p. 16. Italics in original.

42. Tiger, 1999.

43. Browne, 2002.

44. For example, Inglehart and Norris, 2003.

45. Men's organizations that address gender issues reflect a wide range of political stances. See Connell, 2005.

46. For the poll data, see, for example, J. Mann, 2000. The poll of 1,500 respondents was commissioned by Deloitte & Touche, a financial services firm, and conducted by Roper-Starch Worldwide.

47. Diekman, Goodfriend, and Goodwin, 2004; Diekman and Goodfriend, 2006.

48. For examples of media reports of women's retreat from high-powered careers, see Belkin, 2003; Story, 2005; Wallis, 2004. For analysis of media claims, see Dunn-Jensen and Stroh, 2007.

49. Ridgeway, 2006a, p. 281.

50. Blau, Brinton, and Grusky, 2006, contains debate about very recent trends in gender equality. See in particular the chapters by Ridgeway on gender as an organizing force in social relations, by England on resistance from the family division of labor, and by R. M. Jackson on the inevitability of continuing change toward gender equality.

51. See Tajfel and Turner, 1979, for a social identity theory analysis of the conditions under which women and other lower-status groups engage in activism to improve their status. See J. M. Jones, 2005a, and Lifetime Women's Pulse Poll, 2006, for public opinion polls.

ABC News/*Washington Post* Poll. 2006. Clinton does well on attributes but still lacks crossover appeal. May 28. http://abcnews.go.com/images/Politics/1012a4HRC.pdf.

Abelson, R. P. 1985. A variance explanation paradox: When a little is a lot. *Psychological Bulletin* 97: 129–133.

Abzug, B. 1996. Women will change the nature of power. In *Women's leadership and the ethics of development*, B. Abzug and D. Jain. UNDP Gender in Development: Resource Room. http://www.sdnp.undp.org/gender/resources/mono4.html#Women%20Will%20Change%20the%20Nature%20of%20Power.

Acker, J. 1990. Hierarchies, jobs, bodies: A theory of gendered organizations. *Gender & Society* 4: 139–158.

———.1995. Feminist goals and organizing processes. In *Feminist organizations: Harvest of the new women's movement*, edited by M. M. Ferree and P. Y. Martin, 137–144. Philadelphia: Temple University Press.

Adams-Roy, J., and J. Barling. 1998. Predicting the decision to confront or report sexual harassment. *Journal of Organizational Behavior* 19: 329–336.

Adler, N. J. (2007). One world: Women leading and managing worldwide. In *Handbook of women in business and management*, edited by D. Bilimoria and S. K. Piderit, 330–355. Cheltenham, UK: Edward Elgar.

Agle, B. R., N. J. Nagarajan, J. A. Sonnenfeld, and D. Srinivasan. 2006. Does CEO charisma matter? An empirical analysis of the relationships among organizational performance, environmental uncertainty, and top management team perceptions of CEO charisma. *Academy of Management Journal* 49: 161–174.

Ajzen, I., and M. Fishbein. 2005. The influence of attitudes on behavior. In *The handbook of attitudes*, edited by D. Albarracín, B. T. Johnson, and M. P. Zanna, 173–221. Mahwah, NJ: Erlbaum.

Allen, T. D. 2006. Rewarding good citizens: The relationship between citizenship behavior, gender, and organizational rewards. *Journal of Applied Psychology* 36: 120–143.

———, L. T. Eby, M. L. Poteet, E. Lentz, and L. Lima, 2004. Career benefits associated with mentoring for protégés: A meta-analysis. *Journal of Applied Psychology* 89: 127–136.

———, D. E. L. Herst, C. S. Bruck, and M. Sutton. 2000. Consequences associated with work-to-family conflict: A review and agenda for further research. *Journal of Occupational Health Psychology* 5: 278–308.

———, and J. E. Russell. 1999. Parental leave of absence: Some not so family-friendly implications. *Journal of Applied Social Psychology* 29: 166–191.

Allmendinger, J., and J. R. Hackman. 1995. The more, the better? A four-nation study of the inclusion of women in symphony orchestras. *Social Forces* 74: 423–460.

Almer, E. D., J. R. Hopper, and S. E. Kaplan. 1998. The effect of diversity-related attributes on hiring, advancement and voluntary turnover judgments. *Accounting Horizons* 12: 1–17.

Alsop, R. 2005. Men do numbers, women do strategy: Recruiters see a clear difference between male and female applicants. *Wall Street Journal*, September 21, R5.

Alvesson, M., and Y. D. Billing. 1992. Gender and organization: Towards a differentiated understanding. *Organization Studies* 13: 73–103.

Ambert, A. 1994. An international perspective on parenting: Social change and social constructs. *Journal of Marriage and the Family* 56: 529–543.

American Bar Association Commission on Women in the Profession. 2006. *A current glance at women in the law 2006*. http://www.abanet.org/women/CurrentGlanceStatistics2006.pdf.

American freshman: Forty-year trends. 2007. Los Angeles: Higher Education Research Institute.

Anders, G. 2005. Depositions require a skill set leaders don't use on the job. *Wall Street Journal*, July 26, A17.

Anderson, D. J., M. Binder, and K. Krause. 2003. The motherhood wage penalty revisited: Experience, heterogeneity, work effort, and work-schedule flexibility. *Industrial & Labor Relations Review* 56: 273–294.

Anderson, L. R., and P. N. Blanchard. 1982. Sex differences in task and social-emotional behavior. *Basic and Applied Social Psychology* 3: 109–139.

Angrist, J., and W. N. Evans. 1998. Children and their parents' labor supply: Evidence from exogenous variation in family size. *American Economic Review* 88: 450–477.

Antilla, S. 2004. Money talks, women don't. *New York Times*, July 21, section A, 19.

Antonakis, J. 2004. On why "emotional intelligence" will not predict leadership effectiveness beyond IQ or the "Big Five": An extension and rejoinder. *Organizational Analysis* 12: 171–182.

———, B. J. Avolio, and N. Sivasubramaniam. 2003. Context and leadership: An examination of the nine-factor full-range leadership theory using the Multifactor Leadership Questionnaire. *Leadership Quarterly* 14: 261–295.

Archer, J. 2000. Sex differences in aggression between heterosexual partners: A meta-analytic review. *Psychological Bulletin* 126: 651–680.

———. 2002. Sex differences in physically aggressive acts between heterosexual partners: A meta-analytic review. *Aggression and Violent Behavior* 7: 313–351.

———. 2004. Sex differences in aggression in real-world settings: A meta-analytic review. *Review of General Psychology* 8: 291–322.

———. 2006a. Cross-cultural differences in physical aggression between partners: A social-role analysis. *Personality and Social Psychology Review* 10: 133–153.

———. 2006b. Testosterone and human aggression: An evaluation of the challenge hypothesis. *Neuroscience and Biobehavioral Reviews* 30: 319–345.

———, and S. M Coyne. 2005. An integrated review of indirect, relational, and social aggression. *Personality and Social Psychology Review* 9: 212–230.

Arendell, T. 2000. Conceiving and investigating motherhood: The decade's scholarship. *Journal of Marriage and the Family* 62: 1192–1207.

Armstrong-Stassen, M. 2005. Coping with downsizing: A comparison of executive-level and middle managers. *International Journal of Stress Management* 12: 117–141.

Artis, J. E., and E. K. Pavalko. 2003. Explaining the decline in women's household labor: Individual change and cohort differences. *Journal of Marriage and the Family* 65, 746–761.

Arun, S. V., T. G. Arun, and V. K. Borooah. 2004. The effect of career breaks on the working lives of women. *Feminist Economics* 10: 65–84.

Arvey, R. D., M. Rotundo, W. Johnson, Z. Zhang, and M. McGue. 2006. The determinants of leadership role occupancy: Genetic and personality factors. *Leadership Quarterly* 17: 1–20.

Astin, H. S., and C. Leland. 1991. *Women of influence, women of vision: A cross-generational study of leaders and social change*. San Francisco: Jossey-Bass.

Atwater, L. E., J. F. Brett, D. Waldman, L. DiMare, and M. V. Hayden. 2004. Men's and women's perceptions of the gender typing of management subroles. *Sex Roles* 50: 191–199.

Atwood, G. 2006. *Big girls do cry but not at work*. Society of Women Engineers: Professional Development. http://www.swe.org/stellent/groups/website/@public/documents/webdoc/swe_000423.pdf.

Auletta, K. 1998. In the company of women. *New Yorker*, April 20, 72–78.

———. 2002. The Howell doctrine. *New Yorker*, June 10, 48–56, 58–64, 66–71.

Aurora and Caliper. 2005. *The DNA of women leaders*. April. http://www.auroravoice.com/pdf/dna_2005.pdf.

Aven, F. F., Jr., B. Parker, and G. M. McEvoy. 1993. Gender and attitudinal commitment to organizations: A meta-analysis. *Journal of Business Research* 26: 63–73.

Avolio, B. J. 1999. *Full leadership development: Building the vital forces in organizations*. Thousand Oaks, CA: Sage.

———, B. M. Bass, and D. I. Jung. 1999. Re-examining the components of transformational and transactional leadership using the Multifactor Leadership Questionnaire. *Journal of Occupational and Organizational Psychology* 72: 441–462.

————, J., W. L. Gardner, F. O. Walumbwa, F. Luthans, and D. R. May. 2004. Unlocking the mask: A look at the process by which authentic leaders impact follower attitudes and behaviors. *Leadership Quarterly* 15, 801–823.

Ayman, R. 2004. Situational and contingency approaches to leadership. In *The nature of leadership*, edited by J. Antonakis, A. T. Cianciolo, and R. J. Sternberg, 148–170. Thousand Oaks, CA: Sage.

Babcock, L., M. Gelfand, D. Small, and H. Stayn. 2006. Gender differences in the propensity to initiate negotiations: A new look at gender variation in negotiation behavior. In *Social psychology and economics*, edited by D. De Cremer, M. Zeelenberg, and J. K. Murnighan, 239–259. Mahwah, NJ: Erlbaum.

————, and S. Laschever. 2003. *Women don't ask: Negotiation and the gender divide*. Princeton, NJ: Princeton University.

Bailyn, L. 2002. Time in organizations: Constraints on, and possibilities for, gender equity in the workplace. In *Advancing women's careers: Research and practice*, edited by R. J. Burke and D. L. Nelson, 262–272. Malden, MA: Blackwell.

Baker, J. G. 2002. The influx of women into legal professions: An economic analysis. *Monthly Labor Review* 125(8): 14–24.

Bales, R. F. 1950. *Interaction process analysis: A method for the study of small groups*. Reading, MA: Addison-Wesley.

Banaji, M. R., and C. D. Hardin. 1996. Automatic stereotyping. *Psychological Science* 7: 136–141.

————, C. D. Hardin, and A. J. Rothman. 1993. Implicit stereotyping in person judgment. *Journal of Personality and Social Psychology* 65: 272–281.

————, K. M. Lemm, and S. J. Carpenter. 2001. The social unconscious. In *Blackwell handbook of social psychology: Intraindividual processes*, edited by A. Tesser and N. Schwarz, 134–158. Malden, MA: Blackwell.

Bargh, J. A., P. Raymond, J. B. Pryor, and F. Strack. 1995. Attractiveness of the underling: An automatic power→sex association and its consequences for sexual harassment and aggression. *Journal of Personality and Social Psychology* 68: 768–781.

Barmby, T. A., M. G. Ercolani, and J. G. Treble. 2002. Sickness absence: An international comparison. *Economic Journal* 112: F315–F331.

Barnett, R. C., and J. S. Hyde. 2001. Women, men, work, and family: An expansionist theory. *American Psychologist* 56: 781–796.

Baron, R. A., J. H. Neuman, and D. Geddes. 1999. Social and personal determinants of workplace aggression: Evidence for the impact of perceived injustice and the Type A behavior pattern. *Aggressive Behavior* 25: 281–296.

Barron, L. A. 2003. Ask and you shall receive? Gender differences in negotiators' beliefs about requests for a higher salary. *Human Relations* 56: 635–662.

Barth, J., and M. R. Ferguson. 2002. Gender and gubernatorial personality. *Women & Politics* 24: 63–82.

Bartunek, J. M., K. Walsh, and C. A. Lacey. 2000. Dynamics and dilemmas of women leading women. *Organization Science* 11: 589–610.

Bass, B. M. 1981. *Stogdill's handbook of leadership: A survey of theory and research*. Rev. ed. New York: Free Press.

————. 1985. *Leadership and performance beyond expectations*. New York: Free Press.

————. 1990. *Bass & Stogdill's handbook of leadership: Theory, research, and managerial applications*. 3rd ed. New York: Free Press.

————. 1998. *Transformational leadership: Industrial, military, and educational impact*. Mahwah, NJ: Erlbaum.

Bauer, T. N., E. W. Morrison, and R. R. Callister. 1998. Organizational socialization: A review and directions for future research. In *Research in personnel and human resources management*, edited by G. R. Ferris. Vol. 16, 149–214. Stamford, CT: Elsevier Science/JAI Press.

Baxter, J., and E. O. Wright. 2000. The glass ceiling hypothesis: A comparative study of the United States, Sweden, and Australia. *Gender & Society* 14: 275–294.

Bayard, K., J. Hellerstein, D. Neumark, and K. Troske. 2003. New evidence on sex segregation and sex differences in wages from matched employee-employer data. *Journal of Labor Economics* 21: 886–922.

Bayard de Volo, L. 2000. Global and local framing of maternal identity: Obligation and the mothers of Matagalpa, Nicaragua. In *Globalizations and social movements: Culture, power, and the transnational public sphere*, edited by J. Guidry, M. D. Kennedy, and M. N. Zald, 127–146. Ann Arbor: University of Michigan Press.

Beatty, S. 2004. Boss talk: Plotting plaid's future; Burberry's Rose Marie Bravo designs ways to keep brand growing and still exclusive. *Wall Street Journal*, September 9, B1, B8.

Becker, G. S. 1985. Human capital, effort, and the sexual division of labor. *Journal of Labor Economics* 3, no. 1, supplement: S33–S58.

Beckham, B., and H. Aronson. 1978. Selection of jury foremen as a measure of the social status of women. *Psychological Reports* 43: 475–478.

Belkin, L. 2003. The opt-out revolution. *New York Times Magazine*, October 26, 42–47, 58, 85–86.

Bell, E. L. J. E., and S. M. Nkomo. 2001. *Our separate ways: Black and white women and the struggle for professional identity.* Boston: Harvard Business School Press.

Bennis, W. 1989. *On becoming a leader.* Reading, MA: Addison-Wesley.

Benoit, B. 2006. Lecturer or listener? Why Merkel may need to work on her assertive side. *Financial Times*, February 21. http://search.ft.com/searchArticle?queryText=Lecturer+or+listenerandy=7andjavascriptEnabled=trueandid=060221000753andx=15.

Berdahl, J. L., and C. Anderson. 2005. Men, women, and leadership centralization in groups over time. *Group Dynamics: Theory, Research, and Practice* 9: 45–57.

———, and C. Moore. 2006. Workplace harassment: Double jeopardy for minority women. *Journal of Applied Psychology* 91: 426–436.

Berger, J., and M. H. Fisek. 2006. Diffuse status characteristics and the spread of value: A formal theory. *American Journal of Sociology* 111: 1038–1079.

Bergman, M. E., R. D. Langhout, P. A. Palmieri, L. M. Cortina, and L. F. Fitzgerald. 2002. The (un)reasonableness of reporting: Antecedents and consequences of reporting sexual harassment. *Journal of Applied Psychology* 87: 230–242.

Berkeley, A. E. 1989. Job interviewers' dirty little secret. *Wall Street Journal*, March 20, 1,14.

Bernardin, H. J., C. M. Hagan, J. S. Kane, and P. Villanova. 1998. Effective performance management: A focus on precision, customers, and situational constraints. In *Performance appraisal: State of the art in practice*, edited by J. W. Smither, 3–48. San Francisco: Jossey-Bass.

The best and worst managers of the year. 2005. *BusinessWeek Online*, January 10. http://www.businessweek.com/magazine/toc/05_02/B39150502manager.htm.

Bettencourt, B. A., and N. Miller. 1996. Gender differences in aggression as a function of provocation: A meta-analysis. *Psychological Bulletin* 119: 422–447.

Betty Dukes et al. v. Wal-Mart Stores, Inc. 2003a. Expert report of William T. Bielby, Ph.D. U.S. District Court, Northern District of California, Case No. C-01-2242 MJJ., February. http://www.walmartclass.com/walmartclass94.pl?wsi=0andwebsys_screen=all_reports_view&websys_id=19

Betty Dukes et al. v. Wal-Mart Stores, Inc. 2003b. Statistical analysis of gender patterns in Wal-Mart workforce by R. Drogin of Drogin, Kakigi & Associates. U.S. District Court, Northern District of California, Case No. C-01-2242 MJJ, February. http://www.walmartclass.com/walmartclass94.pl?wsi=0&websys_screen=all_reports_view&websys_id=18.

Betty Dukes et al. v. Wal-Mart Stores, Inc. 2003c. Declaration of Gretchen Adams in support of plaintiffs' motion for class certification. U.S. District Court, Northern District of California, Case No. C-01-2242 MJJ, April. http://www.walmartclass.com/staticdata/walmartclass/declarations/Adams_Gretchen.htm

Beutel, A. M., and M. M. Marini. 1995. Gender and values. *American Sociological Review* 60: 436–448.

Beyer, S. 1990. Gender differences in the accuracy of self-evaluations of performance. *Journal of Personality and Social Psychology* 59: 960–970.

Bianchi, S. M. 2000. Maternal employment and time with children: Dramatic change or surprising continuity? *Demography* 37: 401–414.

———, M. A. Milkie, L. C. Sayer, and J. P. Robinson. 2000. Is anyone doing the housework? Trends in the gender division of household labor. *Social Forces* 79: 191–228.

———, J. P. Robinson, and M. A. Milkie. 2006. *Changing rhythms of American family life.* New York: Russell Sage Foundation.

Bielby, D. D., and W. T. Bielby. 1984. Work commitment, sex-role attitudes, and women's employment. *American Sociological Review* 49: 234–247.

———, and W. T. Bielby. 1988. She works hard for the money: Household responsibilities and the allocation of work effort. *American Journal of Sociology* 93: 1031–1059.

Bielby, W. T., and Bielby, D. D. 1989. Family ties: Balancing commitments to work and family in dual earner households. *American Sociological Review* 54: 776–789.

Biernat, M. 2003. Toward a broader view of social stereotyping. *American Psychologist* 58: 1019–1027.

———, C. S. Crandall, L. V. Young, D. Kobrynowicz, and S. M. Halpin. 1998. All that you can be: Stereotyping of self and others in a military context. *Journal of Personality and Social Psychology* 75: 301–317.

———, and D. Kobrynowicz. 1997. Gender- and race-based standards of competence: Lower minimum standards but higher ability standards for devalued groups. *Journal of Personality and Social Psychology* 72: 544–557.

————, M. Manis, and T. B. Nelson. 1991. Stereotypes and standards of judgment. *Journal of Personality and Social Psychology* 66: 5–20.

————, and T. K. Vescio. 2002. She swings, she hits, she's great, she's benched: Implications of gender-based shifting standards for judgment and behavior. *Personality and Social Psychology Bulletin* 28: 66–77.

Bilimoria, D. 2000. Building the business case for women corporate directors. In *Women on corporate boards of directors: International challenges and opportunities*, edited by R. J. Burke and M. C. Mattis, 25–40. Dordrecht: Kluwer Academic.

Bittman, M., P. England, L. Sayer, N. Folbre, and G. Matheson. 2003. When does gender trump money? Bargaining and time in household work. *American Journal of Sociology* 109: 186–214.

————, and J. Wajcman. 2000. The rush hour: The character of leisure time and gender equity. *Social Forces* 79: 165–189.

Björkqvist, K. 1994. Sex differences in physical, verbal, and indirect aggression: A review of recent research. *Sex Roles* 30: 177–188.

Black, C. 2001. Protestant neighbors bought Catholic newspapers from her. In *How Jane won: 55 successful women share how they grew from ordinary girls to extraordinary women*, edited by S. Rimm and S. Rimm-Kaufman, 78–83. New York: Crown Business.

Black, J. 2003. The women of tech. *BusinessWeek Online*, May 29. http://www.businessweek.com/technology/content/may2003/tc20030529_2635_tc111.htm?chan=search.

Blair, I. V., and M. R. Banaji. 1996. Automatic and controlled processes in stereotype priming. *Journal of Personality and Social Psychology* 70: 1142–1163.

Blair-Loy, M. 2003. *Competing devotions: Career and family among women executives*. Cambridge, MA: Harvard University Press.

Blau, F. D., M. C. Brinton, and D. B. Grusky, eds. 2006. *The declining significance of gender?* New York: Russell Sage Foundation.

————, and L. M. Kahn. 2006a. The gender pay gap: Going, going . . . but not gone. In *The declining significance of gender?* edited by F. D. Blau, M. C. Brinton, and D. B. Grusky, 37–66. New York: Russell Sage Foundation.

————, and L. M. Kahn. 2006b. The U. S. gender pay gap in the 1990s: Slowing convergence. *Industrial and Labor Relations Review* 60: 45–66.

————, and L. M. Kahn. 2007. The gender pay gap: Have women gone as far as they can? *Academy of Management Perspectives* 21: 7–23.

Blinder, A. 1973. Wage discrimination: Reduced form and structural estimates. *Journal of Human Resources* 8: 436–455.

Boehm, C. 1999. *Hierarchy in the forest: The evolution of egalitarian behavior*. Cambridge, MA: Harvard University Press.

Boise, L., and M. B. Neal. 1996. Family responsibilities and absenteeism: Employees caring for parents versus employees caring for children. *Journal of Managerial Issues* 8: 218–238.

Boldry, J., W. Wood, and D. A. Kashy. 2001. Gender stereotypes and the evaluation of men and women in military training. *Journal of Social Issues* 57: 689–705.

Bolino, M. C., and W. H. Turnley. 2003. Counternormative impression management, likeability, and performance ratings: The use of intimidation in an organizational setting. *Journal of Organizational Behavior* 24: 237–250.

Bond, J. T., C. Thompson, E. Galinsky, and D. Prottas. 2002. *Highlights of the national study of the changing workforce*. New York: Families and Work Institute.

Bond, M. A., L. Punnett, J. L. Pyle, D. Cazeca, and M. Cooperman. 2004. Gendered work conditions, health, and work outcomes. *Journal of Occupational Health Psychology* 9: 28–45.

Bono, J. E., and M. H. Anderson. 2005. The advice and influence networks of transformational leaders. *Journal of Applied Psychology* 90: 1306–1314.

————, and T. A. Judge. 2004. Personality and transformational and transactional leadership: A meta-analysis. *Journal of Applied Psychology* 89: 901–910.

Boraas, S., and W. M. Rodgers III. 2003. How does gender play a role in the earnings gap? An update. *Monthly Labor Review* 126 (3): 9–15.

Borkowski, S. C., and Y. J. Ugras. 1998. Business students and ethics: A meta-analysis. *Journal of Business Ethics* 17: 1117–1127.

Borman, W. C. 2004. The concept of organizational citizenship. *Current Directions in Psychological Science* 13: 238–241.

Boulis, A. 2004. The evolution of gender and motherhood in contemporary medicine. *Annals of the American Academy of Political and Social Science* 596: 172–206.

Bowen, C., J. K. Swim, and R. R. Jacobs. 2000. Evaluating gender biases on actual job performance of real people: A meta-analysis. *Journal of Applied Social Psychology* 30: 2194–2215.

Bowler, M., R. E. Ilg, S. Miller, E. Robinson, and A. Polivka. 2003. *Revisions to the Current Population Survey effective in January 2003.* http://www.bls.gov/cps/rvcps03.pdf.

Bowles, H. R., L. Babcock, and L. Lai. 2007. Social incentives for gender differences in the propensity to initiate negotiations: Sometimes it does hurt to ask. *Organizational Behavior and Human Decision Processes* 103: 84–103.

———, L. Babcock, and K. L. McGinn. 2005. Constraints and triggers: Situational mechanics of gender in negotiation. *Journal of Personality and Social Psychology* 89: 951–965.

Bowman, G. W., N. B. Worthy, and S. A. Greyser. 1965. Are women executives people? *Harvard Business Review* 43(4): 14–28, 164–178.

Brackett, M. A., S. E. Rivers, S. Shiffman, N. Lerner, and P. Salovey. 2006. Relating emotional abilities to social functioning: A comparison of self-report and performance measures of emotional intelligence. *Journal of Personality and Social Psychology* 91: 780–795.

Bradley, R. 2005. *Harvard rules: The struggle for the soul of the world's most powerful university.* New York: HarperCollins.

Brady, S., and G. Salvatore. 2005. With children: Leading an integrated life. In *Enlightened power: How women are transforming the practice of leadership*, edited by L. Coughlin, E. Wingard, and K. Hollihan, 151–166. San Francisco: Jossey-Bass.

Brancato, C. K., and D. J. Patterson. 1999. *Board diversity in U.S. corporations: Best practices for broadening the profile of corporate boards.* New York: Conference Board.

Brass, D. J. 1985. Men's and women's networks: A study of interaction patterns and influence in an organization. *Academy of Management Journal* 28: 327–343.

———. 2001. Social capital and organizational leadership. In *The nature of organizational leadership: Understanding the performance imperatives confronting today's leaders*, edited by S. J. Zaccaro and R. J. Klimoski, 132–152. San Francisco, CA: Jossey-Bass.

Brazelton, T. B. 1988. *What every baby knows.* New York: Ballentine Books.

Brescoll, V., and M. LaFrance. 2004. The correlates and consequences of newspaper reports of research on sex differences. *Psychological Science* 15: 515–520.

Brett, J. M., and L. K. Stroh. 1997. Jumping ship: Who benefits from an external labor market career strategy? *Journal of Applied Psychology* 82: 331–341.

———, and L. K. Stroh. 2003. Working 61 hours a week: Why do managers do it? *Journal of Applied Psychology* 81: 67–78.

Bridges, S., and K. Mumford. 2001. Absenteeism in the UK: A comparison across genders. *Manchester School* 69: 276–284.

Bridges, W. P. 2003. Rethinking gender segregation and gender inequality: Measures and meanings. *Demography* 40: 543–568.

Brooks, C., and C. Bolzendahl. 2004. The transformation of U.S. gender role attitudes: Cohort replacement, social-structural change, and ideological learning. *Social Science Research* 33: 106–133.

Browne, K. R. 1999. *Divided labours: An evolutionary view of women at work.* New Haven, CT: Yale University Press.

———. 2002. *Biology at work: Rethinking sexual equality.* New Brunswick, NJ: Rutgers University Press.

Bryant, W. K., and C. D. Zick. 1996a. Are we investing less in the next generation? Historical trends in time spent caring for children. *Journal of Family and Economic Issues* 17: 365–391.

———, and C. D. Zick. 1996b. An examination of parent-child shared time. *Journal of Marriage and the Family* 58: 227–237.

Budig, M. J. 2002. Male advantage and the gender composition of jobs: Who rides the glass escalator? *Social Problems* 49: 258–277.

———, and P. England. 2001. The wage penalty for motherhood. *American Sociological Review* 66: 204–225.

Buller, D. J. 2005. *Adapting minds: Evolutionary psychology and the persistent quest for human nature.* Cambridge, MA: MIT Press.

Burgess, D., and E. Borgida. 1999. Who women are, who women should be: Descriptive and prescriptive gender stereotyping in sex discrimination. *Psychology, Public Policy, and Law* 5: 665–692.

Burgoon, M., T. S. Birk, and J. R. Hall. 1991. Compliance and satisfaction with physician-patient communication: An expectancy theory interpretation of gender differences. *Human Communication Research* 18: 177–208.

———, J. P. Dillard, and N. E. Doran. 1983. Friendly or unfriendly persuasion: The effects of violations by males and females. *Human Communication Research* 10: 283–294.

Burke, C. S., K. C. Stagl, C. Klein, G. F. Goodwin, E. Salas, and S. M. Halpin. 2006. What type of leadership behaviors are functional in teams? A meta-analysis. *Leadership Quarterly* 17: 288–307.

Burke, R. J., and M. C. Mattis. 2000. *Women on corporate boards of directors: International challenges and opportunities.* Dordrecht: Kluwer Academic.

———, and C. A. McKeen. 1996. Gender effects in mentoring relationships. *Journal of Social Behavior and Personality* 11(5): 91–104.

Burns, G. 2006. Bringing new energy to ADM. *Chicago Tribune*, December 29, section 1, 29.

Burns, J. M. 1978. *Leadership.* New York: Harper and Row.

Burt, R. S. 1992. *Structural holes: The social structure of competition.* Cambridge, MA: Harvard University Press.

———. 1998. The gender of social capital. *Rationality & Society* 10: 5–46.

Bushman, B. J., and C. A. Anderson. 2001. Media violence and the American public: Scientific facts versus media misinformation. *American Psychologist* 56: 477–489.

Buss, D. M. 1981. Sex differences in the evaluation and performance of dominant acts. *Journal of Personality and Social Psychology* 40: 147–154.

———. 1995. Evolutionary psychology: A new paradigm for psychological science. *Psychological Inquiry* 6: 1–30.

———, ed. 2005. *The handbook of evolutionary psychology.* Hoboken, NJ: Wiley.

———, and D. T. Kenrick. 1998. Evolutionary social psychology. In *The handbook of social psychology,* edited by D. T. Gilbert, S. T. Fiske, and G. Lindzey, 4th ed., Vol. 2, 982–1026. Boston: McGraw-Hill.

Butler, A. B., and A. Skattebo. 2004. What is acceptable for women may not be for men: The effect of family conflicts with work on job-performance ratings. *Journal of Occupational and Organizational Psychology* 77: 553–564.

Buttner, E. H., and M. McEnally. 1996. The interactive effect of influence tactic, applicant gender, and type of job on hiring recommendations. *Sex Roles* 34: 581–591.

Bylsma, W. H., and B. Major. 1994. Social comparisons and contentment: Exploring the psychological costs of the gender wage gap. *Psychology of Women Quarterly* 18: 241–249.

Byrne, D., and J. H. Neuman. 1992. The implications of attraction research for organizational issues. In *Issues, theory, and research in industrial/organizational psychology,* edited by K. Kelly, 29–70. Amsterdam: Elsevier Science.

Byrnes, J. P., D. C. Miller, and W. D. Schafer. 1999. Gender differences in risk taking: A meta-analysis. *Psychological Bulletin* 125: 367–383.

Cadsby, C. B., and E. Maynes. 2005. Gender, risk aversion, and the drawing power of equilibrium in an experimental corporate takeover game. *Journal of Economic Behavior and Organizations* 56: 39–59.

Caiazza, A., A. Shaw, and M. Werschkul. 2004. *Women's economic status in the states: Wide disparities by race, ethnicity, and region.* Washington, DC: Institute for Women's Policy Research. http://www.iwpr.org/pdf/R260.pdf.

Caliper. 2005. *The qualities that distinguish women leaders.* http://www.caliperonline.com/womenstudy/WomenLeaderWhitePaper.pdf.

Campbell, A. 1999. Staying alive: Evolution, culture, and women's intrasexual aggression. *Behavioral and Brain Sciences* 22: 203–214.

———. 2004. Female competition: Causes, constraints, content, and contexts. *Journal of Sex Research* 41: 16–26.

———. 2005. Aggression. In *The handbook of evolutionary psychology,* edited by D. Buss, 628–652. Hoboken, NJ: Wiley.

Campbell, R. 1996. Letter to the editor. *Wall Street Journal,* April 12, A11.

Canady, A. 2001. She was a "twofer." In *How Jane won: 55 successful women share how they grew from ordinary girls to extraordinary women,* edited by S. Rimm and S. Rimm-Kaufman, 164–168. New York: Crown Business.

Cappelli, P., and M. Hamori. 2005. The new road to the top. *Harvard Business Review* 83 (1): 25–32.

Cardwell, D. 2006. Born to the elite, New York's chief city planner sweats the details of the streets. *New York Times,* January 15, A16.

Carli, L. L. 1989. Gender differences in interaction style and influence. *Journal of Personality and Social Psychology* 56: 565–576.

———. 1990. Gender, language, and influence. *Journal of Personality and Social Psychology* 59: 941–951.

———. 1999. Gender, interpersonal power, and social influence. *Journal of Social Issues* 55: 81–99.

———. 2001a. Assertiveness. In *Encyclopedia of women and gender: Sex similarities and differences and the impact of society on gender,* edited by J. Worell, 157–168. San Diego, CA: Academic Press.

———. 2001b. Gender and social influence. *Journal of Social Issues* 57: 725–741.

————. 2004. Gender effects on persuasiveness and compliance gaining: A review. In *Perspectives on persuasion, social influence and compliance gaining*, edited by J. S. Seiter and R. H. Gass, 133–148. Boston: Allyn and Bacon.

————. 2006a. Gender issues in workplace groups: Effects of gender and communication style on social influence. In *Gender and communication at work*, edited by M. Barrett and M. J. Davidson, 69–83. Burlington, VT: Ashgate.

————. 2006b. Gender and social influence: Women confront the double bind. Paper presented at the 26th International Conference of Applied Psychology, Athens, Greece, July.

————, and W. Fung. 1997. Gender differences in the prisoner's dilemma game: A meta-analysis. Presented at the 105th Annual Convention of the American Psychological Association, Chicago, IL, August.

————, S. J. LaFleur, and C. C. Loeber. 1995. Nonverbal behavior, gender, and influence. *Journal of Personality and Social Psychology* 68: 1030–1041.

————, and C. Olm-Shipman. 2004. *Gender differences in task and social behavior: A meta-analytic review.* Unpublished research, Wellesley College, Wellesley, MA.

Carras, M. 1979. *Indira Gandhi: In the crucible of leadership: A political biography.* Boston: Beacon.

Carroll, J. 2006. *Americans prefer male boss to a female boss.* September 1. Gallup Brain, http://brain.gallup.com.

Carroll, S. J. 2001. Introduction. In *The impact of women in public office*, edited by S. J. Carroll, xi–xxvi. Bloomington: Indiana University Press.

Carter, D. A., B. J. Simkins, and W. G. Simpson. 2003. Corporate governance, board diversity, and firm value. *Financial Review* 38: 33–53.

Cash, T. F., B. Gillen, and D. S. Burns. 1977. Sexism and "beautyism" in personnel consultant decision making. *Journal of Applied Psychology* 62: 301–311.

Cassirer, N., and B. F. Reskin. 2000. High hopes: Organizational positions, employment experiences, and women's and men's promotion aspirations. *Work and Occupations* 27: 438–463.

Catalyst. 2001. *Women in corporate leadership: Comparisons among the US, the UK, and Canada.* http://www.catalyst.org/files/fact/US,%20UK,%20Canada%20WICL%20Comparisons.pdf.

————. 2002. *2002 Catalyst census of women corporate officers and top earners of Canada.* http://www.catalyst.org/files/fact/2002%20Canadian%20COTE%20Fact%20Sheet.pdf.

————. 2003. *Workplace flexibility is still a woman's advancement issue.* http://www.catalyst.org/files/view/Workplace%20Flexibility%20Is%20Still%20a%20Women%27s%20Advancement%20Issue.pdf.

————. 2004a. *Advancing African-American women in the workplace: What managers need to know.* http://www.catalyst.org/files/full/Advancing%20African-American%20Women%20in%20Workplace.pdf.

————. 2004b. *The bottom line: Connecting corporate performance and gender diversity.* http://catalyst.org/files/full/financialperformancereport.pdf.

————. 2004c. *Women and men in U.S. corporate leadership: Same workplace, different realities?* http://www.catalyst.org/files/full/Women%20and%20Men%20in%20U.S.%20Corporate%20Leadership%20Same%20Workplace,%20Different%20Realities.pdf

————. 2005a. *Quick takes: Women in management in Canada.* http://www.catalyst.org/files/quicktakes/Quick%20Takes%20-%20Women%20in%20Management%20in%20Canada.pdf.

————. 2005b. *Women "take care," men "take charge": Stereotyping of U.S. business leaders exposed.* http://www.catalyst.org/files/full/Women%20Take%20Care%20Men%20Take%20Charge.pdf.

————. 2006a. *Connections that count: The informal networks of women of color in the United States.* http://www.catalyst.org/files/full/Women%20of%20Color%20-%20Connections%20that%20count.pdf.

————. 2006b. *2005 Catalyst census of women board directors of the Fortune 500.* http://www.catalyst.org/files/full/2005%20WBD.pdf.

————. 2006c. *2005 Catalyst census of women corporate officers and top earners of the Fortune 500.* http://www.catalyst.org/files/full/2005%20COTE.pdf.

Cave, D. 2006. Madam speaker, after her first year of firsts. *New York Times*, December 30, B10.

CBS News/*New York Times*. 2006. *A woman for president.* February 5. http://www.cbsnews.com/htdocs/pdf/020306woman.pdf#search=%22a%20woman%20for%20president%20CBS%20News%2FNew%20York%20Times%20Poll%22.

Cejka, M. A., and A. H. Eagly. 1999. Gender-stereotypic images of occupations correspond to the sex segregation of employment. *Personality and Social Psychology Bulletin* 25: 413–423.

Center for American Women and Politics. 2005. *Sex differences in voter turnout: Fact sheet.* http://www.cawp.rutgers.edu/~cawp/Facts/sexdiff.pdf.

———. 2006. *Women appointed to presidential cabinets: Fact sheet.* http://www.cawp.rutgers.edu/Facts/Officeholders/fedcab.pdf.

———. 2007a. *Women in elective office 2007: Fact sheet.* http://www.cawp.rutgers.edu/Facts/Officeholders/elective.pdf.

———. 2007b. *Women of color in elective office 2007: Fact sheet.* http://www.cawp.rutgers.edu/Facts/Officeholders/color.pdf.

Center for Women's Business Research. 2007. *Top facts about women-owned businesses.* http://www.cfwbr.org/facts/index.php.

Chambliss, E., and C. Uggen. 2000. Women and men in elite law firms: Reevaluating Kanter's legacy. *Law and Social Inquiry* 25: 41–68.

Chatman, J. A., A. D. Boisnier, J. L. Berdahl, S. E. Spataro, and C. Anderson. 2005. The typical, the rare, and the outnumbered: Disentangling the effects of historical typicality and numerical distinctiveness at work. Working paper, University of California at Berkeley.

Chemers, M. M. 1997. *An integrative theory of leadership.* Mahwah, NJ: Erlbaum.

Cheng, M. N. 1998. Women conductors: Has the train left the station? *Harmony* no. 6: 81–90.

Chevalier, A. 2004. Motivation, expectations, and the gender pay gap for UK graduates. Discussion Paper No. 1101. Institute for the Study of Labor, Bonn, Germany.

Chin, J. L. 2004. 2003 Division 35 presidential address: Feminist leadership: Feminist visions and diverse voices. *Psychology of Women Quarterly* 28: 1–8.

Chronicle of Higher Education. 2006. Executive compensation 53, no. 14 (November 24), section B.

Cialdini, R. B. 2001. *Influence: Science and practice.* Boston: Allyn and Bacon.

Ciulla, J. B. 2004. Ethics and leadership effectiveness. In *The nature of leadership,* edited by J. Antonakis, A. T. Cianciolo, and R. J. Sternberg, 302–327. Thousand Oaks, CA: Sage.

Clift, E., and T. Brazaitis. 2000. *Madam President: Shattering the last glass ceiling.* New York: Scribner.

Clymer, A. 2001. Book says Nixon considered a woman for Supreme Court. *New York Times,* September 27, A16.

Coeds. 2007. *New York Times,* January 7, Education Life, 12–13.

Cohen, D., R. E. Nisbett, B. F. Bowdle, and N. Schwarz. 1996. Insult, aggression, and the Southern culture of honor: An "experimental ethnography." *Journal of Personality and Social Psychology* 70: 945–960.

Cohen, F., S. Solomon, M. Maxfield, T. Pyszczynski, and J. Greenberg. 2004. Fatal attraction: The effects of mortality salience on evaluations of charismatic, task-oriented, and relationship-oriented leaders. *Psychological Science* 15: 846–851.

Cohen, L. E., J. P. Broschak, and H. A. Haveman. 1998. And then there were more? The effect of organizational sex composition on the hiring and promotion of managers. *American Sociological Review* 63: 711–727.

Coleman, C. 2001. Rowing crew taught her to excel, one stroke at a time. In *How Jane won: 55 successful women share how they grew from ordinary girls to extraordinary women,* edited by S. Rimm and S. Rimm-Kaufman, 159–163. New York: Crown Business.

Collins, D. 1997. The ethical superiority and inevitability of participatory management as an organizational system. *Organization Science* 8: 489–507.

Collins, G. 1998. Why the women are fading away. *New York Times Magazine,* October 25, 54–55.

Collins, J. C. 2001. *Good to great: Why some companies make the leap . . . and others don't.* New York: HarperCollins.

Colvin, G. 2004. Power 25: The most powerful people in business. *Fortune* at *CNNMoney.com,* August 9. http://money.cnn.com/magazines/fortune/fortune_archive/2004/08/09/377903/index.htm.

———. 2006. Catch a rising star. *Fortune* at *CNNMoney.com,* January 30. http://money.cnn.com/magazines/fortune/fortune_archive/2006/02/06/8367928/index.htm.

Committee of 200. 2002. *The C200 business leadership index 2002: Annual report on women's clout in business.* Chicago: Committee of 200.

Conger, J. A., and R. N. Kanungo. 1998. *Charismatic leadership in organizations.* Thousand Oaks, CA: Sage.

Conlin, M. 2002. She's gotta have "it." *BusinessWeek Online,* July 22. http://www.businessweek.com/magazine/content/02_29/b3792112.htm?chan=search.

Connell, R. W. 2003. Scrambling in the ruins of patriarchy: Neo-liberalism and men's divided interests in gender change. In *Gender—from costs to benefits,* edited by U. Pasero, 58–69. Wiesbaden, Germany: Westdeutscher Verlag.

———. 2005. Change among the gatekeepers: Men, masculinities, and gender equality in the global arena. *Signs: Journal of Women in Culture and Society* 30: 1801–1825.

Conway, M., M. T. Pizzamiglio, and L. Mount. 1996. Status, communality, and agency: Implications for stereotypes of gender and other groups. *Journal of Personality and Social Psychology* 71: 25–38.

Copeland, C. L., J. E. Driskell, and E. Salas. 1995. Gender and reactions to dominance. *Journal of Social Behavior and Personality* 10: 53–68.

Correll, S. J. 2001. Gender and the career choice process: The role of biased self-assessments. *American Journal of Sociology* 106: 1691–1730.

———. 2004. Constraints into preferences: Gender, status, and emerging career aspirations. *American Sociological Review* 69: 93–133.

———, S. Benard, and I. Paik. 2007. Getting a job: Is there a motherhood penalty? *American Journal of Sociology* 112: 1297–1338.

Corrigall, E. A., and A. M. Konrad. 2006. The relationship of job attribute preferences to employment, hours of paid work, and family responsibilities: An analysis comparing women and men. *Sex Roles* 54: 95–111.

Cortina, L. M., and S. A. Wasti. 2005. Profiles in coping: Responses to sexual harassment across persons, organizations, and cultures. *Journal of Applied Psychology* 90: 182–192.

Coser, L. 1974. *Greedy institutions: Patterns of undivided commitment.* New York: Free Press.

Costa, P. T., Jr., A. Terracciano, and R. R. McCrae. 2001. Gender differences in personality traits across cultures: Robust and surprising findings. *Journal of Personality and Social Psychology* 81: 322–331.

Cotton, J. L., and J. M. Tuttle. 1986. Employee turnover: A meta-analysis and review with implications for research. *Academy of Management Review* 11: 55–70.

Council on Foundations. 2006. *2006 Grantmakers salary and benefits report: Executive summary.* Washington, DC: Council on Foundations. http://www.cof.org/Learn/content.cfm?itemnumber=9124&navItem Number=1983.

Cowan, R. S. 1976. Two washes in the morning and a bridge party at night: The American housewife between the wars. *Women's Studies* 3: 147–172.

———. 1983. *More work for mother: The ironies of household technologies from the open hearth to the microwave.* New York: Basic Books.

Cox, T. H., and C. V. Harquail. 1991. Career paths and career success in the early career stages of male and female MBAs. *Journal of Vocational Behavior* 39: 54–75.

Craig, J. M., and C. W. Sherif. 1986. The effectiveness of men and women in problem-solving groups as a function of group gender composition. *Sex Roles* 14: 453–466.

Creswell, J. 2006. How suite it isn't: A dearth of female bosses. *New York Times*, December 17, Business 1, 9, 10.

Crick, N. R., J. F. Casas, and D. A. Nelson. 2002. Toward a more comprehensive understanding of peer maltreatment: Studies of relational victimization. *Current Directions in Psychological Science* 11: 98–101.

———, and J. Grotpeter. 1995. Relational aggression, gender and social-psychological adjustment. *Child Development* 66: 710–722.

Crittenden, A. 2004. *If you've raised kids, you can manage anything: Leadership begins at home.* New York: Gotham Books.

Crocker, J., and B. Major. 1989. Social stigma and self-esteem: The self-protective properties of stigma. *Psychological Review* 96: 608–630.

Crosby, F. J. 1982. *Relative deprivation and working women.* New York: Oxford University Press.

———. 1984. The denial of personal discrimination. *American Behavioral Scientist* 27: 371–386.

———. 2004. *Affirmative action is dead: Long live affirmative action.* New Haven, CT: Yale University Press.

———, A. Iyer, and S. Sincharoen. 2006. Understanding affirmative action. *Annual Review of Psychology* 57: 585–611.

Cross, S. E., and L. Madson. 1997. Models of the self: Self-construals and gender. *Psychological Bulletin* 122: 5–37.

Cuddy, A. J. C., S. T. Fiske, and P. Glick. 2004. When professionals become mothers, warmth doesn't cut the ice. *Journal of Social Issues* 60: 701–718.

Dahlerup, D., ed. 2006. *Women, quotas and politics.* New York: Routledge, Taylor & Francis Group.

Dall'Ara, E., and A. Maass. 1999. Studying sexual harassment in the laboratory: Are egalitarian women at higher risk? *Sex Roles* 41: 681–704.

Daly, M., and M. Wilson. 1988. *Homicide.* New York: A. de Gruyter.

Darity, W. A., Jr., and P. L. Mason. 1998. Evidence on discrimination in employment: Codes of color, codes of gender. *Journal of Economic Perspectives* 12: 63–90.

Darley, J. M., and P. H. Gross. 1983. A hypothesis-confirming bias in labeling effects. *Journal of Personality and Social Psychology* 44: 20–33.

Darwin, C. 1871. *The descent of man and selection in relation to sex.* London: Murray.

Dasgupta, N., and S. Asgari. 2004. Seeing is believing: Exposure to counterstereotypic women leaders and its effect on the malleability of automatic gender stereotyping. *Journal of Experimental Social Psychology* 40: 642–658.

Daubman, K. A., and H. Sigall. 1997. Gender differences in perceptions of how others are affected by self-disclosure of achievement. *Sex Roles* 37: 73–89.

Davenport, D. B. 2003. Lessons learned. In *Some leaders are born women! Stories and strategies for building the leader within you,* edited by J. E. Gustafson, 113–116. Anthem, AZ: Leader Dynamics.

Davidson, M. J., and R. J. Burke. 2004. *Women in management worldwide: Facts, figures and analysis.* Aldershot, England: Ashgate.

Davies, P. G., S. J. Spencer, and C. M. Steele. 2005. Clearing the air: Identity safety moderates the effects of stereotype threat on women's leadership aspirations. *Journal of Personality and Social Psychology* 88: 276–287.

Davies-Netzley, S. A. 1998. Women above the glass ceiling: Perceptions on corporate mobility and strategies for success. *Gender & Society* 12: 339–355.

Davis, J. A., T. W. Smith, and P. V. Marsden. 2005. *General social surveys, 1972–2004.* 2nd ICPSR version. Chicago, IL: National Opinion Research Center [producer], 2005. Storrs, CT: Roper Center for Public Opinion Research, University of Connecticut / Ann Arbor, MI: Inter-university Consortium for Political and Social Research / Berkeley, CA: Computer-assisted Survey Methods Program (http://sda .berkeley.edu), University of California [distributors].

Davison, H. K., and M. J. Burke. 2000. Sex discrimination in simulated employment contexts: A meta-analytic investigation. *Journal of Vocational Behavior* 56: 225–248.

Dawkins, R. 1989. *The selfish gene.* New York: Oxford University Press.

Dean, C. 2005. For some girls, the problem with math is that they're good at it. *New York Times,* February 1, F3.

Deaux, K., and M. Kite. 1993. Gender stereotypes. In *Psychology of women: A handbook of issues and theories,* edited by F. L. Denmark and M. A. Paludi, 107–139. Westport, CT: Greenwood Press.

———, and B. Major. 1987. Putting gender into context: An interactive model of gender-related behavior. *Psychological Review* 94: 369–389.

Delli Carpini, M. X., and E. R. Fuchs. 1993. The year of the woman: Candidates, voters, and the 1992 elections. *Political Science Quarterly* 108: 29–36.

DeMott, B. 2000. *Killer woman blues: Why Americans can't think straight about gender and power.* Boston: Houghton Mifflin.

de Pater, I. E. 2005. *Doing things right or doing the right thing: A new perspective on the gender gap in career success.* Doctoral dissertation, University of Amsterdam.

———, and A. E. M. Van Vianen. 2006. Gender differences in job challenge: A matter of task preferences or task allocation? Paper presented at the annual meeting of the Society for Industrial and Organizational Psychology, New York, April.

Deutsch, C. H. 2002. At Xerox, the Chief earns (grudging) respect. *New York Times,* June 2, section 3, 1.

———. 2004. At lunch with: Sheila W. Wellington; In a marriage of equals, why create obstacles? *New York Times Online,* August 29. http://select.nytimes.com/search/restricted/article?res=F10D14F63A5A0C7 A8EDDA10894DC404482

———. 2005. Inside the news: Behind the exodus of executive women: Boredom. *New York Times,* May 1, section 3, 4.

Devine, D. J., L. D. Clayton, B. B. Dunford, R. Seying, and J. Pryce. 2000. Jury decision making: 45 years of empirical research. *Psychology, Public Policy, and Law* 7: 622–727.

Devine, P. G., M. J. Monteith, J. R. Zuwerink, and A. J. Elliot. 1991. Prejudice with and without compunction. *Journal of Personality and Social Psychology* 60: 817–830.

de Zárate, R. O. 2007. *Women rulers currently in office.* http://www.terra.es/personal2/monolith/00 women5.htm.

DiBerardinis, J. P., K. Ramage, and S. Levitt. 1984. Risky shift and gender of the advocate: Information theory versus normative theory. *Group & Organization Studies* 9: 189–200.

Diekman, A. B., and A. H. Eagly. 2000. Stereotypes as dynamic constructs: Women and men of the past, present, and future. *Personality and Social Psychology Bulletin* 26: 1171–1188.

———, A. H. Eagly, A. Mladinic, and M. C. Ferreira. 2005. Dynamic stereotypes about women and men in Latin America and the United States. *Journal of Cross-Cultural Psychology* 36: 209–226.

———, and W. Goodfriend. 2006. Rolling with the changes: A role congruity perspective on gender norms. *Psychology of Women Quarterly* 30: 369–383.

———, W. Goodfriend, and S. A. Goodwin. 2004. Dynamic stereotypes of power: Perceived change and stability in gender hierarchies. *Sex Roles* 50: 201–215.

Di Leonardo, M. 1992. The female world of cards and holidays: Women, families, and the work of kinship. In *Rethinking the family: Some feminist questions*, edited by B. Thorne and M. Yalom, rev. ed., 246–261. Boston: Northeastern University Press.

Dindia, K., and D. J. Canary, eds. 2006. *Sex differences and similarities in communication.* 2nd ed. Mahwah, NJ: Erlbaum.

Dirks, K. T., and D. L. Ferrin. 2002. Trust in leadership: Findings and implications for research and practice. *Journal of Applied Psychology* 87: 611–628.

Dobbins, G. H., and S. J. Platz. 1986. Sex differences in leadership: How real are they? *Academy of Management Review* 11: 118–127.

Dobryznski, J. H. 2006. Cherchez la femme. *Wall Street Journal*, August 4, A16.

Dollar, D., R. Fisman, and R. Gatti. 2001. Are women really the "fairer" sex? Corruption and women in government. *Journal of Economic Behavior & Organization* 46: 423–429.

Dorfman, P. W., and R. J. House. 2004. Cultural influences on organizational leadership: Literature review, theoretical rationale, and GLOBE project goals. In *Culture, leadership, and organizations: The GLOBE study of 62 societies*, edited by R. J. House, P. J. Hanges, M. Javidan, P. W. Dorfman, and V. Gupta, 51–73. Thousand Oaks, CA: Sage.

Dorning, M. 2005. How much bossiness is too much? Bolton's behavior puts issue on federal agenda. *Chicago Tribune*, May 12, section 1, 1, 24.

Douglas, S. J., and M. W. Michaels. 2004. *The mommy myth: The idealization of motherhood and how it has undermined women.* New York: Free Press.

Dowd, M. 2006. New themes for the same old songs. *New York Times*, September 6, A21.

Dreher, G. F. 2003. Breaking the glass ceiling: The effects of sex ratios and work-life programs on female leadership at the top. *Human Relations* 56: 541–562.

———, and T. H. Cox, Jr. 1996. Race, gender, and opportunity: A study of compensation attainment and establishment of mentoring relationships. *Journal of Applied Psychology* 81: 297–308.

———, and T. H. Cox, Jr. 2000. Labor market mobility and cash compensation: The moderating effects of race and gender. *Academy of Management Journal* 43: 890–900.

Driscoll, D., and C. R. Goldberg. 1993. *Members of the club: The coming of age of executive women.* New York: Free Press.

Driskell, J. E., B. Olmstead, and E. Salas. 1993. Task cues, dominance cues, and influence in task groups. *Journal of Applied Psychology* 78: 51–60.

———, and E. Salas. 2005. The effect of content and demeanor on reactions to dominance behavior. *Group Dynamics: Theory, Research, and Practice* 9: 3–14.

Duehr, E. E., and J. E. Bono. 2006. Men, women, and managers: Are stereotypes finally changing? *Personnel Psychology* 59: 815–846.

Dunning, D., and D. A. Sherman. 1997. Stereotypes and tacit inference. *Journal of Personality and Social Psychology* 73: 459–471.

Dunn-Jensen, L. M., and L. K. Stroh. 2007. Myths in the media: How the news media portray women in the workforce. In *Handbook of women in business and management*, edited by D. Bilimoria and S. K. Piderit, 13–33. Cheltenham, UK: Edward Elgar.

Dwyer, S., O. C. Richard, and K. Chadwick. 2003. Gender diversity in management and firm performance: The influence of growth orientation and organizational culture. *Journal of Business Research* 56: 1009–1019.

Eagly, A. H. 1983. Gender and social influence: A social psychological analysis. *American Psychologist* 38: 971–981.

———. 1987. *Sex differences in social behavior: A social-role interpretation.* Hillsdale, NJ: Erlbaum.

———. 2005. Achieving relational authenticity in leadership: Does gender matter? *Leadership Quarterly* 16: 459–474.

———, and L. L. Carli. 2003a. The female leadership advantage: An evaluation of the evidence. *Leadership Quarterly* 14: 807–834.

————, and L. L. Carli. 2003b. Finding gender advantage and disadvantage: Systematic research integration is the solution. *Leadership Quarterly* 14: 851–859.

————, and A. B. Diekman. 2005. What is the problem? Prejudice as an attitude-in-context. In *On the nature of prejudice: Fifty years after Allport*, edited by J. F. Dovidio, P. Glick, and L. Rudman, 19–35. Malden, MA: Blackwell.

————, and A. B. Diekman. 2006. Examining gender gaps in sociopolitical attitudes: It's not Mars and Venus. *Feminism & Psychology* 16: 26–34.

————, A. B. Diekman, M. C. Johannesen-Schmidt, and A. M. Koenig. 2004. Gender gaps in sociopolitical attitudes: A social psychological analysis. *Journal of Personality and Social Psychology* 87: 796–816.

————, M. C. Johannesen-Schmidt, and M. L. van Engen. 2003. Transformational, transactional, and laissez-faire leadership styles: A meta-analysis comparing women and men. *Psychological Bulletin* 129: 569–591.

————, and B. T. Johnson. 1990. Gender and leadership style: A meta-analysis. *Psychological Bulletin* 108: 233–256.

————, and S. J. Karau. 1991. Gender and the emergence of leaders: A meta-analysis. *Journal of Personality and Social Psychology* 60: 685–710.

————, and S. J. Karau. 2002. Role congruity theory of prejudice toward female leaders. *Psychological Review* 109: 573–598.

————, S. J. Karau, and M. G. Makhijani. 1995. Gender and the effectiveness of leaders: A meta-analysis. *Psychological Bulletin* 117: 125–145.

————, S. J. Karau, J. B. Miner, and B. T. Johnson. 1994. Gender and motivation to manage in hierarchic organizations: A meta-analysis. *Leadership Quarterly* 5: 135–159.

————, M. G. Makhijani, and B. G. Klonsky. 1992. Gender and the evaluation of leaders: A meta-analysis. *Psychological Bulletin* 111: 3–22.

————, and A. Mladinic. 1994. Are people prejudiced against women? Some answers from research on attitudes, gender stereotypes, and judgments of competence. In *European review of social psychology*, edited by W. Stroebe and M. Hewstone, Vol. 5, 1–35. New York: Wiley.

————, and V. J. Steffen. 1984. Gender stereotypes stem from the distribution of women and men into social roles. *Journal of Personality and Social Psychology* 46: 735–754.

————, and V. J. Steffen. 1986. Gender and aggressive behavior: A meta-analytic review of the social psychological literature. *Psychological Bulletin* 100: 309–330.

————, and W. Wood. 1982. Inferred sex differences in status as a determinant of gender stereotypes about social influence. *Journal of Personality and Social Psychology* 43: 915–928.

————, and W. Wood. 1999. The origins of sex differences in human behavior: Evolved dispositions versus social roles. *American Psychologist* 54: 408–423.

————, W. Wood, and A. Diekman. 2000. Social role theory of sex differences and similarities: A current appraisal. In *The developmental social psychology of gender*, edited by T. Eckes and H. M. Trautner, 123–174. Mahwah, NJ: Erlbaum.

————, W. Wood, and M. C. Johannnesen-Schmidt. 2004. The social role theory of sex differences and similarities: Implications for partner preferences. In *The psychology of gender*, edited by A. H. Eagly, A. Beall, and R. J. Sternberg, 2nd ed., 269–295. New York: Guilford Press.

Eccles, J. S. 2001. Achievement. In *Encyclopedia of women and gender: Sex similarities and differences and the impact of society on gender*, edited by J. Worell, Vol. 1, 43–53. San Diego: Academic Press.

Eddleston, K. A., J. F. Veiga, and G. N. Powell. 2006. Explaining sex differences in managerial career satisfier preferences: The role of gender self-schema. *Journal of Applied Psychology* 91: 437–445.

Ellemers, N., D. de Gilder, and H. van den Heuvel. 1998. Career-oriented versus team-oriented commitment and behavior at work. *Journal of Applied Social Psychology* 83: 717–730.

————, D. de Gilder, and S. A. Haslam. 2004. Motivating individuals and groups at work: A social identity perspective on leadership and group performance. *Academy of Management Review* 29: 459–478.

Elliot, M. 2004. Men want change too. *Time*, March 22, 59.

Elliott, J. R., and R. A. Smith. 2004. Race, gender, and workplace power. *American Sociological Review* 69: 365–386.

Ellyson, S. L., J. F. Dovidio, and C. E. Brown. 1992. The look of power: Gender differences in visual dominance behavior. In *Gender, interaction, and inequality*, edited by C. L. Ridgeway, 50–80. New York: Springer-Verlag.

Elsass, P. M., and L. M. Graves. 1997. Demographic diversity in decision-making groups: The experiences of women and people of color. *Academy of Management Review* 22: 946–973.

Else-Quest, N. M., J. S. Hyde, H. H. Goldsmith, and C. A. Van Hulle. 2006. Gender differences in temperament: A meta-analysis. *Psychological Bulletin* 132: 33–72.

Ely, R. J. 1995. The power in demography: Women's social constructions of gender identity at work. *Academy of Management Journal* 38: 589–634.

———, and D. E. Meyerson. 2000. Theories of gender in organizations: A new approach to organizational analysis and change. *Research in Organizational Behavior* 22: 103–151.

———, D. E. Meyerson, and M. N. Davidson. 2006. Rethinking political correctness. *Harvard Business Review* 84(9): 78–87.

———, M. Scully, and E. Foldy, eds. 2003. *Reader in gender, work, and organization*. Malden, MA: Blackwell.

Ember, C. R. 1978. Myths about hunter–gatherers. *Ethnology* 17: 439–448.

Emrich, C. G., F. L. Denmark, and D. N. Den Hartog. 2004. Cross-cultural differences in gender egalitarianism: Implications for societies, organizations, and leaders. In *Culture, leadership, and organizations: The GLOBE study of 62 societies*, edited by R. J. House, P. J. Hanges, M. Javidan, P. W. Dorfman, and V. Gupta, 343–394. Thousand Oaks, CA: Sage.

England, P. 1992. *Comparable worth: Theories and evidence*. New York: Aldine de Gruyter.

———. 2005. Gender inequality in labor markets: The role of motherhood and segregation. *Social Politics* 12: 264–288.

———. 2006. Toward gender equality: Progress and bottlenecks. In *The declining significance of gender?* edited by F. D. Blau, M. C. Brinton, and D. B. Grusky, 245–264. New York: Russell Sage Foundation.

———, P. Allison, and X. Wu. In press. Does bad pay cause occupations to feminize, does feminization reduce pay, and how can we tell with longitudinal data? *Social Science Research*.

Epitropaki, O., and R. Martin. 2004. Implicit leadership theories in applied settings: Factor structure, generalizability, and stability over time. *Journal of Applied Psychology* 89: 293–310.

Erhardt, M. L., J. D. Werbel, and C. B. Shrader. 2003. Board of director diversity and firm financial performance. *Corporate Governance* 11: 102–111.

Erkut, S. 2001. *Inside women's power: Learning from leaders*. Wellesley, MA: Wellesley Centers for Women.

European Commission. 2006. *Decision-making in the top 50 publicly quoted companies*. December 4. http://europa.eu.int/comm/employment_social/women_men_stats/out/measures_out438_en.htm.

Evenson, R. J., and R. W. Simon. 2005. Clarifying the relationship between parenthood and depression. *Journal of Health and Social Behavior* 46: 341–358.

Ewing, M. E., L. A. Gano-Overway, C. F. Branta, and V. D. Seefeldt. 2002. The role of sport in youth development. In *Paradoxes of youth and sport*, edited by M. Gatz, M. A. Messner, and S. J. Ball-Rokeach, 31–47. Albany, NY: SUNY Press.

Fagenson, E. A. 1990. Perceived masculine and feminine attributes examined as a function of individuals' sex and level in the organizational power hierarchy: A test of four theoretical perspectives. *Journal of Applied Psychology* 75: 204–211.

———, and J. J. Jackson. 1994. The status of women managers in the United States. In *Competitive frontiers: Women managers in a global economy*, edited by N. J. Adler and D. N. Israeli, 388–404. Oxford: Blackwell.

Falbo, T., M. D. Hazen, and D. Linimon. 1982. The costs of selecting power bases or messages associated with the opposite sex. *Sex Roles* 8: 147–157.

Families and Work Institute. 2005. *Generation and gender in the workplace*. New York: Families and Work Institute. http://familiesandwork.org/eproducts/genandgender.pdf.

Farrell, W. 2005. *Why men earn more: The startling truth behind the pay gap and what women can do about it*. New York: American Management Association.

Fazio, R. H., and M. A. Olson. 2003. Implicit measures in social cognition research: Their meaning and use. *Annual Review of Psychology* 54: 297–327.

Featherstone, L. 2004. *Selling women short: The landmark battle for workers' rights at Wal-Mart*. New York: Basic Books.

Federal Bureau of Investigation. 2004. *Crime in the United States 2004: Uniform crime reports*. http://www.fbi.gov/ucr/cius_04/.

Federal Glass Ceiling Commission. 1995a. *Good for business: Making full use of the nation's human capital: The environmental scan: A fact-finding report of the Federal Glass Ceiling Commission*. Washington, DC: United States Government Printing Office.

———. 1995b. *A solid investment: Making full use of the nation's human capital*. Washington, DC: U.S. Government Printing Office.

Feingold, A. 1994. Gender differences in personality: A meta-analysis. *Psychological Bulletin* 116: 429–456.

Feldman-Summers, S., D. E. Montano, D. Kasprzyk, and B. Wagner. 1980. Influence attempts when competing views are gender-related: Sex as credibility. *Psychology of Women Quarterly* 5: 311–320.

Fenwick, S. L. 2001. From candy striper to hospital COO. In *How Jane won: 55 successful women share how they grew from ordinary girls to extraordinary women*, edited by S. Rimm and S. Rimm-Kaufman, 141–145. New York: Crown Business.

Ferdman, B. M. 1999. The color and culture of gender in organizations: Attending to race and ethnicity. In *Handbook of gender and work*, edited by G. Powell, 17–34. Thousand Oaks, CA: Sage.

Fiedler, F. E. 1967. *A theory of leadership effectiveness*. New York: McGraw-Hill.

Filardo, A. K. 1996. Gender patterns in African American and white adolescents' social interactions in same-race, mixed-gender groups. *Journal of Personality and Social Psychology* 71: 71–82.

Finder, A., P. D. Healy, and K. Zernike. 2006. President of Harvard resigns, ending stormy 5-year tenure. *New York Times Online*, February 22. http://www.nytimes.com/20006/02/22/education.

Finkelstein, S., and D. C. Hambrick. 1996. *Strategic leadership: Top executives and their effects on organizations.* Minneapolis/St. Paul: West Publishing Company.

Fiorina, C. 2006. *Tough choices: A memoir.* New York: Portfolio of Penguin Group.

Firth, M. 1982. Sex discrimination in job opportunities for women. *Sex Roles* 8: 891–901.

Fisher, A. 2006. Avoiding the dreaded B-word: How women executives can stand up for themselves without being labeled uncooperative or worse. *Fortune* at *CNN.Money.com*, October 3. http://209.85 .165.104/search?q=cache:AZse3AT0320J:money.cnn.com/2006/09/29/news/economy/mpw.bword .fortune/index.htm+%22woman+boss%22+bitchy&hl=en&gl=us&ct=clnk&cd=3.

Fisher, R., B. M. Patton, and W. K. Ury. 1991. *Getting to yes: Negotiating agreement without giving in.* Boston: Houghton Mifflin.

Fiske, A. P., N. Haslam, and S. T. Fiske. 1991. Confusing one person with another: What errors reveal about the elementary forms of social relations. *Journal of Personality and Social Psychology* 60: 656–674.

Fiske, S. T. 1998. Stereotyping, prejudice, and discrimination. In *The handbook of social psychology*, edited by D. T. Gilbert, S. T. Fiske, and G. Lindzey, 4th ed., Vol. 2, 357–411. Boston: McGraw-Hill.

———, D. N. Bersoff, E. Borgida, K. Deaux, and M. E. Heilman. 1991. Social science research on trial: Use of sex stereotyping research in Price Waterhouse v. Hopkins. *American Psychologist* 46: 1049–1060.

———, and L. E. Stevens. 1993. What's so special about sex? Gender stereotyping and discrimination. In *Gender issues in contemporary society: Claremont symposium on applied social psychology*, Vol. 6, 173–196. Newbury Park, CA: Sage.

Fitzgerald, L. F., F. Drasgow, C. L. Hulin, M. J. Gelfand, and V. J. Magley. 1997. Antecedents and consequences of sexual harassment in organizations: A test of an integrated model. *Journal of Applied Psychology* 82: 578–589.

Fix, M., and M. A. Turner, eds. 1998. *A national report card on discrimination in America: The role of testing.* Washington, DC: Urban Institute. http://www.urban.org/UploadedPDF/report_card.pdf.

Fletcher, J. K. 1999. *Disappearing acts: Gender, power, and relational practice at work.* Cambridge, MA: MIT Press.

———. 2004. The paradox of postheroic leadership: An essay on gender, power, and transformational change. *Leadership Quarterly* 15: 647–661.

Flynn, F. J., and D. R. Ames. 2006. What's good for the goose may not be as good for the gander: The benefits of self-monitoring for men and women in task groups and dyadic conflicts. *Journal of Applied Psychology* 91: 272–281.

Foels, R., J. E. Driskell, B. Mullen, and E. Salas. 2000. The effects of democratic leadership on group member satisfaction: An integration. *Small Group Research* 31: 676–701.

Foley, L. A., and M. A. Pigott. 1997. The influence of forepersons and nonforepersons on mock jury decisions. *American Journal of Forensic Psychology* 15: 5–17.

Fondas, N. 1992. A behavioral job description for managers. *Organizational Dynamics* 21: 47–58.

———. 1997. Feminization unveiled: Management qualities in contemporary writings. *Academy of Management Review* 22: 257–282.

Forret, M. L., and T. W. Dougherty. 2004. Networking behaviors and career outcomes: Differences for men and women? *Journal of Organizational Behavior* 25: 419–437.

Fortune 50 most powerful women in business. 2006. *Fortune* at *CNN.Money.com*, October 16. http://money .cnn.com/magazines/fortune/mostpowerfulwomen/2006/index.html.

Foschi, M. 1996. Double standards in the evaluation of men and women. *Social Psychology Quarterly* 59: 237–254.

————. 2000. Double standards for competence: Theory and research. *Annual Review of Sociology* 26: 21–42.

————, L. Lai, and K. Sigerson. 1994. Gender and double standards in the assessment of job applicants. *Social Psychology Quarterly* 57: 326–339.

————, K. Sigerson, and M. Lembesis. 1995. Assessing job applicants: The relative effects of gender, academic record, and decision type. *Small Group Research* 26: 328–352.

Fox, R. L., and J. L. Lawless. 2004. Entering the arena? Gender and the decision to run for office. *American Journal of Political Science* 48: 264–280.

Franke, G. R., D. F. Crown, and D. F. Spake. 1997. Gender differences in ethical perceptions of business practices: A social role theory perspective. *Journal of Applied Psychology* 82: 920–934.

Frankel, L. P. 2004. *Nice girls don't get the corner office: 101 unconscious mistakes women make that sabotage their careers*. New York: Warner Business Books.

Fried-Buchalter, S. 1997. Fear of success, fear of failure, and the imposter phenomenon among male and female marketing managers. *Sex Roles* 37: 847–859.

Friedman, C., and K. Yorio. 2006. *The girl's guide to being a boss (without being a bitch): Valuable lessons, smart suggestions, and true stories for succeeding as the chick-in-charge*. New York: Morgan Road Books.

Friedman, S. A. 1996. *Work matters: Women talk about their jobs and their lives*. New York: Viking.

Frissen, V. A. J. 2000. ICTs in the rush hour of life. *The Information Society* 16: 65–75.

From one male bastion to the other. 2006. *Business Week Online*, May 15. http://www.businessweek.com/magazine/content/06_20/b3984060.htm?campaign_id=search.

Fuchs Epstein, C., F. Olivares, P. Graham, F. N. Schwartz, M. R. Siegel, J. Mansbridge, et al. 1991. Ways men and women lead. *Harvard Business Review* 69(1): 150–158.

Fuegen, K., M. Biernat, E. Haines, and K. Deaux. 2004. Mothers and fathers in the workplace: How gender and parental status influence judgments of job-related competence. *Journal of Social Issues* 60: 737–754.

Fukuyama, F. 1998. Women and the evolution of world politics. *Foreign Affairs* 77(5): 24–40.

Fuller, J. 2007. 2 leaders tell us about ourselves. *Chicago Tribune*, February 2, section 1, 19.

Galinsky, E., K. Salmond, J. T. Bond, M. B. Kropf, M. Moore, and B. Harrington. 2003. *Leaders in a global economy: A study of executive women and men*. New York: Families and Work Institute.

Gardiner, M., and M. Tiggemann. 1999. Gender differences in leadership style, job stress and mental health in male- and female-dominated industries. *Journal of Occupational and Organizational Psychology* 72: 301–315.

Gardner, W. L., and S. Gabriel. 2004. Gender differences in relational and collective interdependence: Implications for self-views, social behavior, and subjective well-being. In *The psychology of gender*, edited by A. H. Eagly, A. E. Beall, and R. J. Sternberg, 2nd ed., 169–191. New York: Guilford Press.

Garvin, D. A. 1993. Building a learning organization. *Harvard Business Review* 71 (4): 78–91.

Gastil, J. 1994. A meta-analytic review of the productivity and satisfaction of democratic and autocratic leadership. *Small Group Research* 25: 384–410.

Gawronski, B. 2003. On difficult questions and evident answers: Dispositional inference from role-constrained behavior. *Personality and Social Psychology Bulletin* 29: 1459–1475.

Geary, D. C. 1998. *Male, female: The evolution of human sex differences*. Washington, DC: American Psychological Association.

Gehrke, K. 2006. Hicks makes history at the Minnesota Orchestra. Minnesota Public Radio, November 7. http://minnesota.publicradio.org/display/web/2006/11/07/sarahhicks/.

Gelfand, M. J., J. L. Raver, L. H. Nishii, and B. Schneider. 2005. Discrimination in organizations: An organizational level systems perspective. In *Discrimination at work: The psychological and organizational bases*, edited by R. L. Dipboye and A. Colella, 89–116. Mahwah, NJ: Erlbaum.

George and Laura Bush: The *People* interview. 2006. *People.com*, December 15. http://www.people.com/people/article/0,,20004374,00.html.

Gergen, D. 2005. Women leading in the twenty-first century. In *Enlightened power: How women are transforming the practice of leadership*, edited by L. Coughlin, E. Wingard, and K. Hollihan, xv–xxix. San Francisco: Jossey-Bass.

Gerhart, B., and S. Rynes. 1991. Determinants and consequences of salary negotiations by male and female MBA graduates. *Journal of Applied Psychology* 76: 256–262.

Gerrard, M., C. Breda, and F. X. Gibbons. 1990. Gender effects in couples' decision making and contraceptive use. *Journal of Applied Social Psychology* 20: 449–464.

Giacalone, R. A., and C. A. Riordan. 1990. Effect of self-presentation on perceptions and recognition in an organization. *Journal of Psychology* 124: 25–38.

Giele, J. Z. 2004. Women and men as agents of change in their own lives. In *Changing life patterns in Western industrial societies*, edited by J. Z. Giele and E. Holst, Advances in life course research, Vol. 8, 299–317. Amsterdam: Elsevier.

Gilbert, D. T. 1998. Ordinary personology. In *The handbook of social psychology*, edited by D. T. Gilbert, S. T. Fiske, and G. Lindzey, 4th ed., Vol. 2, 89–150. Boston: McGraw-Hill.

Gill, M. J. 2004. When information does not deter stereotyping: Prescriptive stereotyping can foster bias under conditions that deter descriptive stereotyping. *Journal of Experimental Social Psychology* 40: 619–632.

Gladwell, M. 2005. *Blink: The power of thinking without thinking*. New York: Little, Brown.

Glass, J. 1990. The impact of occupational segregation on working conditions. *Social Forces* 68: 779–796.

———, and V. Camarigg. 1992. Gender, parenthood, and job-family compatibility. *American Journal of Sociology* 98: 131–151.

Glick, P. 1991. Trait-based and sex-based discrimination in occupational prestige, occupational salary, and hiring. *Sex Roles* 25: 351–378.

———, and S. T. Fiske. 1996. The Ambivalent Sexism Inventory: Differentiating hostile and benevolent sexism. *Journal of Personality and Social Psychology* 3: 491–512.

———, and S. T. Fiske. 2001a. An ambivalent alliance: Hostile and benevolent sexism as complementary justifications for gender inequality. *American Psychologist* 56: 109–118.

———, and S. T. Fiske. 2001b. Ambivalent sexism. In *Advances in experimental social psychology*, edited by M. P. Zanna, Vol. 33, 115–188. San Diego: Academic Press.

Gmelch, W. H., P. K. Wilke, and N. P. Lovrich. 1986. Dimensions of stress among university faculty: Factor-analytic results from a national study. *Research in Higher Education* 24: 266–286.

Gneezy, U., M. Niederle, and A. Rustichini. 2003. Performance in competitive environments: Gender differences. *Quarterly Journal of Economics* 118: 1049–1074.

———, and A. Rustichini. 2004. Gender and competition at a young age. *American Economic Review* 94: 377–381.

Goldberg, C. B., L. M. Finkelstein, E. L. Perry, and A. M. Konrad. 2004. Job and industry fit: The effects of age and gender matches on career progress outcomes. *Journal of Organizational Behavior* 25: 807–829.

Goldberg, P. 1968. Are women prejudiced against women? *Trans-Action* 5: 316–322.

Goldberg, S. 1993. *Why men rule: A theory of male dominance*. Chicago: Open Court.

Goldin, C. 1997. Career and family: College women look to the past. In *Gender and family issues in the workplace*, edited by F. Blau and R. Ehrenberg, 20–64. New York: Russell Sage Foundation.

———. 2006. The rising (and then declining) significance of gender. In *The declining significance of gender?* edited by F. D. Blau, M. C. Brinton, and D. B. Grusky, 67–101. New York: Russell Sage Foundation.

———, L. F. Katz, and I. Kuziemko. 2006. The homecoming of American college women: The reversal of the college gender gap. National Bureau of Economic Research Working Paper No. 121139. http://www.nber.org/papers/w12139.

———, and C. Rouse. 2000. Orchestrating impartiality: The impact of "blind" auditions on female musicians. *American Economic Review* 90: 715–741.

Gomez-Mejia, L. R., J. E. McCann, and R. C. Page. 1985. The structure of managerial behaviors and rewards. *Industrial Relations* 24: 147–154.

Goode, W. J. 1960. A theory of role strain. *American Sociological Review* 25: 483–496.

Goodman, C. K. 2005. Gen X dads struggle to balance work and home lives. *New York Times*, March 21, C3.

Goodman, E. 2004. Little mention of woman for VP. *Boston Globe*, July 8, A11.

Goodman, J. S., D. L. Fields, and T. C. Blum. 2003. Cracks in the glass ceiling: In what kinds of organizations do women make it to the top? *Group & Organization Management* 28: 475–501.

Goodwin, S. A., and S. T. Fiske. 2001. Power and gender: The double-edged sword of ambivalence. In *Handbook of the psychology of women and gender*, edited by R. K. Unger, 358–366. Hoboken, NJ: Wiley.

Gorman, E. H. 2005. Gender stereotypes, same-gender preferences, and organizational variation in the hiring of women: Evidence from law firms. *American Sociological Review* 70: 702–728.

Graham, K. 1997. *Personal history*. New York: Knopf.

Graves, L. M., and G. N. Powell. 1996. Sex similarity, quality of the employment interview and recruiters' evaluation of actual applicants. *Journal of Occupational and Organizational Psychology* 69: 243–261.

Green, C. A., and M. A. Ferber. 2005. The long-run effect of part-time work. *Journal of Labor Research* 26: 323–333.

Greene, B. A., and T. K. DeBacker. 2004. Gender and orientations toward the future: Links to motivation. *Educational Psychology Review* 16: 91–120.

Greenhaus, J. H., and G. N. Powell. 2006. When work and family are allies: A theory of work-family enrichment. *Academy of Management Review* 31: 72–92.

Greenstein, T. N. 2000. Economic dependence, gender, and the division of labor in the home: A replication and extension. *Journal of Marriage and the Family* 62: 322–335.

Griffen, R. W., and Y. P. Lopez. 2005. "Bad behavior" in organizations: A review and typology for future research. *Journal of Management* 31: 988–1005.

Griffeth, R. W., P. W. Hom, and S. Gaertner. 2000. A meta-analysis of antecedents and correlates of employee turnover: Update, moderator tests, and research implications for the next millennium. *Journal of Management* 26: 463–488.

Gronau, R. 1988. Sex-related wage differentials and women's interrupted labor careers—the chicken or the egg. *Journal of Labor Economics* 6: 277–301.

Groves, K. S. 2005. Gender differences in social and emotional skills and charismatic leadership. *Journal of Leadership and Organizational Studies* 11: 30–46.

Gruber, J. E. 1998. The impact of male work environments and organizational policies on women's experiences of sexual harassment. *Gender & Society* 12: 301–320.

Grzelakowski, M. 2005. *Mother leads best: 50 women who are changing the way organizations define leadership.* Chicago: Dearborn Trade Publishing.

Grzywacz, J. G., and N. F. Marks. 2000. Reconceptualizing the work-family interface: An ecological perspective on the correlates of positive and negative spillover between work and family. *Journal of Occupational Health Psychology* 5: 111–126.

Guastello, D. D., and S. J. Guastello. 2003. Androgyny, gender role behavior, and emotional intelligence among college students and their parents. *Sex Roles* 49: 663–673.

Gupta, D., R. L. Oaxaca, and N. Smith. 2006. Swimming upstream, floating downstream: Comparing women's relative wage progress in the United States and Denmark. *Industrial and Labor Relations Review* 59: 243–266.

Gupta, S. 1999. The effects of transitions in marital status on men's performance of housework. *Journal of Marriage and the Family* 61: 700–711.

Gutek, B. A. 2001. Women and paid work. *Psychology of Women Quarterly* 25: 379–393.

———, and B. Morasch. 1982. Sex-ratios, sex-role spillover, and sexual harassment of women at work. *Journal of Social Issues* 38(4): 55–74.

Hackman, M. Z., A. H. Furniss, M. J. Hills, and T. J. Patterson. 1992. Perceptions of gender-role characteristics and transformational and transactional leadership behaviours. *Perceptual and Motor Skills* 75: 311–319.

Hall, J. A. 2006. Women's and men's nonverbal communication: Similarities, differences, stereotypes, and origins. In *The SAGE handbook of nonverbal communication*, edited by V. L. Manusov and M. L. Patterson, 201–218. Thousand Oaks, CA: Sage.

———, and J. D. Carter. 1999a. Gender-stereotype accuracy as an individual difference. *Journal of Personality and Social Psychology* 77: 350–359.

———, and J. D. Carter. 1999b. Unpublished data. Northeastern University, Boston.

———, E. J. Coats, and L. S. LeBeau. 2005. Nonverbal behavior and the vertical dimension of social relations: A meta-analysis. *Psychological Bulletin* 131: 898–924.

Halpern, D. F. 2000. *Sex differences in cognitive abilities.* 3rd ed. Mahwah, NJ: Erlbaum.

———. 2001. Sex difference research: Cognitive abilities. In *Encyclopedia of women and gender: Sex similarities and differences and the impact of society on gender*, edited by J. Worrell, Vol. 2, 963–971. San Diego: Academic Press.

Hamilton, D. L., and R. K. Gifford. 1976. Illusory correlation in interpersonal perception: A cognitive bias of stereotypic judgments. *Journal of Experimental Social Psychology* 12: 392–407.

Hanisch, K. A. 1996. An integrated framework for studying the outcomes of sexual harassment: Consequences for individuals and organizations. In *Sexual harassment in the workplace: Perspectives frontiers and response strategies*, edited by E. S. Stockdale, 174–198. Thousand Oaks, CA: Sage.

Harmon, M., senior producer. 2006. *The nightly business report: One on one with Susan Gharib*, October 11. Miami: NBR Enterprises. http://www.pbs.org/nbr/site/onair/gharib/061011_gharib/.

Harper, S., and B. F. Reskin. 2005. Affirmative action at school and on the job. *Annual Review of Sociology* 31: 357–379.

Harris, C. R. 2003. A review of sex differences in sexual jealousy, including self-report data, psychophysiological responses, interpersonal violence, and morbid jealousy. *Personality and Social Psychology Review* 7: 102–128.

Hass, N. 2005. Hollywood's new old girls' network. *New York Times*, April 24, section 2, 1, 13.

Hayden, B., M. Deal, A. Cannon, and J. Casey. 1986. Ecological determinants of women's status among hunter/gatherers. *Human Evolution* 1: 449–473.

Hays, S. 1996. *The cultural contradictions of motherhood*. New Haven, CT: Yale University Press.

Hazan, C., and L. M. Diamond. 2000. The place of attachment in human mating. *Review of General Psychology* 4: 186–204.

Heatherington, L., A. B. Burns, and T. B. Gustafson. 1998. When another stumbles: Gender and self-presentation to vulnerable others. *Sex Roles* 38: 889–913.

———, K. A. Daubman, C. Bates, A. Ahn, H. Brown, and C. Preston. 1993. Two investigations of "female modesty" in achievement situations. *Sex Roles* 29: 739–754.

Heckman, J. J. 1998. Detecting discrimination. *Journal of Economic Perspectives* 12: 101–116.

Heffernan, M. 2002. The female CEO ca. 2002. *Fast Company* 61 (August): 9, 58, 60, 62, 64, 66.

———. 2004. *The naked truth: A working woman's manifesto on business and what really matters*. San Francisco: Jossey-Bass.

Heifetz, R. A. 1994. *Leadership without easy answers*. Cambridge, MA: Harvard University Press.

Heilman, M. E. 1983. Sex bias in work settings: The lack of fit model. *Research in Organizational Behavior* 5: 269–298.

———. 1996. Affirmative action's contradictory consequences. *Journal of Social Issues* 52: 105–109.

———. 2001. Description and prescription: How gender stereotypes prevent women's ascent up the organizational ladder. *Journal of Social Issues* 57: 657–674.

———, and S. L. Blader. 2001. Assuming preferential selection when the admissions policy is unknown: The effect of gender rarity. *Journal of Applied Psychology* 86: 188–193.

———, C. J. Block, and R. F. Martell. 1995. Sex stereotypes: Do they influence perceptions of managers? *Journal of Social Behavior and Personality* 10: 237–252.

———, C. J. Block, R. F. Martell, and M. C. Simon. 1989. Has anything changed? Current characterizations of men, women, and managers. *Journal of Applied Psychology* 74: 935–942.

———, and J. J. Chen. 2005. Same behavior, different consequences: Reactions to men's and women's altruistic citizenship behavior. *Journal of Applied Psychology* 90: 431–441.

———, R. F. Martell, and M. C. Simon. 1988. The vagaries of sex bias: Conditions regulating the undervaluation, equivaluation, and overvaluation of female job applicants. *Organizational Behavior and Human Decision Processes* 41: 98–110.

———, and T. G. Okimoto. 2007. Why are women penalized for success at male tasks? The implied communality deficit. *Journal of Applied Psychology* 92: 81–92.

———, and L. R. Saruwatari. 1979. When beauty is beastly: The effects of appearance and sex on evaluations of job applicants for managerial and nonmanagerial jobs. *Organizational Behavior and Human Decision Processes* 23: 360–372.

———, A. S. Wallen, D. Fuchs, and M. M. Tamkins. 2004. Penalties for success: Reactions to women who succeed in male gender-typed tasks. *Journal of Applied Psychology* 89: 416–427.

Heldman, C., S. J. Carroll, and S. Olson. 2005. "She brought only a skirt": Print media coverage of Elizabeth Dole's bid for the Republican presidential nomination. *Political Communication* 22: 315–335.

Helfat, C. E., D. Harris, and P. J. Wolfson. 2006. The pipeline to the top: Women and men in the top executive ranks of U.S. corporations. *Academy of Management Perspectives* 20(4): 42–64.

Helgesen, S. 1990. *The female advantage: Women's ways of leadership*. New York: Currency/Doubleday.

Hemphill, J. K., and A. E. Coons. 1957. Development of the Leader Behavior Description Questionnaire. In *Leader behavior: Its description and measurement*, edited by R. M. Stogdill and A. E. Coons, 6–38. Columbus, OH: Bureau of Business Research, Ohio State University.

Hepworth, W., and A. Towler. 2004. The effects of individual differences and charismatic leadership on workplace aggression. *Journal of Occupational Health Psychology* 9: 176–185.

Herbert, B. 2006. Hillary can run, but can she win? *New York Times*, May 19, A29.

Hewlett, S. A. 2002. *Creating a life: Professional women and the quest for children*. New York: Talk Miramax Books.

———, and C. B. Luce. 2005. Off-ramps and on-ramps: Keeping talented women on the road to success. *Harvard Business Review* 38 (3): 43–46, 48, 50–54.

Hill, J. L., J. Waldfogel, J. Brooks-Gunn, and W. Han. 2005. Maternal employment and child development: A fresh look using newer methods. *Developmental Psychology*, 41, 833–850.

Hill, M. 2003. Where have all the sisters gone? In *The difference "difference" makes: Women and leadership*, edited by D. L. Rhode, 98–101. Stanford, CA: Stanford Law and Politics.

Hines, M. 2004. *Brain gender*. New York: Oxford University Press.

Hirsch, B. T. 2004. Why do part-time workers earn less? The role of worker and job skills. IZA Discussion Paper No. 1261. Institute for the Study of Labor, Bonn, Germany.

Hochschild, A. R. 1997. *The time bind: When work becomes home and home becomes work*. New York: Metropolitan Books.

Hogan, R., and R. B. Kaiser. 2005. What we know about leadership. *Review of General Psychology* 9: 169–180.

Hogue, M., and J. D. Yoder. 2003. The role of status in producing depressed entitlement in women's and men's pay allocations. *Psychology of Women Quarterly* 27: 330–337.

Hollands, J. 2002. *Same game, different rules: How to get ahead without being a bully broad, ice queen, or "Ms. Understood."* New York: McGraw-Hill.

Holtgraves, T., and B. Lasky. 1999. Linguistic power and persuasion. *Journal of Language and Social Psychology* 18: 196–205.

Hosoda, M., and D. L. Stone. 2000. Current gender stereotypes and their evaluative content. *Perceptual and Motor Skills* 90: 1283–1294.

House, R. J., P. J. Hanges, M. Javidan, P. W. Dorfman, and V. Gupta, eds. 2004. *Culture, leadership, and organizations: The GLOBE study of 62 societies*. Thousand Oaks, CA: Sage.

Howell, J. P., and D. L. Costley. 2006. *Understanding behaviors for effective leadership*. Upper Saddle River, NJ: Pearson Prentice Hall.

Hoyt, C. L., and J. Blascovich. In press. Leadership efficacy and women leaders' responses to stereotype activation. *Group Processes and Intergroup Relations*.

Huddy, L., and N. Terkildsen. 1993. The consequences of gender stereotypes for women candidates at different levels and types of office. *Political Research Quarterly* 46: 503–525.

Hudson, K. 2001. She learned to pass tests from the boys. In *How Jane won: 55 successful women share how they grew from ordinary girls to extraordinary women*, edited by S. Rimm and S. Rimm-Kaufman, 117–121. New York: Crown Business.

Huffman, M. L. 2004. Gender inequality across local wage hierarchies. *Work and Occupations* 31: 323–344.

———, and L. Torres. 2002. It's not only "who you know" that matters: Gender, personal contacts, and job lead quality. *Gender & Society* 16: 793–813.

Hull, K. E., and R. L. Nelson. 2000. Assimilation, choice, or constraint? Testing theories of gender differences in the careers of lawyers. *Social Forces* 79: 229–264.

Hultin, M. 2003. Some take the glass escalator, some hit the glass ceiling? Career consequences of occupational sex segregation. *Work and Occupations* 30: 30–61.

Hunt, J. G. 2004. What is leadership? In *The nature of leadership*, edited by J. Antonakis, A. T. Cianciolo, and R. J. Sternberg, 19–47. Thousand Oaks, CA: Sage.

———, K. B. Boal, and R. L. Sorenson. 1990. Top management leadership: Inside the black box. *Leadership Quarterly* 1: 41–65.

Huston, A. C., and S. R. Aronson. 2005. Mothers' time with infant and time in employment as predictors of mother-child relationships and children's early development. *Child Development* 76: 467–482.

Hyde, J. S. 1984. How large are gender differences in aggression? A developmental meta-analysis. *Developmental Psychology* 20: 722–736.

———. 2005. The gender similarities hypothesis. *American Psychologist* 60: 581–592.

Hymowitz, C. 2004. Through the glass ceiling. *Wall Street Journal*, November 8, R1, R3.

———. 2006a. The 50 women to watch. *Wall Street Journal*, November 20, R1.

———. 2006b. In the lead: Women tell women: Life in the top jobs is worth the effort. *Wall Street Journal*, November 20, B1.

———, and T. C. Schellhardt. 1986. The glass ceiling: Why women can't seem to break the invisible barrier that blocks them from top jobs. *Wall Street Journal*, March 24, special supplement, 1, 4.

Ibarra, H. 1997. Paving an alternative route: Gender differences in managerial networks. *Social Psychology Quarterly* 60: 91–102.

Ilies, R., N. Hauserman, S. Schwochau, and J. Stibal. 2003. Reported incidence rates of work-related sexual harassment in the United States: Using meta-analysis to explain reported rate disparities. *Personnel Psychology* 56: 607–631.

Inglehart, R., and P. Norris. 2003. *Rising tide: Gender equality and cultural change around the world.* New York: Cambridge University Press.

International Institute for Democracy and Electoral Assistance and Stockholm University. 2007. *Global database of quotas for women.* http://www.quotaproject.org.

Inter-Parliamentary Union. 2007. *Women in national parliaments* (situation as of February 28, 2007). http://www.ipu.org/wmn-e/world.htm.

Ishida, H., K-H. Su, and S. Spilerman. 2002. Models of career advancement in organizations. *European Sociological Review* 18: 179–198.

It wasn't so easy for Roosevelt, either. 2005. *New York Times,* July 31, Education Life, 36.

Ito, T. A., and G. R. Urland. 2003. Race and gender on the brain: Electrocortical measures of attention to the race and gender of multiply categorizable individuals. *Journal of Personality and Social Psychology* 85: 616–626.

Izraeli, D. N. 1983. Sex effects or structural effects? An empirical test of Kanter's theory of proportions. *Social Forces* 62: 153–165.

———. 1984. The attitudinal effects of gender mix in union committees. *Industrial and Labor Relations Review* 37: 212–221.

Jackman, M. R. 1994. *The velvet glove: Paternalism and conflict in gender, class, and race relations.* Berkeley: University of California Press.

Jackson, R. A., and M. A. Newman. 2004. Sexual harassment in the federal workplace revisited: Influences on sexual harassment by gender. *Public Administration Review* 64: 705–717.

Jackson, R. M. 1998. *Destined for equality: The inevitable rise of women's status.* Cambridge, MA: Harvard University Press.

Jacobs, B. A. 2002. Where the boys aren't: Non-cognitive skills, returns to school and the gender gap in higher education. *Economics of Education Review* 21: 589–598.

Jacobs, J. A. 1992. Women's entry into management: Trends in earnings, authority, and values among salaried managers. *Administrative Science Quarterly* 37: 282–301.

———, and G. Gerson. 2004. *The time divide: Work, family, and gender inequality.* Cambridge, MA: Harvard University Press.

Jacobs, R. L., and D. C. McClelland. 1994. Moving up the corporate ladder: A longitudinal study of the leadership motive pattern and managerial success in women and men. *Consulting Psychology Journal: Practice & Research* 46: 32–41.

Jacobsen, J. P. 1998. *The economics of gender.* 2nd ed. Malden, MA: Blackwell.

———, and L. M. Levin. 1995. Effects of intermittent labor force attachment on women's earnings. *Monthly Labor Review* 118(9): 14–19.

Jaffee, S., and J. S. Hyde. 2000. Gender differences in moral orientation: A meta-analysis. *Psychological Bulletin* 126: 703–726.

Jago, A. G., and V. H. Vroom. 1982. Sex differences in the incidence and evaluation of participative leader behavior. *Journal of Applied Psychology* 67: 766–783.

Jalalzai, F. 2004. Women political leaders: Past and present. *Women & Politics* 26: 85–108.

James, D., and J. Drakich. 1993. Understanding gender differences in amount of talk: A critical review of research. In *Gender and conversational interaction,* edited by D. Tannen, 281–312. New York: Oxford University Press.

Janzen, B. L., and N. Muhajarine. 2003. Social role occupancy, gender, income adequacy, life stage and health: A longitudinal study of employed Canadian men and women. *Social Science and Medicine* 57: 1491–1503.

Jarrell, S. B., and T. D. Stanley. 2004. Declining bias and gender wage discrimination? A meta-regression analysis. *Journal of Human Resources* 39: 828–838.

Jayne, M. E. A., and R. L. Dipboye. 2004. Leveraging diversity to improve business performance: Research findings and recommendations for organizations. *Human Resource Management* 43: 409–424.

Jenkins, P. 1998. *Moral panic: Changing concepts of the child molester in modern America.* New Haven, CT: Yale University Press.

Johnson, B. T., and A. H. Eagly. 2000. Quantitative synthesis of social psychological research. In *Handbook of research methods in social and personality psychology,* edited by H. T. Reis and C. M. Judd, 496–528. New York: Cambridge University Press.

Johnson, M. P., and K. J. Ferraro. 2000. Research on domestic violence in the 1990s: Making distinctions. *Journal of Marriage and the Family* 62: 948–963.

Jones, D. 2006a. Not all successful CEOs are extroverts. *USA Today Online,* June 7. http://www.usatoday.com/money/companies/management/2006-06-06-shy-ceo-usat_x.htm.

———. 2006b. Women-led firms lift stock standing. *USA Today Online*, December 27. http://www
.usatoday.com/money/companies/management/2006-12-27-women-ceos-usat_x.htm

Jones, J. M. 2005a. *Gender differences in views of job opportunity: Fifty-three percent of Americans believe opportunities are equal.* August 2. Gallup Brain, http://brain.gallup.com.

———. 2005b. *Nearly half of Americans think U.S. will soon have a woman president.* October 4. Gallup Brain,
http://brain.gallup.com.

Judge, T. A., J. E. Bono, R. Ilies, and M. W. Gerhardt. 2002. Personality and leadership: A qualitative and
quantitative review. *Journal of Applied Psychology* 87: 765–780.

———, D. M. Cable, J. W. Boudreau, and R. D. Bretz, Jr. 1995. An empirical investigation of the predictors
of executive career success. *Personnel Psychology* 48: 485–519.

———, A. E. Colbert, and R. Ilies. 2004. Intelligence and leadership: A quantitative review and test of theoretical propositions. *Journal of Applied Psychology* 89: 542–552.

———, and R. F. Piccolo. 2004. Transformational and transactional leadership: A meta-analytic test of
their relative validity. *Journal of Applied Psychology* 89: 901–910.

———, R. F. Piccolo, and R. Ilies. 2004. The forgotten ones? The validity of consideration and initiating
structure in leadership research. *Journal of Applied Psychology* 89: 36–51.

———, C. J. Thoresen, J. E. Bono, and G. K. Patton. 2001. The job satisfaction–job performance relationship: A qualitative and quantitative review. *Psychological Bulletin* 127: 376–407.

Judiesch, M. K., and K. S. Lyness. 1999. Left behind? The impact of leaves of absence on managers' career
success. *Academy of Management Journal* 42: 641–651.

Juran, J. M. 1988. *Juran on planning for quality.* New York: Free Press.

Kabacoff, R. L. 1998. Gender differences in organizational leadership: A large sample study. Paper presented at the annual meeting of the American Psychological Association, San Francisco, August.

Kalev, A., F. Dobbin, and E. Kelly. 2006. Best practices or best guesses? Assessing the efficacy of corporate
affirmative action and diversity polities. *American Sociological Review* 71: 589–617.

Kanter, R. M. 1977. *Men and women of the corporation.* New York: Basic Books.

———. 1997. *Rosabeth Moss Kanter on the frontiers of management.* Boston: Harvard Business School Press.

Kaplan, H., K. Hill, J. Lancaster, and A. M. Hurtado. 2000. A theory of human life history evolution: Diet,
intelligence, and longevity. *Evolutionary Anthropology* 9: 156–185.

Kark, R. 2004. The transformational leader: Who is (s)he? A feminist perspective. *Journal of Organizational
Change Management* 17: 160–176.

Kasof, J. 1993. Sex bias in the naming of stimulus persons. *Psychological Bulletin* 113: 140–163.

Kathlene, L. 1994. Power and influence in state legislative policymaking: The interaction of gender and
position in committee hearing debates. *American Political Science Review* 3: 560–576.

———. 2001. Words that matter: Women's voice and institutional bias in public policy formation. In
The impact of women in public office, edited by S. J. Carroll, 22–49. Bloomington: Indiana University
Press.

Kaufman, G., and P. Uhlenberg. 2000. The influence of parenthood on the work effort of married men
and women. *Social Forces* 78: 931–947.

Kay, F. M., and J. Hagan. 1998. Raising the bar: The gender stratification of law-firm capital. *American Sociological Review* 63: 728–743.

———, and J. Hagan. 1999. Cultivating clients in the competition for partnership: Gender and the organizational restructuring of law firms in the 1990s. *Law & Society Review* 33: 517–555.

Keith, K., and A. McWilliams. 1997. Job mobility and gender-based wage differentials. *Economic Inquiry* 35:
320–333.

———, and A. McWilliams. 1999. The returns to mobility and job search by gender. *Industrial and Labor
Relations Review* 52: 460–477.

Kelleher, D., P. Finestone, and A. Lowy. 1986. Managerial learning: First notes from an unstudied frontier.
Group and Organization Studies 11: 169–202.

Kellerman, B. 2003. You've come a long way baby—And you've got miles to go. In *The difference "difference" makes: Women and leadership*, edited by D. L. Rhode, 53–58. Stanford, CA: Stanford Law and
Politics.

Kellett, J. B., R. H. Humphrey, and R. G. Sleeth. 2002. Empathy and complex task performance: Two
routes to leadership. *Leadership Quarterly* 13: 523–544.

Kelley, J., and N. D. DeGraaf. 1997. National context, parental socialization, and religious belief: Results
from 15 nations. *American Sociological Review* 62: 639–659.

Keltner, D., D. H. Gruenfeld, and C. Anderson. 2003. Power, approach, and inhibition. *Psychological Review* 110: 265–284.

Kenney, R. A., B. M. Schwartz-Kenney, and J. Blascovich. 1996. Implicit leadership theories: Defining leaders described as worthy of influence. *Personality and Social Psychology Bulletin* 22: 1128–1143.

Kenrick, D. T., M. R. Trost, and J. M. Sundie. 2004. Sex roles as adaptations: An evolutionary perspective on gender differences and similarities. In *The psychology of gender*, edited by A. H. Eagly, A. Beall, and R. J. Sternberg, 2nd ed., 65–91. New York: Guilford Press.

Kilbourne, B. S., P. England, G. Farkas, K. Beron, and D. Weir. 1994. Returns to skill, compensating differentials, and gender bias: Effects of occupational characteristics on the wages of white women and men. *American Journal of Sociology* 100: 689–719.

Killeen, L. A., E. López-Zafra, and A. H. Eagly. 2006. Envisioning oneself as a leader: Comparisons of women and men in Spain and the United States. *Psychology of Women Quarterly* 30: 312–322.

Kimball, M. M. 1995. *Feminist visions of gender similarities and differences*. Binghampton, NY: Haworth Press.

King, J., and G. Gomez. 2007. *The American college president: 2007 edition*. Washington, DC: American Council on Education, Center for Policy Analysis.

Klein, K. E. 2006. Minting women millionaires. *BusinessWeek Online*, May 11. http://www.businessweek.com/print/smallbiz/content/may2006/sb20060511_780723.htm.

Klenke, K. 1997. Women in the leadership and information labyrinth: Looking for the thread of Adriadne. *Women in Leadership* 1: 57–70.

Klerman, J. A., and A. Leibowitz. 1999. Job continuity among new mothers. *Demography* 36: 145–155.

Kling, K. C., J. S. Hyde, C. J. Showers, and B. N. Buswell. 1999. Gender differences in self-esteem: A meta-analysis. *Psychological Bulletin* 4: 470–500.

Klumb, P. L., and T. Lampert. 2004. Women, work, and well-being 1950–2000: A review and methodological critique. *Social Science & Medicine* 58: 1007–1024.

Knapp, M. L., and J. A. Hall. 2002. *Nonverbal communication in social interaction*. 5th ed. Stamford, CT: Wadsworth/Thompson Learning.

Knauft, B. M. 1991. Violence and sociality in human evolution. *Current Anthropology* 32: 391–409.

Knight, G. P., R. A. Fabes, and D. A. Higgins, 1996. Concerns about drawing causal inferences from meta-analyses: An example in the study of gender differences in aggression. *Psychological Bulletin* 119: 410–421.

Koch, S. C., R. Luft, and L. Kruse. 2005. Women and leadership—20 years later: A semantic connotation study. *Social Science Information* 44(1): 9–39.

Koenig, A. M., and A. H. Eagly. 2007. The sources of stereotypes: How observations of groups' social roles shape stereotype content. Unpublished manuscript, Northwestern University.

Kolb, D. M., and J. Williams. 2000. *The shadow negotiation: How women can master the hidden agendas that determine bargaining success*. New York: Simon and Schuster.

Konrad, A. M., and J. Pfeffer. 1991. Understanding the hiring of women and minorities in educational institutions. *Sociology of Education* 64: 141–157.

———, J. E. Ritchie, Jr., P. Lieb, and E. Corrigall. 2000. Sex differences and similarities in job attribute preferences: A meta-analysis. *Psychological Bulletin* 126: 593–641.

Kossek, E. E., and M. D. Lee. 2005. *Making flexibility work: What managers have learned about implementing reduced-load work*. Summary of findings from Phase II of Alfred P. Sloan Grant # 2002-6-11. Michigan State University and McGill University. http://flex-work.lir.msu.edu/.

Kramer, L., and S. Lambert. 2001. Sex-linked bias in chances of being promoted to supervisor. *Sociological Perspectives* 44: 111–127.

Kramer, R. M. 2006. The great intimidators. *Harvard Business Review* 84(2): 88–96.

Kramer, V. W., A. M. Konrad, and S. Erkut. 2006. *Critical mass on corporate boards: Why three or more women enhance governance*. Executive summary. Wellesley, MA: Wellesley Centers for women. http://www.wcwonline.org/pdf/CriticalMassExecSummary.pdf.

Kray, L. J., A. D. Galinsky, and L. Thompson. 2002. Reversing the gender gap in negotiations: An exploration of stereotype regeneration. *Organizational Behavior and Human Decision Processes* 87: 386–409.

Krishnan, H. A., and D. Park. 2005. A few good women—on top management teams. *Journal of Business Research* 58: 1712–1720.

Kuhn, P., and F. Lozano. 2005. The expanding workweek? Understanding trends in long work hours among U.S. men, 1979–2004. National Bureau of Economic Research Working Paper No. W11895. http://www.nber.org/papers/w11895.

———, and C. Weinberger. 2005. Leadership skills and wages. *Journal of Labor Economics* 23: 395–436.

Kunda, Z., and L. Sinclair. 1999. Motivated reasoning with stereotypes: Activation, application, and inhibition. *Psychological Inquiry* 10: 12–22.

———, and S. J. Spencer. 2003. When do stereotypes come to mind and when do they color judgment? A goal-based theoretical framework for stereotype activation and application. *Psychological Bulletin* 129: 522–544.

———, and P. Thagard. 1996. Forming impressions from stereotypes, traits, and behaviors: A parallel-constraint-satisfaction theory. *Psychological Review* 103: 284–308.

LaFarge, A. 2001. Her wish is to make an enduring contribution. In *How Jane won: 55 successful women share how they grew from ordinary girls to extraordinary women*, edited by S. Rimm and S. Rimm-Kaufman, 110–116. New York: Crown Business.

LaFrance, M., E. L. Paluck, and V. Brescoll. 2004. Sex changes: A current perspective on the psychology of gender. In *The psychology of gender*, edited by A. H. Eagly, A. Beall, and R. J. Sternberg, 2nd ed., 328–344. New York: Guilford Press.

Lahelma, E., S. Arber, K. Kivelä, and E. Roos. 2002. Multiple roles and health among British and Finnish women: The influence of socioeconomic circumstances. *Social Science and Medicine* 54: 727–740.

Laland, K. N., and G. R. Brown. 2002. *Sense and nonsense: Evolutionary perspectives on human behavior*. New York: Oxford University Press.

Lam, S. S. K., and G. F. Dreher. 2004. Gender, extra-firm mobility, and compensation attainment in the United States and Hong Kong. *Journal of Organizational Behavior* 25: 791–805.

Landau, M. J., S. Solomon, J. Greenberg, F. Cohen, T. Pyszczynski, J. Arndt, C. H. Miller, D. M. Ogilvie, and A. Cook. 2004. Deliver us from evil: The effects of mortality salience and reminders of 9/11 on support for President George W. Bush. *Personality and Social Psychology Bulletin* 9: 1136–1150.

Landino, R. A., and S. V. Owen. 1988. Self-efficacy in university faculty. *Journal of Vocational Behavior* 33: 1–14.

Langewiesche, W. 2003. Columbia's last flight: The inside story of the investigation—and the catastrophe it laid bare. *Atlantic Monthly*, November, 58–64, 66–74, 76–78, 80–82, 84–87.

Lauterbach, K. E., and B. J. Weiner. 1996. Dynamics of upward influence: How male and female managers get their way. *Leadership Quarterly* 7: 87–107.

Lawless, J. L. 2004. Women, war and winning elections: Gender stereotyping in the post-September 11th era. *Political Research Quarterly* 57: 479–490.

Lawrence, T. B., and V. Corwin. 2003. Being there: The acceptance and marginalization of part-time professional employees. *Journal of Organizational Behavior* 24: 923–943.

Leary, M. R., K. M. Patton, A. E. Orlando, and W. Wagoner Funk. 2000. The impostor phenomenon: Self-perceptions, reflected appraisals, and interpersonal strategies. *Journal of Personality* 68: 725–756.

Lee, D. M., and J. M. Alvares. 1977. Effects of sex on descriptions and evaluations of supervisory behavior in a simulated industrial setting. *Journal of Applied Psychology* 62: 405–410.

Lee, P. M., and E. H. James. 2007. She-E-Os: Gender effects and investor reactions to the announcements of top executive appointments. *Strategic Management Journal* 28: 227–241.

Lee, Y., L. J. Jussim, and C. R. McCauley, eds. 1995. *Stereotype accuracy: Toward appreciating group differences*. Washington, DC: American Psychological Association.

Lemm, K. M., M. Dabady, and M. R. Banaji. 2005. Gender picture priming: It works with denotative and connotative primes. *Social Cognition* 23: 218–241.

Lepowsky, M. 1993. *Fruit of the motherland: Gender in an egalitarian society*. New York: Columbia University Press.

Levering, R., and M. Moskowitz. 2006. Best companies to work for 2006: How we pick the 100 best. *Fortune* at *CNNMoney.com*. http://money.cnn.com/.element/ssi/sections/mag/fortune/bestcompanies/2006/how.popup.html.

Levinson, R. M. 1982. Sex discrimination and employment practices: An experiment with unconventional job inquiries. In *Women and work: Problems and perspectives*, edited by R. Kahn-Hut, A. N. Daniels, and R. Colvard, 54–65. New York: Oxford University Press.

Lewin, K., R. Lippitt, and R. K. White. 1939. Patterns of aggressive behavior in experimentally created "social climates." *Journal of Social Psychology* 10: 271–299.

Lewis, G. 1998. Continuing progress toward racial and gender pay equality in the federal service. *Review of Public Administration* 18: 23–40.

Liden, R. C. 1985. Female perceptions of female and male managerial behavior. *Sex Roles* 12: 421–432.

Lifetime Women's Pulse Poll. 2006. Generation why? March. http://www.pollingcompany.com/cms/files/Executive%20Summary%20Layout%20FINAL.pdf.

Likert, R. 1961. *New patterns of management*. New York: McGraw-Hill.

Lillie, C. R. 2003. Multicultural women and leadership opportunities: Meeting the challenges of diversity in the American legal profession. In *The difference "difference" makes: Women and leadership*, edited by D. Rhode, 102–108. Stanford, CA: Stanford Law and Politics.

Lim, S., and L. M. Cortina. 2005. Interpersonal mistreatment in the workplace: The interface and impact of general incivility and sexual harassment. *Journal of Applied Psychology* 90: 483–496.

Lindner, M. 2001. Girl scouting, ballroom dancing, and dyslexia gave her confidence. In *How Jane won: 55 successful women share how they grew from ordinary girls to extraordinary women*, edited by S. Rimm and S. Rimm-Kaufman, 68–73. New York: Crown Business.

Lipman-Blumen, J. 1996. *The connective edge: Leading in an interdependent world*. San Francisco: Jossey-Bass.

———. 2005. *The allure of toxic leaders: Why we follow destructive bosses and corrupt politicians—and how we can survive them*. New York: Oxford University Press.

Lippa, R. A. 1998a. Gender-related individual differences and the structure of vocational interests: The importance of the people-things dimension. *Journal of Personality and Social Psychology* 74: 996–1009.

———. 1998b. The nonverbal display and judgment of extraversion, masculinity, femininity, and gender diagnosticity: A lens model analysis. *Journal of Research in Personality* 32: 80–107.

Lips, H. M. 2000. College students' visions of power and possibility as moderated by gender. *Psychology of Women Quarterly* 24: 39–43.

———. 2001. Envisioning positions of leadership: The expectations of university students in Virginia and Puerto Rico. *Journal of Social Issues* 57: 799–813.

Lipsey, M. W., and D. B. Wilson. 2001. *Practical meta-analysis*. Thousand Oaks, CA: Sage.

Littlepage, G., W. Robison, and K. Reddington. 1997. Effects of task experience and group experience on group performance, member ability, and recognition of expertise. *Organizational Behavior and Human Decision Processes* 69: 133–147.

Lizza, R. 2007. The invasion of the Alpha male Democrats. *New York Times*, January 7, Week in Review, 1, 3.

Lockheed, M. E. 1985. Sex and social influence: A meta-analysis guided by theory. In *Status, rewards, and influence*, edited by J. Berger and M. Zelditch, Jr., 406–429. San Francisco: Jossey-Bass.

Loden, M. 1985. *Feminine leadership: Or how to succeed in business without being one of the boys*. New York: Times Books.

Lord, R. G., D. J. Brown, J. L. Harvey, and R. J. Hall. 2001. Contextual constraints on prototype generation and their multi-level consequences for leadership perceptions. *Leadership Quarterly* 12: 311–338.

———, C. L. de Vader, and G. M. Alliger. 1986. A meta-analysis of the relation between personality traits and leadership perceptions: An application of validity generalization procedures. *Journal of Applied Psychology* 71: 402–410.

———, and K. J. Maher. 1993. *Leadership and information processing: Linking perceptions and performance*. New York: Routledge.

Lovenduski, J., and P. Norris. 2003. Westminster women: The politics of presence. *Political Studies* 51: 84–102.

Low, B. S. 2000. *Why sex matters: A Darwinian look at human behavior*. Princeton, NJ: Princeton University Press.

Lowe, K. B., K. G. Kroeck, and N. Sivasubramaniam. 1996. Effectiveness correlates of transformational and transactional leadership: A meta-analytic review of the MLQ literature. *Leadership Quarterly* 7: 385–425.

Lucas, J. W. 2003. Status processes and the institutionalization of women as leaders. *American Sociological Review* 68: 464–480.

Lundberg, S., and E. Rose. 2000. Parenthood and the earnings of married men and women. *Labour Economics* 7: 689–710.

Lundgren, L. M., J. Fleischer-Cooperman, R. Schneider, and T. Fitzgerald. 2001. Work, family, and gender in medicine: How do dual-earners decide who should work less? In *Working families: The transformation of the American home*, edited by R. Hertz and N. L. Marshall, 251–269. Berkeley: University of California Press.

Luthans, F. 1988. Successful vs. effective real managers. *Academy of Management Executive* 2(2): 127–132.

———, F., R. M. Hodgetts, and S. A. Rosenkrantz. 1988. *Real managers*. Cambridge, MA: Ballinger.

Lynch, J. P. 2002. Trends in juvenile violent offending: An analysis of victim survey data. Office of Juvenile Justice and Delinquency Prevention, U. S. Department of Justice. http://www.ncjrs.gov/pdffiles1/ojjdp/191052.pdf.

Lyness, K. S., and M. E. Heilman. 2006. When fit is fundamental: Performance evaluations and promotions of upper-level female and male managers. *Journal of Applied Psychology* 91: 777–785.

———, and M. K. Judiesch. 1999. Are women more likely to be hired or promoted into management positions? *Journal of Vocational Behavior* 54: 158–173.

————, and M. K. Judiesch. 2001. Are female managers quitters? The relationships of gender, promotions, and family leaves of absence to voluntary turnover. *Journal of Applied Psychology* 86: 1167–1178.

————, and D. E. Thompson. 1997. Above the glass ceiling? A comparison of matched samples of female and male executives. *Journal of Applied Psychology* 82: 359–375.

————, and D. E. Thompson. 2000. Climbing the corporate ladder: Do female and male executives follow the same route? *Journal of Applied Psychology* 85: 86–101.

Maass, A., M. Cadinu, G. Guarnieri, and A. Grasselli. 2003. Sexual harassment under social identity threat: The computer harassment paradigm. *Journal of Personality and Social Psychology* 85: 853–870.

MacCoun, R. J. 1998. Biases in the interpretation and use of research results. *Annual Review of Psychology* 49: 259–287.

MacDonald, E., and C. R. Schoenberger. 2006. The world's most powerful women: No. 7, Sallie Krawcheck. *Forbes.com.*, August 31. http://www.forbes.com/lists/2006/11/06women_Sallie-Krawcheck_DFBE.html.

Madden, M. E. 2005. 2004 Division 35 presidential address: Gender and leadership in higher education. *Psychology of Women Quarterly* 29: 3–14.

Magley, V. J., C. L. Hulin, L. F. Fitzgerald, and M. DeNardo. 1999. Outcomes of self-labeling sexual harassment. *Journal of Applied Psychology* 84: 390–402.

Maier, M. 1999. On the gendered substructure of organizations: Dimensions and dilemmas of corporate masculinity. In *Handbook of gender & work*, edited by G. N. Powell, 69–93. Thousand Oaks, CA: Sage.

Mainiero, L. A. 1994. On breaking the glass ceiling: The political seasoning of powerful women executives. *Organizational Dynamics* 22(4): 4–20.

Major, B. 1994. From social inequality to personal entitlement: The role of social comparisons, legitimacy appraisals, and group membership. In *Advances in experimental social psychology*, edited by M. P. Zanna, Vol. 26, 293–355. San Diego: Academic Press.

Mallabar, J. 2006. First person: When you give up a successful career. *Saturday Guardian*, April 2, Family section, 3.

Mandel, H., and M. Semyonov. 2005. Family policies, wage structures, and gender gaps: Sources of earnings inequality in 20 countries. *American Sociological Review* 70: 949–967.

Mandell, B., and S. Pherwani. 2003. Relationship between emotional intelligence and transformational leadership style: A gender comparison. *Journal of Business and Psychology* 17: 387–404.

Mann, E. S. 2005. Familialism in Nicaragua: Reproductive and sexual policy regimes, 1979–2002. Paper presented at meeting of Research Committee 19 of International Sociological Association, Chicago, September. http://www.northwestern.edu/rc19/Mann.pdf.

Mann, J. 2000. Who says a woman can't be president? We do. *Washington Post*, January 28, C11.

Manning, A., and B. Petrongolo. 2006. The part-time pay penalty for women in Britain. IZA Discussion Paper No. 2419. Institute for the Study of Labor, Bonn, Germany.

Mansfield, H. G. 2006. *Manliness*. New Haven, CT: Yale University Press.

Manuel, T., S. Shefte, and D. J. Swiss. 1999. *Suiting themselves: Women's leadership styles in today's workplace*. Cambridge, MA: Radcliffe Public Policy Institute.

Marini, M. M., P. Fan, E. Finley, and A. M. Beutel. 1996. Gender and job values. *Sociology of Education* 69: 49–65.

Markoff, J. 1999. Hewlett-Packard picks rising star at Lucent as its chief executive. *New York Times*, July 20, C1.

Marks, S. R. 1977. Multiple roles and role strain: Some notes on human energy, time, and commitment. *American Sociological Review* 42: 921–936.

Martell, R. F., D. M. Lane, and C. G. Emrich. 1996. Male-female differences: A computer simulation. *American Psychologist* 51: 157–158.

————, C. Parker, C. G. Emrich, and M. S. Crawford. 1998. Sex stereotyping in the executive suite: "Much ado about something." *Journal of Social Behavior and Personality* 13: 127–138.

Martin, A. 2005. *The changing nature of leadership: A CCL research report*. Greensboro, NC: Center for Creative Leadership. http://www.ccl.org/leadership/pdf/research/NatureLeadership.pdf.

Martin, P. Y. 1990. Rethinking feminist organizations. *Gender & Society* 4: 182–206.

————. 2003. "Said and done" versus "saying and doing": Gender practices, practicing gender at work. *Gender & Society* 17: 342–366.

Martinez, G. M., A. Chandra, J. C. Abma, J. Jones, and W. D. Mosher. 2006. *Fertility, contraception, and fatherhood: Data on men and women from Cycle 6 of the 2002 National Survey of Family Growth*. U.S. Department of Health and Human Services, National Center for Health Statistics, Vital and Health Statistics, Series 23, No. 26. http://www.cdc.gov/nchs/data/series/sr_23/sr23_026.pdf.

Mastekaasa, A. 2000. Parenthood, gender, and sickness absence. *Social Science and Medicine* 50: 1827–1842.

Matschiner, M., and S. K. Murnen. 1999. Hyperfemininity and influence. *Psychology of Women Quarterly* 23: 631–642.

Matsui, C. 2001. Growing up in the best of two worlds. In *How Jane won: 55 successful women share how they grew from ordinary girls to extraordinary women*, edited by S. Rimm and S. Rimm-Kaufman, 122–127. New York: Crown Business.

Mattingly, M. J., and S. M. Bianchi. 2003. Gender differences in the quantity and quality of free time: The U. S. experience. *Social Forces* 81: 99–1030.

Maume, D. J., Jr. 1999a. Glass ceilings and glass escalators: Occupational segregation and race and sex differences in managerial promotions. *Work and Occupations* 26: 483–509.

———. 1999b. Occupational segregation and the career mobility of white men and women. *Social Forces* 77: 1433–1459.

———. 2004. Is the glass ceiling a unique form of inequality? Evidence from a random-effects model of managerial attainment. *Work and Occupations* 31: 250–274.

———, and P. Houston. 2001. Job segregation and gender differences in work-family spillover among white collar workers. *Journal of Family and Economic Issues* 22: 171–189.

Mayer, J. D., P. Salovey, and D. R. Caruso. 2004. Emotional intelligence: Theory, findings, and implications. *Psychological Inquiry* 15: 197–215.

McBroom, P. 1986. *The third sex: The new professional woman*. New York: W. Morrow.

McCall, L. 2001. *Complex inequality: Gender, class, and race in the new economy*. New York: Routledge.

McCall, M. W., Jr., M. M. Lombardo, and A. M. Morrison. 1988. *The lessons of experience: How successful executives develop on the job*. Lexington, MA: Lexington Books.

McCauley, C. D. 2004. Successful and unsuccessful leadership. In *The nature of leadership*, edited by J. Antonakis, A. T. Cianciolo, and R. J. Sternberg, 199–221. Thousand Oaks, CA: Sage.

———, M. N. Ruderman, P. J. Ohlott, and J. E. Morrow. 1994. Assessing the developmental components of managerial jobs. *Journal of Applied Psychology* 79: 544–560.

McClelland, D. C. 1985. *Human motivation*. Glenview, IL: Scott, Foresman.

———, and R. E. Boyatzis. 1982. Leadership motive pattern and long-term success in management. *Journal of Applied Psychology* 67: 737–743.

McClure, E. B. 2000. A meta-analytic review of sex differences in facial expression processing and their development in infants, children, and adolescents. *Psychological Bulletin* 126: 424–453.

McCrae, R. R., and P. T. Costa. 2003. *Personality in adulthood: A five-factor theory perspective*. New York: Guilford Press.

McElroy, J. C., P. C. Morrow, and S. N. Rude. 2001. Turnover and organizational performance: A comparative analysis of the effects of voluntary, involuntary, and reduction-in-force turnover. *Journal of Applied Psychology* 86: 1294–1299.

McIntyre, S., D. J. Moberg, and B. Z. Posner. 1980. Preferential treatment in preselection decisions according to sex and race. *Academy of Management Journal* 23: 738–749.

McLean, B., and P. Elkind. 2004. *The smartest guys in the room: The amazing rise and scandalous fall of Enron*. New York: Portfolio.

McMunn, A., M. Bartley, R. Hardy, and D. Kuh. 2006. Life course social roles and women's health in midlife: Causation or selection? *Journal of Epidemiology and Community Health* 60: 484–489.

McPherson, M., L. Smith-Lovin, and J. M. Cook. 2001. Birds of a feather: Homophily in social networks. *Annual Review of Sociology* 27: 415–444.

Mehdorn, H. 2006. Letter to the editor. *Financial Times*, March 13. FT.com, http://search.ft.com/searchArticle?queryText=Lecturer+or+listenerandy=7andjavascriptEnabled=true&id=060313000697&x=15.

Melamed, T., and N. Bozionelos. 1992. Gender differences in the personality features of British managers. *Psychological Reports* 71: 979–986.

Mendell, A. 1996. *How men think: The seven essential rules for making it in a man's world*. New York: Fawcett Columbine.

Mero, J., and P. Sellers. 2003. Power—Do women really want it? *Fortune*, October 13, 80–100.

Merrill-Sands, D., J. Kickul, and C. Ingols. 2005. Women pursuing leadership and power: Challenging the myth of the "opt out revolution." *CGO Insights, Briefing Note No. 20*, February. http://www.simmons.edu/som/docs/centers/insights_20.pdf.

———, and D. M. Kolb. 2001. Women as leaders: The paradox of success. *CGO Insights: Briefing Note No. 9*, April. http://www.simmons.edu/som/docs/centers/insights_9.pdf.

Meyerson, D. E. 2001. *Tempered radicals: How people use difference to inspire change at work.* Boston: Harvard Business School Press.

———, and J. K. Fletcher. 2000. A modest manifesto for shattering the glass ceiling. *Harvard Business Review* 78(1): 126–136.

Meyersson Milgrom, E. M., and T. Petersen. 2006. The glass ceiling in the United States and Sweden: Lessons from the family-friendly corner of the world, 1970 to 1990. In *The declining significance of gender?* edited by F. D. Blau, M. C. Brinton, and D. B. Grusky, 67–101. New York: Russell Sage Foundation.

Milkie, M. A., S. M. Bianchi, M. J. Mattingly, and J. P. Robinson. 2002. Gendered division of childrearing: Ideals, realities, and the relationship to parental well-being. *Sex Roles* 47: 21–38.

———, M. J. Mattingly, K. M. Nomaguchi, S. M. Bianchi, and J. P. Robinson. 2004. The time squeeze: Parental statuses and feelings about time with children. *Journal of Marriage and the Family* 66: 739–761.

Miller, D. T., B. Taylor, and M. L. Buck. 1991. Gender gaps: Who needs to be explained? *Journal of Personality and Social Psychology* 61: 5–12.

Miller, L. C., L. L. Cooke, J. Tsang, and F. Morgan. 1992. Should I brag? Nature and impact of positive and boastful disclosures for women and men. *Human Communication Research* 18: 364–399.

Miller, M. 2005. Listen to my wife. *New York Times*, May 25, A27.

Milwid, B. 1990. *Working with men: Professional women talk about power, sexuality, and ethics.* Hillsboro, OR: Beyond Words Publishing.

Mineham, C. E. 2005. An introduction. *Regional Review*, Federal Reserve Bank of Boston, Quarter 1. http://www.bos.frb.org/economic/nerr/rr2005/q1/introduction.pdf

Miner, J. B. 1993. *Role motivation theories.* New York: Routledge.

———, and N. S. Raju. 2004. Risk propensity differences between managers and entrepreneurs and between low- and high-growth entrepreneurs: A reply in a more conservative vein. *Journal of Applied Psychology* 89: 3–13.

Mintzberg, H. 1979. *The structuring of organizations: A synthesis of the research.* Englewood Cliffs, NJ: Prentice Hall.

Mitra, A. 2003. Access to supervisory jobs and the gender wage gap among professionals. *Journal of Economic Issues* 37: 1023–1044.

Mnookin, S. 2004. *Hard news: The scandals at the* New York Times *and their meaning for American media.* New York: Random House.

Moore, D. 1992. Discrimination and deprivation: The effects of social comparisons. *Social Justice Research* 4: 49–64.

Moore, D. P., and E. H. Buttner. 1997. *Women entrepreneurs: Moving beyond the glass ceiling.* Thousand Oaks, CA: Sage Publications.

Moore, D. W. 2003. Little prejudice against a woman, Jewish, black, or Catholic presidential candidate. June 10. Gallup Brain, http://brain.gallup.com.

———. 2005. Gender stereotypes prevail on working outside the home: Modest backlash among women against working; men warming up to staying home. August 17. Gallup Brain, http://brain.gallup.com.

Moore, G. 1988. Women in elite positions: Insiders or outsiders? *Sociological Forum* 3: 566–585.

———. 1990. Structural determinants of men's and women's personal networks. *American Sociological Review* 55: 726–735.

———. 2004. Mommies and daddies on the fast track in other wealthy nations. *Annals of the American Academy of Political and Social Science* 596: 208–213.

Moreland, R. L., and J. M. Levine. 2001. Socialization in organizations and work groups. In *Groups at work: Theory and research,* edited by M. E. Turner, 69–112. Mahwah, NJ: Erlbaum.

Morrill, C. 1995. *The executive way: Conflict management in corporations.* Chicago: University of Chicago Press.

Morris, B. 2002. Trophy husbands: Arm candy? Are you kidding? While their fast-track wives go to work, stay-at-home husbands mind the kids. They deserve a trophy for trading places. *Fortune,* October 14, 78–82, 86, 90, 94, 98.

Morris, M., and B. Western. 1999. Inequality in earnings at the close of the twentieth century. *Annual Review of Sociology* 25: 623–657.

Morrison, A. M. 1992. *The new leaders.* San Francisco: Jossey-Bass.

———, and M. A. von Glinow. 1990. Women and minorities in management. *American Psychologist* 45: 200–208.

Morse, J., and A. Bower. 2002. The party crasher. *Time*, December 30, 52 ff.

Moskowitz, D. S., E. J. Suh, and J. Desaulniers. 1994. Situational influences on gender differences in agency and communion. *Journal of Personality and Social Psychology* 66: 753–761.

Munson, L. J., A. G. Miner, and C. Hulin. 2001. Labeling sexual harassment in the military: An extension and replication. *Journal of Applied Psychology* 86: 293–303.

Murray, A. 2007. Business: Behind Nardelli's abrupt exit; Executive's fatal flaw: Failing to understand new demands on CEOs. *Wall Street Journal*, January 4, A1, A12.

Murrell, A. J., J. E. Olson, and I. H. Frieze. 1995. Sexual harassment and gender discrimination: A longitudinal study of women managers. *Journal of Social Issues* 51: 139–149.

Musteen, M., V. L. Barker III, and V. L. Baeten. 2006. CEO attributes associated with attitude toward change: The direct and moderating effects of CEO tenure. *Journal of Business Research* 59: 604–612.

Myers, W. 2005. Keeping a gentle grip on power. *U.S. News & World Report*, October 31. http://www.usnews.com/usnews/news/articles/051031/31whitman.htm.

Nadis, S. 1999. Women scientists unite to combat cowboy culture. *Nature* 398: 361.

Naff, K. C. 1994. Through the glass ceiling: Prospects for the advancement of women in the federal civil service. *Public Administration Review* 54: 507–514.

National Center for Health Statistics. 2006. *Body measurements*. http://www.cdc.gov/ndhs/fastats/bodymeas.htm.

Nelson, R. L., and W. P. Bridges. 1999. *Legalizing gender inequality: Courts, markets, and unequal pay for women in America*. Cambridge, UK: Cambridge University Press.

Neuman, J. H., and R. A. Baron. 1998. Workplace violence and workplace aggression: Evidence concerning specific forms, potential causes, and preferred targets. *Journal of Management* 24: 391–419.

Neumark, D., with the assistance of R. J. Bank, and K. D. Van Nort. 1996. Sex discrimination in restaurant hiring: An audit study. *Quarterly Journal of Economics* 111: 915–941.

Newman, M. A., R. A. Jackson, and D. D. Baker. 2003. Sexual harassment in the federal workplace. *Public Administration Review* 63: 472–483.

Newport, F. 2001. Americans see women as emotional and affectionate, men as more aggressive: Gender specific stereotypes persist in recent Gallup poll. February 21. Gallup Brain, http://brain.gallup.com.

Ng, T. W. H., L. T. Eby, K. L. Sorensen, and D. C. Feldman. 2005. Predictors of objective and subjective career success: A meta-analysis. *Personnel Psychology* 58: 367–408.

NICHD Early Child Care Research Network. 2006. Child care effect sizes for the NICHD study of early childcare and youth development. *American Psychologist*, 61, 99–116.

Niederle, M., and L. Vesterlund. 2005. Do women shy away from competition? Do men compete too much? National Bureau of Economic Research Working Paper No. 11474. http://www.nber.org/papers/w11474.

Nieva, V. G., and B. A. Gutek. 1981. *Women and work: A psychological perspective*. New York: Praeger.

Noonan, M. C., and M. E. Corcoran. 2004. The mommy track and partnership: Temporary delay or dead end? *Annals of the American Academy of Political and Social Science* 596: 130–150.

Northouse, P. G. 2004. *Leadership: Theory and practice*. 3rd ed. Thousand Oaks, CA: Sage.

Oaxaca, R. L. 1973. Male-female wage differentials in urban labor markets. *International Economic Review* 14: 693–709.

Offermann, L. R., J. K. Kennedy, Jr., and P. W. Wirtz. 1994. Implicit leadership theories: Content, structure, and generalizability. *Leadership Quarterly* 5: 43–58.

Ohlott, P. J., M. N. Ruderman, and C. D. McCauley. 1994. Gender differences in managers' developmental job experiences. *Academy of Management Journal* 37: 46–67.

Olian, J. D., D. P. Schwab, and Y. Haberfeld. 1988. The impact of applicant gender compared to qualifications on hiring recommendations: A meta-analysis of experimental studies. *Organizational Behavior and Human Decision Processes* 41: 180–195.

Olsson, S. 2006. "We don't need another hero!": Organizational storytelling as a vehicle for communicating a female archetype of workplace leadership. In *Gender and communication at work*, edited by M. Barrett and M. J. Davidson, 195–210. Burlington, VT: Ashgate.

O'Neill, J. 2003. Catching up: The gender gap in wages, circa 2000. *American Economic Review* 93: 309–314.

———, and S. Polachek. 1993. Why the gender gap in wages narrowed in the 1980s. *Journal of Labor Economics* 11: 205–228.

Ones, D. S., and C. Viswesvaran. 1998. Gender, age, and race differences on overt integrity tests: Results across four large-scale job applicant data sets. *Journal of Applied Psychology* 83: 35–42.

———, C. Viswesvaran, and F. L. Schmidt. 1993. Comprehensive meta-analysis of integrity test validities: Findings and implications for personnel selection and theories of job performance. *Journal of Applied Psychology* 78: 679–703.

Oppenheimer Funds and Mass Mutual Financial Group. 2002. Successful women business executives don't just talk a good game . . . they play(ed) one. http://www.massmutual.com/mmfg/pdf/boardroom.pdf.

Osterman, P. 1995. Work/family programs and the employment relationship. *Administrative Science Quarterly* 40: 681–700.

Ott, E. M. 1989. Effects of the male-female ratio at work: Policewomen and male nurses. *Psychology of Women Quarterly* 13: 41–57.

Otto, C. 2001. Visualizing success made a difference. In *How Jane won: 55 successful women share how they grew from ordinary girls to extraordinary women*, edited by S. Rimm and S. Rimm-Kaufman, 99–103. New York: Crown Business.

Pallier, G. 2003. Gender differences in self-assessment of accuracy on cognitive tasks. *Sex Roles* 48: 265–276.

Panczer, L. M. 2002. Women, representation, and public policy in the 103rd Congress. Doctoral dissertation, University of Missouri, Saint Louis. *Dissertation Abstracts International* 62: 3553-A.

Paolillo, J. G. P. 1981. Manager's self assessments of managerial roles: The influence of hierarchical level. *Journal of Management* 7: 43–52.

Paris, L. D., J. P. Howell, P. W. Dorfman, and P. Hanges. 2007. *Gender differences in implicit leadership theories: The moderating effects of culture and industry*. Manuscript submitted for publication.

Parker, P. S., and d. t. ogilvie. 1996. Gender, culture, and leadership: Toward a culturally distinct model of African-American women executives' leadership strategies. *Leadership Quarterly* 7: 189–214.

Pavett, C. M., and A. W. Lau. 1983. Managerial work: The influence of hierarchical level and functional specialty. *Academy of Management Journal* 26: 170–177.

Pear, R. 2006. Married and single parents spending more time with children, study finds. *New York Times Online*, October 17. http://select.nytimes.com/search/restricted/article?res=F30E11FA35540C748 DDDA90994DE404482.

Pearson, A. 2002. *I don't know how she does it: The life of Kate Reddy, working mother*. New York: Knopf.

Perse, E. M., A. I. Nathanson, and D. M. McLeod. 1996. Effects of spokesperson sex, public service announcement appeal, and involvement on evaluations of safe-sex PSAs. *Health Communications* 8: 171–189.

Peter, K., and L. Horn. 2005. *Gender differences in participation and completion of undergraduate education and how they have changed over time*. NCES 2005-169. U.S. Department of Education, National Center for Education Statistics. http://nces.ed.gov/pubs2005/2005169.pdf.

Petersen, T., I. Saporta, and M. L. Seidel. 2000. Offering a job: Meritocracy and social networks. *American Journal of Sociology* 106: 763–816.

Petrides, K. V., and A. Furnham. 2000. Gender differences in measured and self-estimated trait emotional intelligence. *Sex Roles* 42: 449–461.

Pew Research Center for the People and the Press. 1997. Motherhood today: A tougher job, less ably done. http://people-press.org/reports/print.php3?ReportID=109.

Pfeffer, J., and A. Davis-Blake. 1987. The effect of the proportion of women on salaries: The case of college administrators. *Administrative Science Quarterly* 32: 1–24.

Phillips, J. S., and R. G. Lord. 1982. Schematic information processing and perception of leadership in problem-solving groups. *Journal of Applied Psychology* 67: 486–492.

Phipps, S., P. Burton, and L. Osberg. 2001. Time as a source of inequality within marriage: Are husbands more satisfied with time for themselves than wives? *Feminist Economics* 7: 1–21.

Plant, E. A., and P. G. Devine. 1998. Internal and external motivation to respond without prejudice. *Journal of Personality and Social Psychology* 75: 811–832.

Podsakoff, P. M., S. B. MacKenzie, J. B. Paine, and D. G. Bachrach. 2000. Organizational citizenship behaviors: A critical review of the theoretical and empirical literature and suggestions for future research. *Journal of Management* 26: 513–563.

Polgreen, L., and L. Rohter. 2006. Where political clout demands a maternal touch. *New York Times Online*, January 22. http://www.nytimes.com/2006/01/22/weekinreview/22roht.html.

Powell, G. N. 1990. One more time: Do male and female managers differ? *Academy of Management Executive* 4(3): 68–75.

———. 1999. Reflections on the glass ceiling: Recent trends and future prospects. In *Handbook of gender & work*, edited by G. N. Powell, 325–345. Thousand Oaks, CA: Sage.

————, and D. A. Butterfield. 1994. Investigating the "glass ceiling" phenomenon: An empirical study of actual promotions to top management. *Academy of Management Journal* 37: 68–86.

————, D. A. Butterfield, and J. D. Parent. 2002. Gender and managerial stereotypes: Have the times changed? *Journal of Management* 28: 177–193.

————, and L. M. Graves. 2003. *Women and men in management*, 3rd ed. Thousand Oaks, CA: Sage.

————, and L. M. Graves. 2006. Gender and leadership: Perceptions and realities. In *Sex differences and similarities in communication*, edited by K. Dindia and D. J. Canary, 2nd ed., 13–98. Mahwah, NJ: Erlbaum.

Pratto, F., J. D. Korchmaros, and P. Hegarty. 2007. When race and gender go without saying. *Social Cognition*, 25: 221–247.

Prentice, D. A., and E. Carranza. 2002. What women and men should be, shouldn't be, are allowed to be, and don't have to be: The contents of prescriptive gender stereotypes. *Psychology of Women Quarterly* 26: 269–281.

————, and D. T. Miller. 2006. Essentializing differences between women and men. *Psychological Science* 17: 129–135.

Price, D. 1997. Lady Justice: Her commitment to the underdog may bring Ruth Bader Ginsburg the court's top job. *Detroit News*, January 3, E1.

Price Waterhouse v. Hopkins, 490 U. S., 228 1989.

Propp, K. M. 1995. An experimental examination of biological sex as a status cue in decision-making groups and its influence on information use. *Small Group Research* 26: 451–474.

Prowse, V. 2005. How damaging is part-time employment to a woman's occupational prospects? IZA Discussion Paper No. 1648. Institute for the Study of Labor, Bonn, Germany.

Pryor, J. B. 1987. Sexual harassment proclivities in men. *Sex Roles* 17: 269–290.

————. 1995. The psychosocial impact of sexual harassment on women in the U. S. military. *Basic and Applied Social Psychology* 17: 581–603.

————, J. L. Giedd, and K. B. Williams. 1995. A social psychological model for predicting sexual harassment. *Journal of Social Issues* 51: 69–84.

————, C. M. LaVite, and L. M. Stoller. 1993. A social psychological analysis of sexual harassment: The person/situation interaction. *Journal of Vocational Behavior* 42: 68–83.

————, and L. M. Stoller. 1994. Sexual cognition processes in men high in the likelihood to sexually harass. *Personality and Social Psychology Bulletin* 20: 163–169.

Purvanova, R. K., J. E. Bono, and J. Dzieweczynski. 2006. Transformational leadership, job characteristics, and organizational citizenship performance. *Human Performance* 19: 1–22.

Putnam, R. D. 2000. *Bowling alone: The collapse and revival of American community*. New York: Simon and Schuster.

Quinn, K. A., N. J. Roese, G. L. Pennington, and J. M. Olson. 1999. The personal/group discrimination discrepancy: The role of informational complexity. *Personality and Social Psychology Bulletin* 25: 1430–1440.

Ragins, B. R. 1999. Gender and mentoring relationships: A review and research agenda for the next decade. In *Handbook of gender & work*, edited by G. Powell, 347–370. Thousand Oaks, CA: Sage.

————, J. M. Cornwell, and J. S. Miller. 2003. Heterosexism in the workplace: Do race and gender matter? *Group & Organization Management* 28: 45–74.

————, and J. L. Cotton. 1999. Mentor functions and outcomes: A comparison of men and women in formal and informal mentoring relationships. *Journal of Applied Psychology* 84: 529–550.

————, and E. Sundstrom. 1989. Gender and power in organizations: A longitudinal perspective. *Psychological Bulletin* 105: 51–88.

————, B. Townsend, and M. Mattis. 1998. Gender gap in the executive suite: CEOs and female executives report on breaking the glass ceiling. *Academy of Management Executive* 12: 28–42.

Ramchandani P., A. Stein, J. Evans, T. G. O'Conner, and the APSPAC team. 2005. Paternal depression in the postnatal period and child development: A prospective population study. *Lancet* 365: 2201–2205.

Rapoport, R., L. Bailyn, J. K. Fletcher, and B. H. Pruitt. 2002. *Beyond work-family balance: Advancing gender equity and workplace performance*. San Francisco: Jossey-Bass.

Rapp, E. 2003. A pep talk for women to end all pep talks. *New York Times*, September 28, 11.

Reinelt, C. 1994. Fostering empowerment, building community: The challenge for state-funded feminist organizations. *Human Relations* 47: 685–705.

Repetti, R. L., K. A. Matthews, and I. Waldron. 1989. Employment and women's health: Effects of paid employment on women's mental and physical health. *American Psychologist* 44: 1394–1401.

Reskin, B. F., and D. B. McBrier. 2000. Why not ascription? Organizations' employment of male and female managers. *American Sociological Review* 65: 210–233

————, D. B. McBrier, and J. A. Kmec. 1999. The determinants and consequences of workplace sex and race composition. *Annual Review of Sociology* 25: 335–361.

Reynolds, J. 2003. You can't always get the hours you want: Mismatches between actual and preferred work hours in the U. S. *Social Forces* 81: 1171–1199.

Rhoads, K. V., and R. B. Cialdini. 2002. The business of influence: Principles that lead to success in commercial settings. In *The persuasion handbook: Developments in theory and practice*, edited by J. P. Dillard and M. Pfau, 513–542. Thousand Oaks, CA: Sage.

Rich, F. 2001. The father figure. *New York Times Magazine*, September 30, 23.

————. 2004. How Kerry became a girlie-man. *New York Times*, September 5, section 2, 1.

Richard, O. C., T. Barnett, S. Dwyer, and K. Chadwick. 2004. Cultural diversity in management, firm performance, and the moderating role of entrepreneurial orientation dimensions. *Academy of Management Journal* 47: 255–266.

Richerson, P. J., and R. Boyd. 2005. *Not by genes alone: How culture transformed human evolution*. Chicago: University of Chicago Press.

Ridgeway, C. L. 1982. Status in groups: The importance of motivation. *American Sociological Review* 47: 76–88.

————. 1987. Nonverbal behavior, dominance, and the basis of status in task groups. *American Sociological Review* 52: 683–694.

————. 1997. Interaction and the conservation of gender inequality: Considering employment. *American Sociological Review* 62: 218–235.

————. 2001. Gender, status, and leadership. *Journal of Social Issues* 57: 637–655.

————. 2006a. Gender as an organizing force in social relations. In *The declining significance of gender?* edited by F. D. Blau, M. C. Brinton, and D. B. Grusky, 265–287. New York: Russell Sage Foundation.

————. 2006b. Status construction theory. In *Contemporary social psychological theories*, edited by P. J. Burke, 301–323. Stanford, CA: Stanford University Press.

————, and C. Bourg. 2004. Gender as status: An expectation states theory approach. In *The psychology of gender*, edited by A. H. Eagly, A. Beall, and R. J. Sternberg, 2nd ed., 217–241. New York: Guilford Press.

Riger, S. 1994. Challenges of success: Stages of growth in feminist organizations. *Feminist Studies* 20: 275–300.

Riggio, R. E. 1986. Assessment of basic social skills. *Journal of Personality and Social Psychology* 51: 649–660.

Rimer, S. 2005. At Harvard, the bigger concern of the faculty is the president's management style. *New York Times*, January 26, A17.

Robinson, D. 1998. Differences in occupational earnings by sex. *International Labour Review* 137: 3–31.

Robinson, J. P., and G. Godbey. 1997. *Time for life: The surprising ways Americans use their time*. University Park: Pennsylvania State University Press.

————, and M. A. Milkie, M. A. 1998.Back to the basics: Trends in and role determinants of women's attitudes towards housework. *Journal of Marriage and the Family*, 60, 205–218.

Roehling, P. V., M. V. Roehling, and P. Moen. 2001. The relationship between work-life policies and practices and employee loyalty: A life course perspective. *Journal of Family and Economic Issues* 22: 141–170.

Rones, P. L., R. E. Ilg, and J. M. Gardner. 1997. Trends in hours of work since the mid-1970s. *Monthly Labor Review*, April, 3–14.

Roper Starch Worldwide. 1995. *The 1995 Virginia Slims opinion poll: A 25-year perspective of women's issues*. New York: Altria Group.

Rose, H., and S. Rose, eds. 2000. *Alas poor Darwin: Arguments against evolutionary psychology*. London: Jonathan Cape.

Rose, S. J., and H. I. Hartmann. 2004. *Still a man's labor market: The long-term earnings gap*. Washington, DC: Institute for Women's Policy Research. http://www.iwpr.org/pdf/C355.pdf.

Rosen, B., and T. H. Jerdee. 1973. The influence of sex-role stereotypes on evaluations of male and female supervisory behavior. *Journal of Applied Psychology* 57: 44–48.

————, and T. H. Jerdee. 1974. Effects of applicant's sex and difficulty of job on evaluations of candidates for management positions. *Journal of Applied Psychology* 59: 511–512.

Rosener, J. B. 1990. Ways women lead. *Harvard Business Review* 68(6): 119–125.

————. 1995. *America's competitive secret: Utilizing women as management strategy*. New York: Oxford University Press.

Rosenthal, C. S. 1998. *When women lead: Integrative leadership in state legislatures*. New York: Oxford University Press.

————, ed. 2002. *Women transforming Congress*. Norman: University of Oklahoma Press.

Rosenthal, P., D. Guest, and R. Peccei. 1996. Gender differences in managers' causal explanations for their work performance: A study in two organizations. *Journal of Occupational and Organizational Psychology* 69: 145–151.

Rosenthal, R. 1990. How are we doing in soft psychology? *American Psychologist* 45: 775–777.

————, and D. B. Rubin. 1982. Comparing effect sizes of independent studies. *Psychological Bulletin* 92: 500–504.

Rosenwasser, S. M., and N. G. Dean. 1989. Gender role and political office: Effects of perceived masculinity/femininity of candidate and political office. *Psychology of Women Quarterly* 13: 77–85.

Rosnow, R. L., and R. Rosenthal. 1989. Statistical procedures and the justification of knowledge in psychological science. *American Psychologist* 44: 1276–1284.

Ross, L., T. M. Amabile, and J. L. Steinmetz. 1977. Social roles, social control, and biases in social-perception processes. *Journal of Personality and Social Psychology* 35: 485–494.

Rosser, M. 2005. Mentoring from the top: CEO perspectives. *Advances in Developing Human Resources* 7: 527–539.

————, and T. M. Egan. 2003. Types and functions of mentoring relationships: A review of the literature. In *Proceedings of the 2003 Academy of Human Resource Development Conference*, edited by S. Lynham and T. M. Egan, 928–934. Minneapolis, MN: Academy of Human Resource Development.

Rost, J. 1991. *Leadership for the 21st century.* New York: Praeger.

Roter, D. L., and J. A. Hall. 2004. Physician gender and patient-centered communication: A critical review of empirical research. *Annual Review of Public Health* 25: 497–519.

————, J. A. Hall, and Y. Aoki. 2002. Physician gender effects in medical communication: A meta-analytic review. *Journal of the American Medical Association* 288: 756–764.

Roth, L. M. 2006. *Selling women short: Gender inequality on Wall Street.* Princeton, NJ: Princeton University Press.

Rotundo, M., D. Nguyen, and P. R. Sackett. 2001. A meta-analytic review of gender differences in perceptions of sexual harassment. *Journal of Applied Psychology* 86: 914–922.

Roxas, J. L., and J. Y. Stoneback. 2004. The importance of gender across cultures in ethical decision-making. *Journal of Business Ethics* 50: 149–165.

Rudman, L. A. 1998. Self-promotion as a risk factor for women: The costs and benefits of counterstereotypical impression management. *Journal of Personality and Social Psychology* 74: 629–645.

————, and P. Glick. 1999. Feminized management and backlash towards agentic women: The hidden costs to women of a kinder, gentler image of middle managers. *Journal of Personality and Social Psychology* 77: 1004–1010.

————, and P. Glick. 2001. Prescriptive gender stereotypes and backlash toward agentic women. *Journal of Social Issues* 57: 743–762.

————, and S. A. Goodwin. 2004. Gender differences in automatic in-group bias: Why do women like women more than men like men? *Journal of Personality and Social Psychology* 87: 494–509.

————, and S. E. Kilianski. 2000. Implicit and explicit attitudes toward female authority. *Personality and Social Psychology Bulletin* 26: 1315–1328.

Rutter, A., and D. W. Hine. 2005. Sex differences in workplace aggression: An investigation of moderation and mediation effects. *Aggressive Behavior* 31: 254–270.

Ryan, C. S. 2002. Stereotype accuracy. In *European review of social psychology*, edited by W. Stroebe and M. Hewstone, Vol. 13, 75–109. Hove, England: Psychology Press/Taylor and Francis.

Ryan, M. K., and S. A. Haslam. 2005a. The glass cliff: Evidence that women are over-represented in precarious leadership positions. *British Journal of Management* 16: 81–90.

————, and S. A. Haslam. 2005b. The glass cliff: Implicit theories of leadership and gender and the precariousness of women's leadership positions. In *Implicit leadership theories: Essays and explorations*, edited by B. Schyns and J. R. Meindel, 137–160. Greenwich, CT: Information Age Publishing.

————, and S. A. Haslam. 2007. The glass cliff: Exploring the dynamics surrounding women's appointment to precarious leadership positions. *Academy of Management Review*, 32, 549–572.

Rynecki, D. 2003. Can Sallie save Citi, restore Sandy's reputation, and earn her $30 million paycheck? *Fortune*, June 9, 68–72.

Sahlstein, E., and M. Allen. 2002. Sex differences in self-esteem: A meta-analytic assessment. In *Interpersonal communication research: Advances through meta-analysis*, edited by A. Allen, R. W. Preiss, B. M. Gayle, and N. Burrell, 59–72. Mahwah, NJ: Erlbaum.

Saint-Germain, M. A. 1993. Women in power in Nicaragua: Myth and reality. In *Women as national leaders*, edited by M. A. Genovese, 70–102. London: Sage.

Salmansohn, K. 1996. *How to succeed in business without a penis: Secrets and strategies for the working woman.* New York: Harmony Books.

Salzman, P. C. 1999. Is inequality universal? *Current Anthropology* 40: 31–44.

Sanday, P. R. 1981. *Female power and male dominance: On the origins of sexual inequality.* New York: Cambridge University Press.

Sandberg, J. F., and S. L. Hofferth. 2001. Changes in children's time with parents: United States, 1981–1997. *Demography* 38: 423–436.

Sargent, A. G. 1981. *The androgynous manager.* New York: AMACOM.

Sayer, L. C., P. N. Cohen, and L. M. Casper. 2004. *The American people: Women, men and work.* New York: Russell Sage Foundation.

Schaller, M., and M. O'Brien. 1992. "Intuitive analysis of covariance" and group stereotype formation. *Personality and Social Psychology Bulletin* 18: 776–785.

Scheepers, D., and N. Ellemers. 2005. When the pressure is up: The assessment of social identity threat in low and high status groups. *Journal of Experimental Social Psychology* 41: 192–200.

———, N. Ellemers, and N. Sintemaartensdijk. 2007. Suffering from the possibility of status loss: Physiological indicators of social identity threat in high status groups. Manuscript submitted for publication.

Schein, V. E. 2001. A global look at psychological barriers to women's progress in management. *Journal of Social Issues* 57: 675–688.

Schmader, T., and M. Johns. 2005. Converging evidence that stereotype threat reduces working memory capacity. *Journal of Personality and Social Psychology* 85: 440–452.

Schmid Mast, M. 2001. Gender differences and similarities in dominance hierarchies in same-gender groups based on speaking time. *Sex Roles* 44: 537–556.

———. 2004. Men are hierarchical, women are egalitarian: An implicit gender stereotype. *Swiss Journal of Psychology* [Schweizerische Zeitschrift für Psychologie—Revue Suisse de Psychologie] 63: 107–111.

Schmidt, F. L., and J. Hunter. 2004. General mental ability in the world of work: Occupational attainment and job performance. *Journal of Personality and Social Psychology* 86: 162–173.

Schmitt, M. T., N. R. Branscombe, and T. Postmes. 2003. Women's emotional responses to the pervasiveness of gender discrimination. *European Journal of Social Psychology* 33: 297–312.

Schneer, J. A., and F. Reitman. 1994. The importance of gender in mid-career: A longitudinal study of MBAs. *Journal of Organizational Behavior* 15: 199–207.

Schneider, J., and K. Cook. 1995. Status inconsistency and gender: Combining revisited. *Small Group Research* 26: 372–399.

Schneider, K. T., S. Swan, and L. F. Fitzgerald. 1997. Job-related and psychological effects of sexual harassment in the workplace: Empirical evidence from two organizations. *Journal of Applied Psychology* 82: 401–415.

Schoen, R., N. M. Astone, K. Rothert, N. J. Standish, and Y. J. Kim. 2002. Women's employment, marital happiness and divorce. *Social Forces* 81: 643–662.

Schor, J. 1991. *The overworked American: The unexpected decline of leisure.* New York: Basic Books.

Schor, S. M. 1997. Separate and unequal: The nature of women's and men's career-building relationships. *Business Horizons* 40(5): 51–58.

Schroeder, P. 1999. And please call me Ms. President. *New York Times*, February 22, A17.

Schubert, R., M. Brown, M. Gysler, and H. W. Brachinger. 1999. Financial decision making: Are women really more risk averse? *American Economic Review* 89: 381–385.

Schutte, N. S., J. M. Malouff, L. E. Hall, D. J. Haggerty, J. T. Cooper, C. J. Golden, and L. Dornheim. 1998. Development and validation of a measure of emotional intelligence. *Personality and Individual Differences* 25: 167–177.

Schwartz, F. N. 1989. Management women and the new facts of life. *Harvard Business Review* 67(1): 65–76.

———, and J. Zimmerman. 1992. *Breaking with tradition: Women and work, the new facts of life.* New York: Warner Books.

Schwartz, S. H., and T. Rubel. 2005. Sex differences in value priorities: Cross-cultural and multimethod studies. *Journal of Personality and Social Psychology* 89: 1010–1028.

Sciolino, E. 2006a. Is France ready to be led by a woman? *International Herald Tribune Online*, April 7. http://www.iht.com/articles/2006/04/06/news/royal.php.

———. 2006b. Gender war à la Française shakes up political arena. *New York Times*, December 26, A10.

Scott, K. A., and D. J. Brown. 2006. Female first, leader second? Gender bias in the encoding of leadership behavior. *Organizational Behavior and Human Decision Processes*, 101: 230–242.

Sczesny, S. 2003a. A closer look beneath the surface: Various facets of the think-manager—think-male stereotype. *Sex Roles* 49: 353–363.

————. 2003b. Führungskompetenz: Selbst- und Fremdwahrnehmung weiblicher und männlicher Führungskräfte [Leadership competence: Self perceptions and others' perceptions of feminine and masculine leadership abilities]. *Zeitschrift für Sozialpsychologie* 34: 133–145.

————, J. Bosak, D. Neff, and B. Schyns. 2004. Gender stereotypes and the attribution of leadership traits: A cross-cultural comparison. *Sex Roles* 51: 631–645.

————, and U. Kühnen. 2004. Meta-cognition about biological sex and gender-stereotypical physical appearance: Consequences for the assessment of leadership competence. *Personality and Social Psychology Bulletin* 30: 13–21.

Seibert, S. E., M. L. Kraimer, and R. C. Liden. 2001. A social capital theory of career success. *Academy of Management Journal* 44: 219–237.

Sellers, P. 2006. Rising star: Mary Minnick, Coca-Cola: Meet corporate America's next generation of leaders. *Fortune Online*, January 24. http://money.cnn.com/2006/01/23/magazines/fortune/stars _minnick_fortune_060206/index.htm

Semadar, A., G. Robins, and G. R. Ferris. 2006. Comparing the validity of multiple social effectiveness constructs in the prediction of managerial job performance. *Journal of Organizational Behavior* 27: 443–461.

Shackelford, S., W. Wood, and S. Worchel. 1996. Behavioral styles and the influence of women in mixed-sex groups. *Social Psychology Quarterly* 59: 284–293.

Shapiro, M., C. Ingols, and S. Blake-Beard. 2007. Optioning in versus "opting out": Women using flexible work arrangements for career success. *CGO Insights* 25: 1–4. http://www.simmons.edu/som/docs/ centers/insights_25.pdf.

Sharpe, R. 2000. As leaders, women rule: New studies find that female managers outshine their male counterparts in almost every measure. *BusinessWeek*, November 20, 74. BusinessWeek Online, http:// www.businessweek.com/common_frames/ca.htm?/2000/00_47/b3708145.htm.

Shelton, B. A., and D. John. 1996. The division of household labor. *Annual Review of Sociology* 22: 299–322.

Shelton, J. N., and J. A. Richeson. 2006. Interracial interactions: A relational approach. In *Advances in experimental social psychology*, edited by M. Zanna, Vol. 38, 121–181. San Diego: Academic Press.

Shrader, C. B., V. B. Blackburn, and P. Iles. 1997. Women in management and firm financial performance: An exploratory study. *Journal of Management Issues* 9: 355–372.

Sicherman, N. 1996. Gender differences in departures from a large firm. *Industrial and Labor Relations Review* 49: 484–505.

Sidanius, J., and F. Pratto. 1999. *Social dominance: An intergroup theory of social hierarchy and oppression.* New York: Cambridge University Press.

Sieber, S. D. 1974. Toward a theory of role accumulation. *American Sociological Review* 39: 567–578.

Silver, R. C., E. A. Holman, D. N. McIntosh, M. Poulin, and V. Gil-Rivas. 2002. Nationwide longitudinal study of psychological responses to September 11. *Journal of the American Medical Association* 288: 1235–1244.

Silverman, I. W. 2003a. Gender differences in delay of gratification: A meta-analysis. *Sex Roles* 49: 451–463.

————. 2003b. Gender differences in resistance to temptation: Theories and evidence. *Developmental Review* 23: 219–259.

Silvestri, M. 2003. *Women in charge: Policing, gender and leadership.* Portland, OR: Willan Publishing.

Simons, T. 2002. Behavioral integrity: The perceived alignment between managers' words and deeds as a research focus. *Organization Science* 13: 18–35.

Sims, C. S., F. Drasgow, and L. F. Fitzgerald. 2005. The effects of sexual harassment on turnover in the military: Time-dependent modeling. *Journal of Applied Psychology* 90: 1141–1152.

Singh, V., S. Vinnicombe, and S. Terjesen. 2007. Women advancing onto the corporate board. In *Handbook of women in business and management*, edited by D. Bilimoria and S. K. Piderit, 304–329. Cheltenham, UK: Edward Elgar.

Singleton, A., and J. Maher. 2004. The "new man" is in the house: Young men, social change, and housework. *Journal of Men's Studies* 12: 227–240.

Smith, P. B., S. Dugan, and F. Trompenaars. 1997. Locus of control and affectivity by gender and occupational status: A 14-nation study. *Sex Roles* 36: 51–77.

Smith, R. A. 2002. Race, gender, and authority in the workplace: Theory and research. *Annual Review of Sociology* 28: 509–542.

Smuts, B. 1995. The evolutionary origins of patriarchy. *Human Nature* 6: 1–32.

Sokolove, M. 2006. Follow me. *New York Times Sports Magazine*, February, 96–101, 116–117.

Solberg, E. J. 1999. Using occupational preference in estimating market wage discrimination: The case of the gender pay gap (decomposition of a reduced-form wage equation). *American Journal of Economics and Sociology* 58: 85–113.

Souchon, N., G. Coulomb-Cabagno, A. Traclet, and O. Rascle. 2004. Referees' decision making in handball and transgressive behaviors: Influence of stereotypes about gender of players? *Sex Roles* 51: 445–453.

South, S. J., and G. Spitze. 1994. Housework in marital and nonmarital households. *American Sociological Review* 59: 327–347.

Spangler, W. D., and R. J. House. 1991. Presidential effectiveness and the leadership motive profile. *Journal of Personality and Social Psychology* 60: 439–455.

Spence, J. T., R. L. Helmreich, and C. K. Holahan. 1979. Negative and positive components of psychological masculinity and femininity and their relationships to self-reports of neurotic and acting out behaviors. *Journal of Personality and Social Psychology* 37: 1673–1682.

Spencer, S. J., S. Fein, C. T. Wolfe, C. Fong, and M. A. Dunn. 1998. Automatic activation of stereotypes: The role of self-image threat. *Personality and Social Psychology Bulletin* 24: 1139–1152.

Spivey, C. 2005. Time off at what price? The effects of career interruptions on earnings. *Industrial and Labor Relations Review* 59: 119–140.

Spock, B. 1946. *Baby and child care*. New York: Meredith Press.

Spragins, E. 2001. Is my mom better than yours? *New York Times*, July 1, section 3, 10.

Spurr, S. J. 1990. Sex discrimination in the legal profession: A study of promotion. *Industrial and Labor Relations Review* 43: 406–417.

Stangor, C., L. Lynch, C. Duan, and B. Glass. 1992. Categorization of individuals on the basis of multiple social features. *Journal of Personality and Social Psychology* 62: 207–218.

Stanley, T. D., and S. B. Jarrell. 1998. Gender wage discrimination bias? A meta-regression analysis. *Journal of Human Resources* 33: 947–973.

Steel, D. 1993. *They can kill you . . . but they can't eat you*. New York: Pocket Books.

Steele, C. M., S. J. Spencer, and J. Aronson. 2002. Contending with group image: The psychology of stereotype and social identity threat. In *Advances in experimental social psychology*, edited by M. P. Zanna, Vol. 34, 379–440. San Diego: Academic Press.

Steinberg, J. 2003. Executive Editor of *The Times* and top deputy step down. *New York Times*, June 5. http://www.nytimes.com/2003/06/05/national/05CND-RESI.html.

Steinpreis, R. E., K. A. Anders, and D. Ritzke. 1999. The impact of gender on the review of curricula vitae of job applicants and tenure candidates: A national empirical study. *Sex Roles* 41: 509–528.

Sternberg, R. J. 2007. A systems model of leadership: WICS. *American Psychologist* 62: 34–42,

Stockdale, M. S. 1998. The direct and moderating influences of sexual-harassment pervasiveness, coping strategies, and gender on work-related outcomes. *Psychology of Women Quarterly* 22: 521–535.

Stone, P., and M. Lovejoy. 2004. Fast-track women and the "choice" to stay home. *Annals of the American Academy of Political and Social Science* 596: 62–83.

Story, L. 2005. Many women at elite colleges set career path to motherhood. *New York Times*, September 20, A1.

Strasser, S. 1982. *Never done: A history of American housework*. New York: Pantheon Books.

Stroh, L. K., J. M. Brett, and A. H. Reilly. 1992. All the right stuff: A comparison of female and male managers' career progression. *Journal of Applied Psychology* 77: 251–260.

Stuhlmacher, A. F., and A. E. Walters. 1999. Gender differences in negotiation outcome: A meta-analysis. *Personnel Psychology* 52: 653–677.

Sullivan, K. M. 2005. Justice in the balance: The precedent-setting life of the all-important swing vote on the high court. *Washington Post*, December 25, Book World, T03.

Sung, H. 2003. Fairer sex or fairer system? Gender and corruption revisited. *Social Forces* 82: 703–723.

A surgeon cuts to the heart of the matter. 1991. *People Weekly*, October 28, 36, 50.

Sutton, C. D., and K. K. Moore. 1985. Executive women—20 years later. *Harvard Business Review* 63(5): 42–66.

Swamy, A., S. Knack, Y. Lee, and O. Azfar. 2001. Gender and corruption. *Journal of Development Economics* 64: 25–51.

Swim, J. K. 1994. Perceived versus meta-analytic effect sizes: An assessment of the accuracy of gender stereotypes. *Journal of Personality and Social Psychology* 66: 21–36.

———, E. Borgida, G. Maruyama, and D. G. Myers. 1989. Joan McKay versus John McKay: Do gender stereotypes bias evaluations? *Psychological Bulletin* 105: 409–429.

———, and L. J. Sanna. 1996. He's skilled, she's lucky: A meta-analysis of observers' attributions for women's and men's successes and failures. *Personality and Social Psychology Bulletin* 22: 507–519.

Swiss, D. J. 1996. *Women breaking through: Overcoming the final 10 obstacles at work*. Princeton, NJ: Peterson's/Pacesetter Books.

Tajfel, H., and J. C. Turner. 1979. An integrative theory of intergroup conflict. In *The social psychology of intergroup relations*, edited by W. G. Austin and S. Worchel, 33–48. Monterey, CA: Brooks/Cole.

Tannen, D. 1990. *You just don't understand: Women and men in conversation*. New York: William Morrow.

Taps, J., and P. Y. Martin. 1990. Gender composition, attributional accounts, and women's influence and likability in task groups. *Small Group Research* 21: 471–491.

Tarsala, M. 2003. eBay's Meg Whitman named CEO of the year by CBS MarketWatch. *Silicon Valley News of Benchmark Capital*, September 18. http://www.benchmark.com/news/sv/2003/09_18_2003.php.

Taylor, S. E., and S. T. Fiske. 1978. Salience, attention, and attribution: Top of the head phenomena. In *Advances in experimental social psychology*, edited by L. Berkowitz, Vol. 11, 249–288. New York: Academic Press.

Tepper, B. J., S. J. Brown, and M. D. Hunt. 1993. Strength of subordinates' upward influence tactics and gender congruency effects. *Journal of Applied Social Psychology* 23: 1903–1919.

Tharenou, P. 1999. Gender differences in advancing to the top. *International Journal of Management Reviews* 1: 111–132.

Third Clinton-Bush-Perot Presidential Debate. 1992. The American presidency project at University of California, Santa Barbara. http://www.presidency.ucsb.edu/showdebate.php?debateid=17.

Thoits, P. A. 1992. Identity structures and psychological well-being: Gender and marital status comparisons. *Social Psychology Quarterly* 55: 236–256.

Thomas-Hunt, M. C., and K. W. Phillips. 2004. When what you know is not enough: Expertise and gender dynamics in task groups. *Personality and Social Psychology Bulletin* 30: 1585–1598.

Tiger, L. 1999. *The decline of males*. New York: Golden Books.

Timberlake, S. 2005. Social capital and gender in the workplace. *Journal of Management Development* 24: 34–44.

Timmons, H. 2006. Tradition-breaking choice to be chief of mining giant. *New York Times*, October 25, C10.

Tischler, L. 2004. Where are the women? *Fast Company*, February, 52–55, 58, 60.

———. 2005. The CEO's new clothes. *Fast Company*, September, 27–28.

Tomaskovic-Devey, D., C. Zimmer, K. Stainback, C. Robinson, T. Taylor, and T. McTague. 2006. Documenting desegregation: Segregation in American workplaces by race, ethnicity, and sex, 1966–2003. *American Sociological Review*, 71, 565–588.

Toner, R. 2007. Women feeling freer to suggest "vote for mom." *New York Times*, January 29, A1, A14.

Tornow, W. W., and P. R. Pinto. 1976. The development of a managerial job taxonomy: A system for describing, classifying, and evaluating executive positions. *Journal of Applied Psychology* 61: 410–418.

Tosi, H. L., and S. W. Einbender. 1985. The effects of the type and amount of information in sex discrimination research: A meta-analysis. *Academy of Management Journal* 28: 712–723.

Trivers, R. L. 1972. Parental investment and sexual selection. In *Sexual selection and the descent of man: 1871–1971*, edited by B. Campbell, 136–179. Chicago: Aldine.

Troemel-Ploetz, S. 1994. "Let me put it this way, John": Conversational strategies of women in leadership positions. *Journal of Pragmatics* 22: 199–209.

Truell, P. 1996. Success and sharp elbows: One woman's path to lofty heights on Wall Street. *New York Times*, July 2, D1.

Turner, N., J. Barling, O. Epitropaki, V. Butcher, and V. B. Milner. 2002. Transformational leadership and moral reasoning. *Journal of Applied Psychology* 87: 304–311.

Twenge, J. M. 1997a. Attitudes toward women, 1970–1995: A meta-analysis. *Psychology of Women Quarterly* 21: 35–51.

———. 1997b. Changes in masculine and feminine traits over time: A meta-analysis. *Sex Roles* 36: 305–325.

———. 2001. Changes in women's assertiveness in response to status and roles: A cross-temporal meta-analysis, 1931–1993. *Journal of Personality and Social Psychology* 81: 133–145.

———, W. K. Campbell, and C. A. Foster. 2003. Parenthood and marital satisfaction: A meta-analytic review. *Journal of Marriage and the Family* 65: 574–583.

The 2006 Global 500: Women CEOs. 2006. *Fortune* at *CNN.Money.com*. http://money.cnn.com/magazines/fortune/global500/2006/womenceos/.

Uggen, C., and A. Blackstone. 2004. Sexual harassment as a gendered expression of power. *American Sociological Review* 69: 64–92.

Uhlmann, E. L., and G. L. Cohen. 2005. Constructed criteria: Redefining merit to justify discrimination. *Psychological Science* 16: 474–480.

Uleman, J. S., L. S. Newman, and G. B. Moskowitz. 1996. People as flexible interpreters: Evidence and issues from spontaneous trait inference. In *Advances in experimental social psychology*, edited by M. P. Zanna, Vol. 28, 211–279. San Diego: Academic Press.

Underwood, M. K. 2003. *Social aggression among girls*. New York: Guilford Press.

United Nations Development Programme. 2006. *Human development report 2006*. New York: United Nations Development Programme. http://hdr.undp.org/hdr2006/pdfs/report/HDR_2006_Tables.pdf.

U.S. Bureau of Justice Statistics. 2005. *Criminal victimization in the United States: Gender by offender*. http://www.ojp.usdoj.gov/bjs/abstract/cvus/gender.htm.

U.S. Bureau of Labor Statistics. 2005a. *Unpublished tabulations from the American Time Use Survey*, Table 8-A. Washington, DC: U.S. Department of Labor.

———. 2005b. *News: Workers on flexible and shift schedules in May 2004*. http://www.bls.gov/news.release/pdf/flex.pdf.

———. 2006a. *Highlights of women's earnings in 2005*. http://www.bls.gov/cps/cpswom2005.pdf.

———. 2006b. *News: American time-use survey—2005 results announced by BLS*. http://www.bls.gov/news.release/pdf/atus.pdf.

———. 2006c. *News: Employment characteristics of families*. http://www.bls.gov/news.release/pdf/famee.pdf.

———. 2006d. *Women in the labor force: A databook*. Report 996. http://www.bls.gov/cps/wlf-databook2006.htm.

———. 2007a. *Historical CPS employment for 1983–99 on the 2002 Census industry and occupational classifications*. http://www.bls.gov/cps/constio198399.htm.

———. 2007b. *News: Work experience of the population in 2005*. http://www.bls.gov/news.release/pdf/work.pdf.

———. 2007c. *Tables from employment and earnings: Annual averages, household data*. http://www.bls.gov/cps/home.htm.

U.S. Census Bureau. 1973. *Statistical abstract of the United States: 1973*. http://www2.census.gov/prod2/statcomp/documents/1973-01.pdf.

———. 1975. *Bicentennial edition: Historical statistics of the United States, Colonial Times to 1970*. http://www2.census.gov/prod2/statcomp/documents/CT1970p1-01.pdf.

———. 2007. *Statistical abstract of the United States: 2007*. Washington, DC. http://www.census.gov/prod/www/statistical-abstract.html.

U.S. Department of Defense. 2005. *Active duty military personnel by rank/grade* (for September 2005). http://siadapp.dior.whs.mil/personnel/MILITARY/Miltop.htm.

U.S. Department of Labor, Women's Bureau. 2006. *20 leading occupations of employed women; full-time wage and salary workers; 2005 annual averages*. http://www.dol.gov/wb/factsheets/20lead2005.htm.

U.S. Equal Employment Opportunity Commission. 2006. *Sex-based discrimination*. http://www.eeoc.gov/types/sex.html.

U.S. Government Accountability Office. 2003. *Women's earnings: Work patterns partially explain difference between men's and women's earnings* (GAO-04-35). http://www.gao.gov/new.items/d0435.pdf.

U.S. Merit Systems Protection Board. 1995. *Sexual harassment in the federal workplace: Trends, progress, continuing challenges*. http://www.mspb.gov/studies/sexhar.pdf.

U.S. National Center for Education Statistics. 2005. *Digest of education statistics, 2005*. http://nces.ed.gov/programs/digest/d05_tf.asp.

U.S. Office of Personnel Management. 2005. *The fact book: Federal civilian workforce statistics*. http://www.opm.gov/feddata/factbook/2005/factbook2005.pdf.

Valian, V. 1998. *Why so slow? The advancement of women*. Cambridge, MA: MIT Press.

van Engen, M. L, R. van der Leeden, and T. M. Willemsen. 2001. Gender, context and leadership styles: A field study. *Journal of Occupational and Organizational Psychology* 74: 581–598.

———, and T. M. Willemsen. 2004. Sex and leadership styles: A meta-analysis of research published in the 1990s. *Psychological Reports* 94: 3–18.

van Knippenberg, A., M. van Twuyver, and J. Pepels. 1994. Factors affecting social categorization processes in memory. *British Journal of Social Psychology* 33: 419–431.

van Knippenberg, D., and M. C. Schippers. 2007. Work group diversity. *Annual Review of Psychology* 58: 515–541.

Van Rooy, D. L., A. Alonso, and C. Viswesvaran. 2005. Group differences in emotional intelligence scores: Theoretical and practical implications. *Personality and Individual Differences* 38: 689–700.

———, and C. Viswesvaran. 2004. Emotional intelligence: A meta-analytic investigation of predictive validity and nomological net. *Journal of Vocational Behavior* 65: 71–95.

Van Steenbergen, E. F., N. Ellemers, and A. Mooijaart. In press. How work and family can facilitate each other: Distinct types of work-family facilitation and outcomes for women and men. *Journal of Occupational Health Psychology*.

Van Velsor, E., and J. B. Leslie. 1995. Why executives derail: Perspectives across time and cultures. *Academy of Management Executive* 9(4): 62–72.

van Vianen, A. E. M., and A. H. Fischer. 2002. Illuminating the glass ceiling: The role of organizational culture preferences. *Journal of Occupational and Organizational Psychology* 75: 315–337.

Van Vugt, M. 2006. Evolutionary origins of leadership and followership. *Personality and Social Psychology Review*, 10, 354–371.

———, S. F. Jepson, C. M. Hart, and D. De Cremer. 2004. Autocratic leadership in social dilemmas: A threat to group stability. *Journal of Experimental Social Psychology* 40: 1–13.

Vecchio, R. P. 2002. Leadership and gender advantage. *Leadership Quarterly* 13: 643–671.

Vinkenburg, C. J., M. L. van Engen, A. H. Eagly, and M. L. Johannesen-Schmidt. 2007. *Beliefs about the leadership styles of women and men in relation to promotion.* Manuscript submitted for publication.

Vinnicombe, S., and J. Bank. 2003. *Women with attitude: Lessons for career management.* New York: Routledge.

Vistnes, J. P. 1997. Gender differences in days lost from work due to illnesses. *Industrial and Labor Relations Review* 50: 304–323.

Vogl, A. J. 2003. An unnatural match? *Across the Board* 40(3): 49–54.

Volkema, R. J. 2004. Demographic, cultural, and economic predictors of perceived ethicality of negotiation behavior: A nine-country analysis. *Journal of Business Research* 57: 69–78.

von Hippel, W., D. Sekaquaptewa, and P. Vargas. 1995. On the role of encoding processes in stereotype maintenance. In *Advances in experimental social psychology*, edited by M. Zanna, Vol. 27, 177–254. San Diego: Academic Press.

Vroom, V. H., and P. W. Yetton. 1973. *Leadership and decision-making.* Pittsburgh, PA: University of Pittsburgh Press.

Wagner, D. G., R. S. Ford, and T. W. Ford. 1986. Can gender inequalities be reduced? *American Sociological Review* 51: 47–61.

Wajcman, J. 1998. *Managing like a man: Women and men in corporate management.* University Park: Pennsylvania State University Press.

Wakin, D. J. 2005. In American orchestras, more women are taking the bow. *International Herald Tribune,* July 27, 10.

Waldfogel, J. 1997. The effect of children on women's wages. *American Sociological Review* 62: 209–217.

———. 1998. The family gap for young women in the United States and Britain: Can maternity leave make a difference? *Journal of Labor Economics* 16: 505–545.

Wallis, C. 2004. The case for staying home. *Time,* March 22, 51–59.

Wal-Mart Class Website. 2004. *Federal judge orders Wal-Mart Stores, Inc., the nation's largest private employer, to stand trial for company-wide sex discrimination: Media advisory,* June 22. http://www.walmartclass.com/walmartclass94.pl?wsi=0&websys_screen=all_press_release_view&websys_id=14.

Walsh, K. C. 2002. Enlarging representation: Women bringing marginalized perspectives to floor debate in the House of Representatives. In *Women transforming Congress,* edited by C. S. Rosenthal, 370–396. Norman: University of Oklahoma Press.

Walsh, M. W. 2001. So where are the corporate husbands? For women at the top, something is missing: Social, wifely support. *New York Times,* June 24, section 3, 1.

Walter, T., and G. Davie. 1998. The religiosity of women in the modern West. *British Journal of Sociology* 49: 640–660.

Walters, A. E., A. F. Stuhlmacher, and L. L. Meyer. 1998. Gender and negotiator competitiveness: A meta-analysis. *Organizational Behavior and Human Decision Processes* 76: 1–29.

Warner, J. 2005. Mommy madness. *Newsweek,* February 21, 42–49.

———. 2007. Trying to imagine a woman in the White House. January 25. *Times Select,* http://warner.blogs.nytimes.com/.

Warr, M., and C. G. Ellison. 2000. Rethinking social reactions to crime: Personal and altruistic fear in family households. *American Journal of Sociology* 106: 551–578.

Warren, E. 2004. No apologies, no regrets. *Chicago Tribune Magazine,* December 5, 13–17, 19, 20, 31.

Washington Post, Kaiser Family Foundation, and Harvard University 2006. *African American men survey.* Menlo Park, CA: Henry J. Kaiser Family Foundation.

Wax, A. L. 2004. Family-friendly workplace reform: Prospects for change. *Annals of the American Academy of Political and Social Science* 596: 36–61.

Wayne, J. H. 2003. Who is a good organizational citizen? Social perception of male and female employees who use family leave. *Sex Roles* 49: 233–246.

Wayne, S. J., and R. C. Liden. 1995. Effects of impression management on performance ratings: A longitudinal study. *Academy of Management Journal* 38: 232–260.

Weber, M. 1968/1925. The types of legitimate domination. In *Economy and society: An outline of interpretive sociology*, edited by G. Roth and C. Wittich, 212–301. New York: Bedminster Press. Original work published 1925.

Weichselbaumer, D., and R. Winter-Ebmer. 2005. A meta-analysis of the international gender wage gap. *Journal of Economic Surveys* 19: 479–511.

Weinberger, C. 2006. Are there racial gaps in high school leadership opportunities? Working Paper, University of California, Santa Barbara. http://econ.ucsb.edu/~weinberg/leadopps.pdf.

———, and P. Kuhn. 2006. The narrowing of the U.S. gender earnings gap, 1959–1999: A cohort-based analysis. National Bureau of Economic Research Working Paper No. 12115. http://www.nber.org/papers/W12115.

Weir, A. 1998. *The life of Elizabeth I*. New York: Ballatine Books.

Wellington, S. 2001. *Be your own mentor: Strategies from top women on the secrets of success*. New York: Random House.

Welsh, S. 1999. Gender and sexual harassment. *Annual Review of Sociology* 25: 169–190.

White, K. 1995. *Why good girls don't get ahead but gutsy girls do: 9 secrets every working woman must know*. New York: Warner Books.

Whitley, B. E., Jr., A. B. Nelson, and C. J. Jones. 1999. Gender differences in cheating attitudes and classroom cheating behavior: A meta-analysis. *Sex Roles* 41: 657–680.

Whitman, C. T. 1999. Christine Todd Whitman in conversation with Ruth B. Mandel and Mary S. Hartman. In *Talking leadership: Conversations with powerful women*, edited by M. S. Hartman, 257–278. New Brunswick, NJ: Rutgers University Press.

Why not many mommy tracks? 1989. *New York Times*, March 13, A18.

Wigboldus, D. H. J., A. Dijksterhuis, and A. van Knippenberg. 2003. When stereotypes get in the way: Stereotypes obstruct stereotype-inconsistent trait inferences. *Journal of Personality and Social Psychology* 84: 470–484.

Wilde, A., and A. B. Diekman. 2005. Cross-cultural similarities and differences in dynamic stereotypes: A comparison between Germany and the United States. *Psychology of Women Quarterly* 29: 188–196.

Wilkie, J. R., M. M. Ferree, and K. S. Ratcliff. 1998. Gender and fairness: Marital satisfaction in two-earner couples. *Journal of Marriage and the Family* 60: 577–594.

Williams, C. L. 1992. The glass escalator: Hidden advantages for men in the "female" professions. *Social Problems* 39: 41–57.

———. 1995. *Still a man's world: Men who do women's work*. Berkeley: University of California Press.

———, P. A. Giuffre, and K. Dellinger. 1999. Sexuality in the workplace: Organizational control, sexual harassment, and the pursuit of pleasure. *American Sociological Review* 25: 73–93.

Williams, J. 2000. *Unbending gender: Why family and work conflict and what to do about it*. New York: Oxford University Press.

Williams, J. E., and D. L. Best. 1990. *Measuring sex stereotypes: A multination study*. Newbury Park, CA: Sage.

Williams, J. M. 1980. Personality characteristics of the successful female athlete. In *Sport psychology: An analysis of athlete behavior*, edited by W. F. Straub, 2nd ed., 353–359. Ithaca, NY: Movement Publications.

Williams, K. Y., and C. A. O'Reilly. 1998. Demography and diversity in organizations: A review of 40 years of research. *Research on Organizational Behavior* 20: 77–140.

Williams, M. L., M. A. McDaniel, and N. T. Nguyen. 2006. A meta-analysis of the antecedents and consequences of pay level satisfaction. *Journal of Applied Psychology* 91: 392–413.

Wilson, D. C. 2006. *When equal opportunity knocks*. April 13. Gallup Brain, http://brain.gallup.com.

Wilson, M., and M. Daly. 1992. The man who mistook his wife for a chattel. In *The adapted mind: Evolutionary psychology and the generation of culture*, edited by J. H. Barkow, L. Cosmides, and J. Tooby, 289–322. New York: Oxford University Press.

Winter, D. G. 1988. The power motive in women—and men. *Journal of Personality and Social Psychology* 54: 510–519.

Wirth, L. 2001. *Breaking through the glass ceiling: Women in management*. Geneva: International Labor Office. http://www.ilo.org/public/english/support/publ/pdf/btgc.pdf.

———. 2004. *Breaking through the glass ceiling: Women in management, update 2004*. Geneva: International Labor Office. http://www.ilo.org/public/english/support/publ/pdf/btgc.pdf.

Woo, D. A., and G. P. S. Khoo. 2006. Corporate culture and leadership: Traditional, legal, and charismatic authority. In *Gender, race, and ethnicity in the workplace: Issues and challenges for today's organizations*, edited by M. F. Karsten, Vol. 1, 79–111. Westport, CT: Praeger.

Wood, R. G., M. E. Corcoran, and P. N. Courant. 1993. Pay differences among the highly paid: The male-female earnings gap in lawyers' salaries. *Journal of Labor Economics* 11: 417–441.

Wood, W., P. N. Christensen, M. R. Hebl, and H. Rothgerber. 1997. Conformity to sex-typed norms, affect, and the self-concept. *Journal of Personality and Social Psychology* 73: 523–535.

———, and A. H. Eagly. 2002. A cross-cultural analysis of the behavior of women and men: Implications for the origins of sex differences. *Psychological Bulletin* 128: 699–727.

———, and C. A. Kallgren. 1988. Communicator attributes and persuasion: Recipients' access to attitude-relevant information in memory. *Personality and Social Psychology Bulletin* 14: 172–182.

———, and S. J. Karten. 1986. Sex differences in interaction style as a product of perceived sex differences in competence. *Journal of Personality and Social Psychology* 50: 341–347.

Woopidoo! 2006a. Quotations: Business quotes by talk show host Oprah Winfry. http://www.woopidoo.com/business_quotes/authors/oprah-winfrey-quotations.htm.

———. 2006b. Quotations: Inspirational business quotes—encouragement quotes. http://www.woopidoo.com/business_quotes/encouragement-quotes.htm.

Wootton, B. H. 1997. Gender differences in occupational employment. *Monthly Labor Review* 120: 15–24.

Wosinska, W., A. J. Dabul, R. Whetstone-Dion, and R. Cialdini. 1996. Self-presentational responses to success in the organization: The costs and benefits of modesty. *Basic and Applied Social Psychology* 18: 229–242.

Wrangham, R. W., J. H. Jones, G. Laden, D. Pilbeam, and N. Conklin-Brittain. 1999. The raw and the stolen: Cooking and the ecology of human origins. *Current Anthropology* 40: 567–577.

Wright, E. O., J. Baxter, and G. E. Birkelund. 1995. The gender gap in workplace authority: A cross-national study. *American Sociological Review* 60: 407–435.

Yang, J. L. 2005a. Alpha females. *Fortune* at *CNN.Money.com*, November 14. http://money.cnn.com/magazines/fortune/fortune_archive/2005/11/14/8360719/index.htm.

———. 2005b. Goodbye to all that. *Fortune* at *CNN.Money.com*, November 14. http://money.cnn.com/magazines/fortune/fortune_archive/2005/11/14/8360706/index.htm.

Yoder, J. D. 2001. Making leadership work more effectively for women. *Journal of Social Issues* 57: 815–828.

———. 2002. 2001 Division 35 presidential address: Context matters: Understanding tokenism processes and their impact on women's work. *Psychology of Women Quarterly* 26: 1–8.

———, and T. L. Schleicher. 1996. Undergraduates regard deviation from occupational gender stereotypes as costly for women. *Sex Roles* 34: 171–188.

———, T. L. Schleicher, and T. W. McDonald. 1998. Empowering token women leaders: The importance of organizationally legitimated credibility. *Psychology of Women Quarterly* 22: 209–222.

———, and L. M. Sinnett. 1985. Is it all in the numbers? A case study of tokenism. *Psychology of Women Quarterly* 9: 413–418.

Young, H. 1990. *One of us: A biography of Margaret Thatcher*. London: Pan.

Yukl, G. 2006. *Leadership in organizations*. 6th ed. Upper Saddle River, NJ: Prentice Hall.

Zaccaro, S. J. 2007. Trait-based perspectives of leadership. *American Psychologist* 62: 6–16.

———, C. Kemp, and P. Bader. 2004. Leader traits and attributes. In *The nature of leadership*, edited by J. Antonakis, A. T. Cianciolo, and R. J. Sternberg, 101–124. Thousand Oaks, CA: Sage.

Zahra, S. A., R. L. Priem, and A. A. Rasheed. 2005. The antecedents and consequences of top management fraud. *Journal of Management* 31: 803–828.

Zaleznik, A. 1977. Managers and leaders: Are they different? *Harvard Business Review* 55(3): 67–78.

Zanna, M. P., F. Crosby, and G. Lowenstein. 1987. Male reference groups and discontent among female professionals. In *Women's career development*, edited by B. Gutek and L. Larwood, 28–41. Newbury Park, CA: Sage.

Zeidner, M., G. Matthews, and R. D. Roberts. 2004. Emotional intelligence in the workplace: A critical review. *Applied Psychology: An International Review* 53: 371–399.

Zelechowski, D. D., and D. Bilimoria. 2003. The experience of women corporate inside directors on the boards of *Fortune* 1000 firms. *Women in Management Review* 18: 376–381.

Zick, C. D., and W. K. Bryant. 1996. A new look at parents' time spent in child care: Primary and secondary time use. *Social Science Research* 25: 260–280.

Zweigenhaft, R. L., and G. W. Domhoff. 1998. *Diversity in the power elite: Have women and minorities reached the top?* New Haven, CT: Yale University Press.

AUTHOR INDEX

Clymer, A., 201n3, 241
Coats, E. J., 217n9, 250
Cohen, D., 205n19, 241
Cohen, F., 132, 223n62, 241, 256
Cohen, G. L., 218n27, 219n52, 269
Cohen, L. E., 213n14, 241
Cohen, P. N., 209n12, 210n32, 266
Colbert, A. E., 206n41, 254
Coleman, C., 113–114, 220n57, 241
Collins, D., 223n59, 241
Collins, G., 24, 203n50, 241
Collins, J. C., 117, 220n72, 227n10, 241
Colvin, G., 203n33, 208n69, 241
Committee of 200, 202n17, 225n56, 230n18, 241
Conger, J. A., 222n45, 241
Conklin-Brittain, N., 205n14, 273
Conlin, M., 116, 220n71, 241
Connell, R. W., 231n32, 231n45, 241
Conway, M., 215n18, 242
Cook, A., 223n62, 256
Cook, J. M., 226n75, 259
Cook, K., 219n41, 266
Cooke, L. L., 218n13, 260
Coons, A. E., 221n25, 251
Cooper, J. T., 207n55, 266
Cooperman, M., 218n33, 237
Copeland, C. L., 217n9, 242
Corcoran, M. E., 211n44, 213n15, 224n3, 261, 273
Cornwell, J. M., 217n63, 263
Correll, S. J., 211n51, 219n50, 242
Corrigall, E. A., 210n31, 210–211n31, 210–211n43, 211n44, 211n50, 211–212n53, 212n57, 242, 255
Cortina, L. M., 219n37, 219n38, 227n25, 236, 242, 257
Corwin, V., 225n68, 256
Coser, L., 140, 224n7, 242
Costa, P. T., Jr., 43, 44t, 205n25, 206n42, 207n52, 207n53, 207n54, 242, 259
Costley, D. L., 220n1, 252
Cotton, J. L., 210n39, 228n52, 242, 263
Coulomb-Cabano, G., 218n16, 268
Council on Foundations, 203n28, 242
Courant, P. N., 213n15, 273
Cowan, R. S., 208n2, 209n16, 242
Cox, T. H., Jr., 213n15, 213n27, 225n58, 228n52, 242, 244
Coyne, S. M., 205n22, 205n23, 234
Craig, J. M., 218n30, 242
Crandall, C. S., 220n60, 236
Crawford, M. S., 216n50, 258
Creswell, J., 229n2, 242
Crick, N. R., 205n22, 242
Crittenden, A., 162, 206n36, 225n68, 227n4, 242
Crocker, J., 214n41, 242
Crosby, F., 225n62, 226n70, 228n37, 228n38, 242, 273

Cross, S. E., 221n20, 242
Crown, D. F., 207n60, 247
Cuddy, A. J. C., 219n50, 242

Dabady, M., 214n8, 256
Dabul, A. J., 218n13, 273
Dahlerup, D., 203n45, 242
Dall'Ara, E., 219n35, 242
Daly, M., 205n15, 205n20, 242, 272
Darity, W. A., Jr., 214n36, 242
Darley, J. M., 214n3, 243
Darwin, C., 204n4, 243
Dasgupta, N., 89, 215n21, 243
Daubman, K. A., 227n26, 243, 251
Davenport, D. B., 166, 227n16, 243
Davidson, M. J., 202n21, 243
Davidson, M. N., 231n30, 246
Davie, G., 207n59, 271
Davies, P. G., 93–94, 216n45, 243
Davies-Netzley, S. A., 224n31, 228n47, 243
Davis, J. A., 98f, 208n9, 243
Davis-Blake, A., 230n29, 262
Davison, H. K., 77, 214n32, 219n48, 220n55, 243
Dawkins, R., 204n4, 243
Deal, M., 204n11, 251
Dean, C., 107–108, 218n29, 243
Dean, N. G., 216n36, 265
Deaux, K., 215n10, 219n50, 219n51, 221n20, 243, 247, 248
DeBacker, T. K., 211n51, 250
De Cremer, D., 222n33, 271
de Gilder, D., 224n27, 230n27, 245
DeGraaf, N. D., 207n59, 254
Delli Carpini, M. X., 203n51, 243
Dellinger, K., 219n39, 272
DeMott, B., 197, 205n31, 231n40, 243
DeNardo, M., 218n31, 219n37, 258
Den Hartog, D. N., 216n47, 229n3, 246
Denmark, F. L., 216n47, 229n3, 246
de Pater, I. E., 225n50, 225n51, 243
Desaulniers, J., 221n23, 261
Deutsch, C. H., 150–151, 225n59, 227n14, 229n64, 243
De Vader, C. L., 206n34, 206n41, 257
Devine, D. J., 204n54, 243
Devine, P. G., 214n5, 243, 262
de Zárate, R. O., 203n47, 243
Diamond, L. M., 204n4, 251
DiBerardinis, J. P., 219n41, 243
Diekman, A. B., 196, 205n18, 207n59, 215n13, 215n14, 216n56, 231n34, 231n39, 231n47, 243, 244, 245, 272
Dijksterhuis, A., 216n43, 272
Di Leonardo, M., 208n1, 244
Dillard, J. P., 217n10, 238
DiMare, L., 216n32, 234
Dindia, K., 220n71, 244
Dipboye, R. L., 231n30, 253

SUBJECT INDEX

Anglo American plc (Anglo Mining), 166
antidiscrimination legislation, 151
Archer Daniels Midland, 47, 176
Argentina, 16, 17
Asian American women, 17, 68, 69f
assertiveness
    assertive task behavior, niceness and, 164–165,
        188, 227n11, 227n13
    ethnicity and, 103, 217n8
    as managerial role, 91
    networking and, 173
    psychological sex differences in, 36–37
    resistance to, 103–104, 217n4, 217n6
    in seeking demanding assignments, 181
    sex differences in, shrinking, 186
    women's self-reports of, 38
assimilation, 84–85
athletics, female participation in, 206–207n51
AT&T, 169
attitudes of men toward women, 196–198
attitude surveys, 10
    on fathers' childcare responsibilities, 52
    on women political leaders, 97, 98f, 99, 99f
    on women's career opportunities, 3
    sex difference on political issues, 194–195
attributions for success and failure, 79
attrition rate. See continuity of employment
authenticity of leaders, 171–173
authority
    authoritative leadership roles, 122
    female assertions of, negative reactions to,
        123, 125–126
    gender gap in, 72–75, 74t
    positive relationships with, 91
    undermined in masculine settings, 188
    of women, legitimizing, 156–157, 226n83
autocratic leaders, 122, 158–159
autocratic leadership style, 122, 125–127, 222n33

Baby and Child Care (Spock), 53–54
Bachelet, Michelle, 95
bachelor's degrees. See educational attainment
Bank of America, 192
barriers to advancement, 139–151, 187. See also
        discrimination; division of labor by gender;
        family responsibilities
    biosocial barriers, 35, 184
    "competency barrier," 164
    demands for long hours, 140–143, 224n10
    inability to obtain desirable assignments,
        148–151
    lack of fit with organizational culture,
        137–138, 146–148
    lack of social capital, 144–146
    travel and relocation requirements, 143
barriers to women's leadership, 2–8
    concrete wall, 2–3, 27

glass ceiling, 2, 4f, 4–5, 6
labyrinth, 2, 5–8
between-occupations wage gap, 71, 213n9,
    213n12
bias
    in explanations of success or failure, 79
    illusory correlation, 191, 230n17
    in personnel practices, 155
    in research studies, 10, 190
    uniform bias against women, 72–75, 73t
Big Five personality traits, 40–43, 41f
    agreeableness, 40, 41, 41f
    conscientiousness, 40, 41, 41f, 43
    extraversion, 40–41, 41f, 42
    intelligence and, 41f, 43, 44f, 45, 206n43
    neuroticism, 40, 41, 41f
    openness to experience, 40, 41, 41f, 42, 43
    women and men compared on, 43–47
Biogen Idec, 178
Biology at Work: Rethinking Sexual Equality
    (Browne), 197
biosocial barriers, 35, 184
biosocial origin theory, 34–35, 205n19
blended leadership style, 163–173, 188
    effective negotiation and, 169–171, 227n31
    feeling authentic in role, 171–173, 228n44
    in female leaders, 123, 221n23–25
    limits in masculine settings, 167–168, 188
    navigating labyrinth and, 161
    "niceness" with assertive task behavior,
        164–165, 188, 227n11, 227n13
    resistance to female leadership and, 166
    taking credit for accomplishments, 168–169,
        227n27
boards of directors, 157–158, 192, 202n22
Brady Corporation, 107, 110
Bravo, Rose Marie, 128, 222n46
breaks from employment. See continuity of
    employment
breakthrough women, 167, 181
Browne, Kingsley, 29, 30, 48, 197, 204n2
BT Retail, 45
"bully" bosses, 39
"bully broads," 106
Burberry, 128
Burden, Amanda, 166
Bush, George H. W., 23
Bush, George W., 23, 98–99, 132, 223n62
BusinessWeek, 21–22, 116
Buss, David, 204n2
Byrne, Jane, 92

Campbell, Kim, 102
Canada, 16, 19, 196
candidate pool, 11, 189
careers
    attitude surveys on opportunities, 3

commitment to, 61–64, 63f, 219n52
momentum of, 57, 154, 186
spouse's help with, 178–179
Carroll, Cynthia, 166
Carter, James Earl, 23
Catalyst Inc., 18, 19, 152, 164, 178, 191
Catz, Safra, 229n67
Center for Public Leadership, 60
CEOs. *See* chief executive officers (CEOs)
challenging assignments
difficulty of obtaining, 148–151
establishing competence in, 164
seeking, assertiveness in, 181
women placed in risky assignments, 151
Chamorro, Violeta, 95
change agents, leaders as, 95
charismatic leadership, 222n45, 223n50
Cheng, Marietta Nien-hwa, 122
Chicago Bears, 134
chief executive officers (CEOs). *See also* executive
positions
female, shareholder prejudice against, 192
increasingly demanding jobs of, 158–159
percentage of women as, 13–14, 26, 27
childbearing, delayed, 175
childcare, 6
attitudes about, 52
comparisons of generations, 51, 208n7
on-site, 153, 226n70
shared with husbands, 140, 142, 175
time demands (*see* time demands of childcare)
childrearing, 209n15, 209n18
by male versus female, 30, 31, 51–54, 53n
working mothers and, 178
Chile, 95
China, 92
Citicorp, 47
Civil Rights Act of 1964, Title VII of, 14
Clinton, Hillary, 8, 165, 183, 227n12
Clinton, William Jefferson, 13, 23, 201n1
Coca-Cola Company, 166
Coleman, Cady, 113–114
collaborative leadership style, 119, 133–134
Collins, Gail, 24
Columbia Pictures, 148
Columbia space shuttle, 127
command-and-control leadership, 48, 119, 132,
159
commitment to paid work versus family, 61–64,
63f, 219n52
common standard, group stereotypes and, 114,
115
communal associations
automatic, 89, 215n22
gender stereotypes and, 86–87, 216n10
communal characteristics, 92, 164–165
communality. *See* expectations of communality

compassion, in women, 46
competence
doubts about women's competence, 110–114,
117, 164
shifting standards of, 114–117, 220n60
"competency barrier," 164
competitiveness
enhanced by gender diversity, 193–194
experimental studies of, 37, 205n29
as managerial role expectation, 91
masculine, displays of, 145–146
psychological sex differences in, 36, 37
toward women, 107
complex economies, gender roles in, 33–34
concrete wall (absolute barrier), 2–3, 27
Conley, Frances, 108, 110, 219n36
conscientiousness
leadership and, 40, 41, 41f, 43
men and women compared on, 44f, 45
contingent reward, 128, 129t, 130, 133
continuity of employment
attrition rate, access to challenging work and,
150–151
breaks from employment, 56–58, 210n35,
210n37, 210n39, 210n44
educational attainment and, 56–57, 153,
225n67
family responsibilities and, 56–60
"female dropouts," 22
flexible or part-time jobs, 59–60, 210–211n43
leaves of absence, 58, 141, 175–176, 210n40
sick days, 58, 210n41
wages and employment patterns, 70
as work-life issue, 175–176
control over resources, social power and, 33
Corporate Coaching International, 149
correlational studies
of benefits of paid employment, 177,
229n57
limitations of, 76, 77
of promotions, 72–75, 73t
of sex discrimination in workplace, 68–76
of wages, 68, 69f, 70–71, 213n9
correspondent inference, 215n15
Couric, Katie, 189
credentials, as barrier to employment, 3
criminal activity
physical aggression (violence), 36, 37, 185,
205n21–22
women less likely to engage in, 46, 207n62
Crist, Peter, 39
cultural context
leadership style and, 131–133
male dominance and, 31–32
cultural norms, 130, 181
cultural shift, in leadership models, 181–182
cultural stereotypes, as male advantage, 92–93

culture
corporate (*see* organizational culture)
female aggressiveness in, 37–38
ideas of communion and agency, 86–87
increasing mother care and, 53–54
masculine language in, 148
masculine/feminine associations in, 85–86
support for meritocracy, 194
Curtin, Karin, 192

decision-making authority, 72
The Decline of Males (Tiger), 197
democratic leadership style, 125–127
depression, in parents, 177, 229n60
descriptive beliefs, 84, 87
developmental job experiences, 148–151
devotion to organization, 140–141, 194
directive behavior
avoiding, 126
combining with support and warmth, 165,
227n11, 227n13
resistance to women's behavior, 103–104
directive leadership style, 125–127
discretionary aspects of leadership, 123, 221n24
discrimination, 1, 67–81
derived from in-group preferences, 155
fostering antidiscrimination legislation, 151
irrational in industrialized societies, 193–194
legal cases about, 143
personal, failure to recognize, 170–171
prejudicial attitudes leading to, 98–99
in salary negotiations, 170, 228n35–37
toll on women's opportunities, 186
work-life issues and, 174–175
in workplace (*see* sex discrimination in
workplace)
diversity goals in organizations, 156, 192–193,
225n62
division of labor by sex. *See also* family
responsibilities
childcare (*see* childcare; time demands of
childcare)
concrete wall and, 3
continuation of, 199
in egalitarian society, 32
glass ceiling and, 4–5
housework, 7, 50f, 50–51, 208n2, 208n4
implications of, 55–56, 209n26
mental associations about men and women,
87–88, 215n15
psychological sex differences and, 35
traditional division of family responsibilities,
7, 187, 195
weakening of, 7–8, 50–53
Dixie Chicks, 38
Dole, Elizabeth, 120, 183, 220n9

domestic work
childcare (*see* childcare; time demands of
childcare)
division of labor, implications of, 55–56,
209n26
greater female responsibility for, 184
housework, 7, 50f, 50–51, 208n2, 208n4
loss of job tenure and, 56–58
paid domestic help, 64–65
of women versus men, 49–56, 64
dominance
female (*see* female dominance)
male (*see* male dominance)
positive forms of, 39
psychological sex differences in, 36–37, 205n15
role in leadership, 38–39
double bind, 101–118
concerns about lack of agency, 110–117, 164,
220n60
expectations of communality and, 102–110
leadership style and, 130–131
vulnerability to prejudice and, 187, 189, 190,
191
double standard, 114–117, 220n60
Drogin, Richard, 74
dropping out. *See* continuity of employment
dual-earner couples, 142
Dubinsky, Donna L., 229n67
Duckworth, Connie K., 202n17
Duke University, 134, 159
Dungy, Tony, 134

eBay, 7, 13, 21, 166
economic advances
gender roles and, 33–34
gender hierarchies in, 33
Edelman, Marian Wright, 89
educational attainment
breaks from employment and, 56–57, 153,
225n67
risk of sexual harassment and, 108, 218n31
views of motherhood and, 54
women's growing advantage in, 14–16, 16f, 21,
202n8
women's wages and, 70–71
EEOC (Equal Employment Opportunity
Commission), 108
EEOC v. Sears, Roebuck & Co., 143
effort per hour of market work, 62–64
egalitarian groups, women in, 125
egalitarian societies, 31–32
8Wings Enterprises, 202n17
Eisenhower, Dwight D., 23
Elizabeth I, 92
emotion, 89–90, 167–168
emotional intelligence, 41, 45, 206n44

female leaders (continued)
   resistance to (see resistance to female
      leadership)
   sex discrimination in evaluations of, 78–79
   of small work groups, 24–26, 26f
   student leaders, 25–26, 26f, 204n55
female leaders, effectiveness of
   company profitability and, 191–192, 230n22
   confidence in, 156–157, 226n83
   gender stereotypes and, 190
   leadership style and, 124
   studies of, 189–190, 230n12–13
female mating strategy, 30–31
female voters, 194
feminine settings
   culturally feminine organizations, 118
   doubts about male competence in, 113
   female competence in, 190
   preference for females in, 77–78, 80
   promotion of males in, 73–74
feminist activism, slowing of, 199
feminist writing on leadership, 222n35
Ferraro, Geraldine, 23
Fidelity Investments, 21
film industry, women in, 20
financial performance of company, 191–192,
   230n22
Financial Times, 167
Fiorina, Carly, 6, 7, 21, 22, 51–52, 110, 113, 120,
   187, 201n15, 229n67
flexible jobs
family responsibilities and, 59–60, 210–211n43
   gender equity and, 152–154, 226n70
   flexitime, 153, 226n70
followers, 124, 164, 169
foraging/pastoral societies, 31–32, 34
Ford, Gerald, 23, 117
Ford Foundation, 20
Fortune magazine
   "best companies to work for," 189
   on financial performance of companies,
      191–192, 230n22
   Fortune 500 companies, 21, 146, 171, 178
   on leader characteristics, 117, 123
   lists of powerful people in business, 21–22,
      178–179
   on women in executive positions, 18–19,
      202n16, 202n19
foundations, women as executives of, 20
France, 16
Freedom of Information Act, 2
Friedman, Caitlin, 106
Fudge, Ann, 150

Gallup polling, 80–81, 99f, 214n41
Gandhi, Indira, 92, 126
Garrison, Karen M., 51–52, 229n67

Gates, Bill, 42
gender. See also mental associations about gender
   social capital and, 144–145
   as strongest basis of classification, 85
   wage gap and, 68, 69f, 70–71, 213n9
gender-congruent roles, 125
gender diversity
   competitiveness enhanced by, 193–194
   differences on political issues, 194–195
   positive and negative effects, 193
gender equality. See also promotions gaps; wage
     gaps
   global trend toward, 184
   male attitudes and, 197
   pause in change toward, 198–199
   profitability of company and, 191–192, 230n22
   role of men in achieving, 180
   societal pressures for, 193–195
   in work-life issues, 178–180, 180f
gender equality, fostering, 151–158, 160
   fairness in evaluation of candidates, 154–156
   flexible jobs, 152–154, 226n70
   legitimizing women's contributions, 156–157,
     226n83
   reducing tokenism, 157–158
   through legislation, 151
gender gap, in authority, 72–75, 74t
gender hierarchies, 33, 88
gender imbalance. See also feminine settings;
     masculine settings
   sexual harassment and, 108, 110
   tokenism, 157
   women disadvantaged by, 108, 218n30
gender inequality, 13–27
   education and, 14–16, 16f
   labor force participation, 14, 15f
   in leadership positions, 16–22, 26
   overview, 13–14
   political leadership, 23–24, 203n51
   in small work groups, 24–26, 26f
gender-neutral settings
   female competence in, 190
   male advantage in, 111–112, 219n43, 219n50
   preference for males in, 77–78
gender norms, leadership style and, 124
gender prejudice, 83–100
   ethnic prejudice and, 99
   experimental studies of, 76–80, 186
   in women's advancement, 1
gender roles, traditional
   double bind and (see double bind)
   expectations of women and, 101
   job attributes and, 60–61, 211n49–51
   in organizational practices, 160
   stereotypes and, 88, 215n16
gender stereotyping, 85–90, 101
   accentuated by emotion, 89–90

agentic/communal associations and, 86–87, 216n10

leader effectiveness and, 190

by people in authority, 155–156

prescriptiveness of, 87

shifting standards and, 114–117, 220n60

social change and, 195–196

social interaction shaped by, 88, 186–187

status differences and, 85, 86, 88, 94

tokenism and, 157

traditional gender roles and, 88, 215n16

unconscious, 85, 86, 94, 215n9

women's leadership undermined by, 93–94

General Social Survey, 98f

Generation X/Y fathers, 51, 208n7

genetic predisposition to leadership, 30, 39, 204n4

Germany, 17, 92, 167

Gillette Company, 117

Ginsburg, Ruth Bader, 2

Giuliani, Rudy, 91

glass ceiling, 2, 4f, 4–5, 6, 73, 183

Glass Ceiling Commission, 4, 5

glass ceiling metaphor, 1, 4, 4f, 6, 7, 183

"glass cliff," 151

glass escalator, 74

global organizations, 19, 127

Goddard Space Flight Center, 168

Goldberg paradigm, 76–77

Golden West Financial, 19

"Goodbye Earl" (song), 38

good-coach leader model, 119, 181–182

"good mother" behaviors, 165

good-teacher leader model, 119, 159, 181–182

governmental positions. See also political leadership

legislatures, 23, 24

promotions, 75, 213n26

Senior Executive Service (federal), 20, 75, 213n26

state governors, 24

women in, 20, 190

women of color in, 203n49

Graham, Katharine, 19, 157

Grasso, Ella, 24

Greck, Todd, 179

Griffin, Joanne, 191, 230n18

Hacker, Andrew, 203n36

Ham, Linda, 127

Hancock, Ellen, 229n67

Harvard Business Review, 3, 121, 152, 221n12

Harvard Business School, 2

Harvard University, 20, 42, 60, 93, 120, 226n95

"having it all," 175–178

health and well-being, multiple life roles and, 176–178, 181

healthy worker effect, 177, 229n57

Hearst Magazines, 177

Hewlett-Packard Company, 6, 7, 21, 51, 110, 120

Heytesbury Limited, 133

hierarchical relationships, male preference for, 37, 222n34

high achievers, working hours of, 141

higher-level positions. See executive positions

higher standard of performance for women, 114–117, 164

high school student leaders, 25–26, 26f, 204n55

Hill, Anita, 24

Hills, Carla Anderson, 23

hiring of women. See recruitment and hiring of women

Hispanics, 17, 68, 69f, 208n9

Hobby, Oveta Culp, 23

Holmes à Court, Janet, 133–134

Holmes à Court, Robert, 133

homemaker role, acceptance of, 62

homosocial reproduction, 155

Hopkins, Ann, 112

Hopkins, Deborah C., 229n67

hormones, 205n19

household responsibilities (housework)

division of labor and, 7, 50f, 50–51, 208n2, 208n4

shared by husbands, 178

time diary studies of, 50, 50f

House of Representatives, 23

How Men Think: The Seven Essential Rules for Making It in a Man's World (Mendell), 162

How To Succeed in Business Without a Penis: Secrets and Strategies for the Working Woman (Salmansohn), 162

Hudson, Katherine, 107, 110–111

humor, influence and, 111

hunter-gatherer societies. See foraging/pastoral societies

husbands

childcare shared with, 140, 142, 175

help with spouse's career, 178–179

housework shared by, 178

stay-at-home husbands, 51–52

women earning more than, 180, 180f

ideal employee model, 139–140

If You've Raised Kids, You Can Manage Anything: Leadership Begins at Home (Crittenden), 162

illusory correlation, 191, 230n17

income loss from employment breaks, 56–57, 59. *See also* continuity of employment

Indianapolis Colts, 134

individualized consideration, 129t, 130

industrialized societies

acceptance of gender equality, 197

discrimination irrational in, 193–194

removal of biosocial barriers in, 35

sex differences in complex economies, 33–34

influence
  challenges in wielding, 112–113, 220*n53*
  increasing, with blended style, 165, 227*n11*,
    227*n13*
  as managerial role, 91
  of women, diminished, 111–112, 219*n43*,
    219*n50*
in-group loyalty, 155
integrative leadership, 222*n45*
intelligence
  Big Five personality traits and, 41*f*, 43, 44*f*, 45,
    206*n43*
  emotional intelligence, 41, 45
  leadership and, 40, 42, 48, 185, 206*n41*
interactions shaped by stereotyping, 88, 186–187
interactive style, typical of female leaders, 121,
    221*n11*
international assignments, 149
international comparisons, 14
  educational attainment, 16
  employment of women, 202*n5*
  leadership positions, 17
  women in executive positions, 19, 202*n22*
  women in politics, 23
interpersonally oriented leadership style
  of male leaders, 134–135
  task orientation and, 124–125, 221*n25*, 222*n29*,
    222*n31*
interpersonal skills, 190

Japan, 16, 17, 92
job attributes, preferences for, 60–61, 211*n49–51*,
    212*n57*
job commitment, 61–64
job interviews, 3, 5
jobs. *See also* work-life issues; workplace hours
  of CEOs, increasing demands of, 158–159
  creative redefinition of job criteria, 112
  design of, to promote gender equity, 152–154,
    226*n70*
  discrimination. *See* sex discrimination in
    workplace
  domestic obligations, loss of tenure and,
    56–58
  effort, 62–64
job satisfaction, 150, 222*n33*
Johnson, Abby, 21
juries, 25, 206*n40*

Kennedy School of Government (Harvard), 60
Kerry, John, 132
*Killer Woman Blues: Why Americans Can't Think
    Straight About Gender & Power* (DeMott),
    197
Kimberly-Clark Corporation, 117
Krawcheck, Sallie, 47, 208*n67*
Krzyzewski, Mike, 134, 159

laboratory experiments. *See* experimental studies
labor force participation
  changes in, 14, 15*f*, 202*n5*, 202*n6*
  consistency of, 186
  educational attainment and, 56–57, 153,
    225*n67*
labyrinth, 2, 5–8
  leadership and information labyrinth, 201*n14*
  leadership behavior and, 163–174
  navigating through, 161–182
  overview, 161–163
  work-life issues, 174–180
laissez-faire leadership style, 128, 129, 129*t*, 130
language of masculine culture, 148
La Roche, Elaine, 120, 220*n6*
law enforcement, masculine culture in, 148
Lay, Kenneth, 46
leader(s), 8. *See also* mental associations about
    leaders
  agentic characteristics of, 90–91, 92, 94–95
  autocratic, changing environment and,
    158–159
  as change agents, 95
  characteristics of, 117, 123
  communal characteristics of, 92
  conflation with ideas about men, 92–93, 94
  feeling of authenticity in role, 171–173, 228*n44*
  female (*see* female leaders)
  male (*see* male leaders; men as natural leaders)
  masculine associations about, 87, 90–91, 92
  meta-analysis of research, 78–79, 125–130,
    129*t*, 189–190, 230*n12–13*
  spontaneous emergence of, 25, 206*n40*
leadership, 8–9. *See also* access to leadership;
    barriers to advancement
  aggregative, 222*n45*
  athletic participation and, 206–207*n51*
  candidate pool for, 11
  changes in norms of, 158–160, 189
  charismatic, 223*n50*
  discretionary aspects of, 123, 221*n24*
  ethical qualities and, 42, 193, 206*n50*
  executive leadership ability, 95
  genetic predisposition to, 30, 39, 204*n4*
  intelligence and, 40, 42, 48, 185, 206*n41*
  management contrasted with, 9
  masculine construal of, 90–94
  mental associations about, 90–96, 101, 137
  personality traits associated with, 39–43, 41*f*,
    47–48, 185–186
  physical attractiveness and, 90
  political (*see* political leadership)
  postheroic, 127
  role of dominance in, 38–39
leadership behavior, 163–174. *See also* leadership
    style
  blended style of (*see* blended leadership style)

building social capital, 161, 173–174, 188
  increasing influence with, 165, 227n11, 227n13
leadership competence standards, 110–114, 164
leadership models
  autocratic, 122
  command-and-control model, 119
  "enlightened parent" model, 162
  good-coach model, 119, 181–182
  good-teacher model, 119, 159, 181–182
leadership positions, 1, 13–27
  absence of equality in, 16–22, 26
  agentic qualities and, 96
  causes of women's ascent to, 185–188
  feeling of authenticity in, 171–173, 228n44
  men in (see male leaders; men as natural
    leaders)
  preference for males in, 77–78
  research studies on, 17f, 17–22
  risk of sexual harassment and, 108, 109f, 110,
    218n31, 218n33
  statistics on, 17f, 17–22, 202n12, 202n14
  stress of, 60
  uniform bias against women and, 72–75, 73t
  women in (see female leaders)
leadership style, 119–135
  blended (see blended leadership style)
  collaborative, 119, 133–134
  debates about, 120–122
  democratic versus autocratic, 125–127,
    222n33
  double bind and, 130–131
  importance of cultural context, 131–133
  job satisfaction and, 222n33
  meta-analysis of research, 124–130, 129t
  overview, 119–120
  similarities and differences of women and
    men, 122–123, 187, 221n23–25
  task versus interpersonal orientation, 124–125,
    221n25, 222n29, 222n31
  transformational, transactional, or laissez-faire,
    127–131, 129t
leaves of absence, 58, 141, 175–176, 210n40
legal profession, 20, 138–139, 142
legislatures, women in, 23, 24
Lepore, Dawn G., 229n67
Liberia, 95, 132
life roles, multiple, importance of, 176
likeability penalty, 104, 117
Lincoln, Abraham, 117
line positions, 18, 150, 164
loss of job tenure, 56–58
Lucent Technologies, 7

male dominance
  acceptance of, 117
  cultural context and, 31–32
  evolutionary psychology theory of, 29–31

masculine image of leadership and, 92–93
  social dominance, 30, 37, 184
male leaders, 1. See also leadership style
  cultural stereotypes as advantage, 92–93
  decreasing predominance of, 25–26
  favoritism toward, 96–97, 97f, 216–217n58–59
  with interpersonally oriented leadership style,
    134–135
  masculine image of political leadership, 23–24,
    92
  mentoring relationships with, 145, 173–174
  political, conflict and, 132–133, 223n63
  preference for, 77
  sex discrimination in workplace and, 80–81,
    214n41
male versus female comparisons. See also
    leadership style; personality traits
  childrearing, 30, 31, 51–54, 53n
  ethical qualities, 46–47, 207n60, 207n62
  mating strategies, 30–31
  of military cadets, 112, 190
  role in family responsibilities, 49–56, 64, 179,
    195
management, leadership contrasted with, 9
management by exception, 128–129, 129t, 130
managerial roles, 90–92, 158–159, 160
managers. See leader(s)
market work, effort per hour of, 62–64
marriage
  wages and, 70
  satisfaction and, 177–178
masculine culture, language of, 148
masculine settings
  doubts about female competence in, 112–113,
    220n53
  leadership style in, 126
  limits of blended leadership style in, 167–168,
    188
  male advantage in, 111–112, 190, 219n43,
    219n50
  masculine image of leadership and, 92–93
  organizational culture as, 145, 146–148,
    225n44
  preference for males in, 77–78
  racism in, 131
  resistance to women in, 105–106, 107, 190–191
  risk of sexual harassment in, 108, 109f, 218n31,
    218n33, 218–219n34
Massachusetts Institute of Technology (MIT), 20
maternal symbolism, in politics, 95–96
mating strategy, male versus female, 30–31
Meier, Golda, 126
men
  advantage in gender-neutral settings, 111–112,
    219n43, 219n50
  attitudes toward women, 196–198
  boastfulness acceptable for, 104

men (continued)
  clear path to leadership, 172–173
  communal characteristics in, 164–165
  competence in feminine settings, 113
  costs of long work hours, 142
  displays of competitive masculinity, 146–147, 225n44
  ethical qualities of, 46–47, 207n60, 207n62
  extraversion in, 41f, 43, 44f, 45
  fathers, childcare responsibilities of, 51, 52, 208n7
  gender equality and, 180, 197
  housework (see household responsibilities [housework])
  husbands (see husbands)
  involvement in family roles, 179, 195
  leisure, 55, 61
  masculine construal of leadership, 90–94
  mental associations about, 86–87
  mental associations about gender and, 92–93
  networking with, 173, 181
  opposition to gender equality, and self-interest, 197
  physical aggression by, 36, 185
  preference for hierarchical relationships, 37, 222n34
  resistance to hiring of women, 107
  sexual harassment by, 108, 197, 218n31, 218n33, 218–219n34
  sexual selection and, 30
men as natural leaders, 29–48
  biosocial origins of sex differences, 34–35, 205n19
  evolutionary psychology theory, 29–31
  male versus female personality traits, 36–39, 43–47, 207n60, 207n62
  "natural ability" theory rejected, 185, 189
  personality traits associated with leadership, 39–43, 41f
  problems with evolutionary analysis, 31–34
mental associations about gender, 83, 85–90
  as advantage for men, 92–93
  content of, 86–87
  female leaders and, 96
  personality traits and, 87–88, 215n15
  sources of, 87–90
  stereotyping and, 88, 186–187
mental associations about leaders, 90–96
  differences in leadership roles, 94–96, 101
  female leaders and, 96
  influence on organizational norms, 137
  masculine construal of leadership, 90–94
mental health, multiple life roles and, 176–178
mentoring relationships, with men, 145, 173–174
Merkel, Angela, 167, 227n22
meta-analysis of research, 10. See also male versus female comparisons
  effect size in, 203–204n52l

on leaders, 78–79, 125–130, 129t, 189–190, 230n12–13
on leadership style, 124–130, 129t
Microsoft Corporation, 42
middle management positions, 18, 20, 190
military, 2
  incidence of sexual harassment in, 108, 109f, 218–219n34
  leadership style and, 126
  ratings of male and female cadets, 112, 190
  shifting standards of competence, 114–115, 220n60
  women in, 20
Minnick, Mary, 166
Mr. and Mrs. Smith (film), 38
MIT (Massachusetts Institute of Technology), 20
MLQ (Multifactor Leadership Questionnaire), 128, 129t
Mockler, Coleman M., 117
modesty
  in female leaders, 105, 110, 156
  self-promotion and, 169, 227n27
"mommy track," 152
Mondale, Walter, 23
morally nontraditional behavior, disapproval of, 46
Morrison, Toni, 89
"motherhood penalty," 57–58
Mulcahy, Anne M., 7, 21, 51–52, 151, 165, 229n67
Multifactor Leadership Questionnaire (MLQ), 128, 129t
Murray, Patty, 95–96

negative reactions
  to female assertions of authority, 123, 125–126
  to female leaders, 117, 166, 172
  to workplace aggression, 38–39
negotiation
  discrimination in salary negotiations, 170, 228n35–37
  effective, blended leadership style and, 169–171, 227n31
  experimental studies of, 37, 205n28
  unscrupulous, women's disapproval of, 46
networking
  to build social capital, 144–145, 173–174
  gender-segregation and, 145–146
  limited female access to, 187–188
  with men as well as women, 146, 173, 181
neuroticism
  leadership and, 40, 41, 41f
  men and women compared on, 41f, 45
neutral contexts. See gender-neutral settings
New Guinea, 32, 204n12
New York City Planning Commission, 166
New York Times, 54, 107, 119–120, 132, 143–144, 150–153, 183
New York Times Magazine, 22, 24, 203n40

politician, CEO as, 158–159

politics

    command-and-control leadership in, 132

    implications of gender/sex differences, 10, 194–195

    maternal symbolism in, 95–96

    sex differences on issues, 194–195

    women in, 23

positive regard for women's caring qualities, 89

postheroic leadership, 127

power. *See* influence

prejudice

    against female leaders, 96–100, 97f–99f, 216–217n58–59

    shareholder prejudice against female CEOs, 192

    against women of color, 99, 103, 217n8

    women vulnerable to, 187, 189, 190, 191, 230n17

prescriptive beliefs, 84, 87, 101–108

presidential cabinets, women in, 23–24

Price Waterhouse, 112

PricewaterhouseCoopers, 112

"prime," 85

Princeton University, 2, 20

Procter & Gamble, 150–151, 169

profitability, effectiveness of leader and, 191–192, 230n22

promotions

    access to, in staff positions, 150

    correlational studies of, 72–75, 73t

    directive behavior and, 103

    evaluations prior to, 112

    in governmental positions, 75, 213n26

    of males in feminine settings, 73–74

    social capital and, 144

promotions gaps, 213n16, 213n17, 213n20. *See also* wage gaps

    access to challenging work and, 149–150

    demands for travel and relocation, 143

    ethnicity and, 72

    nondiscriminatory determinants of, 76, 213n28

    sex discrimination and, 80

psychological commitment to paid work, 61–64, 63f, 219n52

psychological sex differences, 35–39. *See also* male versus female comparisons; personality traits

    aggressiveness, 36

    biosocial origin theory for, 34–35, 205n19

    division of labor by gender and, 35

    dominance, assertiveness, and competitiveness, 36–37

psychological variables, in correlational studies, 76

psychology of prejudice, 83–100, 195–196. *See also* resistance to female leadership

    advancement of women and, 195–196

    against female leaders, 96–100, 97f–99f, 216–217n58–59

    mental associations about gender, 83, 85–90

    mental associations about leaders, 90–96, 101, 137

    overview, 83–84, 186–187, 195–196

    stereotypes as social constructions, 84–85

public sphere, male dominance in, 30, 37, 184

quid pro quo harassment, 218n31

Quinn, Christine, 126

quitting. *See* continuity of employment

quota systems, for women in politics, 23, 203n45

race. *See* ethnicity

racism, in masculine domains, 131

Raines, Howell, 119–120

Reagan, Ronald, 23

recruitment and hiring of women

    candidate pool, 11, 189

    gender equity in, fostering, 154–156

    job criteria and, 112

    male resistance to, 107

    need for culturally feminine skills, 159

    reforming, gender equity and, 154–156

    transparency in, 154–155

regression analysis, of wage gap, 67, 70–71

relationship-building capabilities

    creating social capital, 173–174

    leadership and, 42–43

relationships

    hierarchical, men's preference for, 37, 222n34

    mentoring relationships with men, 145, 173–174

    positive, with authority, 91

religiosity, in women and men, 46

relocation, demands for, 143

research methods, 9–10

    bias in, 10, 190, 201n22

    correlational (*see* correlational studies)

    effect size in, 203–204n52

    experimental. *See* experimental studies

    longitudinal studies, advantages of, 71, 177, 229n58

    meta-analysis of (*see* meta-analysis of research)

    shifting standards (*see* shifting standards of competence)

resistance to female leadership, 101–118. *See also* female leaders

    African American females, 131

    blended leadership style and, 166

    as double bind, 101–117

    doubts about agency, 110–117, 164, 220n60

    expectations of communality, 102–110

    sexual harassment as, 108, 218n31, 218n33, 218–219n34

"reverse engineering" by evolutionary psychologists, 34

status differences, stereotyping and, 85, 86, 88, 94
stay-at-home husbands, 51–52
stay-at-home mothers, long-term health of, 177, 229n57
Steel, Dawn, 148, 166
stereotypes
  about gender (*see* gender stereotyping)
  automaticity of, 85–86
  cultural, as male advantage, 92–93
  denial of opportunity due to, 113
  influence of, lack of awareness about, 155–156
  norms about type of employment, 150
  racial, 115, 220n65
  shifting standards of competence, 114–117, 220n60
stereotype threat, 93–94, 216n46
stress
  caused by gender diversity, 193
  created by employment norms, 142
  of leadership positions, 60
  of work-life issues, 176
student leaders, 25–26, 26f, 204n55
subsistence patterns, social change and, 32–34
success, bias in explanations of, 79
Summers, Lawrence, 93, 120, 226n95
Sun Oil, 192
Supreme Court, 24
surveys. *See* attitude surveys
Sweden, 16, 17, 23, 202n22
Switzerland, 23
symphony orchestras, 20, 203n30

talent pool, 11, 189
task competence, 171
task-oriented leadership style, 124–125
technology industry, 6–7
tempered radicals, 172, 228n44
terrorism, effects of, 132
Thatcher, Margaret, 92, 126
"think manager-think male," 92
Thoman, G. Richard, 165
Thomas, Clarence, 24
"Through the Glass Ceiling" (Hymowitz), 5–6
TIAA-CREF, 157
time demands of childcare
  changes in, 52–54, 53f
  division of labor and, 55–56, 209n26
  shifting to spouse, 140
  work-family trade-offs, 138–139
time diary studies
  of childrearing, 51, 209n24
  of housework, 50, 50f
Time magazine, 22, 91, 203n40
time off. *See* continuity of employment
Title VII of Civil Rights Act of 1964, 14
tokenism, reducing, 157–158. *See also* feminine settings; masculine settings

toughness in women, doubts about, 116–117, 220n71
traditional views of parent roles, 56
transactional leadership style, 128, 129t, 130, 133
transformational leadership style, 127–128, 129t, 130, 133–134, 222n45, 222n48, 223n50–51
transparency
  of authentic leaders, 171–172
  in recruitment, 154–155
travel, demands for, 143

undesirable qualities ascribed to other sex, 87
United Kingdom, 16, 17, 92, 151
United States, 17f, 17–18, 92, 196
University of Michigan, 20
University of Pennsylvania, 20
unscrupulous negotiation tactics, 46
U.S. Congress
  Glass Ceiling Commission, 4
  House of Representatives, 23
  Senate, 23, 24
U.S. military academies, 2
USA Today, 191

vacations, rarity of, 141
Vanatinai society (New Guinea), 32, 204n12
Vaz, Patricia, 45–46
verbal aggression, 38–39, 104
vulnerability to prejudice, 187, 189, 190, 191, 230n17

wage gaps. *See also* promotions gaps
  between-occupations gap, 71, 213n9, 213n12
  ethnicity and, 68, 69f
  gender and, 68, 69f, 70–71, 213n9
  nondiscriminatory determinants of, 76, 213n28
  studies of, 67, 70, 71, 80, 213n9
  within-occupation gap, 71, 213n9
wages
  continuity of employment and, 70
  correlational studies of, 68, 69f, 70–71, 213n9
  discrimination in salary negotiations, 170, 228n35–37
  educational attainment and, 70–71
  effective negotiation of, 169–171, 227n31
  entry of women into occupations and, 193
  income losses from employment disconti-
    nuity, 56–57, 59
Wall Street Journal, 4, 5–6, 83, 131–132, 192
  on CEOs, 158
  lists of women in corporate positions, 21–22
  poll of MBA recruiters, 159
Wal-Mart, 147
Wal-Mart sex discrimination case, 74–75, 155
Washington Post, 19, 157
Waters, Mary, 159
Watkins, Sherron, 46

Alice H. Eagly is a professor, department chair of psychology, and James Padilla Chair of Arts and Sciences at Northwestern University. She is also a faculty fellow in Northwestern's Institute for Policy Research. Previously she held faculty positions at Michigan State University, University of Massachusetts in Amherst, and Purdue University. She obtained her PhD from the University of Michigan. Her research and writing pertain mainly to the study of gender, attitudes, prejudice, cultural stereotypes, and leadership. She received the Distinguished Scientist Award of the Society for Experimental Social Psychology, the Donald Campbell Award for Distinguished Contribution to Social Psychology, the Carolyn Wood Sherif Award of the Society for the Psychology of Women, and the Interamerican Psychologist Award. In addition to numerous journal articles and chapters in edited volumes, Eagly is the author of two books, *Sex Differences in Social Behavior: A Social Role Interpretation* and (with coauthor Shelly Chaiken) *The Psychology of Attitudes*, and is the coeditor of four books, including *The Psychology of Gender*.

Linda L. Carli, an associate professor in the department of psychology at Wellesley College, has conducted extensive research on the effects of gender on women's leadership; group interaction, communication, and influence; and reactions to adversity, resulting in more than seventy-five scholarly articles, chapters, and presentations. Currently, she is focusing her research on gender discrimination and the challenges faced by professional women. She is active in professional organizations in psychology and management and serves on the executive board of the Society for the Psychology of Women. She was the coeditor (with Alice Eagly) of a volume of the *Journal of Social Issues* that focused on women leaders. At Wellesley, she teaches courses in organizational and applied psychology. She has also developed and conducted diversity training workshops and negotiation and conflict resolution workshops for women leaders and has lectured widely on gender and diversity for business, academic, and other organizations. She holds a PhD in social psychology from the University of Massachusetts at Amherst.